Pacific
and the
Economi

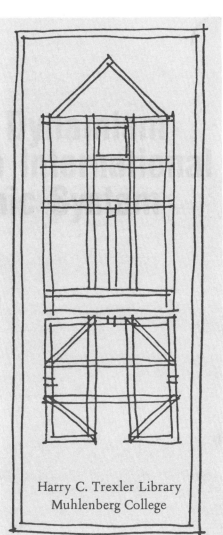

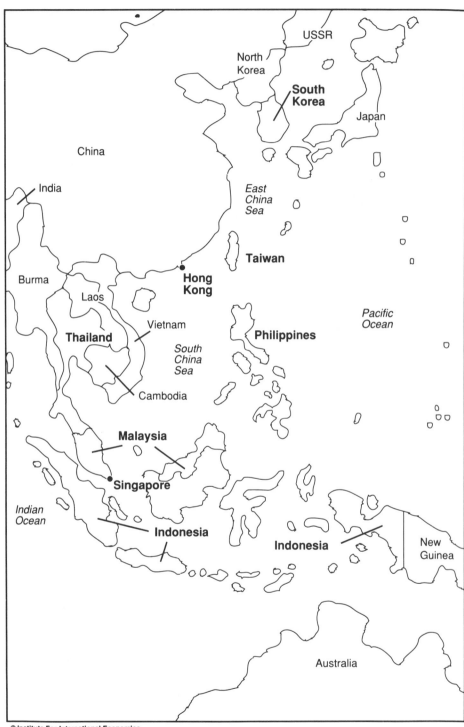

USSR

North
Korea

**South
Korea**

Japan

China

India

East
China
Sea

Taiwan

Burma

Laos

**Hong
Kong**

Thailand

Vietnam

Philippines

Pacific
Ocean

South
China
Sea

Cambodia

Malaysia

Indian
Ocean

•Singapore

Indonesia

Indonesia

New
Guinea

Australia

C. FRED BERGSTEN
MARCUS NOLAND
Editors

Pacific Dynamism and the International Economic System

INSTITUTE FOR INTERNATIONAL ECONOMICS
Washington, DC
in association with
THE PACIFIC TRADE AND DEVELOPMENT CONFERENCE SECRETARIAT
THE AUSTRALIAN NATIONAL UNIVERSITY
1993

C. Fred Bergsten, Director, was Assistant Secretary for International Affairs of the US Treasury (1977–81); Assistant for International Economic Affairs to the National Security Council (1969–71); and a Senior Fellow at the Brookings Institution (1972–76), the Carnegie Endowment for International Peace (1981), and the Council on Foreign Relations (1967–68). He is the author of 21 books on a wide range of international economic issues, including *America in the World Economy: A Strategy for the 1990s* (1988), *The United States–Japan Economic Problem* (1987), *American Multinationals and American Interests* (1978), *The Dilemmas of the Dollar* (1976), and *World Politics and International Economics* (1975).

Marcus Noland is a Research Fellow at the Institute, as well as Visiting Assistant Professor of Economics at The Johns Hopkins University. He was formerly Visiting Professor of Policy Science at Saitama University in Japan and a visiting scholar at the Korean Development Institute. He has written many articles on international economics, and is the author of *Pacific Basin Developing Countries: Prospects for the Future* (1990) and coauthor of *Japan in the World Economy* (1988).

INSTITUTE FOR INTERNATIONAL ECONOMICS
11 Dupont Circle, NW
Washington, DC 20036-1207
(202) 328-9000   FAX: (202) 328-5432

C. Fred Bergsten, *Director*
Christine F. Lowry, *Director of Publications*

Printed in the United States of America
95 94 93 4 3 2 1

Library of Congress Cataloging-in-Publication Data

Bergsten, C. Fred
  Pacific dynamism and the international economic system / C. Fred Bergsten and Marcus Noland.
    p.   cm.
  Includes bibliographical references and index.

  1. International economic relations. 2. Pacific Area—Foreign economic relations. 3. Pacific Area—Economic integration. I. Title.
  HF1359.N65   1993
  337.9—dc20   92-37824
                                           CIP

ISBN 0-88132-196-6 (paper)

Cover design by Michelle Fleitz.

Cover photograph by permission of NASA: "Earth from Apollo 17."

The views expressed in this publication are those of the author. This publication is part of the overall program of the Institute, as endorsed by its Board of Directors, but does not necessarily reflect the views of individual members of the Board or the Advisory Committee.

Marketed and Distributed outside the USA and Canada by Longman Group UK Limited, London

*Dedicated to the memory of
Dr. Saburo Okita (1914–93),
a dynamic leader of global and
regional economic affairs and long-time
participant in the PAFTAD series,
among whose many contributions was his
chairmanship of the PAFTAD
International Steering Committee.*

Contents

Preface   ix

Contributors   xiii

I Introduction and Overview

Introduction and Overview *C. Fred Bergsten and
Marcus Noland*   3

II The International Economic System: Past, Present, and Future

1 Global Trade Flows: Old Structures, New Issues, Empirical
Evidence *Richard J. Grant, Maria C. Papadakis,
and J. David Richardson*   17

2 The Uruguay Round and the GATT: Whither the Global
System? *John Whalley*   65

3 Globalism and Regionalism: Complements or Competitors?
Soogil Young   111

III Regional Institutional Arrangements

4 The Existing Bloc Expanded? The European Community,
EFTA, and Eastern Europe *Per Magnus Wijkman*   135

5 NAFTA and Pacific Partnership: Advancing Multilateralism?
H. Edward English and Murray G. Smith   159

6 The Pacific: An Application of a General Theory of Economic
Integration *Peter Drysdale and Ross Garnaut*   183

7 Subregional Economic Zones: A New Motive Force in
Asia-Pacific Development *Chia Siow Yue and Lee Tsao Yuan*   225

IV Systemic Implications of Pacific Dynamism

8 Changing Patterns of Direct Investment and the Implications
for Trade and Development *Shujiro Urata* 273

9 The Yen and the International Monetary System *Takatoshi Ito* 299

10 Human Capital Flows *Glenn A. Withers* 323

11 Economic Growth, Environmental Issues, and Trade
Kym Anderson 341

12 Implications of the Post-Cold War Politico-Security
Environment on the Pacific Economy *Hadi Soesastro* 365

Index 389

Preface

The Asia-Pacific region has been the most dynamic part of the world economy for the past quarter century. The United States remains the world's largest national economy and trading nation. Japan has emerged as a technological leader and the world's largest creditor country. China has had the world's fastest growth rate for the last decade and has launched fundamental economic reforms that could make it the single largest economy within the foreseeable future. The developing countries of East Asia have tripled their share of global income and trade.

The Asia-Pacific region has also been the only major geographical area without intergovernmental institutions to facilitate its expanding economic ties. Its rapid integration has been wholly market-driven. However, subregional arrangements are now beginning to emerge. The United States and Canada (and now Mexico), and Australia and New Zealand as well, have launched innovative trade pacts that may be models for broader regional and/or global negotiations. The Asia Pacific Economic Cooperation (APEC) group has recently been created to begin the process of regionwide cooperation.

The nexus between this Pacific dynamism and its associated institutional arrangements, and the international economic system, will be one of the most fascinating and potentially most important phenomena of the next decade or so. The present volume, *Pacific Dynamism and the International Economic System*, addresses this set of questions. It is based on the 20th Pacific Trade and Development Conference (PAFTAD 20), hosted here at the Institute for International Economics in Washington in September 1992. The PAFTAD series has traditionally brought together preeminent economic thinkers from both sides of the Pacific, and PAFTAD 20 was no exception.

This volume provides a foundation for understanding and foreseeing the impact of this dynamic region on the international economic system and includes a number of suggestions for how the process might evolve most effectively. It begins with an assessment of the basic building blocks: the determinants of international trade flows, the status and prospects for the Uruguay Round of global trade negotiations, and the relationships between globalism and regionalism. We then turn to the world's current and prospective regional arrangements: the European Community and its potential expansion, the North American Free Trade Area, the possibilities for the Pacific Rim, and—on a different tack—subregional zones within that broad area. We turn finally to five functional issues that will play central roles in the emerging agenda: foreign direct investment, the role of the yen and related monetary questions, international labor migration, trade and the environment, and security.

In the course of organizing the conference, and in the preparation of this volume, the editors have received indispensable assistance from the PAFTAD

International Steering Committee and PAFTAD Secretariat under the leadership of Professors Peter Drysdale and Hugh Patrick. In addition, the host-country steering committee—comprising Richard Cooper, Lawrence Krause, and Robert Lawrence along with the editors—was of enormous help in planning the agenda and making assignments. We also thank Valerie Norville and Michael Treadway for their skillful and painstaking work in editing the papers for publication.

We also want to express our deep appreciation for the enormous contribution of the late Dr. Saburo Okita to PAFTAD 20 and many earlier conferences in the series. Dr. Okita was a member of the concluding panel of PAFTAD 20 and provided his usual wise and insightful commentary. He had been a previous chairman of the PAFTAD International Steering Committee and was a member of the Board of Directors of the Institute for International Economics during 1981–87. Dr. Okita was Japan's appointee to the Eminent Persons Group (of which I am the appointee of the United States and chairman) created by the 1992 APEC Ministerial meeting to recommend a strategy for Asia-Pacific economic cooperation, the topic of PAFTAD 20. It was characteristic of Dr. Okita's commitment to these issues that he was discussing them with me on the telephone when he collapsed and died in February 1993. We dedicate this volume to his memory.

The Institute for International Economics is a private nonprofit institution for the study and discussion of international economic policy. Its purpose is to analyze important issues in that area, and to develop and communicate practical new approaches for dealing with them. The Institute is completely nonpartisan.

The Institute is funded largely by philanthropic foundations. Major institutional grants are now being received from the German Marshall Fund of the United States, which created the Institute with a generous commitment of funds in 1981, and from the Ford Foundation, the William and Flora Hewlett Foundation, the William M. Keck, Jr. Foundation, the C. V. Starr Foundation, and the United States–Japan Foundation. A number of other foundations and private corporations also contribute to the highly diversified financial resources of the Institute. About 14 percent of the Institute's resources in our latest fiscal year were provided by contributors outside the United States, including about 6 percent from Japan.

The Board of Directors bears overall responsibility for the Institute and gives general guidance and approval to its research program—including identification of topics that are likely to become important to international economic policymakers over the medium run (generally, one to three years), and which thus should be addressed by the Institute. The Director, working closely with the staff and outside Advisory Committee, is responsible for the development of particular projects and makes the final decision to publish an individual study.

The Institute hopes that its studies and other activities will contribute to building a stronger foundation for international economic policy around the world. We invite readers of these publications to let us know how they think we can best accomplish this objective.

C. FRED BERGSTEN
Director
April 1993

Contributors

Host:

C. FRED BERGSTEN
Institute for International Economics

Guest Speaker:

SENATOR JOHN D. ROCKEFELLER IV

Authors

Kym Anderson
General Agreement on Tariffs and
    Trade

C. Fred Bergsten
Institute for International Economics

Peter Drysdale
Australia-Japan Research Centre

H. Edward English
Carleton University

Ross Garnaut
Australian National University

Richard J. Grant
Syracuse University

Takatoshi Ito
Hitotsubashi University

Marcus Noland
Institute for International Economics

Maria C. Papadakis
Syracuse University

J. David Richardson
Syracuse University
Institute for International Economics

Murray G. Smith
Carleton University

Hadi Soesastro
Centre for Strategic and
    International Studies

Shujiro Urata
Waseda University

John Whalley
University of Western Ontario

Per Magnus Wijkman
European Free Trade Association

Glenn A. Withers
La Trobe University

Lee Tsao Yuan
National University of Singapore

Chia Siow Yue
National University of Singapore

Soogil Young
Korea Development Institute

Discussants

Florian Alburo
University of the Philippines

Mohamed Ariff
University of Malaya

Taeho Bark
Korea Institute for International
    Economic Policy

Allan Bollard
New Zealand Institute of Economic
    Research

Edward K.Y. Chen
University of Hong Kong

Jeffrey Frankel
University of California at Berkeley

Junichi Goto
Kobe University

Edward M. Graham
Institute for International Economics

Chun-Tien Hu
Sun Yat-Sen Institute for Social
    Sciences and Philosophy

Gary C. Hufbauer
Institute for International Economics

Lawrence Krause
University of California

Justin Yifu Lin
Development Research Center

Yuzuru Ozeki
International Monetary Fund

Mari Pangestu
Centre for Strategic and
    International Studies

Hugh Patrick
Columbia University

Luis F. Rubio
Centro De Investigacion para el
    Desarrollo

Jeffrey J. Schott
Institute for International Economics

Hee-Yhon Song
Korea Development Institute

Somsak Tambunlertchai
Thammasat University

George Tavlas
International Monetary Fund

John Whalley
University of Western Ontario

Rong I Wu
Fair Trade Commission, the
    Executive Yuan

Ippei Yamazawa
Hitotsubashi University

Introduction and Overview

Introduction and Overview

C. FRED BERGSTEN AND MARCUS NOLAND

Over the past quarter century, the Asia-Pacific region has been the most dynamic part of the world economy. Japan has emerged as a technological leader and the world's largest creditor country. The developing countries of East Asia have tripled their share of world income and trade. China has launched fundamental economic reforms that could one day make it the world's largest economy. The United States and Canada (and now Mexico) on the one hand, and Australia and New Zealand on the other, have entered into innovative free trade agreements that may be models for future global pacts.

Politics lags economics, however, and the rising economic importance of the Asia-Pacific region has not been fully reflected in international economic policymaking. The world's leading economic organizations still exhibit a tilt toward the Atlantic. The region itself has none of the institutional infrastructure, such as the North Atlantic Treaty Organization (NATO) and the Organization for Economic Cooperation and Development (OECD), that prevails across the Atlantic. This is a timely juncture at which to examine the interaction between Pacific dynamism and the global economic system.

That interaction will be affected substantially by two historical transformations that are drastically altering the global economic order. The most directly relevant is economic tripolarity: the onset of the three roughly equal economic superpowers of Japan, the United States, and the uniting Europe. Neither America nor any other country can now dominate the world economy. Hence, economic conflict becomes much more possible. Collective economic leadership is essential to avoid such an outcome.

Achieving such collective leadership is rendered more difficult by the second historic transformation: the end of the Cold War. The Cold War placed a security blanket over relations among the major industrial democracies, providing their political leaders with an overriding incentive to avoid economic and other conflicts that might disrupt their anti-Communist alliance systems. Hence, economic disputes were always settled cooperatively. The end of the Cold War pulls the security blanket aside, however, and makes conflict much more possible.

In a world of three economic superpowers without mutual security concerns to bind them together, two paths of systemic evolution are most plausible. One is toward collective leadership to revitalize an open and globally oriented economic order. The other is toward regional blocs grouped around each of the three poles.

It is impossible to determine at this point which trend is more likely. The Group of Seven and the Uruguay Round of the General Agreement on Tariffs and Trade (GATT), as noted in the next section, are faltering badly in their efforts to maintain an effective global approach. The European Community (EC) and the North American Free Trade Agreement (NAFTA) are faring somewhat better at the regional level though, as also noted below, they, too, are experiencing significant difficulties.

The outcome will turn in part on the growth prospects of the world economy, the Asia-Pacific region itself, and of the United States—the largest and most influential actor in the system. Unfortunately, world economic growth is likely to remain quite modest, even sluggish, for the next few years. Each of the major growth poles faces obstacles that could inhibit the resumption of robust growth.

In the United States, the enormous debts built up during the 1980s fueled the longest uninterrupted period of peacetime economic expansion in US history. Once the economy entered a recession, however, the debt overhang prolonged the downturn and inhibited recovery. The accumulated debt constrained the spending plans of households and firms, while preventing forceful countercyclical actions by the government. As a consequence, the economy stagnated for four years, and the subsequent expansion has been far weaker than normal.

In Europe, the costs of German reunification have proved far greater than originally anticipated. Huge budget deficits resulted, and the ensuing highly restrictive monetary policy of the German authorities has constrained growth throughout Europe. In Japan, the government faces the difficult task of managing asset deflation while maintaining the health of the financial system. In both cases, the authorities are beginning to pursue more expansionary policies, but rapid recovery still seems distant.

The brightest spot in the growth picture is the developing countries of East Asia. Despite their high trade dependence, they have been able to maintain high rates of growth, even with weakness in the developed countries, through a combination of rising domestic demand and intraregional trade. The rapidly rising incomes of these groups will make them highly coveted markets for trade and investment for the indefinite future.

Trade Policies

Under these circumstances, one can paint a bleak picture for trade policy prospects in both the Asia-Pacific region and globally. Each of the three major initiatives under way—the Uruguay Round, European integration, and the NAFTA—could fail or at least falter badly. The momentum toward European integration has been slowed by the disarray in the exchange rate mechanism and by internal disputes over agricultural policy in the context of the Uruguay Round, and approval of the Maastricht Treaty is by no means certain. The Uruguay Round has stalled, halting the momentum toward trade liberalization, just as slower growth prompts new protectionist pressures. It could collapse and fail, leaving the multilateral trading system in disrepair. The NAFTA agreement will be delayed by the additional negotiations sought by President Clinton and could be further delayed (or even rejected) by the Congress.

Movement toward protectionism, bilateralism, and managed trade are thus quite possible. However, they are by no means the most likely outcome. Europe, for all its problems, will probably stay on track toward further and deeper integration. The 1992 process will be completed largely on schedule. Economic and Monetary Union (EMU) will proceed.

In fact, Economic and Monetary Union could proceed faster than anyone now thinks. The Europeans created the European Monetary System (EMS) in the first place for reasons that ranged far beyond economics or finance but rather derived from European politics. Giscard d'Estaing and Helmut Schmidt concluded in 1978 that Europe needed a major boost. They also wanted to go down in history as the people who provided that momentum. They thus decreed the EMS, over the objections of the Bundesbank and all their economic and financial advisers, and the experiment worked.

A similar scenario could evolve with EMU. Helmut Kohl and François Mitterand will want to restore economic and financial momentum, and therefore political momentum, to Europe. They will want to go down in history as the people who put Europe on the path to a single currency. It could happen in 1994.

We also know that Europe is going to remain almost totally preoccupied with Europe for some time to come. That could preclude any significant new global cooperation among the economic superpowers. We now know that the main global impact of European integration is not trade diversion but attention diversion. (A similar phenomenon befell the United States with respect to NAFTA.) When you focus in one direction, you cannot focus in too many others at the same time, no matter how large your country or your government.

Here in the Western Hemisphere, the probability is very high that the Congress will ratify the NAFTA. It will not make much difference for the United States in economic terms. Gary Clyde Hufbauer and Jeffrey J. Schott, in their 1993 book, *NAFTA: An Assessment*, have laid out the largest estimates of its job impact, and even the gross number is less than the normal monthly turnover in the US labor force. NAFTA is even less important for Canada. Mexico has already liberalized. For Mexico, NAFTA is essentially an insurance policy against a reversion by future Mexican governments to the bad policies of the past.

It is possible that a few other Latin American countries may dock onto the NAFTA over the next few years. When President Bush proposed the Enterprise for the Americas Initiative (EAI), virtually every country in the hemisphere indicated a great interest in responding. They all forgot about the "devil to the north" once the offer was made.

However, the United States has made very clear that NAFTA is a different kind of trade negotiation. Historically, North-South trade negotiations have proceeded on the presumption of asymmetrical, nonreciprocal concessions in favor of the southern country. The northern country was asked to make concessions to the developing country far in excess of what it asked in return. NAFTA and the EAI are the opposite. The United States has said, first to Mexico and then to Chile and others in the hemisphere, that they must liberalize their economies before it will talk.

So Chile, which has liberalized everything, is the only Latin American country that now qualifies. It is the only conceivable docker to the NAFTA agreement over the next few years. Brazil's whole liberalization program remains in question; therefore, the Southern Cone arrangement is doubtful at this time. It is hard to imagine any other Latin American countries qualifying to participate within the next three to five years.

In short, what we are seeing in the Western Hemisphere does not add up to a new bloc. Canada and Mexico are close US neighbors. Some cynics have even said they long ago became the 13th and 14th Federal Reserve districts. There is no deep integration *a la* Europe. That will not happen for decades, if ever.

There is modest trade diversion in NAFTA but no new trade barriers. It is fully compatible with the global economic system. It is thus hard to believe that NAFTA would propel East Asia into developing a defensive bloc of its own, despite the East Asian Economic Group (EAEG) proposal. Asia's economic interest is global, as is that of the Western Hemisphere and certainly the United States. The most desirable world scenario would permit both Asia and the Western Hemisphere to pursue their fundamental global interests.

The most uncertain outlook, however, is for the Uruguay Round and thus the GATT system. The number-one source of unanimity in our profession is the need to bring the Uruguay Round to a successful conclusion. The global trading system has eroded. All but four of OECD's 24 member countries have increased their trade barriers over the last decade, including a dose of managed trade. The European Community is managing its trade with Eastern Europe as it begins to develop relations in that direction.

The great irony is that the erosion of the global trading system is precipitated by the countries that originally created and tried to maintain and nurture that system. The United States and Western Europe are the chief villains. Countries around the world that have shunned that system for decades are now clamoring to get in. The former socialist economies and all of Latin America, many of which formerly stood aside, now want to enter GATT.

These new liberalizers in the developing world, and to some extent the emerging market economies such as China and others, are now the real leaders of the world trading system. They are the ones that are moving in the right direction. The Cairns Group was an institutional manifestation of this process, a group of medium powers and developing countries coming together to give critical impetus to the Uruguay Round and push it as hard as it could.

We may be seeing some convergence in world trade policies: those that have been most liberal are now restricting a bit; those that have been most restrictive are now liberalizing. Countries from both ends of the spectrum may thus be moving toward the middle.

But even a successful Uruguay Round would not comprehensively address all of the issues on the international trade agenda. The bicycle theory suggests that you have to keep moving forward toward greater liberalization or you fall back toward protection and mercantilist action. At the end of every round—the Kennedy Round and the Tokyo Round, in particular—pent-up protectionist pressures did in fact emerge and lead to a great deal of backsliding in the years before the launch of the next. It will thus make a great deal of sense to move immediately on to a new set of negotiations after the end of this round, particularly if its outcome is not as great as one would hope.

The agenda of such a round could include issues of both procedure and substance. Future negotiations might focus more on rules of competition than on market access. They will have to confront trade and investment, trade and the environment, and ultimately trade and migration. There will be a need to reform Article 24 and the relationship between global and regional trade arrangements. GATT could become involved in establishing a framework for military trade. All of these areas are important to the international trading system. Some are outside the traditional norms but could be brought into the next round of discussion. The crucial point is that successful conclusion of the Uruguay Round would significantly reduce the momentum toward major non-GATT initiatives including those in the Asia Pacific.

Asian Pacific Economic Integration

A failure of the Uruguay Round will lead to considerable interest in developing new trading arrangements across the Pacific, perhaps based on the Asia Pacific Economic Cooperation (APEC) group. Successful implementation of NAFTA at the same time, with its modest discrimination against Asia and its symbolic implication that North America "is going regional like Europe," could add to such pressures. Under such circumstances, a Pacific Free Trade Area (PAFTA) could push the world toward two rather than three major trading areas—a decidedly superior outcome.

If the Uruguay Round is successfully concluded, there will be much less pressure for new formal trading arrangements across the Pacific in the foreseeable future. Global arrangements will remain much more important to the United States than the NAFTA or other regional arrangements. However, supplementary trans-Pacific arrangements that go beyond the GATT outcome could still be desirable.

However, there are several problems with proposals for a major trade deal across the Pacific. On the one hand, the Europeans would get a free ride if it were done on a most-favored-nation basis. On the other hand, huge discrimination against Europe and much of the rest of the world would result if they were left outside. A possible reconciliation is to proceed on a conditional MFN basis, but this dilemma will prove difficult to surmount.

In addition, a trans-Pacific deal would have to overcome US-Japan economic tensions. A complete rupture in relations between the US and Japan is highly unlikely; the trade, investment, diplomatic, and security interdependencies are simply too great. At the same time, a US-Japan free trade agreement is very unlikely because the conventional wisdom in the United States holds that an agreement with Japan on tangible trade barriers is irrelevant. In most sectors, Japan already has the lowest overt tariffs and nontariff barriers among the industrial countries. Nonetheless, the belief that the Japanese market is effectively closed to trade and investment is widely held in both business and government circles. The real barriers are thought to be related to competition policy, *keiretsu*, and the like. These issues have been addressed in the Structural Impediments Initiative (SII) talks but are very difficult to grapple with there, much less in an FTA.

A significant trans-Pacific deal might emerge, however, if the Uruguay Round failed. In the United States, there would be movement toward increased emphasis on Super 301–type tactics, managed trade deals, and regional initiatives. Japan would have a difficult time forming a bloc that excluded the United States. Indeed, given its economic, political, and security stake in its relationship with the United States, it is not in Japan's interests to do so. Both the United States and Japan might thus attempt to convert APEC into a free trade area (PAFTA). This could create a trans-Pacific bloc consisting of APEC, NAFTA, and perhaps some of the more liberal Latin American countries such as Chile. The result would be a two-bloc world: the EC and PAFTA. In comparison to an open global system, this is a decidedly second-best option. But it is also decidedly less bad than a world of three blocs, or one that is fragmented into a large number of subregional arrangements.

Alternatively, APEC could evolve gradually into an "Asian OECD." It could be a forum for extensive consultation but without a large secretariat. Among the obvious possible missions would be to promote multilateral trade liberalization and strengthen the GATT, harmonize economic policies not covered under the GATT, provide a neutral forum for the United States and Japan to discuss issues of regional interest currently conducted on a bilateral basis (e.g., exchange rate policies), and perhaps develop common approaches to the evolving security concerns in the region. In addition to an Asian OECD, more and more Asian countries will enter the OECD itself. Korea will certainly enter soon. Others in the area, as they come into the higher income club, should join the OECD and become members in order to enable it to continue to play its role as a forum for discussion among the higher income countries.

Conclusions

The future course of the world economy depends in part on when and how the United States gets its domestic house in order, restoring its competitiveness and self-confidence and adjusting to the loss of its dominance in this post–Cold War era. It depends in part on how the European Community completes its integration and how soon it will again look outward. It depends in part on how Japan adjusts to its new global responsibilities and on the degree to which the rest of the world accords to Japan the global role that its economic and other achievements deserve.

Meanwhile, the rest of Asia will continue to grow rapidly. It will increase its world role and force itself onto the stage in many ways. It will assure itself of a major place in any new world order, whatever that may look like.

The nexus between this Pacific dynamism and the international economic system will be one of the most fascinating, and most important, phenomena of the next decade or so. This volume, based on the Pacific

Trade and Development (PAFTAD) 20 conference, attempts to provide a foundation for understanding and foreseeing the likely course of events. We begin with an assessment of the basic building blocks: the determinants of international trade flows, the status and prospects for the Uruguay Round, and the relationships between globalism and regionalism.

The first paper by Richard J. Grant, Maria C. Papadakis, and J. David Richardson surveys trends in global trade and recent intellectual advances in the analysis of these trends. Grant, Papadakis, and Richardson find that intraindustry and intrafirm trade account for growing shares of world trade, especially for the rapidly developing countries of East Asia. They also uncover some evidence of an increasing regional orientation of trade.

The welfare implications for these developments are ambiguous. It is likely that the growth of intraindustry trade represents welfare-enhancements beyond the conventional gains from trade. Similarly, intrafirm trade may involve beneficial technology transfer in addition to the standard gains from trade. Yet intrafirm trade may also foster oligopolistic behavior, and the existing international trade regime is particularly weak in checking such behavior. Moreover, the growth of intraregional trade may challenge the very relevance of the GATT system as currently constituted. The first of these challenges is taken up in the succeeding paper by John Whalley, and the second is addressed in the paper that follows by Soogil Young.

Whalley argues that, regardless of the outcome of the Uruguay Round, a fundamental reassessment of the trading system is necessary. He envisions a system in which global economic performance, not nondiscrimination and multilateralism, is the central organizing principle. Whalley proposes a less state-oriented system in which access rights and rights of redress would be shared by all agents (including individuals, firms, and governments).

Young takes a similar, performance-oriented view, posing the question of whether regional arrangements accelerate or retard the growth of world trade and welfare. He answers by arguing that emerging blocs in Europe and North America are not likely to be welfare-reducing as long as the blocs refrain from raising external barriers to third parties. Unfortunately, Young concludes that this proviso is unlikely to be realized: external barriers are likely to be raised in sectors experiencing acute adjustment difficulties, and hence the new regionalism *is* a threat to the world as a whole and the dynamic exporters of East Asia in particular.

The next four papers examine these regional developments in greater detail. Per Wijkman addresses developments in Europe. He argues that the accession of the European Free Trade Association countries to the European Community is unlikely to result in higher external barriers to trade. The Eastern European countries are an entirely different matter, however. When these countries become EC members, they are likely to lobby for higher external barriers and to use EC contingent protection policies to the detriment of East Asian countries.

Wijkman also derives several lessons from the European experience for prospective blocs. He argues that integration is most likely to occur when there is already considerable intramember trade dependency, when there is a hegemon or core economy, and when there are political as well as economic motives for integration. The NAFTA appears to meet these criteria; in the cases of proposed integration schemes for the Asia Pacific, the answer is less clear.

H. Edward English and Murray G. Smith return to the theme of regionalism and globalism in their paper on the NAFTA. They point out that even the NAFTA has been regarded as a supplement to, rather than a substitute for, the global system: the NAFTA negotiators would have apparently preferred to address some knotty issues such as agricultural trade in the Uruguay Round rather than in the NAFTA. Consequently, English and Smith see future regional developments as highly contingent on the outcome of the Uruguay Round. Failure of the Round would present policymakers with a number of options; English and Smith would prefer to reconstitute a liberal system as broadly as possible, pointing to a superregional trans-Pacific organization (such as a PAFTA) as a possibility.

Potential developments in the Pacific are taken up in the two following papers, with Peter Drysdale and Ross Garnaut assessing the prospects for integration via intergovernmental agreement and Chia Siow Yue and Lee Tsao Yuan examining the prospects for subregional economic zones. Drysdale and Garnaut make the important point that, unlike much of the rest of the world, there has been a clear trend toward trade liberalization and greater openness throughout the Asia Pacific. Indeed, for the most part, reforms have been undertaken unilaterally for the conventional reasons of gains from trade and competition—what they term the "prisoner's delight," as opposed to the traditional notion of the "prisoner's dilemma." Faced with growing regionalism elsewhere, Drysdale and Garnaut propose a model of "open regionalism" to simultaneously strengthen the global system and enhance integration within the trans-Pacific APEC region.

Chia and Lee's paper is microeconomic in focus, examining the phenomenon of rapidly growing subregional economic zones. Their conceptualization of this emerging phenomenon focuses on the role of policy in encouraging private cross-border investment flows. Happily, foreign direct investment is the topic of the first of five functional issue papers that conclude the volume.

In this paper, Shujiro Urata describes the pattern of foreign direct investment in the Asia Pacific and analyzes the impact of these investment flows on the Asia-Pacific economies. Urata emphasizes Japanese firms' role as investors, responding to permanent changes in comparative costs brought on by exchange rate changes beginning in the mid-1980s. For recipients, foreign direct investment can bring technology transfer, greater market integration, and increased foreign exchange. At the same time, Urata notes that foreign investment is sometimes associated with environmental degradation and foreign domination of the host-country economy.

The importance of Japan as a financier is also reflected in the use of the yen internationally, the topic of the next paper in the volume. Takatoshi Ito observes that, although there has been some increase in the use of the yen as an invoice currency or reserve currency by central banks, the pace has not been as fast as the growth of either Japan's shares of world income or capital exports. He suggests that the yen's slow development as a key currency is due to Japan's relatively closed financial markets at home and its problematic political relationships abroad.

Capital is not the only factor of production that is mobile internationally. In the third functional area paper, Glenn A. Withers addresses the issue of labor mobility and migration. He notes that labor flows are substantial and increasing both globally and within the Asia-Pacific region. He goes on to analyze the impact of these flows on both sender and recipient economies and begins to develop a set of recommendations for a new global policy regime.

Another functional area in which the international policy regime is in its infancy is that of environmental policy. Kym Anderson takes up the nexus of issues involving international trade, economic growth, and the environment. Anderson predicts that the current green wave will have a greater impact on policy than its predecessor did in the 1970s. Anderson examines both the actual impact that trade liberalization could have on the environment and the political economy of policy formation, where policymakers may be motivated by both altruistic environmental and particularistic national competitiveness concerns.

The final paper in this volume addresses the implications of the post–Cold War politico-security environment for regional economic relations. Hadi Soesastro identifies four central issues: trends in the regional politico-security environment, the changing nature of global political relations, the "Asianization" of security issues in the Asia Pacific, and the possibility of trans-Pacific economic conflicts. He ends up returning to a theme that runs throughout this volume, namely, the tension between global and regional institution building. Soesastro argues that the possible dissolution of the world into three rival blocs is the greatest threat to global prosperity. The issue, then, is what to do to avoid this.

He proposes a two-part strategy. First, the NAFTA countries should cease any enlargement in the NAFTA in exchange for the East Asian countries forswearing any attempt to create a trade bloc in the Western Pacific. Then the countries of the Asia Pacific should commit to making

APEC "compellingly attractive." Soesastro regards this as a more flexible approach than attempting to construct a PAFTA.

The conference that this volume is based on concluded with a final overview panel. One of the participants in that final panel was Dr. Saburo Okita, whose untimely death in February 1993 deprived the world of one of its greatest economic statesmen—and one of the most influential sponsors of both Pacific dynamism and close ties between the countries of the Pacific and the rest of the world. Dr. Okita was a long-time participant in the PAFTAD conference series and made major contributions to virtually all of its 20 sessions over a period of 24 years. His remarks at PAFTAD 20 were typically thoughtful, creative, and provocative. We all deeply regret his passing and dedicate this volume to his memory.

II

The International Economic System: Past, Present, and Future

1

Global Trade Flows: Old Structures, New Issues, Empirical Evidence

RICHARD J. GRANT, MARIA C. PAPADAKIS,
J. DAVID RICHARDSON

The purpose of this paper is to assess recent trends in global trade patterns and new thinking about their determinants and policy implications.

The first part of the paper begins with some traditional measures of broad and sectoral openness, barriers, and competitiveness, along with traditional perspectives on the economic and political determinants of these measures. Traditional measures and perspectives have, however, been subject to increasing skepticism in the past several decades, and newer perspectives have challenged them.

In the second part of the paper, we summarize these newer perspectives, of which the most important concern the roles of nonprice competition, large firms, technology, governments, regional groupings, and even chance in international trade. We describe trends, characteristics, and determinants of trade in categories suggested by the newer perspectives: intraindustry trade, intracorporate trade, high-technology trade, and intrabloc trade. We find indicators that intraindustry trade has continued to grow as a share of overall national trade, though most rapidly for the rapidly developing countries of East and Southeast Asia. We also detect growth in intrafirm trade, and since 1980 (but not before) in trade for high-technology categories, both as shares of overall trade. Finally, trends in intraregional trade are quite varied, though we infer possible acceler-

The authors are, respectively, Assistant Professor of Geography; Assistant Professor of Public Administration and Senior Research Associate in the Technology and Information Policy Program; and Professor of Economics at the Maxwell School of Citizenship and Public Affairs, Syracuse University. Richardson is a Visiting Fellow at the Institute for International Economics.

ation in its importance since 1984 for European, North American, and Pacific blocs, and this acceleration can be measured in several ways.

The implications of these conclusions for policy and the Pacific outlook vary. The strong growth of intraindustry trade in East and Southeast Asia suggests considerable gains from trade, even beyond those traditionally measured. These gains are best viewed as productivity enhancements. Growth in intrafirm trade has, at best, mixed benefits. On the one hand, it facilitates global market integration and technological diffusion. But oligopolistic practices may be fostered as well, and current international institutions regulate cross-national corporate competition poorly, if at all. Recent growth in high-technology trade also earns mixed reviews for similar reasons. Productive innovation is surely embodied in the goods traded, yet larger shares of trade fall under the intellectual-property protection that both encourages ongoing innovation and defends entrenched market power. Finally, current multilateralism may pertain less and less to growing intraregional trade and institutions, suggesting the possible need for a new international policy regime.

Traditional Perspectives and Measures

Traditional measures of the importance and determinants of international trade remain arguably valuable for interpreting and forecasting trends and for modifying policy. Yet other important trends, especially since 1985, suggest the growing importance of newer measures and perspectives concerning technology, regionalism, and the competitive structure of both industries and firms. These perspectives also give more emphasis to the identity and preferences of the demanders of traded goods, which are often firms themselves rather than the traditional "consumers."

Trends in Three Traditional Measures

Traditional analysis of international trade has two main concerns: the overall "openness" of countries, especially the way border barriers limit that openness, and the sectoral structure of countries' trade—whether some sectors are more open than others and why it matters. Modern analysis, discussed later in the paper, amplifies these concerns and adds new ones: the benefits and costs of two-way trade within any given sector, whether trade in high-technology sectors is unique, the trade performance of multinational firms in contrast to countries, and of blocs of countries as well as that of each bloc member.

Recent trends in traditional measures are quite striking. Table 1 records the trends in a familiar measure of openness: the ratio of goods and services exports to GDP. Several aspects are notable.[1] One is the very

---

1. One aspect that is familiar is the rough correlation of this measure of openness with

Table 1 Openness ratios, 1965 and 1990 (exports of goods and nonfactor services to GDP multiplied by 100)

By income level and country	1965	1990
Low-income economies	8	18
Middle-income economies	17	25[a]
High-income economies	12	20
China	4	18
Indonesia	5	26
Philippines	17	28
Thailand	16	38
Malaysia	42	79
Korea, Rep.	9	32
Singapore	123	190
Hong Kong	71	137
New Zealand	21	28
Australia	14	17
Japan	11	11
Canada	19	25
United States	5	10

a. 1989 figure from World Bank (1991), table 9, 220.

Source: World Bank (1992), table 9, 234–35.

strong worldwide growth in openness, as measured by export dependence. Another is the very marked "coming out" of fairly closed economies such as China, Korea, Indonesia—and the United States! Still another is how closed Japan remains, though the United States is comparable, and how little change there has been in this measure of its openness. Finally, the smaller *entrepot* economies—Singapore, Hong Kong, and Malaysia—naturally stand out above the rest, but even their trend toward openness is strong. The lesson from these trends is that insulation is declining: international trade is becoming an ever more important influence on domestic prosperity.[2]

One explanation for the trends indicated in table 1 is trade liberalization. It is well appreciated that tariffs have declined to fairly modest levels, as summarized in table 2. What is not as well appreciated is how ubiquitously nontariff barriers (NTBs) have grown. Few countries have been exempt. Few sectors have been exempt. Table 3 documents these counter-

country size. Small countries tend naturally to be more export-dependent; large countries less so because many shipments of their small subregions fall within national boundaries. In the extreme, of course, by this measure, the world economy as a whole is "closed."

2. Some claim that there is only a 20th century trend in this direction, and that openness in the 19th century was much like that of today. See, for example, Gagnon and Rose (1990). But for evidence that the trend toward greater openness is in fact at least 250 years old, see, for example, the *Economic Report of the President 1992*, 193–95. The aberrant period, in which openness shrank, was 1913–50.

Table 2   Tariff rates in selected sectors for various regions, 1988
(weighted average percentages[a])

Region	High Technology	Sophisticated Extractive	Simple Extractive	Low Wage	Food
US	2.7	1.4	4.0	15.8	10.9
Japan	3.6	1.8	.2	15.3	15.1
EC (12)	6.3	1.4	2.3	12.1	9.8
Canada	5.2	2.0	1.4	18.6	2.9
Australia[b]	10.6	5.8	2.0	22.6	6.3
New Zealand	13.4	7.2	1.2	21.9	7.7
Sweden	5.5	.5	.3	10.5	2.2
Colombia	26.3	19.1	21.7	53.5	24.6
Morocco	27.5	45.0	25.0	45.0	29.2
Hong Kong	0.0	0.0	0.0	0.0	0.0
Hungary	10.9	2.2	4.1	9.2	11.8
Indonesia	13.3	7.3	6.9	23.5	13.7
ASEAN[c]	18.4	23.6	20.8	19.7	20.1

ASEAN = Association of Southeast Asian Nations
a. The weighted average tariff rates are derived from the General Agreement of Tariff and Trade *Trade Policy Review* (various issues and years) GATT: Geneva. The classification of commodities is based on work by Smith and White (1990) that derives a theoretically relevant classification of commodities. They suggest that there are 5 different levels of processing of commodities and that 3 particular commodities in each category provide a good representation of bundles of commodities that flow together in the international economy. These categories are arranged in a continuum ranging from the highest tech category to the lowest. The commodities representing each category are at the two-digit SITC code. The five categories and three commodities representing each category are as follows: 1) the high tech category "machinery-non- electrical," "artificial resins, plastics, cellose esters and ethers" and "manufactures of metal, not specified elsewhere"; 2) the sophisticated extractive category "paper, paperboard, and articles of paper pulp," "pulp and waste paper," and "gas, natural and manufacture"; 3) the simple extractive category "oil seeds and oleaginous fruit," "animal oils and fats," and "cereals and cereal preparations"; 4) the low wage category "articles of apparel and clothing accessories," "footwear," and "travel goods, handbags and similar containers"; and 5) the food products category "meat and meat preparations," "dairy products and bird's eggs," and "crude animal and vegetable materials, not elsewhere specified."
b. Tariff rates reported for Australia are for 1986.
c. Tariff average rates for ASEAN states are from the Philippine Tariff Commission for 1985 and are reported in Ariff and Loong-Hoe (1988:30).

Sources: GATT Trade Policy Reports 1990 and Ariff and Loong-Hoe, (1988).

liberalizing trends, using a traditional rough measure, and shows a dramatic increase in the use of NTBs among countries of the Organization for Economic Cooperation and Development (OECD) since 1966.[3] Ap-

---

3. A major problem with any NTB index is that relevant worldwide information is often insufficient and incomplete. Laird and Yeats (1990), the source for table 3, use the United Nations Conference on Trade and Development (UNCTAD) Data Base on Trade Measures, which is compiled from government publications and other official sources such as General Agreement on Tariff and Trade (GATT) reports. Their reliance on official sources may cause the importance of some NTBs to be understated where there is a lack of "transparency" or where measures such as voluntary export restraints (VERs) are not typically listed in national reports. Bearing these problems in mind, we believe that their NTB index is still useful in making comparisons over time and between states. This is the purpose of our use of this index, and as such, we implicitly assume that measurement problems in the table are stable over time and space.

Table 3 Nontariff barrier frequency indices for commodities[a]

Country	High technology		Sophisticated extractive		Simple extractive		Low-wage		Food		All commodities	
	1966	1986	1966	1986	1966	1986	1966	1986	1966	1986	1966	1986
Japan	36	25	17	29	0	59	9	43	51	99	34	50
US	39	62	46	.1	14	31	20	99	14	54	27	57
EC	4	51	5	38	4	28	5	95	38	96	15	58
OECD	19	58	3	39	4	41	7	89	36	89	17	54

OECD = Organization for Economic Development and Cooperation

a. The classification of commodity categories is the same as in table 2. The frequency index refers to the percentage of commodities affected in some manner by NTBs. We adopt a similar stance to Laird and Yeats (1990) and believe that rather than discussing NTB rates in percentage terms (as is common in research on tariffs), it is more appropriate to measure the percentage of products affected in some manner by NTBs. NTBs are different from tariff barriers in that, rather than introducing flat NTB rates, governments have considerable discretion and flexibility in implementing different NTBs, which can range from quotas, embargoes to packaging, and labeling restrictions, etc.

Source: After Laird and Yeats (1990). Note: Categories will not add up due to different categories used.

Table 4   Freight and insurance factors, 1965 and 1987 (ratio of imports inclusive of freight and insurance costs to imports without such costs)

By income level and country	1965	1987
Small low-income economies	1.023	1.140
Developing economies	1.102	1.096
Industrial economies	1.081	1.044
China	1.090	1.090
Indonesia	1.100	1.120
Philippines	1.107	1.067
Thailand	1.110	1.108
Malaysia	1.056	1.105
Korea, Rep.	1.092	1.056
Singapore	1.064	1.060
Hong Kong	1.100	1.100
New Zealand	1.079	1.082
Australia	1.114	1.085
Japan	1.214	1.025
Canada	1.032	1.025
United States	1.082	1.044

Source: International Monetary Fund, *Supplement on Trade Statistics* (supplement to *International Financial Statistics*), no. 15, 1988, 66–69.

proximately half of all commodities traded were subject to some type of NTB in 1986, and the food category stands out as especially highly protected.

So when the liberalizing and counter-liberalizing trends of tables 2 and 3 are combined, it is not clear that they provide an important explanation of the increased openness shown in table 1. Another candidate for explaining table 1 is decreased transportation, communication, and transfer costs. But these are notoriously hard to measure and would facilitate both domestic and international commerce unless the costs sharply declined for international commerce alone. Table 4 records one very rough measure: the ratio of imports inclusive of freight and insurance costs to imports without these charges. Downward trends are present only for the industrialized countries; other trends seem random.

Table 5 records trends in the sectoral structure of trade. Several aspects are notable. Manufactures trade has grown strongly,[4] especially once the 1970s' surge in fuels and mining trade is taken into account. The strongest growth of all is in capital goods, particularly in machinery, transportation equipment, and—as figure 1 shows—goods thought to embody rapidly

---

4. It stands in sharp contrast to growth in manufacturing *output* as a share of domestic output, which tends to fall over time in advanced industrial countries, and to rise only for nascent industrial countries. See World Bank (1987), especially chapter 3.

Table 5   Composition of world trade, 1965–90

GATT breakdown[a] (shares of total world trade)	1970	1980	1990
Merchandise			
Agriculture	16½	12½	10
Mining	12	22	11½
Manufactures	50	45½	57
(Not specified)	2½	3	2½
Capital goods	29½	26½	37
Commercial services[b]	19	17	19

World Bank breakdown (shares of total world merchandise imports)	1965[c]	1979[d]	1985[e]	1990
Food	18	12	10	9
Fuels	10	20	19	11
Other primary commodities	17	9	8	8
Manufactures	55	58	62	73
Machinery, transport	23	25	29	34

a. GATT (1992, table 1); GATT (1990, table 8); GATT (1989, 9).
b. Commercial services include shipping and other passenger, port, and transportation services; travel goods and services other than passenger services acquired by persons staying for a year or less in an economy where they are not resident); and other private services (communications, advertising, brokerage, management, professional and technical services). Commercial services do not include investment income on unrequited transfers, whether official or private (e.g., migrants, transfers, workers' remittances). See GATT (1989, box 2).
c. World Bank (1992, table 15).
d. Total-import weighted average of averages for industrial market economies (weight = 0.758), middle-income economies (weight = 0.209), and low-income economies (weight = 0.034). World Bank (1982, table 10, 128–29).
e. Total-import weighted average of averages for industrial market economies (weight = 0.735) and developing economies (weight = 0.265). See World Bank (1987, table 12).

improving technologies. By contrast, trade in agricultural and other primary commodities has grown weakly; their share of world exports has been in continual decline for 25 years. Trade in commercial services has grown at rates below manufactures trade but above other trade so that the service share of world exports is fairly stable.

The lessons from these trends are that the composition of trade is shifting toward goods with rapid technological evolution, toward heterogenous goods (away from homogeneous goods), and toward producer goods (away from consumer goods). These shifts are clearly linked to intraindustry and intrafirm trade and to innovation, all discussed below, and have important implications for policy and for the determinants of trade, to which we turn next.

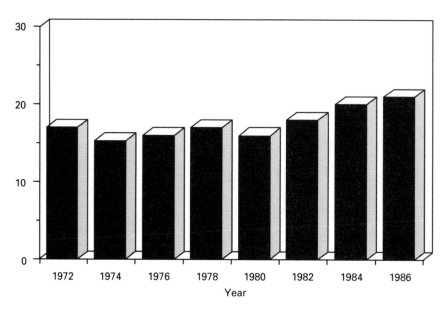

Figure 1. High-technology exports as a percentage of all manufactures exports. Note: OECD-11 exports to the rest of the world. High-tech industries are aerospace, electronic components and equipment, drugs and medicines, electrical machinery, office machines and computers, and instruments.

Empirical Estimation of Traditional Trade Theories

Traditional trade theories emphasize the way that international trade reflects and embodies a region's endowments of the primary factors of production—labor, capital, land, natural resources—relative to world standards. Under a (fairly stringent) set of conditions, a region's exports will embody the services of factors in which it is relatively abundant by world standards, and its imports will embody services of its relatively scarce factors. That is, its exports will tend to be those goods whose production requires its abundant factors intensively, and its imports those goods whose production requires its scarce factors intensively. When estimated with data, these theories have had reasonable but not startling predictive performance. The usual approach is to employ measures of factor abundance or intensity, respectively, to explain statistically the variation in exports and imports, or their differences across regions or industries. Deardorff (1984) is an excellent survey; Leamer (1992a) is a more recent survey with an emphasis on method. Leamer (1984) is an impressive example of such estimation.[5]

---

5. Kotlikoff and Leamer (1987) estimate variants of these theories' predictions for value added, factor demands, and wages across countries, with similarly modest conclusions.

More recent estimation, however, has tended to ratify the endowments perspectives even more weakly. Bowen, Sveikauskas, and Leamer (1987), for example, find that simple qualitative implications of the theories fail against a data set for 12 factors in 27 countries. For example, the implied net trade in a country's factors, as embodied in its goods traded, does not line up very closely with a measure of the relative abundance of its factors. And the rankings of the factors implicitly exported or imported as embodied in goods should, but do not, correspond to the rankings of the factors by their abundance. In careful statistical testing of competing hypotheses for "failure" of the traditional view, the authors find clear dominance for an explanation that emphasizes measurement errors in the data and differing technological competence (i.e., factor productivities) across countries. The latter finding is especially interesting for the support it gives to newer technology-based trade theories, discussed below.

Maskus (1991), using more recent data for 28 to 38 countries[6], supports these conclusions. Measurement error corrupts simple tests of traditional perspectives, but direct international comparisons of technologies (factor intensities and productivity) for various industries show revealing differences across countries and industries. Industrial countries have higher productivity than semi-industrialized countries, which themselves surpass developing countries, but the differences are least pronounced in the most capital-intensive industries.[7] Industrial countries also generally use more capital-intensive techniques.

Noland (1990), however, finds stronger results from traditional endowments regressions in a panel approach, for a cross-section across countries and years.[8] The panel approach, sampling endowments across several years, may reduce their measurement error.[9] For each of 46 commodities, exports or imports are related reasonably strongly to nine traditional factor endowments. An auxiliary set of time-series autoregressions for his factor endowments allows him to project the commodity composition and intensity of trade in the year 2000 for eight smaller Asian economies.[10]

---

6. Maskus' basic data are for 1984; Bowen, Leamer, and Sveikauskas' are for the 1960s. Maskus collects explicit factor input intensities for each industry in each country, subject to some data gaps; Bowen, Leamer, and Sveikauskas rely on scalar multiples of US factor intensities to characterize the rest of their countries.

7. And the differences nearly vanish when "purchasing-power parity" versions of exchange rates (based on overall GNPs) are used to make comparisons instead of measured exchange rates.

8. 1968, 1972, 1976, 1980, 1984.

9. Only 1984 data are used in Noland (1991a), with measurement error and productivity gaps playing significant and explicit roles (see especially pp. 15–16) as they do for Bowen, Leamer, Sveikauskas, and Maskus.

10. Hong Kong, Singapore, Taiwan, Korea, Malaysia, Thailand, Indonesia, and the Philippines.

Smith (1991, 1992) also finds stronger results from augmented endowments regressions in a panel of exports across 51 US states and three years.[11] Her augmentation, a patent-based measure of technological endowments with strong explanatory power, underlines again the significance of technology in its own right as a determinant of trade. Smith (1992) also detects evidence of geographical agglomeration from a study of the residual exports left "unexplained" by endowments. That is, exports of certain products tend to cluster in certain states at the expense of others. This suggests that pure locational factors may matter in addition to the location of endowments, and thereby influence inter- and intra-regional trade patterns.

Petri (1991) and Noland (forthcoming) also augment traditional endowments regressions to draw several provocative conclusions about the importance of corporate structure and industrial policy in Japanese trade patterns.[12] In a study of Japan's world export shares and home import shares across industries, Petri finds both shares to be significantly positively related to oligopolistic concentration, and import penetration to be significantly negatively related to business's and government's share of overall demand. In a study of Japan's industry-by-industry residual exports—those left unexplained by traditional endowments-based regressions—Noland finds them positively correlated to government R&D subsidies and (usually) to capital subsidies, though not to effective rates of protection.[13]

The general conclusion of recent contributions to this literature is that endowments-based explanations of trade patterns are foundational but inadequate in themselves. Technology, scale, corporate structure, and policy play important complementary roles.[14]

In other words, endowments-based traditional trade should be supplemented but cannot be easily dismissed. The apparatus alone is broadly

---

11. States include the District of Columbia. Years are 1987, 1988, and 1989.

12. Petri's regressions explain scaled trade across industries by measures of industry factor intensity in using various endowments. But Petri's conclusions may not be robust in light of Maskus' (1991) conclusion that this type of cross-industry approach to traditional endowments-based perspectives performs reasonably well for Germany, Japan, and the United States only, and not for the other 24 countries in his extensive data set.

13. The endowments-based regressions are across 29 trading partners for each of 15 industries; the policy correlations come from regressions across the 15 industry residuals for each of three years.

14. That this conclusion is not new, but may have been forgotten, is illustrated by the closing paragraph of Gary Hufbauer's 1970 classic in the same spirit (Hufbauer 1970, 193):

> What can be said about an evaluation which finds virtue everywhere? Considering the unlikely, indeed almost improbable, statistics used in certain instances, the discovery of little truths in every nook is perhaps surprising. Much better to pour academic hot oil on two or three accounts than to broadcast olive branches!

Table 6 Physical capital formation, 1965 and 1990 (gross domestic investment to GDP multiplied by 100)

By income level and country	1965	1990
Low-income economies	19	31
Middle-income economies	21	23
High-income economies	23	22
China	24	39
Indonesia	8	36
Philippines	21	22
Thailand	20	37
Malaysia	20	34
Korea, Rep.	15	37
Singapore	22	39
Hong Kong	36	28
New Zealand	28	22
Australia	28	21
Japan	32	33
Canada	26	21
United States	20	16

n.a. = not available

Source: World Bank (1992), table 9, 234–35.

consistent with important trends. To see this, consider the trends in endowments summarized in tables 6 and 7. These tables are striking for contrasts of several kinds:

- Physical capital formation rates across disparate countries diverged between 1965 and 1990.

- Physical capital formation declined in the English-speaking Pacific countries over the quarter century; it marked time in Japan (and the Philippines); it rose strongly everywhere else.

- Secondary education participation rates across disparate countries converged between 1965 and 1990; tertiary education participation rates remained quite different.[15]

- Rates of growth of tertiary education participation rates over this quarter century are not strikingly different across countries, even though the base rates are.[16]

---

15. In 1965 both low- and middle-income economies had secondary education participation rates that were one-third to one-half as high as those in high-income economies. By 1990 middle-income economies had converged to where high-income economies were in 1965, at participation rates that run from half as high to just as high as those in the high-income economies. Convergence is much less marked, however, for low-income economies.

16. Mean rates of tertiary education participation rates essentially double for most countries,

Table 7 Human capital formation, 1965 and 1990 (percentage of
age group enrolled in secondary/tertiary education)[a]

World	1965	1990
Low-income economies	20/2	38/n.a.
Middle-income economies	26/7	55/17
High-income economies	61/21	95/42

13 Countries		
China	24/0	44/2
Indonesia	12/1	47/7[b]
Philippines	41/19	73/28
Thailand	14/2	28/16
Malaysia	28/2	59/7
Korea, Rep.	35/6	86/38
Singapore	45/10	69/12[b]
Hong Kong	29/5	73/13[b]
New Zealand	75/15	88/41
Australia	62/16	82/32
Japan	82/13	96/31
Canada	56/26	105/66
United States	86[c]/40	89/63
Average (mean)	45.3/11.9	72.2/27.4
Average dispersion (standard deviation)	24.0/11.1	21.5/19.9
Scaled dispersion (coefficient of variation = standard deviation ÷ mean)	0.53/0.93	0.30/0.73

a. Secondary age groups vary according to country, but are most commonly the population
12–17 years old. Tertiary age group is the population 20–24 years old. Tertiary enrollment
includes vocational schools, two-year colleges, and some adult education and correspondence program enrollments.
b. 1985 figure from World Bank (1988), table 30, pp. 288–89.
c. 1960 figure from World Bank (1982), table 23, p. 155.

Source: World Bank (1992), table 29, 274–75.

The trade implications of these endowments trends, using traditional
categories and theorems, are that aggregate exports would grow more
rapidly in Asian than in other countries, as would output itself; Asian
exports of capital-intensive and semiskilled, labor-intensive goods would
grow especially rapidly compared with those of other countries (which
might well shrink); and Asian countries would find themselves less successful exporters of highly skilled labor-intensive goods (e.g., super-

---

whether low or high participation to start. There is slight convergence, seen in the dispersion
across countries not quite doubling, but the convergence is much less marked than for
secondary education.

computers, in contrast to computer chips), and possibly even increasingly import-dependent in such high-end goods.[17]

Trade and industrial policies may indeed play a role in the account just summarized, though they are often alone credited with the "successes" tallied. Corporate structure, scale economies, and technology (apart from that embodied in education) no doubt all play some role. But disentangling the correlated, joint contributions of physical and human capital formation, trade policy, structure, scale, and technology is a subtle task.[18] Appendix A summarizes the literature that focuses all the explanatory power on policy, along with its supporting evidence, largely historical.

At the end of the day, there is one important reason for expecting lower and lower explanatory power from the traditional endowments-based approaches to trade patterns. It is the growing international mobility of endowments such as machinery and equipment,[19] research and development (R&D),[20] managerial capital, and professionally skilled capital of all kinds (e.g., engineering, marketing, legal, and financial services). Their movement across borders can substitute for goods that embody them. Properly speaking, they should be viewed as tradeables themselves, rather than as endowments (Leamer 1984, 22–23). Only immobile endowments should appear as explanatory variables in traditional empirical estimation. The primary vehicle for this increased international factor mobility is, of course, the multinational firm. Its role is discussed below.

Perspectives and Measures for Newer Issues

Traditional explanations of trade patterns seem most in need of empirical and historical supplementation on matters of policy influence, technology,

---

17. For example, Petri (1992, 72) finds that Japan's shares of world exports become smaller and import dependence rises as technological intensity increases among those industries in the top 20 percent of industries ranked by technological intensity.

18. The attempt by the Industry Commission of Australia (1990) to do so ended giving almost all weight to sensible capital formation and other determinants and almost no weight to trade or industrial policy.

19. Indeed, world trade in capital goods has risen in just 10 years from 26½ to 37 percent of world trade in goods and services, according to table 5, more than triple the level of either agricultural trade or mining trade.

20. According to Brainard (1992, table 1), between 1978–79 and 1987–88, R&D expenditures from foreign sources increased eighteenfold in Italy, eightfold in Canada, fivefold in Norway and Sweden, fourfold in Denmark and the United Kingdom, threefold in France and Japan, but by only 20 percent in Germany. According to the same source, over this same period British pharmaceutical companies increased the proportion of their R&D personnel who were employed abroad from 14 to 28 percent.

Table 8 Traditional and newer approaches to explaining international trade patterns empirically

Approach	Variables of Concern	Determinants
Traditional	Exports, imports, or net exports.	Factor endowments
Intraindustry	Transformations of ratio of net exports to summed exports plus imports.	Traditional determinants plus measures of potential for product differentiation and scale economies
Intracorporate	Trade among or within multinational firms as a share of overall trade.	Traditional determinants plus determinants of vertical and horizontal integration
Technology-based	Trade in high-technology sectors as a share of overall trade.	Traditional determinants, especially factors important to research and development; government policy toward technology, intellectual property
Intraregional	Trade among neighbors or peer countries as a share of overall trade.	Proximity; political affinity; government policy toward regional alliances; health of global (GATT) regime

and on the roles of potential scale economies, scope economies, externalities, product differentiation, and imperfect competition.

The potential for policy to shape comparative advantage via some influence on endowments is obvious. More interesting is how policy's potential for shaping comparative advantage may be enhanced by departures from the norms and assumptions of the traditional approach. Important candidates are technological differences, scale and scope economies, externalities, and imperfect competition. These, in fact, all have significant roles in undergirding the case for "infant industry" exceptions to traditional free-trade policy recommendations and in explaining the phenomena called intraindustry trade, intrafirm trade, technological-gap trade, and product life-cycle trade.

In this part of the paper we examine the significance, measures, and determinants of several of these newer perspectives on comparative advantage and policy.

Table 8 provides a visual ordering of the four newer perspectives reviewed below. The table identifies what it is these approaches try to explain about international trade (in other words, what the dependent variable is), and how they do so (with what independent variables). While the perspectives overlap, they do not necessarily contradict each other or even traditional trade theory. We begin first with a discussion of intraindustry trade, which leads naturally to intrafirm trade issues.[21] We then take up the role of technology and policy-defined comparative advantage, and finish with the effects of regionalism on trade patterns.

Intraindustry Trade

The "oldest" of the newer perspectives is the intraindustry account of geographical and commodity trade patterns. It began inductively, with Grubel and Lloyd's (1975) measures of how frequently developed countries recorded both large exports and imports of goods in the same commodity classifications. This would not tend to happen, according to traditional endowments-based reasoning.[22] But explanations of monopolistic competition and product differentiation soon provided a theoretical basis for measured intraindustry trade, a basis that could be appended conveniently to endowments-based accounts.[23] Products were recognized as differing on the demand side as well as in production and supply. Quality, durability, serviceability, proximity, and fashionability were admitted as dimensions that matter to buyers as well as price, and as ways that sellers could compete with each other in addition to price competition. It should then be no surprise to see simultaneous exports and imports of goods that differ in quality and durability, for instance, even if their factor requirements, commodity classification, and price were the same. It is even less surprising with any fixed cost or scale economies involved in producing or marketing a given variety, since each country's firms will then find it profitable to specialize in a limited number of niches within the quality, durability, etc. dimensions.[24]

---

21. Modern thinking about intraindustry trade begins with imperfect competition in which a firm is more than a mere competitive automaton.

22. Traditional reasoning was that goods in the same commodity classification, at suitable levels of disaggregation, would have very similar factor requirements in production. Therefore, either a particular country or the rest of the world ought to have competitive and comparative advantage in *all* goods in that classification, with positive exports and zero imports. Simultaneous exports and imports were considered an anomaly.

23. Greenaway and Milner (1986) is an exhaustive treatment. More recent general contributions include Gray (1988), Greenaway (1987), Greenaway and Milner (1987), and Globerman and Dean (1990). Hart and McDonald (1992) is a noteworthy and recent monograph focussed on measurement. Bilateral and multilateral measures of intra-industry trade are calculated: for Canada, Mexico, and the United States; for both manufactures and agricultural goods, at three different levels of aggregation; and for each year from 1962 through 1987.

24. Which particular niches a country decides to specialize in may be a matter of chance, history, or government policy that identifies some niches as socially desirable and others as undesirable. Thus there is an arbitrary or policy-sensitive element in the pattern of comparative advantage, as discussed below. This tends to be true, however, because of the assumed scale economies; neither differentiated products nor intraindustry trade are necessary parts of the account.

Trends

For many countries, intraindustry trade in manufactures has been growing—very rapidly for various newly industrializing economies (NIEs),
more slowly if at all for the most industrialized countries (except Japan,
where there has been rapid recent growth, but only enough to restore
the levels of 25 years ago). Table 9 records trends and projections.[25]
Intraindustry trade shares vary positively with the level of a country's
development, both cross-sectionally and over time. France and other
European countries seem to have especially high intensities of intraindustry trade, and Japan seems to have especially low intensities.[26]

Characteristics and Significance

One of the most important characteristics of intraindustry trade is the
distinctive benefits it provides, in addition to the traditional gains from
trade. One distinctive benefit is "variety," but a more meaningful char-
acterization would be "precision": buyers are able to purchase items that
meet their precise needs for quality, durability, serviceability, etc. This is
especially beneficial when the buyer is another firm and the commodity
is a machine, a semiprocessed good, or a professional service. Then the
benefit is measured by enhanced productivity of the purchasing firm, not
by some vague measure of consumer tastes for fashion. Another benefit
to productivity in this case is input cost-savings that might stem from
the ability of a niche supplier of producer goods to spread fixed costs
over a global market or to realize scale economies at a global level. Still
another benefit is the constraint on oligopolistic market power that globally free entry (free trade) allows. It invites producers in new countries
to occupy unfilled niches, often quite close (adjacent) to niches occupied
by powerful incumbent firms, thereby reducing their power. In sum,
intraindustry trade enhances not only traditional efficiency and price
performance, but also quality, productivity, selection, divisibility, work-
ability of competition and, so on.

A second purported characteristic of intraindustry trade is its allegedly
low adjustment costs in the face of trade liberalization. It has become an

---

25. The measure of intraindustry trade is standard and varies between 0 (no intraindustry
trade) and 100 (all trade is intraindustry). The measure is 100 (1 the absolute value of the
difference between exports and imports divided by the sum of exports and imports).

26. Lincoln (1990, chapter 3) documents Japan's low intensity of intraindustry trade in
considerable detail. It is especially low in motor vehicles, power-generating equipment, and
telecommunications equipment. It is not especially low for any particular one of Japan's
trading partners, however, given their stage of development. Ravenhill (1992) shows how
much of Japan's recent resurgence in intraindustry trade is concentrated in its declining
sectors, with competitive exporting sectors maintaining their historically low intensity of
intraindustry trade relative to other sectors.

Table 9 Intraindustry trade indexes for manufactures

Country	1968[a] 1970[b]	1975[b]	1980	1984[b]	1988[a] 1989[b]	2000[a]
Indonesia	7				17	42
Philippines	6				34	30
Thailand	7				39	34
Malaysia	15				48	47
Korea, Rep.	16/19	36	38	46	53/44	51
Singapore	48[a]		67	75	70/73	64
Hong Kong	35				39	32
Taiwan	31[a]		35	40	54/45	61
Japan	32	26	29	26	34	
United States	57	62	60	61	67	
France	78	78	82	80	84	

a. From Noland (1990), left entry when there are two.
b. From Ravenhill (1992)/Lincoln (1990), right entry when there are two.

Sources: Ravenhill (1992), table 3, updating Lincoln (1990), table 3.2, p. 47; Noland (1990).

article of faith that the European Community's early liberalization succeeded because of intraindustry trade; few industries disappeared in any of the original six members, although all rationalized production by reducing the number of varieties they produced and lengthening the production runs of the varieties retained. Rarely is the faith questioned, even as it applies the same adjustment nonchalance to any other liberalization exercise that features large shares of intraindustry trade. This is strange, because the basic mechanism of trade liberalization in the face of scale economies tends to concentrate production in some regions and extinguish it in others. There is no guarantee that each region will retain comparative advantage in at least one or two varieties of every industry group. And regions are able by policy to prey on each others' perceived strategic niches.[27] Thus adjustment costs may be unusually high, not low, in regions whose pattern of intraindustry trade leads to widespread industry closure after liberalization.[28]

A related characteristic is the alleged political-economic stability of intraindustry trade (Marvel and Ray 1987). Pressures to protect some firms against imports are naturally resisted by other, more export-oriented firms in the same industry that fear retaliation in their export markets. Lawrence (1987) and Ravenhill (1992), correspondingly, argue that Japan's

---

27. See Krugman (1992, 435–38) for a brief and recent account of the theory behind this possibility.

28. Richardson (1989, 15–16 and 38–39) provides a fuller account, including a graphical demonstration. See also the caution expressed by Greenaway and Milner (1987, 47–48 and 51) on this issue. If rising fixed costs of R&D, or anything else, are today causing even more concentration of global production and/or joint ventures, then the high adjustment-cost story may be increasingly relevant as the number of "sites for concentration" shrink.

low intraindustry trade has made it highly susceptible to protectionist pressure from its trading partners because they lack counter-protectionist firms in the same industry that export to Japan.

One final characteristic of intraindustry trade is less normative. Its intensity seems to differ markedly across industries (not surprising), but these differences themselves vary markedly across countries (more surprising).[29] Nothing in the work summarized below on determinants helps to explain this "double difference" in patterns across-industries-across-countries.

Determinants

Intraindustry trade, as normally conceived, emphasizes product differentiation and scale economies in contrast to the more conventional factor endowments. It also emphasizes technologically volatile products because of the way rapid technological change creates differentiated varieties of similar products and dynamic scale economies.

Early empirical studies of intraindustry trade featured measurement of the phenomenon rather than statistical estimation of its determinants. The same was true of traditional endowments-based studies, which began with Leontief's paradoxical measurements of the capital and labor embodied in US exports and imports. Unlike endowments-based empirical research, however, that on intraindustry trade has emphasized correlates rather than determinants. Thus the typical research shows the intensity of intraindustry trade to be positively correlated with per capita incomes and overall market size, and negatively correlated with trade barriers, distance, and the difference in per capita incomes between two countries. None of these variables has anything very directly to do with product differentiation or scale economies or technology, though they may well be correlated.[30] Only a few studies measure industry-level proxies for the more direct theoretical underpinnings of intraindustry trade.[31] And none

---

29. Park and Park (1991), in figures 3.1 and 3.2, for example, derive matched time plots of intraindustry trade intensity for the United States and Japan in four different sectors. Intraindustry trade in capital-intensive goods falls sharply in the United States from 1974 through 1987; it remains flat at very low levels in Japan. Intraindustry trade in labor-intensive goods falls sharply in the United States and rises sharply in Japan. In high-technology goods the pattern is a sharp rise in the United States and little trend in Japan. Only raw material–intensive goods show similar patterns (modest decline).

30. Bergstrand (1989, 1990) shows how to interpret and empirically document such influences using a fairly traditional endowments model modified to allow for monopolistic competition and preference maps (tastes) that vary with per capita income.

31. Balassa and Bauwens (1988), for example, include the coefficient of variation among export unit values of subaggregate categories as a measure of product differentiation and two measures of potential for scale economies, one of which is the share of marketing, planning, and support costs in total costs for each industry.

seem to address seemingly obvious questions.[32] One is whether there is greater intraindustry trade in high-technology industries, as suggested above, or in industries where factor requirements are similar across the subaggregate groups making up the industry (an implication of the view that adjustment costs of openness to intraindustry trade are low). Another is how the determinants of vertical intraindustry trade—between products at various stages of fabrication—differ from those of horizontal intraindustry trade, that is, those between products at the same stage.

Intracorporate Trade

Multinational, multiple-product firms are the natural vehicles by which scale and scope economies are captured; by which externalities and spillovers across borders, agents, and activities can be audited, evaluated, and "internalized"; and by which technological change can be diffused without loss of proprietary ownership. Thus among other things, these multinational corporations (MNCs) are important vehicles for the intraindustry trade described above and the technology-based trade described below.

Trends

Virtually all measures of the importance of MNCs in international trade trend upward. Several have been of special interest. One is the share of home and foreign MNCs in a country's own exports and imports. A second is the share of a country's own MNCs in world exports and imports. A third is the share of a country's trade that is carried out within MNCs rather than between them or with other agents.[33] The first indicates the influence of MNCs in a country's trade, the second reflects the competitive and comparative advantage of a country's firms relative to those

---

32. Leamer (1992a, 33) quips, "This area of research has a special difficulty forming interesting empirical questions because the linkage of the theory and the data analyses of necessity is often casual."

33. As this paper is concerned primarily with determinants of geographical and sectoral trade patterns, a brief allusion may suffice to a closely related issue of trade *volume*. The issue is whether more overseas activity by MNCs increases or decreases their trade with their home country. Some say that it displaces exports; others that it enhances them. Some say that it increases imports at the expense of home production; others that it has no effect. Bergsten, Horst, and Moran (1978, chapter 3), is still one of the most careful studies, though dated. They find for the United States that early MNC investment in sales, marketing, and distribution facilities abroad enhances exports but that subsequent additional investment has no effect. They also could detect no effect on US imports. Lipsey (1991), in a more recent study, is similarly eclectic, finding that the correlates of export and import intensity of foreign affiliates in the United States vary with industry and size and age of the affiliate.

Table 10 US, US multinational parent, and overseas affiliate[a] shares of world exports of manufactures, 1966–88
(percentages)

	1966	1977	1982	1985	1988
US	17.1	13.2	14.6	13.4	11.9
US MNC parents	10.7	9.2	9.4	9.4	8.1
US MNC affiliates[a]	6.6	8.3	8.2	8.9	8.9
US MNC Total	17.3	17.5	17.6	18.3	17.0

MNC = multinational corporation
a. Majority-owned overseas affiliates of US multinational parent firms.

Source: Lipsey (1991), tables on pp. 12 and 13 and related text, and Lipsey and Kravis (1991), table 1.

elsewhere in the world, and the third measures the MNC-internalization (as opposed to market-centeredness) of a country's trade.

In all measures, US data is richer than that of other countries. Table 10 shows first how US MNC parents have accounted for increasing shares of US exports because the second line of the table declines more slowly over time than the first. It shows second that US MNCs and their affiliates have maintained a very steady 17 to 18 percent of world exports even in the face of declining US shares of world exports measured geographically. Table 11 shows that the world export competitiveness of both the United States and its MNCs has been especially marked in high-technology goods,[34] with a slight positive trend between 1977 and 1988, and especially low in low-technology goods, with a slight negative trend over the same period.

Not all of such trade is intracorporate, however, which is a category of special interest because of the suspicions that intracorporate transactions are less governed by the normal price/cost determinants than arm's-length transactions are, and that transactions among affiliates and their parents are least likely to be market-determined. Table 12 shows that between 30 and 50 percent of exports by various countries' MNC parents go to their affiliates abroad, and that, wherever a time comparison is possible, these shares are increasing.

Larger perhaps than MNC shares in cross-border transactions are their shares in intraborder—domestic—transactions. Here data on trends and importance is fragmentary at best.[35] But what there is suggests growing

---

34. Kravis and Lipsey (1988) show this to be true of US services "exports" as well.

35. Julius (1990), Kester (1992, chapter 1 and appendix A), and Stevens (1990) are three recent contributions that discuss the methods and pros and cons of an alternative or supplemental set of "trade" accounts, recording trade not just across borders (the traditional accounts),

**Table 11   US and US multinational firms[a] shares of world
exports, selected categories, 1977–88** (percentages)

	1977	1982	1985	1988
"High technology" manufactures[b]				
US	18.8	22.0	20.7	21.5
US MNCs	28.8	33.3	32.6[c]	31.1[c]
"Medium technology" manufactures[b]				
US	15.6	15.9	14.3	12.8
US MNCs	26.5	24.1	24.7[c]	23.7[c]
"Low technology" manufactures[c]				
US	8.3	9.1	7.5	6.8
US MNCs	8.3	8.1	8.3[c]	7.5[c]

MNC = multinational corporation
a. US multinational firms encompass US parent firms and their majority-owned overseas affiliates.
b. Technology level is defined by the research and development intensities of the industries from which the exports originate; classification carried out by the National Bureau of Economic Research from United Nations trade data.
c. Figures were extrapolated from 1982 on the basis of the industry of the affiliate.

Source: Lipsey (1991), table on p. 19 and related text, and Lipsey and Kravis (1991), table 5.

shares of foreign firms in US internal transactions (Graham and Krugman 1991) and growing penetration of overseas activities by MNCs from all countries except the United States. Lipsey (1989) shows, for example, strong upward trends in ratios of employment abroad to employment at home, or of assets abroad to assets at home, for MNCs from Britain, Canada, Germany, Japan, Korea, and the Netherlands. Such ratios for US MNCs plateau in 1977 midway between high ratios for Britain and low ratios for Germany and Japan.

One problem in all these tabulations is the crude rigidity of the categorizations. Measures of trade influenced by "joint ventures," "strategic alliances," consortia, and trading companies do not exist in more than snapshot form,[36] although such trade would be presumably influenced by the same factors as intrafirm trade.

Characteristics and Significance

There are a number of reasons for emphasizing the influence of MNCs generally in international trade, and for the importance of intracorporate

---

but between domestic and foreign firms within a nation's borders. Among other methodological and policy issues discussed, the definitions of domestic and foreign firms are fundamental, of course.

36. See, for example, Soete (1991), summarizing snapshots by Hagedoorn and Schakenraad (1990).

Table 12   Intrafirm trade as a percentage of trade by national MNC parents (exports by MNC parents to affiliates abroad as a percentage of exports from MNC parents resident in country noted)

Country	Share	Year
Belgium	37	1968
	53	1976
United Kingdom	29	1976
West Germany	34	1966
	44	1974
United States	28	1982
	37	1989

Sources: US Department of Commerce (1986), table 2; (1991), table 6; and Greenaway (1987), table 3, citing Van Den Bulcke (1985), table 1, and Panic and Joyce (1980).

transactions. One is that it underlines the value of newer models of imperfect competition and trade, and calls into question traditional conclusions based on perfect competition. It similarly signals the multi-dimensionality of competition—over quality, durability, etc.—that underlies intraindustry and high-tech trade. And it suggests an antitrust or competition-policy lens for trade policy and its global regulatory institutions that fits uneasily into competitive, GATT-centered frames. Finally, to the extent that MNCs do have geographical spheres of influence,[37] their growing importance may be an independent cause of the regionalization discussed below.

But MNCs are not monolithic. The nationality of the MNC seems to matter. Blomström, Kravis, and Lipsey (1988) find, for example, that developing-host-country export patterns of US and Swedish MNC affiliates, unlike those of Japanese MNCs, were more similar to their home-country (US and Swedish) export patterns than to the export patterns of other host-country firms.

Japan has been the focus of considerable attention. Noland (1991) finds a measure of the intensity of *keiretsu* linkage among an industry's firms to be positively associated with the industry's net exports and negatively associated with its gross imports, controlling for the normal market determinants. And Lawrence (1992) interprets the very high shares of Japanese imports that are intrafirm trade to be an entry-deterrence device against foreign firms wanting to compete for Japanese sales.

As MNCs' trade presence grows and as the amount of R&D they perform abroad grows (Brainard 1992, particularly table 1), diffusion of technology from country to country is greater, and the "national"

---

37. See, for example, Urata's (1992) paper for this conference.

appropriability of technology is less and less feasible. Somewhat strangely, this characteristic enhances traditional trade theory's assumption of cross-national technological comparability and undermines the potential for successful "techno-nationalism"—policy that seeks to prevent diffusion of a "nation's" technology across its borders.

Finally, MNCs have clearly enhanced the vertical integration of the world's economies, encouraging trade in capital and intermediate goods,[38] as well as vertical intraindustry trade.

Determinants

Whether and to what degree trade involving MNCs is different from other trade is still one of the most important unanswered questions in empirical analysis and for policy. At the level of broad aggregates, corporate structure does seem to help explain trade patterns in the case of Japan, as discussed above.[39] At a finely detailed level, however, corporate structure can clearly matter, and sometimes for products deemed significant for symbolic or strategic reasons.[40]

The poles in the controversy are the following. At one extreme are those who feel that MNCs are the quintessential competitive firms, the unitary agents who are able on a global scale to transfer and diffuse technology, to measure and compare costs, and to detect the vagaries of how best to compete in price, quality, and service across countries. The "MNC-as-a-veil" pole draws succor from empirical research such as that of Bresnahan and Reiss (1991), showing that most of the distance between pure monopoly and pure competition is traversed by the time a fourth or fifth firm is added to a well-defined market.[41] At the other extreme are those who emphasize the oligopolistic nature of MNCs and therefore the ways their actions are often dictated by considerations other than product-by-product variable resource costs. Such nontraditional determinants of MNC investment and trade include strategic entry-deterrence,

---

38. See Casson (1992) and table 5 above.

39. But we are unaware of research on other countries similar to that of Noland (1991a and b) or Petri (1992).

40. For example, virtually all US exporters of the thin notebook computers (Apple, IBM, Tandy, Toshiba) shifted their production to Ireland and East Asian locations when the United States levied steep antidumping duties on active-matrix display screens, an important component of the computers. It is not surprising that *some* production and exports would shift, of course. That virtually all shifted illustrates the way that multinational corporate structure can overlay traditional determinants of trade patterns with considerations such as exploiting economies of scope and geographical diversification of capacity to ensure against risks of adverse events such as trade-policy decisions.

41. This research is based on a statistical sample of 202 geographically distinct markets for professional services such as dentistry, medicine, and plumbing. The argument in the text construes the conclusion as applicable to a single integrated global market.

cross-subsidization of one product line by another or of one region's customers by another's (dumping), cross-subsidization of current sales (that would be unprofitable otherwise) by expected future (profitable) sales, allocation of fixed costs across borders and joint costs across product lines, and so on.[42] None of these seem very closely or directly related to traditional resource costs or factor endowments. All of them suggest that policy questions need to be addressed more from the perspective of industrial organization and regulation, and less from traditional trade-policy perspectives.[43]

Technology, Innovation, and Trade

Contemporary empirical research on endowments-based, intraindustry, and intracorporate trade suggests the growing influence of technology. Productivity, product differentiation, economies of scale, and the international diffusion of R&D are all technology-induced and have a substantial impact on trade patterns. Perspectives on the economic role of technology are not of recent vintage, however, and may be traced back at least to Ricardo.

In almost all instances, technology-based accounts of international trade constitute dynamic explanations of comparative advantage and international competition. Technology trade theory explicitly rejects the stringent assumptions governing technology in traditional factor endowments models[44] and has moved through two major generations of thought. The first was the early technology gap and product cycle theory, advanced in seminal works by Posner (1961), Hirsch (1965), Hufbauer (1966), and Vernon (1966). Current second-generation theories are far more sensitive to the nature of technological change and innovation, and to their unique dynamics and determinants. Second-generation technology trade theory argues that it is the full matrix of innovative capabilities—technological innovation, intellectual property rights, institutional dynamics—rather

---

42. One determinant of special note is insurance. Considerable anecdotal support exists for MNCs insuring themselves against uncertainty by consciously proliferating sources of their inputs and customers for their outputs. Sometimes the uncertainty is connected with unstable politics in input-supplying countries, sometimes with volatile input prices, sometimes with persistent real-exchange-rate realignment, and sometimes with unpredictable export-control regimes. The resulting "insurance capacity" can give the illusion of *excess* capacity. That it is not in fact "excess" is an implication of the theory of insurance. Furthermore, apart from the political factors, one might expect the locational pattern of excess capacity to match the locational pattern of primary capacity, since low costs are a goal in either case.

43. Graham and Richardson (manuscript) "Global Competitor Policies: Issues in Trade and Industrial Economics."

44. Namely, that technology is exogenous, equally possessed by trading partners, and freely and easily available across national boundaries. As we have seen above, empirical research makes these assumptions especially suspect.

than the introduction of innovations themselves, that engenders competitiveness and comparative advantage. While first-generation theories incorporated exogenous technological variables to help predict interindustry patterns of trade specialization, second-generation approaches explore the root determinants of that specialization via explanations of endogenous technological change, innovation, and R&D. Also unlike the original technology gap and product cycle theories, which can be reasonably regarded as supply-oriented accounts of comparative advantage, much present thinking is evenhandedly demand-oriented too.[45] Endogenous growth theory is by far the most formalized example of these latter new technology trade theories,[46] but a rich descriptive literature on the relationship between technical change and trade may be found within the competitiveness rubric (Dosi and Soete 1988; Porter 1990; Cohen and Zysman 1987; Spence and Hazard 1988; Landau and Rosenberg 1986).

In spite of the richer conception of technology in second-generation technology trade theories, they are still ambiguous about the exact relationship between technical change and trade patterns, and hence about the trade impacts of technical change. Contemporary technology trade theories may still be broadly categorized as either supply- or demand-oriented and still contain large doses of first-generation thinking regarding technology gaps and product cycles. As the first of the technology trade theories, technology gap theory was advanced for understanding global shifts in comparative advantage. Nations introduced innovations from which they were able to realize monopoly rents from trade during an international diffusion lag; subsequently, comparative advantage was lost to the innovator and claimed by the imitator. The emphasis in gap theory is on relatively long lags and the "ownership" of technology, making technology essentially a factor endowment. It is thus not inappropriate to regard technology gap theory as a structural-supply account of trade, complementary to traditional factor endowments models.

Because of the intensive R&D investments required for radical technological change, many believe that technology gaps can be systematically created and maintained through policy and innovation, giving rise to sustained interindustry specializations among nations. Such thinking is still what lies behind the rush for high-tech leads in materials, biotech-

---

45. Comparative advantage is a supply-side, structural determinant of international trade advantage based on principles of relative cost. Cost advantages are implicitly understood to lead to price competitiveness. Competitiveness, as it is used in a modern microeconomic context, means something qualitatively different. That is the ability of a product or producer to prevail in the marketplace due to a host of competitive factors: price, quality, service, channels of distribution, the attributes of a good, consumer taste, and so forth. From this perspective, competitiveness is importantly demand-driven, and flows to the products and producers best able to meet the structure and need of market demand.

46. See Nelson and Winter (1982) and Grossman and Helpman (1991), discussed below.

nology, aerospace, and microelectronics, as well as the greater attentiveness to trends in high-technology trade more generally. Through ongoing technological innovation and lead times, technology gaps can presumably form immutable endowments that provide long-term comparative advantage. The Achilles heel of this theory, however, is that some technological fields lend themselves to sustained national appropriability and others do not, *and it is the nature of the technology itself which determines this.*[47]

While technology gap theory emphasizes gaps and time lags as the key innovation-related trade determinants, product cycle theory emphasizes the movement from unstable, first-generation innovations to standardized, mass market (capital or consumer) goods. First-generation product cycle theories were supply accounts like their technology gap precursor, yet the growing contemporary literature on innovation—technological, commercial, organizational—indicates that product cycle behavior may be appropriately perceived as *demand-induced* dynamics.[48] Producer competition along cycles is often characterized by rapid and strategic product differentiation; the ability to dominate or prolong the expansion phase of a cycle is a function of the supplier's capacity to produce high-quality goods and ancillary servicing that appeal to a variety of consumer tastes at increasingly lower costs. Hence manufacturing technology, learning by doing, innovation lead times, marketing, and the functional interfaces of the firm all figure prominently in the competitive and comparative advantage of firms/nations in a product cycle (Porter 1990; Freeman 1982; Rosenbloom 1989).

These more recent neo-gap–cycle theories suggest interesting hypotheses about the relationship between technology, innovation, and international trade flows. Technology gap theory clearly has comparative advantage implications, which is that technological leaders do better in leading growth sectors, while the "behind countries" will perform better in laggard industrial sectors (e.g., those with less innovation potential). Similarly, due to demand dynamics and the roles of product differentiation and economies of scale in product cycle theory, we might expect that

---

47. Teece (1986) describes, at least at the firm level, the determinants of appropriability of such technological regimes; Perez and Soete (1988) discuss the macro- and microeconomic barriers and opportunities for national appropriability or imitative success.

48. Note that while product cycles are essentially demand-driven, much technology gap theory is really "closet" long wave theory. At the policy level, technology gap theory is often blended with Schumpeterian long wave theory; this conceptual synthesis is especially the case when trade analysis is being conducted through science and technology "lenses," since Schumpeter's account of long cycles, creative destruction, and industrial revolutions has been a primary rationale for government technology policy. In any event, long waves are induced by supply-sided technological change, creating a structural advantage to the innovating country. Multiple, successive, and cumulative product cycles then build on the new technology to sustain long waves through decades.

greater convergence in the pace of innovation among countries will result in greater intraindustry trade between them.

What remains to be established is whether technology constitutes the central determinant of trade flows, as is suggested by technology trade theories, or if it instead interacts with endowments in more complex and complementary ways.[49]

Trends

The OECD is the only organization that reports comparable technology trade data across countries on an ongoing basis, and only for the OECD member countries.[50] Even though Dosi and Soete (1988) point out that the international "club of innovators" is confined to countries within the OECD, it would nevertheless be worthwhile to capture the role of the East Asian and other NIEs in global patterns of high-technology trade because they play host to multinational corporations, which are the repositories of much R&D. Nevertheless, the behavior of the so-called OECD-11 is in itself instructive. The long-standing presumption that technologically intense goods have a leading place in the growth of world trade is not entirely born out by the data in figure 1. Using the OECD classification,[51] it appears that high-tech as a share of total manufactures exports from the OECD-11 to the rest of the world was constant from 1972–80 and then expanded rapidly after that point. While the 1972–86 period is an admittedly short snapshot of the post-war era, data reported

---

49. One of the best recent attempts to integrate technology with other growth and trade variables is Grossman and Helpman's (1991) model of endogenous innovation, growth, and trade. The model features the kind of Schumpeterian process that is often alleged to undermine traditional policy perspectives based on assumptions of perfect competition. In Grossman and Helpman's treatment, successful innovators earn the right to price above cost but need to expend resources, especially on human capital for R&D or reverse engineering, and are under constant pressure from new entrants to the process of producing information. Some specific information can be appropriated, but more general information cannot. The latter creates a positive spillover from R&D activities that can only sometimes be kept within national boundaries. Merchandise trade involves both inter- and intraindustry flows of goods. The assumption that the marginal product of additions to the knowledge stock does not diminish creates a form of economies of scale from simultaneous additions to all inputs. Expectations matter, and historical accidents and temporary government policies can all matter "forever." Out of this structure comes an ordered cornucopia of scenarios in which trade (and industrial and technological) policies matter—sometimes along traditional lines ("free" trade is often wise), and sometimes along the lines of industrial activism (strategic government promotion of selected activities is sometimes wise).

50. Data series, in turn, are most readily available only for the OECD-11.

51. OECD considers the following six industries (out of approximately 21) to be high-technology: aerospace, office machines and computers, electronic equipment and components, drugs and medicine, instruments, and electrical machinery and equipment.

in Grimwade (1989) confirm the relatively limited role of high-tech goods in historical world trade growth. In his data on the shifting commodity composition of world manufactures trade from 1955 to 1985, only the "office and telecommunications" sector shows an appreciably large increase in its share of total manufactures trade.[52] It is possible, of course, that trade in these categories grew faster within the OECD-11 than toward the rest of the world. That would create "regionalizing" trends among the richer nations alone and might be a stimulus to intraindustry trade among them as well.

There are interesting country-of-origin characteristics among the OECD-11 in terms of high-technology trade performance. As reflected in figure 1, export growth in high-tech from 1972–86 outpaced that of total manufactured goods; however, the United States was the only one of the 11 major industrialized countries for which high-tech export growth lagged that of all manufactures (table 13). Curiously enough, with the exception of Japan, the export growth of high-tech manufactures from these other countries was below the OECD-11 average, though above the growth of manufactures in general. Japan was clearly the pacesetter in high-tech exports, with a 27 percent higher rate of growth than the OECD-11 average. The United States also contributed to the strong growth performance of high-tech exports, albeit right at the average.

What is apparent from the manufactures export data is that while all of these major countries were experiencing positive expansion in trade, Japan and the United States definitely led the trade growth for the group as a whole. These nations are the only two to demonstrate above-average export growth for both total manufactures and high-tech trade, but with slightly different emphasis for each. Japan's comparative advantage grew especially in high-tech exports while that of the US grew in other manufacturing sectors. Many underlying causes of these overall trends suggest themselves. The most important is that the European countries are still in a period of technological catch-up, as evidenced by the stronger pace of their high-tech exports relative to total manufactures yet their lower rates of high-tech export expansion compared with Japan and the United States. This is a pattern one would expect during periods of technological diffusion.

The relation of high-technology trade to overall trade performance is also shown to be complex when comparative advantage and net export performance are compared. Papadakis (1992) finds that the United States demonstrates revealed comparative advantage in all six industries that the OECD classifies as high-tech. Yet three of these industries—office and

---

52. The leading growth sectors were chemicals, motor vehicles, and office and telecommunications equipment. Note that Grimwade's categories do not perfectly match the OECD industrial classes and could therefore be masking high-tech leads (for example, drugs and medicines are subsumed within the chemicals sector).

Table 13 Growth index[a] trends in high-technology and total manufactures exports by the OECD-11, 1972–86
(1.00 = OECD-11 average annual rate of growth)

Country	Total manufactures exports	High-tech exports	High-tech relative to total manufactures
US	1.25	1.01	.93
Japan	1.16	1.27	1.27
Germany	.96	.91	1.10
France	.89	.95	1.24
UK	.78	.91	1.35
Italy	.98	.96	1.13
Canada	.86	.81	1.10
Australia	.55	.72	1.51
Netherlands	.88	.78	1.02
Sweden	.85	.89	1.21
Belgium	.81	.79	1.13

OECD = Organization for Economic Cooperation and Development
a. Data are average annual growth rate indexes. An index of 1.00 reflects the average annual rate of growth for all OECD-11 countries combined. The high-tech to total manufactures index is simply each country's average annual rate of growth in high-tech exports relative to its individual growth rate in all manufactures exports.

computing machines, electronics, and electrical machinery—also registered substantial worsening in their net trade position during the 1980s, and these three sectors account for roughly one-fifth of the total manufactures trade decline from 1982–86. Trade recovery since 1987 has only modestly changed this comparative advantage-net export anomaly. Office machines continued to erode finally into a net deficit (from a surplus of $6 billion in 1982); the deficit in electronics has improved only marginally, principally as a consequence of the slowdown in US imports that commenced with slower domestic growth in 1989–90; trends for electrical machinery are harder to read, but by 1989 the surplus in this industry was nowhere near its pre-1982 levels (US Department of Commerce 1992). As Walker (1979, 35) observes, "Innovation is necessary but not a sufficient condition for competitive success—other factors help *sustain* a country's position in world markets." The role of MNCs, for example, cannot be neglected in explaining the contrast between comparative advantage and net balance of trade trends. Statistics may make a competitive industry look uncompetitive in world markets relative to other industries in the same country, if the industry can easily exploit its advantage by investing in production facilities overseas" (Walker 1979, 71). Tables 10 and 11 provide evidence to support this view of the impact of MNCs on trade trends. However, the industries in which US multinationals demonstrate the highest global competitive advantage—food, chemicals, nonelectrical machinery—do not coincide with those high-tech industries for which comparative advantage and competitiveness indicators conflict with one another.

Characteristics and Significance

There is a strong theoretical basis for presuming that technology has a significant role in international trade flows, a role which is empirically verified. However, observing the effects of technology is not to be confused with isolating its effects. Policy based on the empirical research should be formed with some caution. For example, a preoccupation with high-technology trade could lead to the neglect of other, equally or more important, sectors. High-tech leadership strategies are institutionally demanding in terms of innovation, requiring a complex system of competitive activities (Freeman 1984). Technology trade strategies cannot be developed in isolation from a nation's overall matrix of innovative capabilities, including its factor endowments. Demonstrable interindustry variations in the impact of technology are also significant policy issues. Generic technology liberalization (or protection) strategies may have no significant impact on trade flows.

First- and even second-generation theories do little to assist policy-making because they lead principally to the conclusions that more technology is better and that innovative capabilities must be fostered to more fully appropriate the rewards of technological leadership. More recent theory is more helpful. For example, Grossman and Helpman (1991) point out that R&D (with large progrowth spillovers) and high-technology manufacturing (with smaller progrowth spillovers) often compete with each other for the same human capital so that a country whose trade and industrial policies favor the latter over the former will often be inhibiting its own growth. Such awareness leads to more discriminating policymaking, as does their conclusion that the case for trade policy intervention becomes weaker as spillovers become more and more internationally diffused and less and less nationally self-confined. Finally, they show that the policy promotion of R&D in countries without comparative advantage in performing R&D can slow growth worldwide; policy promotion of R&D in locations where it is done most efficiently would therefore have greater global welfare effects.[53]

What is often neglected in technology and trade discussions, but for which there is theoretical justification and empirical evidence, are the welfare effects of the technology diffusion process. As the industrialized nations struggle to create high-tech leads, there is room for growth and trade expansion by virtue of imitation, a lesson not lost to Japan in its early postwar development or for several of the Pacific NIEs.

---

53. Grossman and Helpman are more careful than our summary to draw the distinction between policies that increase growth rates and those that increase national economic welfare. Not all that do the first do the second, and vice versa.

Determinants

For all its importance, general effects of technology on international trade are hard to establish empirically. Case-study literature both substantiates and refutes product cycle and technology gap approaches. Statistical studies on the relationship between R&D and trade performance also reflect limited generalizability (e.g., strong interindustry differences). This class of empirical work fits orthodox trade theory since it uses R&D as a supplement to factor endowments to explain export composition. It has no strong theoretical underpinnings because it assumes that R&D reflects a qualitative dimension of labor endowments, although R&D is treated empirically as a separate independent variable. Thus Gruber, Mehta, and Vernon (1967) proclaim, "All roads lead to a link between export performance and R&D," and they find that the US export position was strongest in the five most R&D-intensive industries. Walker (1979) substantiates a relationship between R&D efforts and trade performance for several countries as well but provides a helpful and important warning: not all industries "fit" the theory of the relationship between relative innovation efforts and trade performance. A handful of industries reflect a positive export correlation with R&D, many more show no correlation, and two are even negatively correlated.[54]

Intrabloc Trade

A special twist in studies on the influence of policy on comparative advantage concerns regional policy. Traditional trade theorists assume states interacting in a global trade system but neglect regional subsystems that might develop to mediate and affect the global regime. Increasingly, some international trade researchers and members of the media argue that the world economy is evolving into a series of regional trading blocs.[55] Regionalism is an old argument; German geopolitical writers in the 1930s proposed a tripartite division of the world economy into large "pan-regions" or autarkic blocs with poles centered on North America, Germany, and Japan (O'Loughlin and van der Wusten 1990). A difference with the argument today is that it is not solely a propaganda statement but a view shared by many trade analysts and policymakers that may affect how they perceive national and international trade policies. Currently, researchers are attempting to define and measure the extent and nature of regionalism with empirical evidence, discussed below.

---

54. The last set of industries presumably are those in which countries not pursuing R&D intensely would find their comparative advantage.

55. Regional trade arrangements have been studied by various researchers (Garten 1989; Schott 1991; Frankel 1991; Lawrence 1991a; but see Anderson and Norheim 1992).

A regional trading bloc can be defined as an association of states that reduces intraregional barriers to trade (and sometimes investment and human capital). Regional trading groupings have three general aims: to generate welfare gains through scale economies, efficiency effects, and trade creation; to increase negotiating leverage with external actors; and to promote regional political cooperation (Schott 1991, 2) and possibly integration.

Trade regions are dynamic, constantly shifting the contours of their orbit. It is generally accepted that regional cohesion and interdependence exists for some time before being formalized in a regional free trade agreement (FTA). Thus regional relativism is not simply a matter of studying FTAs but a more complex issue of delineating regional parallels and contrasts and studying the growth or decline of regions across time and space. A variety of opinions exist as to how many regional blocs there currently are. Some argue for the existence of a tripolar economy (Garten 1989), others cast doubts on the formation of at least one of these poles (Frankel 1991; Petri 1992), and a few argue for regional political groupings of five (Smith and White 1990) and eight (Nierop 1989).

No consensus exists on the criteria for measuring regional trading blocs.[56] All rely on measures of intraregional contact and parallelism. But international trade theory is particularly weak on this issue. Indeed, the matter is made worse by researchers adopting different regional classifications[57] and regional indicators, and then comparing their findings as if they were directly comparable. Agreeing on a regional classification of

---

56. Schott (1991, 2) suggests that blocs exhibit four characteristics: similar levels of GNP per capita, compatible trading regimes, geographical proximity, and political commitment to regional organization. Del la Torre and Kelly (1992) measure the effectiveness of regional arrangements by the degree to which they keep to implementation deadlines and the extent to which the level of intraregional trade increases. Frankel (1991) measures bloc formation by examining levels of intraregional trade and investment flows and by ascertaining to what extent there is growing use of a regional currency. *The Economist* cites three factors that are important in bloc construction: intraregional trade, growing international use of regional currency, and growth in intraregional foreign direct investment ("A Survey of the Yen Bloc." *The Economist*, 15 July 1989).

57. Schott (1991, 1) defines the North American bloc as US, Canada, and Mexico; the European Community as the EC-12; and East Asia as a modified group of Asia Pacific Economic Cooperation (APEC), to include Australia, Hong Kong, Indonesia, Japan, Korea Malaysia, New Zealand, the Philippines, Singapore, Taiwan, and Thailand. Lawrence (1991, 29) denotes the Western Hemisphere as US, Canada, and Latin America; Western Europe as the EC plus the European Free Trade Association (EFTA); and Southeast Asia as Japan, Korea, Taiwan, Hong Kong, Singapore, Malaysia, Thailand, Indonesia, and the Philippines. Garten (1987, 15–16) delineates North America as the US, Mexico, Canada, and the Caribbean; Western Europe as the EC; and East Asia as "virtually every country bordering the Pacific Rim."

the Pacific Rim or East Asia is particularly problematic and a large no-menclature persists (USITC 1992).[58]

At present, the answer to the question of whether trading blocs are evolving depends on which region we consider and how we define the membership of the grouping. Some change in the membership patterns of regional groupings is found in studies by Nierop (1989) and Smith and White (1990), suggesting that we need to direct some attention to the dynamic nature of regions and not simply view them as static entities, as is common in most studies.

Trends

More than 50 FTAs, customs unions, and preferential trading arrange-ments have been initiated since the Second World War (Schott 1991, 3). Regional trading blocs come in a variety of shapes and sizes.[59] Many have not lasted, such as the Council for Mutual Economic Assistance (CMEA or COMECON), and some, especially those composed of industrialized states, have been more successful than those in the Third World.[60]

Two methods for measuring the strength of bloc formation and the impact of the bloc on the trade system are of interest: a formal measure and a political measure. The first method delineates the bloc by a formal FTA. The second method defines regions "politically" by shared mem-bership patterns in intergovernmental organizations. For political regions, trade is viewed as "following the flag," and salient economic ties may lead eventually to the formation of a formal regional trading bloc. The first method is useful in assessing the current trends while the second method may be useful for speculating on future developments.

An East Asian or Pacific bloc is especially difficult to identify. Japan has no formal free trade zone or customs union with any country (the

---

58. During the 1960s and 1970s, when it was in vogue in geographical and international relations research to classify and delineate functional and nonfunctional regions, there were similar obstacles (Russett 1967; Thompson 1973; Berry, Conkling, and Ray 1976). Delineating trade regions should be more straightforward because of the emphasis on economic and geographic criteria over less measurable criteria (political, cultural, etc.), but this is not to say that economic factors can be divorced from other factors and that the interrelationships are the same in each region.

59. See Belous and Hartley (1990) for detailed information on regional groupings' member-ships, goals, and dates of establishment.

60. De la Torre and Kelly (1992) review the impact of regional trade arrangements in Latin America (Latin American Free Trade Agreement , Central American Common Market, Carribean Community, , etc.) and sub-Saharan Africa (Economic Organization of West African States, Economic Community of Central African States, Southern African Develop-ment Coordination Conference, etc.) and note that political interest in these arrangements has not always translated into effective implementation of these goals, and that the overall impact of these regional organizations on trade has been limited.

only industrial country not to), perhaps the result of the memory of Japan's military attempt to form a "Co-Prosperity Sphere" before the Second World War. No positive discriminatory trade measures have been enacted toward East Asian states in the way the US has for Canada (and Mexico in the near future) or the EC has for Europeans. Nonetheless, the concept of an East Asian trading bloc is frequently advanced in the literature, so we form one hypothetically, yet formally, in table 15. Some see such a bloc emerging as the result of the countries of the region coalescing in a "flying geese" pattern around the region's dominant economy, Japan. Others regard the growing interest in Pacific Basin initiatives as the catalyst for a new trading bloc, with both the US and Japan at the core (so that the US blocks Japanese economic dominance in the region). This expanded bloc is formed in table 16. Thus the consequences of both potential blocs are examined empirically.

There are several complicating issues for measuring the extent of bloc formation. There is no widely accepted measure of regional interdependence. Relying on percentage changes in the level of intraregional trade may not be always reliable.[61] Complicating the interpretation of the intraregional trade measure is the continued growth in intracorporate trade, where foreign MNCs internationalize their operations to locate within the boundaries of other regional groupings—sometimes replacing trade. The impact of a range of schemes (e.g., Generalized System of Preferences (GSP), the Caribbean Basin Initiative, the Fourth Lomé Convention etc.) on maintaining South-North trade flows and impeding intra-South trade also complicates the issue.

Tables 14 and 15 decompose trade (exports plus imports) undertaken by countries in the various regions into percentages of total intraregional and total interregional trade. The shares highlight the general trends within regions of the global trading system and provide useful cross-regional measures of bloc formation or fragmentation.

Characteristics

Table 14 shows fairly stable historical levels of intraregional trade for each bloc across time; in the 1970s the measures rise slightly in North America and East Asia and decline in the EC. Measures for each bloc rise more rapidly in the 1980s. The EC trend corresponds to the general attitude toward the integration process in the Community, "Euro-pessimism" in the 1970s, and "Euro-optimism" in the 1980s. By 1984 all three

---

61. Exogenous growth in external trade could cause even faster growth in intraregional trade by catalyzing input-output linkages within the region. We are indebted to Robert Lawrence for this note of caution.

Table 14 Tripolarity? Intraregional and interregional trade[a] among actual and potential formal blocs, 1972—90
(percentages of total trade)

Pole	1972	1976	1980	1984	1988	1990
North America[b]						
Intraregional	30.4	31.5	32.3	34.0	36.0	36.3
With EC	19.1	18.1	18.6	18.4	18.6	18.1
With East Asia	18.7	19.6	18.2	18.3	28.6	28.0
EC[c]						
Intraregional	60.2	62.2	50.6	53.1	58.9	59.1
With N. America	9.9	8.1	8.7	9.5	8.9	10.8
With E. Asia	5.2	5.6	4.9	6.3	6.9	7.4
East Asia[d]						
Intraregional	30.3	31.7	32.8	33.4	37.2	38.0
With N. America	19.1	22.5	22.1	29.1	31.8	28.0
With EC	12.2	12.1	12.2	12.5	13.8	14.8
ASEAN[e]						
intra-regional	14.3	14.1	16.3	18.3	17.4	17.6

ASEAN = Association of Southeast Asian Nations
EC = European Community
a. Exports plus imports.
b. North American Pole: US, Canada, and Mexico.
c. European Pole: 1972 EC-6: France, Italy, Germany, Netherlands, Belgium, Luxembourg; 1976 plus UK, Ireland, and Denmark; 1984 plus Greece; 1988 plus Spain and Portugal.
d. East Asian Pole: Malaysia, Hong Kong, Indonesia, Japan, South Korea, Australia, New Zealand, Taiwan, Papua New Guinea, Singapore and the Philippines.
e. ASEAN: Indonesia, Malaysia, the Philippines, Thailand and Singapore 1984 plus Brunei.

Source: International Monetary Fund, *Direction of Trade Statistics.*

poles behave very similarly. The level of intraregional trade is highest in the EC region, reflecting Europe's regional economic cooperation since the Treaty of Rome in 1957. The region of the Association of Southeast Asian Nations (ASEAN) is not highly integrated in terms of intraregional trade. Current trade patterns and trends suggest, however, that inter-regional trade is becoming increasingly significant for each regional arrangement.

Some have looked at the general evidence and concluded that Japan is secretly attempting to form a "yen bloc" in East Asia ("A Survey of the Yen Bloc." *The Economist*, 15 July 1989). In interpreting the East Asian intraregional trade share, we need to discount for the rapid growth of output and trade that the region has experienced since the late 1970s. The increase in measured intraregional trade could be entirely due to the increase in economic size of the countries involved. As Frankel (1991, 7) notes, "Incorporating a regional bias term shows that the East Asian bias

Table 15 Political polarity? Intraregional and interregional trade[a] among blocs with political affinity, 1972–90
(percentages of total trade)

Blocs	1972	1976	1980	1984	1988	1990
Western Europe						
Intraregional	64.9	67.8	62.5	64.4	67.5	71.2
Latin America	4.5	3.1	3.8	3.0	2.3	2.4
Pacific Rim	15.7	12.9	15.2	16.7	15.8	15.1
Arab Region	4.9	5.1	10.9	8.2	3.4	3.0
Africa	3.1	3.8	3.2	3.6	2.8	2.8
Latin America						
Intraregional	19.7	20.8	25.7	23.8	23.0	22.9
Western Europe	16.9	20.0	26.7	21.6	18.2	18.9
Pacific Rim	59.8	47.5	37.1	43.9	56.6	56.9
Arab Region	.2	3.3	8.7	3.3	.2	.2
Africa	1.1	.8	1.6	1.1	1.0	.9
Pacific Rim						
Intraregional	48.8	50.5	50.7	53.6	54.0	56.0
Western Europe	25.7	18.7	16.4	16.6	20.2	21.4
Arab Region	10.5	11.1	12.5	15.3	11.7	11.0
Africa	3.1	3.1	3.1	3.1	3.1	3.1
Latin America	4.8	3.3	3.6	3.3	3.4	3.3
Arab Region						
Intraregional	4.7	5.9	6.4	4.9	6.0	5.7
Western Europe	52.5	47.4	40.8	38.3	38.2	37.0
Latin America	.9	1.2	5.0	3.3	3.0	2.7
Pacific Rim	36.7	36.8	45.1	49.1	50.1	51.2
Africa	.9	.9	1.7	1.2	1.2	.9
Africa						
Intraregional	9.1	8.0	5.5	6.0	6.1	6.2
Western Europe	59.1	58.2	58.8	58.9	56.6	54.9
Latin America	1.2	3.0	3.0	2.6	2.7	3.8
Pacific Rim	22.0	22.8	22.1	25.8	27.4	27.2
Arab Region	2.8	4.6	5.5	3.7	2.2	2.7

a. Exports plus imports.

b. World Political Affinity Regions. After Nierop (1988). Nierop's methodology used cluster analysis of common membership patterns of intergovernmental organizations (IGOs) to form the political regions.

c. Western Europe: Ireland, UK, France, Spain, Portugal, W.Germany, Denmark, Netherlands, Norway, Sweden, Finland, Italy, Switzerland, Austria, Iceland, Yugoslavia, Greece, Turkey; in 1990 add East Germany, Poland, Czechoslovakia, Hungary, Romania, Bulgaria, and Albania.

d. Latin America: Argentina, Belize, Bolivia, Brazil, Chile, Colombia, Costa Rica, Ecuador, El Salvador, Guatemala, French Guiana, Guyana, Honduras, Dominican Republic, Mexico, Nicaragua, Panama, Paraguay, Peru, Surinam, Uruguay, Venezuela; 1980 excludes Dominican Republic and Guyana.

e. Pacific Rim: US, Canada, Australia, Papua New Guinea, Japan, Indonesia, Malaysia, India, Pakistan, Bangladesh, Thailand, Philippines, South Korea, New Zealand; 1980 adds Sri Lanka, Pakistan, Kampuchea, Vietnam, Iran, Burma, Laos, Afghanistan, and Bangladesh.

f. Arab Region: Morocco, Algeria, Tunisia, Libya, Egypt, Sudan, Iraq, Jordan, Syria, Kuwait; in 1980, includes Qatar, Saudi Arabia, United Arab Emirates, Lebanon, Oman, North Yemen, South Yemen, Sudan, Mauritania, and Somalia.

g. Africa: Mauritania, Senegal, Guinea, Guinea Bissau, Sierra Leone, Cote d'Ivoire, Ghana, Burkina Faso, Togo, Benin, Niger, Nigeria, Chad, Central African Republic, Cameroon, Zaire, Congo, Gabon, Zambia, Malawi, Rwanda, Tanzania, Kenya, Uganda; 1980 includes Botswana, Gambia, Malawi, and Mauritania. Note: Rather than subdividing Africa into Francophone and Anglophone, we treated Africa as one region due to its small share of total world trade.

Source: International Monetary Fund, *Direction of Trade Statistics.*

Table 16 Internalization and business-government relations in the NIEs: the multidimensional process

Dimension	Import Substitution Phase	Export Promotion Phase	Investment in Foreign Markets
Status of comparative advantage	Being created at the factors level	Moving from factors to products	Stabilizing at the firm level
Government role	Create, lead, and protect	Promote and help	Remote control
Corporate role	Follow and negotiate	Equal partner	Leader
Market structure	Monopolistic	Mixed	Competitive
Macro policy	Accumulate human capital and technology	Large savings and investment	Decline in the growth of savings

NIEs = newly industrializing economies

Source: Aggarwal and Agmon (1990), 177.

toward within-region trade actually diminishes in the 1980s."[62] In light of this, the evidence of a yen bloc is weak and fragmentary at best.[63]

As expected, the levels of intraregional trade are appreciably lower in regions of the developing world—Africa, Latin America, and the Arab regions— and show little or negative trend (table 15). Former colonial ties, while they have undergone some change, seem to have persisted in most cases.

Comparisons between tables 16 and 15 are instructive. Within-region trade is higher in the political region of Western Europe than within the formal region of EC-12, and greater within the Pacific Rim region than within either of the "formal" regions at opposite ends of the Pacific Basin (North America and the hypothetical East Asia). This is revealing and suggests that "trade indeed follows the flag." Intraregional trade in political regions may be the best single indicator of possible future regional

---

62. Following Frankel (1991), take the simplest case and imagine that there was no intraregional bias in 1980 and that each East Asian country traded within the region at the latter's weight in world trade (15 percent). Multiply this by a regional bias term to explain the actual share reported in table 14 (33 percent in 1980), and then our regional bias term is 2.18 (or, .33 divided by 15). Holding this regional bias term constant and multiplying it by the region's weight in 1990 world trade (20 percent), we would expect intraregional trade to be 43.6 percent. Actual intraregional trade is 38 percent, which is 6.3 percent lower than expected, so intraregional trade may have declined in the 1980s.

63. Saxonhouse (1991), for example, finds none using a generalized econometric approach based on factor endowments.

developments. Thus Pacific regional trading arrangements seem to have more promise than East Asian.

Looking toward the future, there is growing evidence that some blocs are expanding. In June 1990 the United States launched an Enterprise for the Americas Initiative seeking to create a Western Hemisphere free trade zone. The US invitation to Latin America has stimulated increased interest in regional initiatives throughout the region.[64] States appear to be seeking to negotiate as a group with the United States and therefore are motivated to agree on common external rules. The EC in October 1991 agreed to form a new common market—the European Economic Area—that includes the seven-member EFTA and will come into existence in January 1993. The growth in trans-Pacific trade indicates the possibility of the formation of a Pacific bloc. The greatest change in the direction of trade is the growth in the share of trade between North America and East Asia (10 percent) and East Asia to North America (11 percent) over the 13-year period. This increase suggests that the North American and East Asian regions are becoming more interdependent. Political ties (Nierop 1989), foreign direct investment, and tourism (Krause 1991) show rising intraregional trends in the Pacific.

Determinants

Geographic proximity, if not contiguity, appears to be one of the most important factors motivating bloc formation. Even for the political regions, political distance is highly correlated with geographic distance. Transport costs are also related to distance; that is, they diminish with propinquity.[65] Proximate locations may share historical experiences, thus assisting the integration process. Other factors may be correlated with distance, such as human and physical investments among geographically and culturally proximate states. These investments include knowledge about a partner's language, culture, markets, and business practices. Some investments may be in public goods (e.g., the information generated by a regional trade promotion agency), and still others can lower the costs of further investments in regional linkages (e.g., investments in a regional airport). Petri (1992) concludes that the full impact of these investments

---

64. Andean states (Bolivia, Colombia, Peru, Ecuador, and Venezuela) have signed an accord to lift all trade barriers to intraregional trade by 1991. Steps are progressing to form the Mercosur common market (comprising Brazil, Argentina, Paraguay, and Uruguay) by the end of 1995.

65. See Petri (1992) for reasons why this relationship is not so simple. He argues that transport costs are not likely to vary much across different bilateral linkages because these costs are highly nonlinear, with much of the cost accounted for in the loading and unloading of products. Furthermore, he argues that transport costs vary greatly with access to different modes of transport: thus it may be cheaper to transport goods over a long distance by sea than over shorter distance by rail or road.

may be highly nonlinear; regional linkages may increase exponentially as each investment makes subsequent investments, subsequent trade, and therefore the profitability of further investments more likely.

Similar levels of economic development (facilitating intraindustry trade), compatible trade policies, and the presence of a leading economy or trading state may also be important determinants. Any inability of the GATT process to solve new issues in international trade may encourage some countries to look for a regional solution. Part of the impetus toward regional integration throughout non-European regions may simply reflect a reaction to events on the European continent.[66] It is also likely that the motivational factors toward regionalism are different in various regions. For example, political and historical factors are important driving forces in the EC; foreign direct investment and technology transfers seem crucial in East Asia. With the demise of the Cold War and the transition to a new world order, politics and accidents of history may become less important than these factors and regional geographic proximity in shaping international trade patterns.

Implications

Increasingly the consumers of traded goods and services are themselves producers—because of the growing shares of capital goods and producer goods in trade, and because of the vertical integration of production through MNCs that occurs without respect to boundaries. In this light, the welfare benefits of open trade and the welfare costs of trade barriers are best conceived as spurring improvements in, or putting the brakes on, productivity, not "utility." Trade may be increasingly vital to national growth and competitiveness and less and less a matter of merely satisfying consumer whims. Asia-Pacific trade seems to reflect these observations sharply, with its strong common trends toward rapidly rising output, standards of living, trade, and investment.

Much of Asia-Pacific trade growth is growth in intraindustry and intrafirm trade. The level of resource-based trade remains significant but has not grown as rapidly. The most important implication of this is that scale economies, intercorporate competition, product differentiation based on the development of new varieties, and policies that seek out national advantage in strategic niches have all played important roles. These are not the traditional endowments-based determinants of trade, and recent conflicts that have arisen have not been easily interpreted using traditional categories, or resolved using traditional trade policies.

---

66. The psychological factor may become less important if the EC continues to have difficulties, which appear to be insurmountable, in political and economic union.

Asia-Pacific trade growth in fact provokes the fundamental question of how much influence policy itself has in creating and maintaining desired patterns of comparative advantage, or in deterring rivals who covet one's own historical pattern.

These policy perspectives also suggest the growing need to integrate trade policy with other policy arenas: domestic competition policies, science and technology policies, policies toward investment and intellectual property. And to the extent that intrafirm, intraregional, and high-technology trade are growing, current institutional regimes may be laboring. The GATT in particular, despite the presence of trade-related intellectual property, trade-related investment measures, and other new issues on the agenda of the Uruguay Round, still seems structurally ill-suited to deal with conflicts and inefficiencies caused by unique corporate cultures and national institutions, with regional and supraregional jurisdictional overlaps, and with activist policy support for research, development, and technological change. Beyond institutional evolution, there seems to be growing value in considering new institutional forms—perhaps multilateral, perhaps regional. It would be truly remarkable if institutional innovation, too, emerged in coming years with an Asian Pacific flavor.

Appendix A: Policy-Determined Comparative Advantage

The new perspectives on international trade—technology, intraindustry, and intracorporate trade—all suggest some possibility for indirect policy-determined comparative advantage. Others direct even more attention to the policy component, believing that trade policy is an important and independent source of competitive/comparative advantage.[67] Proponents of this perspective argue that comparative advantage is "created" as opposed to "inherited."[68] There are two dimensions to this argument: one, that government and corporate activism has influence over and beyond the level normally considered in traditional models of international trade, and two, that comparative advantage is dynamic.

The argument for "making" comparative advantage has a tradition dating back to a study by Taussig (1927), which revealed that comparative advantage is determined not only by a country's natural endowments

---

67. This approach combines two different traditions: a business school approach and an economics and political-economy approach. Our view is that this approach fuses ideas from the two traditions by combining industrial organization theories with traditional trade theory.

68. Classic international trade theorists view comparative advantage as static, reflecting the country's slow-to-change natural factor endowments.

but also by its social, political, and educational system.[69] Contemporary adherents of this view center their attention on the state, which actively intervenes in a host of practices (ranging from specific export promotion to import prohibitions to broadly drawn infrastructural policies and industrial targeting[70]) that adjust and may eventually determine comparative advantage.[71] A particular variant of this argument concentrates on the role of strategic trade policy to "perfect" markets, especially those that encourage technological progress and growth.[72] Particular attention is devoted toward the so-called "engineered" success of Japan and the Asian NICs. For example, it is alleged that the role of the government is essential in explaining the inconsistencies between the NICs' domestic factor endowments and the relatively sophisticated nature of the activities of their firms in foreign markets.

The stock of factors that a country enjoys at a particular time are believed to be less important than the rate at which it upgrades and deploys them in particular industries, especially in the high-technology sector. Studies show how countries of different size, history, and culture actively try to direct national comparative advantage.[73] Most emphasize

---

69. Taussig (1927, 57–58) pointed to Germany's well-trained chemists and lab assistants as the basis for that country's comparative advantage in chemical dyes and other chemical products.

70. See Krugman (1992) for a recent survey.

71. There is a growing literature that highlights how government actions influence the competitiveness of the state's exports (Yamamura and Yasuba 1987). These studies are not confined to case studies of the NICs and Japan. Cooper (1987, 249) lists 11 actions of the US government that directly intervene in the market, and Porter (1990) examines international competitiveness for 10 of the world's largest trading states.

72. As Richardson (1990, 109) notes, there are only modest efforts in the literature to keep trade (border) policy analytically distinct from industrial (sectoral) policy. This is in part because the former is often used as an instrument of the latter, and in part because international mobility of corporate capital causes many contemporary trade disputes to be essentially disputes over sharp trade consequences of industrial policies that do not discriminate at the border. There is also a common doubt in the literature as to whether government can efficiently target more than a few sectors for specific subsidization.

73. Aggarwal and Agmon (1990) examine government-directed comparative advantage in India, Singapore, and South Korea. Johnson (1982) sheds light on the role of the Ministry of International Trade and Industry (MITI) in Japan in upgrading and developing the economy around higher value and higher technologically based industry. Okimoto (1989) deemphasizes the role of MITI and casts MITI in the broader context of the complex system within which it operates. He stress MITI's general adherence to market-conforming methods of government intervention, a philosophical tenet that has kept the state from succumbing to the temptation of a political quick fix. Okimoto (1989) finds similarities between the Japanese approach to the market and their aesthetic view of bonsai and traditional Japanese gardens: instead of letting nature take its natural course, humans actually adapt, structure, highlight, and improve what nature produces.

market-conforming trade policies and note differentiated policies across industrial sectors.

Recognizing that the effects of government actions are wide, insofar as government provides for inland transportation, education, efficient banking and other financial transactions that indirectly influence trade policy, what is of interest is government and corporate activity beyond this.

Aggarwal and Agmon (1990) attempt a first cut at documenting sequential stages of government and corporate activism in the shaping and creating of comparative advantage in the NICs: that is, import substitution, export promotion, and foreign direct investment. They note that the distribution of the weight between government- and corporate-led changes as the process moves from one stage to the next, believing that the lead of the government is important in directing initial changes but is generally replaced by the corporate sector. This study provides a suitable general framework for studying the creation of comparative advantage but advances us little toward an understanding of the contribution of individual policies and of the different mixes of policies required to create or even modify comparative advantage.[74]

References

Aggarwal, Raj, and Tamir Agmon. 1990. "The International Success of Developing Country Firms: Role of Government-Directed Comparative Advantage." *Management International Review* 30, no. 2: 163–80.

Balassa, Bela, and Luc Bauwens. 1988. *Changing Trade Patterns in Manufactured Goods: An Econometric Investigation.* Amsterdam: North-Holland.

Belous, Richard S., and Rebecca S. Hartley, eds. 1990. *The Growth of Regional Trading Blocs in the Global Economy.* Washington: The National Planning Association.

Bergsten, C. Fred, Thomas Horst, and Theodore H. Moran. 1978. *American Multinationals and American Interests.* Washington: The Brookings Institution.

Bergstrand, Jeffrey H. 1990. "The Heckscher-Ohlin-Samuelson Model, The Linder Hypothesis and the Determinants of Bilateral Intraindustry Trade." *The Economic Journal* 100 (December): 1216–29.

Berry, Brian J., Edgar C. Conkling, and D. Michael Ray. 1976. *The Geography of Economic Systems.* Englewood Cliffs: Prentice-Hall.

Berry, Brian, J. 1991. *Long-Wave Rhythms in Economic Development and Political Behavior.* Baltimore: The Johns Hopkins University Press.

Blomström, Magnus, Irving B. Kravis, and Robert E. Lipsey. 1988. "Multinational Firms and Manufactured Exports From Developing Countries." Working Paper Series No. 2493, National Bureau of Economics Research, Inc.

Blomström, Magnus, Irving B. Kravis, and Robert E. Lipsey. 1993. "The Competitiveness of Countries and Their Multinational Firms." In Lorraine Eden and Evan Potter, eds., *Multinationals in the Global Political Economy.* London: Macmillan. Forthcoming.

---

74. The Industry Commission of Australia's (1990) monograph is a start.

Bowen, Harry P., Edward E. Leamer and Leo Sveikauskas 1987. "Multicountry, Multifactor Tests of the Factor Abundance Theory." *American Economic Review* 77 (December): 791–809.

Brainard, Robert. 1992. "Internationalizing R&D." *OECD Observer* 174 (February/March): 7–10.

Bresnahan, Timothy F., and Peter C. Reiss. 1991. "Entry and Competition in Concentrated Markets." *Journal of Political Economy* 99: 977–1009.

Cohen, Stephen S., and John Zysman. 1987. *Manufacturing Matters*. New York: Basic Books, Inc.

Cooper, Richard N. 1987. "Industrial Policy and Trade Distortions." In D. Salvatore, ed., *The New Protectionist Threat to World Welfare*. New York: North-Holland.

Deardorff, Alan V. 1984. "Testing Trade Theories and Predicting Trade Flows." In Ronald W. Jones and Peter B. Kenen, eds. *Handbook of International Economics: Volume I*. Amsterdam: North-Holland.

Deardorff, Alan V., and Robert M. Stern. 1989. "Current Issues in Trade Policy: An Overview." In R. M. Stern, ed., *U.S. Trade Policies in a Changing World Economy*. Cambridge: The MIT Press.

de la Torre, Augusto, and Margaret R. Kelly. 1992. "Regional Trade Arrangements." *International Monetary Fund Occasional Paper* 93. Washington: International Monetary Fund.

Dosi, G., and L. Soete. 1988. "Technical Change and International Trade." In Giovanni Dosi et al., eds., *Technical Change and Economic Theory*. London: Pinter.

Drysdale, Peter, and Ross Garnaut. 1992. "The Pacific: An Application of a General Theory of Economic Integration." Paper prepared for the Twentieth Pacific Trade and Development Conference, Washington, D.C., 10–12 September.

Frankel, Jeffrey A. 1991. "Is a Yen Bloc Forming in Pacific Asia?" In Richard O'Brien, ed., *Finance and the International Economy: 5. The AMEX Bank Review Prize Essays*. New York: Oxford University Press.

Freeman, Christopher. 1982. *The Economics of Industrial Innovation*. Cambridge, MA: The MIT Press.

Gagnon, Joseph, and Andrew K. Rose. 1990. "Why Hasn't Trade Grown Faster Than Income? Inter-Industry Trade Over the Past Century." International Finance Discussion Papers, Board of Governors of the Federal Reserve System, Number 371, January.

Gagnon, Joseph E., and Andrew K. Rose. 1992. "How Pervasive Is the Product Cycle? The Empirical Dynamics of American and Japanese Trade Flows." Working Paper No. 3946, National Bureau of Economic Research, (January).

Garten, Jeffrey E. 1989. "Trading Blocs and the Evolving World Economy." *Current History* (January): 15–56.

Globerman, Steven, and James W. Dean. 1990. "Recent Trends in Intraindustry Trade and Their Implications for Future Trade Liberalization." *Weltwirtschaftliches Archiv* 126.

Goldstein, Joshua S. 1988. *Long Cycle: Prosperity and War in the Modern Age*. New Haven: Yale University Press.

Gray, H. Peter. 1988. "Intraindustry Trade: An Untidy Phenomenon," *Weltwirtschaftliches Archiv* 124: 221–29.

Greenaway, David. 1987. "Intraindustry Trade, Intra-Firm Trade and European Integration: Evidence, Gains and Policy Aspects." *Journal of Common Market Studies* (December).

Greenaway, David, and Chris Milner. 1986. *The Economics of Intraindustry Trade*. Oxford: Basil Blackwell.

Greenaway, David, and Chris Milner. 1987. "Intraindustry Trade: Current Perspectives and Unresolved Issues." *Weltwirtschaftliches Archiv* 123.

Grinwade, Nigel. 1989. *International Trade: New Patterns of Trade, Production, and Investment*. London: Routledge.

Grossman, Gene M., and Elhanan Helpman. 1991. *Innovation and Growth in the Global Economy*. Cambridge, MA: MIT Press.

Grubel, H.G., and P.J. Lloyd. 1975. *Intraindustry Trade: The Theory and Measurement of International Trade in Differentiated Products*. London: Macmillan.

Gruber, W. H., D. Mehta, and R. Vernon. 1967. "The R&D Factor in International Trade and International Investment of United States Industries." *Journal of Political Economy* 75: 20–34.

Hagedoorn, J., and J. Schakenraad. 1990. "Leading Companies and the Structure of Strategic Alliances in Core Technologies." MERIT Research Memorandum 90-001, Maastricht.

Hart, Tracy, and Bradley J. McDonald. 1992. *Intraindustry Trade Indexes for Canada, Mexico, and the United States*, 1962-87. US Department of Agriculture, Agricultural Economic Research Service 9206.

Helpman, E. 1987. "Imperfect Competition and International Trade: Evidence from Fourteen Industrialised Countries." *Journal of the Japanese and International Economies* 1 (June).

Hirsch, S. 1965. "The United States Electronics Industry in International Trade." *National Institute Economic Review* (November).

Hooper, Peter, and J. David Richardson, eds. 1991. *International Economic Transactions: Issues in Measurement and Empirical Research*. Chicago: The University of Chicago Press.

Hufbauer, G. C. 1970. "The Impact of National Characteristics and Technology on the Commodity Composition of Trade in Manufactured Goods." In Raymond Vernon, ed., *The Technology Factor in International Trade*. New York: National Bureau for Economic Research.

Hufbauer, G. C. 1966. *Synthetic Materials and the Theory of International Trade*. London: Duckworth.

Hughes, Kirsty. 1986. "Exports and Innovation: A Simultaneous Model." *European Economic Review* 30: 383–99.

Industry Commission, Australia. 1990. *Strategic Trade Theory: The East Asian Experience*. Information paper. Canberra (November).

Johnson, Chalmers. 1984. *MITI and the Japanese Miracle: The Growth of Industrial Policy, 1925–75*. Stanford: Stanford University Press.

Jones, Ronald W., and Peter B. Kenen, eds. 1984. *Handbook of International Economics: Volume I*. Amsterdam: North-Holland.

Jones, Ronald W., and Anne O. Krueger, eds. 1990. *The Political Economy of International Trade: Essays in Honor of Robert E. Baldwin*. Cambridge, MA: Basil Blackwell.

Julius, DeAnne. 1990. *Global Companies & Public Policy: The Growing Challenges of Foreign Direct Investment*. New York: Council on Foreign Relations Press for the Royal Institute of International Affairs.

Keesing, D. 1967. "The Impact of Research and Development on United States Trade." *Journal of Political Economy* 57: 38–48.

Kester, Anne Y., ed. 1992. *Behind the Numbers: U.S. Trade in the World Economy*. Report of a Panel on Foreign Trade Statistics chaired by Robert E. Baldwin. Washington: National Academy Press.

Kondratieff, Nikolai. 1984. *The Long Wave Cycle*. Originally published in German in 1928. Translated by Guy Daniels, with an introduction by Julian M. Snyder. New York: Richardson and Snyder.

Kotlikoff, Laurence J., and Edward E. Leamer. 1987. "Empirical Tests of Alternative Models of International Growth." In William H. Branson and Colin Bradford, eds., *Trade and Structural Change in Pacific Asia*. Chicago: The University of Chicago Press.

Krause, Lawrence B. 1991. "Regionalism in World Trade: The Limits of Economic Interdependence." *Harvard International Review* 13 (Summer) 4–6.

Kravis, Irving B., and Robert E. Lipsey. 1988. "Production and Trade in Services by U.S. Multinational Firms." Working Paper No. 2615. National Bureau of Economic Research, Inc. (June).

Krugman, Paul. 1984. "Import Protection as Export Promotion: International Competition in the Presence of Oligopoly and Economies of Scale." In H. Kjerzkowski, ed., *Monopolistic Competition and International Trade*. Oxford: Clarendon Press.

Krugman, Paul, ed. 1991. *Trade with Japan: Has the Door Opened Wider?"* Chicago: The University of Chicago Press.

Krugman, Paul. 1992. "Does the New Trade Theory Require a New Trade Policy?" *The World Economy* 15 (July): 423.

Kuczynski, Thomas. 1980."Have There Been Differences Between the Growth Rates of the Development of the Capitalist World Economy Since 1850? An Application of Cluster Analysis in Time Series Analysis." In Jerome Clubb and Erwin Scheuch, eds., *Historical Social Research*. Stuttgart: Klett-Cotta.

Laird, Sam, and Alexander Yeats, 1990. "Trends in Nontariff Barriers of Developed Countries 1966-86." *Weltwirtschaftliches Archiv* (Review of World Economies) 126: 299–325.

Landau, Ralph, and Nathan Rosenberg, eds. 1986. *The Positive Sum Strategy*. Washington: National Academy Press.

Lawrence, Robert Z. 1991a. "Emerging Regional Arrangements: Building Blocs or Stumbling Blocs?" In Richard O'Brien, ed., *Finance and the International Economy: 5. The AMEX Bank Review Prize Essays*. New York: Oxford University Press.

Lawrence, Robert Z. 1991b. "How Open is Japan?" In Krugman, ed., *Trade with Japan: Has the Door Opened Wider?* Chicago: The University of Chicago Press.

Leamer, Edward E. 1984. *Sources of International Comparative Advantage*. Cambridge, MA: The MIT Press.

Leamer, Edward E. 1990. "The Structure and Effects of Tariff and Nontariff Barriers in 1983." *The Political Economy of International Trade: Essays in Honor of Robert E. Baldwin*. Cambridge, MA: Basil Blackwell.

Leamer, Edward E. 1992a. "Testing Trade Theory." *Working Paper No. 3957*. Cambridge, MA: National Bureau of Economic Research, Inc.

Leamer, Edward E. 1992b. "Wage Effects of a U.S.-Mexican Free Trade Agreement." Working Paper No. 3991, National Bureau of Economic Research, Inc. (February).

Lincoln, Edward J. 1990. *Japan's Unequal Trade*. Washington: The Brookings Institution.

Lipsey, Robert E. 1989. "The Internationalization of Production." Working Paper No. 2923, National Bureau of Economic Research, Inc., (April).

Lipsey, Robert E. 1991. "Foreign Direct Investment in the United States and U.S. Trade." *The Annals of the American Academy of Political and Social Science* (July): 76–90.

Lipsey, Robert E. 1991. "The Competitiveness of the U.S. and of U.S. Firms." Prepared for the 11th Ministry of Finance-NBER Joint Conference on The Competitiveness of US Industries and its Implications on US-Japan Relationships in the Future, Tokyo, Japan, 10–11 September.

Lipsey, R., and Irving B. Kravis. 1987. "The Competitiveness and Comparative Advantage of U.S. Multinationals." *Banca Nazionale del Laroro Quarterly Review* 161: 147–65.

Little, Jane Sneddon. 1991. "Intra-Firm Trade and U.S. Protectionism: Thoughts Based on a Small Survey." *New England Economic Review* (January/February): 42– 51.

Mandel, Ernest. 1980. *Long Waves of Capitalist Development*. New York: Cambridge University Press.

Mansfield, Edwin, Anthony Romeo, and Samuel Wagner. 1986. "Foreign Trade and U.S. Research and Development." *The Review of Economics and Statistics* 61: 49–52.

Marvel, Howard P., and Edward John Ray. 1987. "Intraindustry Trade: Sources and Effects on Protection." *Journal of Political Economy* 95: 1278–91.

Maskus, Keith. 1983. *The Changing Structure of Comparative Advantage in American Manufacturing*. Ann Arbor, MI: UMI Research Press.

Maskus, Keith E. 1991. "Comparing International Trade Data and Product and National Characteristics Data for the Analysis of Trade Models." In Hooper and Richardson, eds., *International Economic Transactions: Issues in Measurement and Empirical Research*. Chicago: The University of Chicago Press.

Modelski, George. 1986. "Long Cycles, Their Spatial Aspects, And The Pacific Rim." Paper presented at the Annual Meeting of the Association of American Geographers, Minneapolis, 5–7 May.

Modelski, George. 1987. *Long Cycles In World Politics*. Seattle: University of Washington Press.

Nelson, Richard, and Sidney Winter. 1982. *An Evolutionary Theory of Economic Change*. Cambridge, MA: The Belknap Press.

Nierop, Tom. 1989. "Macro-regions and the Global Institutional Network, 1950– 1980." *Political Geography Quarterly* 8 (January) 43–65.

Noland, Marcus. 1990. *Pacific Basin Developing Countries: Prospects for the Future*. Washington: Institute for International Economics.

Noland, Marcus. 1991. "Public Policy, Private Preferences, and the Japanese Trade Pattern." Manuscript, Washington, D.C., (January).

Noland, Marcus. N.d. "The Impact of Industrial Policy on Japan's Trade Specialization." *Review of Economics and Statistics*. Forthcoming.

Okimoto, Daniel I. 1989. *Between MITI and the Market: Japanese Industrial Policy for High Technology*. Stanford: Stanford University Press.

O'Louglin, John, and Herman van der Wusten. 1990. "Political Geography of Panregions." *The Geographical Review* 80 no. 1: 1–20.

Papadakis, Maria. 1992. "Changing International Relations and U.S.-Japanese Competitiveness." In W. Harry Lambright and Dianne Rahm, eds., *Technology and U.S. Competitiveness*. Connecticut: Greenwood Press.

Park, Yung Chul, and Won-Am Park. 1991. "Changing Japanese Trade Patterns and the East Asian NICs." In Krugman, ed., *Trade with Japan: Has the Door Opened Wider?* Chicago: The University of Chicago Press.

Patrick. Hugh. 1991. *Pacific Basin Industries in Distress*. New York: Columbia University Press.

Perez, Carlota, and Luc Soete. 1988. "Catching Up in Technology: Entry Barriers and Windows of Opportunity." In Giovanni Dosi et al., eds., *Technical Change and Economic Theory*. London: Pinter.

Petri, Peter A. 1991a. "Market Structure, Comparative Advantage, and Japanese Trade under the Strong Yen." In Krugman, ed., *Trade with Japan: Has the Door Opened Wider?* Chicago: The University of Chicago Press.

Petri, Peter A. 1991b. "The East Asian Trading Bloc: An Analytical History." Prepared for NBER Conference on the U.S. and Japan in Pacific Asia. Del Mar, CA: 2–5 April.

Petri, Peter A. 1992. "The East Asian Trading Bloc: An Analytical History." Presented at NBER Conference on the United States and Japan in Pacific Asia, Del Mar, CA, 2–5 April 1992.

Porter, Michael E. 1990. *The Competitive Advantage of Nations*. Free Press: New York.

Posner, M.V. 1961. "International Trade and Technological Change." *Oxford Economic Papers* 13, 3 (October).

Ravenhill, John. 1992. "Managing Pacific Trade Relations; Economic Dynamism and Political Immobilism." In Richard Higgott, Richard Leaver, and John Ravenhill, eds., *Pacific Economic Relations in the 1990s: Conflict or Cooperation?* London: Allen and Unwin.

Richardson, J. David. 1989. "Empirical Estimates of Gains from Trade Liberalization Under Imperfect Competition: A Survey." *OECD Economic Studies* 12 (Spring) 7–51.

Richardson, J. David. 1990. "The Political Economy of Strategic Trade Policy." *International Organization* 44, no. 1: 107–35.

Rosenbloom, Richard S., ed. 1989. Research on Technological Innovation, Management, and Policy. Research volumes published annually. Greenwich, CT: Jai Press, Inc.

Russett, Bruce M. 1967. *International Regions and the International System: A Study in Political Ecology*. Chicago: Rand and McNally and Company.

Schott, Jeffrey J. 1991. "Trading Blocs and the World Trading System." *The World Economy* 14 (March): 1–17.

Schumpeter, Joseph A. 1939. *Business Cycles*. New York: McGraw-Hill.

Smith, David A., and Douglas R. White. 1990. "Structure and Dynamics in the Global Economy: Network Analysis of International Trade 1965–80." Paper presented at the

Conference on Commodity Flows in the Pacific Rim, The University of California at Santa Barbara, California, 13–15 November.

Smith, Pamela J. 1991. "Knowledge Capital, Scale Economics, and U.S. State Comparative Advantage: an Empirical Study." Manuscript, 24 September.

Smith, Pamela J. 1992. "Geographic Scale Economies in an Endowments-Based Model of U.S. State Trade." Manuscript, 5 May.

Soete, Luc. 1991. "National Support Policies for Strategic Industries: The International Implications." OECD, Strategic in a Global Economy: Policy Issues for the 1990s. Paris.

Spence, A. Michael, and Heather A. Hazard. 1988. International Competitiveness. Cambridge, MA: Ballinger Pub. Co.

Stevens, Guy V.G. 1990. "The 'Net Foreign Sales Balance' of DeAnne Julius." Internal correspondence, Board of Governors of the Federal Reserve System, 25 July.

Taussig, Frank W. 1927. International Trade. New York: Macmillan.

Thompson, W. R. 1973. "The Regional Subsystem: A Conceptual Explication and a Propositional Inventory." International Studies Quarterly 17, 89–117.

Thompson, William R. 1991. "Long-Waves, Technological Innovation, and Relative Decline." International Organization 42 (Spring) 201–33.

Urata, Shujiro. 1992. "Foreign Direct Investment and Economic Development in Pacific Asia." Prepared for the PAFTAD Conference, 10–12 September.

US Department of Commerce. 1986. "US Merchandise Trade Associated with US Multinational Companies." Survey of Current Business (May): 55.

US Department of Commerce. 1991. "US Direct Investment Abroad: 1989 Benchmark Survey Results." Survey of Current Business (October): 29.

US International Trade Commission. 1992. Regional Organizations in the Asian Pacific Region. Washington: US International Trade Commission, USITC Publication 20436 (April).

Van Duijn, Jaap. 1983. The Long Wave in Economic Life. Boston: Allen and Unwin.

Vernon, R. 1966. "International Investment and International Trade in the Product Cycle." Quarterly Journal of Economics (May): 190–207.

Vernon, Raymond, ed. 1970. The Technology Factor in International Trade. NY: National Bureau for Economic Research.

Walker, W. B. 1979. Industrial Innovation and International Trading Performance. Greenwich, CT: JAI Press, Inc..

Wallerstein, Immanuel. 1979. The Capitalist World-Economy. New York: Cambridge University Press.

Wallerstein, Immanuel. 1984. The Politics of the World-Economy. New York: Cambridge University Press.

Wallerstein, Immanuel. 1989. "The Capitalist World-Economy: Middle-Run Prospects." Alternatives 14, 279–88.

Wallerstein, Immanuel. 1991. Geopolitics and Geoculture. New York: Cambridge University Press.

Yamamura, Kozo, and Yasukichi Yasuba. 1987. The Political Economy of Japan, vol. 1. Stanford: Stanford University Press.

2

The Uruguay Round and the GATT: Whither the Global System?

JOHN WHALLEY

Introduction

This paper looks beyond the Uruguay Round (if and when it concludes), and tries to assess both how the trading system might evolve and what realistic options for expanding world trade might be. This is, of course, a task made especially difficult by uncertainty over the outcome of the Round, which is still in doubt as of this writing.[1]

The outcome (or lack of one) to the round will clearly be an important factor in determining how the trading system develops in the 1990s. While hardly a coherent and integrated system now, a complete breakdown in the negotiations raises the prospect of an even more patchwork system in the future, perhaps with a slow withering away of the General Agreement on Tariffs and Trade (GATT), in the sense that GATT disciplines are increasingly not observed, panel formation is progressively blocked, and panel rulings are increasingly implemented in token fashion. A major result, on the other hand, may prove enough to demonstrate a firm belief on the part of the large powers in the need for a system from which new system strengthening could emerge. An intermediate result presumably yields a mix of these two elements and a scenario under which the GATT

John Whalley is Director of the Centre for the Study of International Economic Relations and Professor of International Trade at the University of Western Ontario. The paper draws on material from The Future of the World Trading System, *coauthored with Colleen Hamilton. The author gratefully acknowledges the helpful comments of Taeho Bark, Marcus Noland, and Jeffrey J. Schott.*

1. See, however, the recent piece by Nguyen, Perroni, and Wigle (1991), which suggests large gains from a successful conclusion to the Round.

process is, in effect, put on ice for several years and kept as a negotiating framework, which could be turned to in the future if the major contracting parties eventually find it useful to do so.

Complicating all this, there are different views as to how important the trading system is both for the performance of the global economy and for that of individual economies. One view is that institutional arrangements tend to be relatively unimportant to economic performance, and tend to follow, not lead, economic developments. Thus the fact that postwar global trade performance has been strong while the GATT system has eroded shows how tangential formalized trade arrangements are to global economic performance. We should perhaps be less concerned with global trade arrangements and more concerned with identifying factors that promote trade performance.

Another view is that, to the contrary, global institutional arrangements are key to global economic performance. According to this argument, if GATT had been in place in the 1930s, we might have avoided the worst of the global depression. And only with this focal point of cooperation established could postwar tariff liberalization proceed, thereby fueling postwar global growth. And if it is now substantially weakened, we risk eventual reversion to global trade wars and even military conflict. Under this view of the world, the systemic focus post-Uruguay Round should be on damage control: defensive as much as launching new initiatives, and restoring cooperation rather than necessarily seeking new liberalization.[2]

Yet another view is that the postwar trading system is largely a child of strategic and not trade concerns and that the end of the Cold War and realigned strategic interests pose the greatest post-Uruguay Round challenge to world trade. The multilateralism of the immediate postwar years was a reflection of the overriding desire to prevent a further world war, and with the onset of the Cold War, multilateral trade arrangements became part of a strategically driven anti-Communist alliance that promoted trade to build the alliance. With the immediate threat of global conflict now removed, the incentive for larger countries to conduct trade policy bilaterally or regionally where they have more leverage, so it is argued, will likely supersede previous strategic interests, with attendant consequences for the trading system.

This paper does not seek to arbitrate these positions; each contains elements of plausibility, but none is the whole story. Instead, I look at three key challenges facing the system after the round: the need to generate yet more access, the need to keep the system open, and the challenge posed by regionalism. In the process, I make two central points about the trading system as it may evolve beyond the round.

---

2. See the discussion in Hamilton and Whalley (1992).

The first is that redesign of the trading system beyond the Uruguay Round, as well as any efforts to further strengthen the system, need to be evaluated relative to today's goals, not those of the 1940s. In my judgment, the views that have percolated up from trade policy circles over the years as to how the global trading system functions and the implications asserted for the post-Uruguay Round trading system have been somewhat romanticized. The idea that we have had a trading system based on clear multilateral rules and disciplines within which significant global trade liberalization has taken place and trade has grown is simply an inaccurate portrayal of what has happened. Instead, the multilateral system has evolved in ways ever more distant from its principles, and system rules have been enforced with only limited vigor and supplemented by all manner of bilateral or plurilateral arrangements. Strong postwar system performance has, to some extent, occurred despite rather than because of the multilateral system.

In the paper, I try to document some of the ways in which the trading system has changed. The global depression and the trade conflicts of the 1930s, and the world war that followed, led to the setting of system goals of the 1940s: nondiscrimination and multilateralism. These, in turn, have shaped the GATT system we have inherited. Sectoral and other derogations from GATT disciplines came into the system first, with special trade rules evolving in agriculture, textiles, steel, autos, and other product areas, and eventually leading to widespread voluntary export restraints (VERs). Regionalism also was part of the system, first with the creation of the European Community and the European Free Trade Association (EFTA), and later with EC enlargement and North American regional arrangements in the 1980s.[3] Nontraditional issues, such as trade-related features of domestic distribution systems, competition policies, environment, and other policies have been more recent additions. And as I will argue later, these developments have both harmed and promoted trade performance. Moves toward further regional arrangements are an example: they weaken multilateral principles through trade diversion but often promote more rapid growth in regional trade.

But system goals are now more explicitly performance-related. Rationalizing global resource allocation and hence improving the performance of the global economy, including higher trade growth, are now taken as goals to aspire toward independent of the choice of institutional framework used to achieve them—multilateral or bilateral, nondiscriminatory and discriminatory. Generating new access, maintaining openness, dealing with new issues, harnessing regionalism for improved performance are the new goals and not nondiscrimination and multilateralism, whose

---

3. Schott (1991) provides an excellent survey of the current situation regarding trading blocs.

value lies more in how they advance performance-oriented goals and less as goals in their own right.

The second central point I make is that GATT rules and disciplines provide only a weak international legal framework to use in preserving existing access and opening new markets. Its principles, such as nondiscrimination and multilateralism, relate largely to the ways in which governments should apply trade-restricting measures one against another. They do not reflect broader-ranging goals to which the trading system would aspire if the overriding objective were to improve the performance of the global economy. A central goal motivated by such concerns might, for instance, be upholding rights of free international access. These would include rights for all agents (individuals, corporations, governments) in all countries to purchase products from abroad free of any border impediments or other restrictions operating within national boundaries, reciprocal rights for agents to export to other countries, and international mobility rights for factors of production (capital and labor).

System strengthening in the Uruguay Round was set as an objective only relative to the weaker disciplines embodied in the GATT, not relative to more ambitious goals. The nondiscrimination and multilateralism principles became the goals of this system strengthening without really being questioned. Beyond the Uruguay Round, my view is that more far-reaching strengthening should be attempted whether the aim be achieving more liberalization or heading off new closing. A stronger set of principles should be agreed to, a set of performance indicators assembled, and new and stronger rights and obligations set out as targets.

As a contract between nations, the GATT's overriding purpose is to limit the extent to which its contracting parties regulate trade. While implicitly proliberalization, it is only indirectly so in execution. The system gives no clear legal rights to individuals, corporations, and other agents as far as trade is concerned, nor does it unambiguously allow them redress if their own or other national governments violate international obligations. Even worse, no evaluation of system performance relative to performance-oriented goals, such as how far rights of international access apply, is ever made.

This piece is not the first to discuss the architecture of the trading system.[4] But in contrast to earlier pieces, here I stress system design from the perspective of the 1990s, not from the standpoint of the GATT system inherited from the 1940s. Future progress in trade liberalization after the Uruguay Round should in my view be judged not by its consistency with multilateral principles such as nondiscrimination but by how far it advances the global economy toward more performance-oriented goals.

---

4. See also Jackson (1969 and 1989), Dam (1970), Hufbauer (1989), GATT (1985b), Camps (1981), Camps and Diebold (1986).

The Present Trading System

The term "system," when applied to global trade, suggests a coordinated and well-organized structure of rules and institutions that oversees and regulates world trade. Like other public policy subsystems (e.g., the tax system, the welfare system), the term suggests consistency and forethought in its overall design, a guiding hand to assist in its inner workings, and self-correcting feedback mechanisms helping it change. However, the present-day global trading system is more of a patchwork quilt of overlapping and seemingly inconsistent trade arrangements.

As table 1 indicates, the larger system (System.T) in practice incorporates four distinct subsystems, each of which interacts with the others.[5] The first, Subsystem.M, covers multilateral trade rules laid down in the GATT and multilateral arrangements negotiated in GATT rounds. The second, Subsystem.D, contains derogations from GATT rules with special arrangements covering textiles, agriculture, other products, and instruments. The third, Subsystem.R, contains the regional (bi- and plurilateral) arrangements in the system, set out in various regional free trade area and customs union agreements. The fourth, Subsystem.NT, contains nontraditional arrangements, which cover areas in which trade and other policy subsystems interact (domestic distribution systems, competition and antitrust policies, investment, environment policy, and others). All four subsystems come together, with own-country (unilateral) trade arrangements specified under domestic law, to provide the current overall framework of trade arrangements, System.T.

When the design of postwar trade and other multilateral institutions was first discussed within the United Nations' system following World War II, it was not intended that the trading system take this form. A broad-ranging International Trade Organization (ITO) had been planned that would set out clear rules governing the use of trade-restricting measures by governments, along with a global institutional structure to oversee them. But the charter for the ITO, negotiated in Havana in 1947, was never ratified, and a more temporary arrangement, the GATT, seen initially as a stepping stone to such an arrangement, instead provided the postwar institutional structure for the conduct of world trade.

The idea behind the GATT was that all signatory countries should agree to broad principles governing the use of trade-restricting measures by other governments and on this basis build a system of rights and obligations between the parties to the agreement. Among these key principles were most-favored nation (MFN) status, set out in Article I and aimed at preventing discrimination among suppliers at national borders, and na-

---

5. Jackson (1989) provides an approach to the system more consistent with a traditional group of issues along the lines of GATT articles.

Table 1 The global trading system (System.T) and its four subsystems

Subsystem.M	Subsystem.D	Subsystem.R	Subsystem.NT
Multilateral trade rules and disciplines that limit country uses of border measures	Derogations from GATT rules and disciplines that have come into system since 1947	Regional trade arrangements negotiated separately from GATT arrangements, although notified to GATT	Loose assembly of arrangements covering various issues related to trade, issues beyond border measures, and nonconventional negotiating approaches and arrangements
Rules and disciplines largely reflected in GATT	Special trade rules for sectors:; agriculture (1947, 1955, 1957), textiles (1962), steel (1977, 1984), computer chips (1986)	Free trade areas, customs unions, trade preferences for small developing countries, inter-developing country trade arrangements	Examples of issues include distribution system in Japan, ownership concentration (*keiretsu* in Japan, *chaebol* in Korea), restrictive business practices
Agreement with 38 articles and key principles: most-favored-nation status (MFN), national treatment, transparency-of-border measures	Voluntary export restraints and other gray-area measures	Examples include EC (1957), EFTA (1959), US-Canada arrangements (1965, 1989), EC-Lomé (1962), CBI (1988), Andean Pact (1962), Australia-New Zealand (1988), Europe (1992), US-Mexico (1987, 1989), current EC-EFTA negotiations	Current high profile issues include trade and environment linkages, and competition policy
Seven negotiating rounds concluded since 1947—latest (Uruguay Round) still under way	Threatened unilateral actions, which, if implemented, could be inconsistent with GATT rules (Section 301 in US)		Non-GATT negotiating approaches and arrangements used, including the US-Japan Structural Impediments Initiative (SII), the Japan-ASEAN Initiative, bilateral pressure on higher-income developing countries
Secretariat in Geneva assists in negotiations and in settling trade disputes			

tional treatment, set out in Article III and aimed at preventing discrimination against foreign products beyond the national border. These two principles remain today as the cornerstones of Subsystem.M.

The GATT was also to establish a process to generate trade-liberalization recording schedules of tariff rates, including any bindings and reductions subsequently agreed to by countries as a result of trade negotiations. Seven GATT negotiating rounds held in the period prior to the Uruguay Round successfully reduced and bound tariffs, although largely tariffs used by developed countries and more heavily for imports of manufactured products than for other product categories.

But since 1947 the other three subsystems have steadily grown in importance, reflecting the characteristic inconsistency of application of GATT principles. Subsystem.D contains a number of clear derogations from the GATT trade arrangements that are inconsistent with key GATT principles such as nondiscrimination and transparency in border measures. These include special GATT rules for agriculture brought into the system in 1947 and since taken further; special trade rules for textiles that grew from temporary restrictions in 1962, affecting only a small number of countries, into the much wider Multi-Fibre Arrangement (MFA) of today; and discriminatory VERs, which came into the system in the 1970s and '80s and cover steel, autos, electronics, computer chips, and other products. In the late 1980s, a new potential derogation was added to the list of potentially GATT-inconsistent measures being used by larger powers against countries that did not lower specific barriers.

Subsystem.R contains regional (bi- or plurilateral) trade arrangements that also run counter to the principles of the GATT. In 1947 these were not envisaged as a central part of the postwar trading system; multilateral trade arrangements in keeping with the preferred approach to security and other concerns were assumed to be the way to proceed. However, from the late 1950s on, the Treaty of Rome (establishing the EC), EFTA, numerous regional developing country arrangements (in Central America, East Africa, the Andean pact, and elsewhere), and more recently the Canada-US, US-Mexico, and other agreements, have all caused regional arrangements to grow in importance.[6]

All these arrangements have been legally accommodated within the GATT system through Article XXIV, which allows regional trade groupings to form even though they are not in keeping with the spirit of MFN. But the latest of these arrangements deal with issues not covered by the GATT, such as labor mobility, financial services, and other matters; they are attractive in that they can be negotiated more quickly than new multilateral arrangements. But the consistency of the multilateral system and the consistent application of its key principles suffer.

---

6. The impacts on global trading patterns are far less clear. See de la Torre and Kelly (1992) and Srinivasan, Wooton, and Whalley (forthcoming).

Subsystem.NT reflects even more recent system evolution. The instruments, areas, and issues it covers, while all related to trade, do not fit within the structure of the disciplines in Subsystem.M. But the political pressures to deal with the trade-related aspects of these issues have been so strong that ways of discussing them have spontaneously evolved, even though they have not been dealt with in Subsystem.M in any central way. Subsystem.NT includes nonconventional negotiations and treaty arrangements (the US-Japan Structural Impediments Initiative, or SII, for instance), new emerging issues not yet under formal multilateral discussion (environmental-trade linkages, competition policy), and a range of nontraditional trade and trade-related issues such as the supposed exclusionary business practices in a number of countries (the *keiretsu* in Japan, the *chaebol* in Korea), trade-restricting effects of domestic distribution systems (again in Japan), coordination of regulation of financial institutions (in Europe 1992, for instance), investment practices (in the US-Canada arrangement), temporary entry for businesspersons (again in the US-Canada arrangement), and other topics not touched on in the multilateral component of the system.

Behind this entire system lies domestic legal and administrative structure. This encompasses trade measures (tariffs, antidumping, and countervailing duties), the setting of product and safety standards, rules controlling trade in toxic and other waste products, and many other laws and regulations affecting trade. The postwar years have seen efforts to harmonize some of these in the GATT and elsewhere: common customs nomenclatures, limits on lengthy or overly complex border procedures, and codes on the use of antidumping and subsidies. But despite these efforts, substantial diversity in practice remains, adding further to the inconsistencies within the system.

Together, these four subsystems of multicountry arrangements and domestic laws make up the global trading system rather than only the system of multilateral rules and disciplines the GATT represents. All are shaped by the wider System.T, which embodies system goals. Linkages between subsystems have grown as each has become progressively more important. Thus, for example, Subsystem.NT has become interlinked with Subsystem.R because of the relative swiftness with which Subsystem.R can begin to deal with issues confronting System.T compared with Subsystem.M.[7] Subsystem.NT also allows for a quick response to current issues. This response is usually in a less consistent manner than one based on multilateral disciplines laid down in advance in Subsystem.M, but the ability (or at least perceived ability) of Subsystem.NT to respond, despite its internal inconsistency, gives it profile and importance.

---

7. One example is US-Canada negotiations concluding agreements in the services and financial service areas in advance of any GATT accords.

But because of Subsystem.M's relative rigidity and ever-wider country participation over the postwar years, its response to new issues and problems has been somewhat cumbersome, which has helped elevate the profiles of Subsystem.D, Subsystem.R, and Subsystem.NT. As a result, since the 1940s the system has evolved away from one in which Subsystem.M was the dominant component of System.T, reflecting the system goals of nondiscrimination and multilateralism, to one in which Subsystem.M is but one (albeit important) component of a System.T.

The framers of the GATT clearly had in mind eventually achieving today's more well-ordered trading system. All-encompassing trade rules and principles were intended to limit national governments' uses of trade-restricting measures. The introduction of new nontariff measures (quotas) was to be prevented; only existing quotas were to be allowed to remain in place. Transparency in border measures (tariffs) was to be achieved, with subsequent reductions to occur through multilateral negotiation. But the coexistence of so many arrangements at different levels and their evolution over the intervening years (with departures from and variations upon basic GATT principles) has meant that de facto the system has become more the accumulation of trade arrangements. There is no necessary consistency across all these arrangements; their relationship to stated system principles varies.

It also follows that if the trading system today is more a collection of policy responses to developments in the global economy than a well-ordered, operational rule-based system, it is also difficult to talk of strengthening, as is promoted in the Uruguay Round. The fact that this has been widely accepted as a needed improvement is a reflection of a growing gap between the system as it has evolved and the GATT system envisaged in the 1940s. This gap, which is reflected in the difference between System.T and System.M, and the divergence between the nondiscrimination and multilateralism principles and the system as it is today, has been filled by more and more non-System.M arrangements, grouped into subsystems System.D, System.R, and System.NT described above.

The distinction this suggests between a concept of a system based on principles and rules and an organizational concept for grouping accumulated trade agreements, is surprisingly important for the way one thinks about the global trading system as it may evolve after the Uruguay Round. If the trading system is largely thought of in terms of GATT-based multilateral rules, it appears natural for global trade policy to focus on sequences of multilateral negotiations that strengthen and enlarge the present system (as in the Uruguay Round). But aspiring to other system goals and principles may actually be better for system performance, since other developments within the trading system affect trade. And these may be deemphasized by an overly heavy focus on the multilateral system component.

Such a focus can also downplay drawbacks of a multilateral rule-based system, such as its relative inflexibility. Long periods are now involved in launching and implementing GATT negotiating rounds.[8] By the time a trade round is actually launched and negotiations completed, some of the issues taken up may no longer be of concern, and other emerging issues, while agreed to be important, may not be easy to deal with if the agenda has already been set. It can be difficult to exploit the give and take of so many negotiating partners across a wide range of negotiating issues; this is a difficulty the Uruguay Round has encountered. Also, the blocking power given to individual countries in multilateral rule-writing negotiations has at times meant that subgroups of countries willing and able to take on more obligations have been unable to do so.

Viewing the global trading system as a preexisting set of multilateral rules and principles that continually have to be strengthened, enlarged, and enriched through complex multilateral negotiating rounds leads naturally to the search for a stronger and better-functioning system, as we have seen. But paradoxically, with each passing year the system has seemed to move even further from nondiscrimination and multilateralism, which are meant to shape it.

If the trading system is instead viewed simply as an organizational framework, reflecting the accumulation of trade arrangements that address issues between all or subsets of countries, deal with specific sectors, and affect particular countries in different ways, the integrity of the system relative to its principles becomes less of an issue. The system is simply an inheritance—an accumulation of negotiated trade arrangements that provides a management framework for world trade. This framework in turn can be harnessed and potentially used to pursue specific performance-related objectives. This is the way in which I propose we think of the trading system in the post-Uruguay Round period: that is, as a framework that can be used to improve global economic performance rather than an end in and of itself.

The goals of the system, like the system itself, should in my view not be taken as fixed: they are security-oriented (multilateralism) when memory of war is strong; they are economic performance-oriented (access-driven) when security concerns weaken, as with the end of the Cold War. It no longer becomes necessary to weigh every trade issue against pre-specified principles, attempting to strengthen the trading system in their name, and only producing multilateral negotiating rounds of ever-growing complexity. System goals can be reassessed, restated, and their implications drawn. Trade management within the inherited structure, as

---

8. After the Tokyo Round was concluded in 1979, the first serious calls for a new round were not made until the 1982 GATT ministerial meeting. It then took until 1986 to gather the necessary support and build political will to launch the Uruguay Round in September 1986.

much as strengthening the trading system, becomes the issue, with corresponding implications for the post-Uruguay Round period.

The trading system of the 1990s differs from the trading system of the 1940s. Today's system reflects a slow, remorseless evolution away from a system dominated by a single set of multilateral rules and disciplines toward a much wider and more complex intertwining of inconsistently applied multilateral disciplines, sectoral arrangements, complex trade instruments, regional trading arrangements, and now a whole range of newer and even more complex concerns.

The trading system will likely witness an ever-closer intertwining of new issues, regionalism, sectoral and other derogations, environment, workers' rights, competition policy, in short, an acceleration over the next few decades of the trends identified above. This is due, in part, to the weakening of the strategic glue underlying the system but also reflects the likelihood of increasingly rapid change in the global economy. Trade policy debate in the 1990s will thus likely witness the end of grand designs, since the complexity of the system will increasingly make it impractical to continue to think in terms of a single set of multilateral rules and disciplines that define the whole system. *De novo* redesign is equally unlikely, given that the 1940s provided a unique window of opportunity, at the end of the Second World War and in light of the experiences of the 1930s, during which new trade rules could be negotiated. New approaches will, therefore, likely be needed to help with key elements of system performance.

Broadening Market Access after the Uruguay Round

Clearly, the postwar trading system has been successful in lowering tariffs on trade in manufactured products between industrial countries, so that relatively few new opportunities for liberalization will remain in this area after the Uruguay Round. But it also remains unclear how to go beyond tariffs and border measures and deal with the trade-restricting effects of domestic policies, how to move beyond manufactured products to significantly liberalize trade in services and other items, how to extend liberalization beyond industrial countries, and how to reverse the sectoral and other forms of nontariff protection in System.D that the eroding postwar system has generated. What may be needed are domestic constituencies in favor of more open trade, a more transparent system, and at least a supplement to the mercantilist bargaining approach used in the GATT to generate new market opening, if not a departure from it.

In the 1990s and beyond, a more open trading system will only result if some way can be found to better support those political forces favoring a more open system, and hence to reinforce existing pressures toward improving market access. During the postwar years, efforts at opening up markets internationally through the GATT system have reflected the premise that mercantilist exchanges of concessions (access to one's own market in return for access abroad) are the best way to proceed. This has been the case even though the concession is typically in the national (as opposed to the sectional) interest. Adherence to this approach has had the two unfortunate side effects that countries either keep protectionist policies as bargaining chips for further mercantilist negotiation,[9] or if they engage in unilateral liberalization, they subsequently also look for credit in multilateral forums. If this acknowledgment is not forthcoming, or if liberalization is not reciprocated, this may be a sufficient basis to stall future global liberalization.[10]

The danger following the Uruguay Round is that weakened multilateral disciplines could be taken to imply that the trading system is likely to generate less additional access. The reduced ability to link access across countries through reciprocity (either multilaterally or bilaterally) under a weakened System.M would then imply less effectiveness in restraining domestic protectionist interests. Domestic producer groups opposing liberalization will likely carry more political weight under such a regime. With more limited prospects for multilateral trade bargaining, interests of exporters in lowering trade barriers yet further in import-competing industries would carry less weight. With weaker links between improved access abroad and lowered barriers at home, generating further improvements in market access may prove more difficult. And committing to international treaties (acceding to GATT), which has long been defended as an effective way to resist domestic protectionist pressures,[11] could also now seem less attractive.

Continued growth of world trade after the round will also likely require concentrating access-generating efforts outside the tariff area. Tariff issues will remain; many developing countries still have high and/or unbound tariffs,[12] and some developed countries, such as Australia, still have a relatively low proportion of their tariffs bound. But removing or weakening impediments to service trade, removing VERs and other quota restrictions, dealing with barriers to trade beyond national borders, and

---

9. Wolf (1986) has argued that Australia has kept higher than otherwise necessary protection on manufacturers, hoping to trade it eventually for global agricultural liberalization.

10. The fate of unilateral trade liberalization in the Philippines since Aquino demonstrates this point, with initial quick liberalization, which then stalled, in part because of the perception of unreciprocated credit multilaterally (Clarete 1989).

11. This was apparently a strong factor in Mexico's decision to join the GATT in 1986.

12. Finger and Laird (1987, 9) report that developing countries' tariffs are, on average, about four times higher than developed countries' tariffs. See also Erzan et al. (1989).

weakening the trade-restricting effects of contingent trade measures (safeguards, antidumping, and countervail) will likely be the larger challenge.

An approach of directly identifying impediments to trade and negotiating on them may also be a helpful way of proceeding, especially if it complements wider, continuing efforts at trade liberalization multilaterally. A so-called "results-oriented" approach to trade negotiations was the one taken in the 1989 SII talks between the United States and Japan, but talks could take a different form in other areas. Complex regulations in restricted service areas might yield further liberalization if the most severe restrictions can be identified and negotiated. Incompatibilities between national standards might be another area amenable to such an approach.

Supporting Protrade Constituencies

Changes in the political calculus that drives trade policy in a number of countries appear to be under way in the early 1990s. There seem to be stronger "antiprotectionist" forces emerging.[13] In such areas as steel and footwear, there is evidence that users of imported products (large industrial users of steel, retailers of footwear) are actively and in some cases successfully opposing trade restrictions.[14] And interest continues to grow in attempts to make the costs of protectionist policies ever more transparent, such as through the reports of the Industries Assistance Commission in Australia, and more recently, the GATT Trade Policy Review Mechanism (TPRM).[15]

Whether these changes alone will provide enough support to those seeking liberalization that they will succeed in generating significant new market access remains to be seen. But consciously adding more transparency to the trade policy process, including through published studies of consumer costs, may be one approach to generating improvements in access. In 1985, for instance, the Leutwiler Report recommended that each country should bring trade policymaking into the open through the use of a "protection balance sheet" that would analyze the costs and benefits of protection. Companies would also be required to reveal any subsidies received.[16]

---

13. See Destler and Odell (1987), who discuss antiprotection groups and coalitions in the United States.

14. See Hamilton's (1989) discussion of the factors underlying the lifting of footwear restrictions in the EC.

15. See Qureshi (1990) for an interesting discussion of the TPRM as "an exercise in transparency or enforcement."

16. See GATT (1985b, 35–37) for more detail.

Providing clear legal rights to groups within countries opposed to protection may be a further step. The GATT system only provides a weak international legal framework within which to maintain openness in the global economy and to seek improvements in market access. Only governments, as contracting parties, have clear rights and obligations; few or no rights exist for other agents, consumers, companies, and associates.[17]

A constructive step could be to enshrine GATT obligations in domestic laws in such a way as to give individuals legal rights to sue their own government for violating their GATT obligations[18]; a related step would be to extend such rights in the form of access to foreign legal systems to pursue remedy. More far-reaching steps would be to extend and redefine the goals of the system along the lines of achieving full implementation of the access rights I set out above: rights of importers to products from abroad free of impediment, rights of exporters to sell abroad, rights of mobility for capital and labor. The system would then be evaluated based on how far it had moved toward these goals.

Competition Policy and Trade

During the 1990s and after the round, linkages between domestic policies and trade seem especially likely to grow further, and the specific linkage to competition (i.e., antitrust) policies is now being widely mentioned as a central component of possible postround negotiating activity. There are many elements in such linkage that will need to be addressed in removing impediments to trade.

First, there are the direct effects on trade that follow from international limits on the reach of competition policies. These are little researched, and to my knowledge there are no quantitative studies giving orders of magnitude of what may be involved, but the policies are widely believed to be important to freeing trade. The most obvious of these involve situations where anticompetitive practices affect countries from outside their borders. Thus, suppliers from countries A and B may collude in their joint activities in country C. These activities may be market-sharing agreements, whereby the two suppliers from countries A and B agree to share the market in country C in some way. There may be informal agreements under which the same two suppliers agree to fix prices in

---

17. Nongovernment rights, such as they are, consist of mechanisms allowing direct private-party access to domestic administrative procedures under the GATT antidumping and subsidies codes (Brand 1990, 12). Under the antidumping code, complaints may be brought against foreign parties selling into domestic markets at less than comparable prices abroad. Under the subsidies code, subsidization is the issue. Issues of injury follow, leading to questions of relief.

18. See the discussion also in Tumlir (1987).

country C. There may be arrangements involving contract tying. In all these ways, the lack of competition between the suppliers from outside the country impinges directly upon the market within the purchasing country and affects trade.

This situation occurs in its most extreme form when all suppliers to a market are outside the country, but similar situations can prevail if only a small portion of the market is serviced by domestic suppliers. It is an area of policy that centrally affects developing countries because of the strong presence of multinational companies in many of their domestic markets. But it is also an issue that arises in mid-sized countries of the Organization for Economic Cooperation and Development (OECD) in which significant portions of the market for a range of manufactured products are met by outside suppliers.

The central issue is the lack of territorial reach of the importing country's domestic competition policy and its inability to control the collusive behavior of foreign suppliers to the domestic market. Advocates of an international negotiation on competition policy, therefore, suggest that measures to extend the reach of competition policy be considered, leading both to freer trade and to larger international gains from specialization, where such practices restrict trade.

The approach generally suggested is to have complaints by affected groups in importing countries examined and if necessary pursued by antitrust agencies in the countries from which the suppliers originate. Problems with such an approach are, however, widely acknowledged. One is the likely asymmetry of the number of such cases across countries, and another is the information sharing required between agencies.

While such an approach may seem to have merit, there have been strong objections from some on the grounds that the trading system traditionally has focused on government-to-government negotiations and arrangements, not rules that constrain private-sector behavior. To extend international trading rules and regimes in ways that deal with private-sector behavior is unworkable since governments would ultimately need to share or at least discuss commercial information, whose integrity in remaining only with foreign governments cannot be assumed. However, the international rule regime in the GATT already encompasses (even if to a small degree) private-sector actions through, for instance, the anti-dumping code, which specifies arrangements under which petitions for antidumping relief by private parties may proceed.

A second element of linkage between competition policy and trade focuses on the implications of the lack of harmonization of competition policy for trade flows. Thus, the lack both of extraterritoriality and of harmonization of competition policies is said to lead to pressures for trade remedy action, and, given concerns over predation, antidumping laws. The absence of antidumping laws within the European Community, due to the European court and structure, has led some to suggest that harmonization of competition policy should be a central objective of future global trade efforts, since it could remove the need for a major component of current trade remedy laws.[19]

A third area where competition law impinges on trade policies, albeit more indirectly, reflects attempted extraterritoriality in some parts of competition laws. Investment restrictions under competition laws of source countries, for instance, may still apply as companies enter other markets and as mergers and acquisitions take place. For instance, there have been cases in which a merger between two parent companies in country A was ruled as inadmissible by competition agencies in country B because of the implications for the two subsidiary companies in country B.[20] Some of these conflicts over extraterritoriality could spill over and elevate tensions in ways that make trade conflict that much more likely.

Changes would be needed to existing multilateral arrangements to deal with such problems. To make competition policy international in reach, courts would need jurisdiction over more than national transactions. This would not only represent a major change in transnational legal structures and the operation of national court systems, it also would involve surrender of jurisdiction by national legislatures to supranational bodies. The willingness of legislatures to agree to such changes is thus a major impediment. To achieve some progress, the approach probably needs to be incremental rather than discrete.

One instance of change in this area, which is often taken to demonstrate what could be feasible elsewhere, is the European Community.[21,22] Firms in individual member states cannot initiate antidumping actions against firms from other member states because competition policy is a Communitywide issue under Article 85 of the Treaty of Rome. Issues involving competition policy are ruled on by the European court, which is empowered to make rulings, levy fines on both firms and national governments, and enforce competition statutes. As a result, antidumping actions are limited to trade matters outside the Community with the associated ben-

19. In a draft report from the European parliament, it was suggested policymakers should consider "a global competition policy to replace dumping measures" (*Financial Times*, 22 November 1990, 8).

20. For example, Julius (1990, 99) cites the case of a New York State court blocking the takeover of a UK-owned mining company by a South African–controlled firm. Since the UK-owned firm had assets in the United States, the New York court was able to block the takeover.

21. See the discussion of European Community antidumping practices in Messerlin (1990), who also notes the industry concentration of antidumping duties on chemicals. The recent volume edited by Trebilcock and York (1990) contains a more wide-ranging discussion of practices in North America, Europe, and other regions.

22. For more discussion of how European Community competition policy works, see IMF (1988, appendix I); European Community (1989, 13–21).

efit of increased flows of trade between European countries. The European court, however, now contains an accumulation of 30 years of jurisprudence, and national governments are willing to both accept and comply with court rulings. In part, this is because of the depth of the wider commitment to the European integration process, which suggests that attempts to achieve similar results quickly elsewhere would probably fail.

A different but more recent example of how limits can be applied to antidumping duties with corresponding implications for competition laws is trade between Australia and New Zealand. Under the bilateral Australia–New Zealand Free Trade Agreement, both countries have jointly agreed to renounce their use of antidumping and countervailing duties against each other, in part because in the past their joint bilateral use has been relatively small. This is to be achieved using a separate body empowered by the two governments to investigate possible transnational violations of antitrust practices. It does not go as far as the European case in seeking to harmonize competition law between the two countries fully by establishing a unified superior court.

There are other recent trade policy developments that implicitly synchronize domestic competition laws. While not removing antidumping duty actions as cross-border impediments, they have the effect of incrementally weakening any harassment in bilateral arrangements. Such attempts are typically bilateral rather than pluri- or multilateral and may well become more common in the 1990s, especially if a weak outcome to the Uruguay Round results and there are difficulties in initiating a new negotiation with competition policy as a major element.

Negotiating Across Culturally Diverse Economic Systems

A further challenge for the trading system is to deal with markets in countries where there are cultural differences in methods of doing business relative to North America and Europe. This issue first became apparent in the 1980s in the trade conflicts between the United States and Japan, which in the postwar years had been the earliest and most rapidly growing of the Asian economies. In the 1990s similar issues may well become more prominent with Korea, Taiwan, and other Asian countries such as Indonesia, Malaysia, and Thailand.

The characteristics of the Japanese economy that have caused the greatest difficulty in its trade relations with the United States are the extreme concentration of ownership and the additional cross-ownership, as represented by the *keiretsu* (conglomerates) with multiple degrees of crossholding.[23] The *keiretsu*, coupled with the heavy focus on production rather

---

23. *Keiretsu* are groupings of firms with common ties or links to the same bank or source of finance with gross holdings of equity and to groups of presidents of firms who jointly have frequent and informal meetings. They have evolved out of the earlier *zaibatsu* con-

than consumption in Japan, even at the household level, and the associated high saving rates, have led those outside the Japanese economic system to view it as collusive, secretive, and riddled with hidden barriers to entry to all sectors.

The difficulties that these features of the Japanese economy pose for trade and investment from other OECD countries are that they have no clear analogues in other countries and that, as a result, they are only partially understood but nonetheless are widely debated in terms of what the policy response should be. There is disagreement in the Western literature as to whether there are, in fact, significant trade barriers in Japan, and whether the inability of US and European firms to penetrate Japanese markets largely reflects the firms' inability to compete or Japanese entry barriers.

One claim is that foreign firms do not produce products that sell in Japan, nor do they learn about Japanese customs and meet other requirements of market penetration in Japan. In the 1970s and into the 1980s, Japan reduced and/or eliminated most of their formal tariff barriers, certainly as far as manufactures are concerned. Liberalization took place as part of the Tokyo Round of GATT negotiations and continued with unilateral liberalization through the late 1970s and into the mid 1980s. The contention is that, beyond tariff barriers, other formal trade barriers are relatively few.[24] There are few quotas and other overtly trade-restricting practices, and those measures that remain have been the subject of repeated government attempts to eliminate them.

The contention from those who argue that Japan substantially restricts trade is that Japanese businesses agree to purchase each other's products at collusive prices.[25] Moreover, the Japanese distribution system, so it is alleged, makes it difficult for foreign suppliers to enter the distribution

---

glomerates that were broken up after the war during the US occupation. See the discussion in Uekusa (1987) and Lincoln (1990), who also point out that the nine largest trading companies in Japan handle 45 percent of exports and 77 percent of imports. See also "Keiretsu, what are they doing, where are they heading?" *Tokyo Business Today*, September 1990, 26–36.

24. In an effort to improve EC relations with Japan, a joint declaration is to be signed in July 1991. The EC wants to see improved and guaranteed access to the Japanese market, but the Japanese are insisting that their efforts at market opening must be recognized. According to a Japanese spokesman, "We've made every effort to change the structure of our economy. It is now up to the exporters to make use of the Japanese market or not" (*Financial Times*, 7 June 1991, 1).

25. Some evidence in favor of this contention is that the vast majority of prosecutions under Japan's antimonopoly laws are for price-fixing agreements (Uekusa 1987). See also the discussion in McMillan (1991) of *dango*, or the art of bid-rigging, in the Japanese construction industry. Japan also recently raised the maximum fine for participating in an illegal cartel to 6 percent of turnover, up from 2 percent. This move was largely a response to the SII talks (*Financial Times*, 15 January 1991, 8).

chain, and both the Japanese government and bureaucracy consistently use practices that support and promote domestic firms over foreign firms.

This sense of Japan as a secretive economy that consistently excludes foreign suppliers was a major impetus in the 1980s behind an EC complaint to a GATT panel that the whole of Japan was a trade-restricting measure and that the operation of the entire Japanese economy restricted imports from the European Community.[26]

The United States generally took a bilateral approach both to gaining improved access to the Japanese market and in restricting Japanese exports in the 1980s.[27] The dramatic increase in the US bilateral trade deficit with Japan between 1980 and 1985 became the symbol of an unfair, closed Japanese trade regime in contrast to the open US marketplace.[28]

Frustrated with the lack of progress, the United States initiated Market-Oriented Sector Selective Talks (MOSS) with Japan in January 1985 with the idea of achieving some degree of liberalization in Japan in four targeted sectors: forest products, medical equipment and pharmaceuticals, electronics (semiconductors excluded), and telecommunications. Discussions were also held later on transportation machinery and auto parts. The talks lasted one year, and while the Japanese made concessions in each area, the success of the talks was varied.[29]

In an effort to accommodate Congress, the United States again pursued a bilateral approach to its trade problems with Japan when it launched the Structural Impediments Initiative (SII) in July 1989, after Japan was named an unfair trader under Super 301. Unlike the MOSS talks, the idea behind the SII negotiations was to deal with problems in both countries by identifying and recommending solutions to what were considered structural impediments to trade. The United States zeroed in on the Japanese saving rate (as too high) and investment, land-use policy, pricing mechanisms, domestic distribution systems, antitrust policy, and the *keiretsu*. In turn, the Japanese targeted the US saving rate (as too low), corporate competitiveness, export promotion, work force training, and education.

---

26. In April 1983, the EC filed a complaint against Japan entitled, "nullification or impairment of benefits and impediment to the attainment of GATT objectives." The EC asserted they had not benefited from successive GATT negotiations with Japan. The dispute was eventually settled bilaterally. GATT (1984, 49–50).

27. Such as in the case of auto VERs, textiles and clothing quotas and discussions to improve US access in beef, citrus, construction, and semiconductors. For details of the US-Japan relationship, see Destler and Sato (1982), Bergsten and Cline (1985), McCullough (1988), *Congressional Quarterly Inc.* (1984).

28. Although it was generally accepted that the imbalance was due to macro factors, largely for political reasons, the Japanese trade regime was blamed. See Bergsten and Cline (1985) for details.

29. See Lincoln (1990) and Low (1990) for details.

Under the SII agreement, reached in June 1990,[30] Japan agreed to ease restrictions on its retail distribution system, increase spending on public works, and improve enforcement of anticompetitive practices. The United States agreed to provide tax credits for personal saving, improve the US education system, and strengthen the Gramm-Rudman budget balancing law (*International Trade Reporter*, 31 May 1989, 684; *The Economist*, 18 November 1989, 15–16; *Financial Times*, 6 April 1990, 26). While the United States admitted some progress had been made in the annual review on May 1991, both sides expressed general dissatisfaction. A particularly contentious issue was the *keiretsu*, where the United States felt there was a "lack of willingness to deal with the problem of cross-shareholding"(*Financial Times*, 24 May 1991, 5).The Japanese evaluation was particularly critical of US corporate policy, especially the fact that some highly paid US executives set their own salaries, which in the Japanese view has a detrimental effect on the morale of employees and corporate saving.

Given these disagreements, both among Westerners and among the Japanese themselves, as to whether there are significant trade and other barriers in Japan, and given the seemingly low level to which the debate has sunk, the prospects for formal future negotiations on trade barriers involving such culturally diverse economies seem poor.[31] These differences also complicate any determination of compliance either with bilateral agreements such as SII or with international standards as represented by the articles of the General Agreement. The issue of collusive business practices in Japan reinforces the pressures for a major focus in future GATT negotiations on restrictive business practices and the benefits that might or might not follow from a multilateral agreement in this area. But some, frustrated with what has been achieved thus far, have instead suggested that there may be benefits from a negotiation focused on performance targets, a negotiation under which Japan would agree to import growth with agreed targets and clearly defined sanctions.

A problem with such negotiations is that they are largely one-sided, with lists of demands for liberalization, to which the Japanese may not continue to agree in the 1990s unless they are offered something in return. Through the 1970s and '80s, Japan seemingly remained largely accom-

---

30. In April 1990 the United States announced that Japan would not be named under its Super 301 provision of the 1988 Omnibus Trade Act for unfair trade practices, citing substantial progress toward market opening on Japan's part.

31. A recent piece in the *Financial Times* ("Trade Warriors Prepare For a New Campaign," 25 January 1991) details the likely list of US demands for further negotiations over the next year. These include a new statement on limiting *keiretsu*, foreign access to Japanese public works projects, improved rights of US lawyers in Japan, further deposit and interstate deregulation in financial services, changes in procurement practices for computers, and removal of testing restrictions on US paper. To some extent, this is happening in the case of semiconductors. For details on the US-Japan semiconductor negotiations, see Hamilton and Whalley (forthcoming).

modating to foreign pressures to open markets and agreed to restrain exports voluntarily, with little asked in the way of a formal quid pro quo. One can argue that Japanese businesses anticipated that they could export around any such impediments (which perhaps they saw as of dubious effectiveness), or that their strategic interests preconditioned a relatively passive response. Europe and the United States have, however, become used to such a relatively passive response from Japan to foreigner's trade policy demands and on that basis might anticipate that in the 1990s similar behavior will occur.

One view in Japan of how to respond to foreign trade policy pressure is that Japan can now say no and would likely say no to a proposal that import performance targets be unilaterally adopted. There are, therefore, new doubts as to whether the negotiating approach used in the 1980s (i.e., SII) will be productive in the 1990s, particularly with the enforcement problems involved.[32]

The enlargement of the trading system to encompass Japan and other Asian economies and the need to continue to generate new access in the 1990s seems to suggest exploring approaches to trade negotiations with these countries different from those used in the 1980s. It further demonstrates the need to move away from multilateral negotiations simply based on a system of trade rules and disciplines. More targeted liberalization efforts in this, as in other areas, seem to be inevitable in the 1990s.

An approach for those seeking access to culturally diverse economies might be more explicitly supporting or pushing for catalytic liberalization—that is, seeking access in one part of the economy that may speed liberalization elsewhere. The United States has already tried such catalytic liberalization, obtaining agreement both from the government of Japan and the local regulatory bodies within prefectures to allow the establishment of US retailers such as Toys-R-Us, K-Mart or Wal-Mart. Once established, the hope has been that they would gain market share and facilitate increased imports from the United States through their retailing operations. Similar catalytic liberalization may be possible in financial, transportation, and other service-related industries.

Clearly, the experience of the 1980s suggests that a different approach to trade policy is needed in dealing with culturally diverse economies from that represented by GATT trade negotiations in the 1960s and '70s. The GATT system as it has evolved reflects the perception in the 1940s

---

32. See also USITC (1990) and Japan Echo (1990) for details on the SII. Dornbusch (1990) contends that the SII approach is misdirected and that the US should concentrate on domestic reforms. In remarks to the US Joint Economic Committee, Clyde Prestowitz (at the time, Senior Fellow at Carnegie Endowment for Peace) asserted the US was "spinning its wheels" trying to open the Japanese market through the SII talks. In his view, the US should accept that some markets are not going to open and should be more pragmatic about cutting deals (*International Trade Reporter*, 18 October 1989, 1349).

that the objective of the trading system was to restore growth in Europe and prevent a return to the high trade barriers of the 1930s. But the GATT system to some degree remains culture-bound and unable to deal directly with the key trade impediments in markets such as Japan.

Improving Market Access Beyond Goods

Part of the motivation for launching the Uruguay Round was to broaden the system of multilateral trade rules as they apply to goods so as to also cover barriers affecting nongoods flows by extending System.M to cover areas now in System.NT. This effort reflected both the desire to reduce or eliminate existing barriers and to put in place firm rules that would head off the introduction of new barriers.[33] This idea, in part, underlies attempts to extend the GATT to cover such new areas as services, trade-related aspects of intellectual property, and trade-related investment issues.[34]

In the early days of the Uruguay Round the belief in the United States and the other large industrial economies was that growing manufactured exports from Japan and other newly industrializing economies (NIEs) in Asia suggested that comparative advantage was changing. Indeed, it was believed that in the 1990s, Japanese and Asian NIEs' comparative advantage would continue to shift away from traditional manufactured products and toward higher technology products and services (Bhagwati 1987; Noland 1990). Since there was no system of international rules to restrain potential trade-restricting practices (Stalson 1985; Diebold and Stalson 1983),[35] the argument was that new rules were needed in these areas both to fend off new protectionism and to achieve new liberalization. In the case of investment (Graham and Krugman 1990; also Guisinger 1987; Hufbauer and Schott 1985), the belief was that trade-related investment practices, such as export performance requirements, could be dealt with through bans or prohibitions, and quite separately from international regulation of investment flows through exchange controls, financing restrictions, local equity participation requirements, investment screening rules, and other impediments.

Even though the outcome of the round is still in the balance, while there is prospect of a major comprehensive agreement in intellectual

---

33. A French proposal in the early 1980s to tax the number of message units relayed on satellite transmissions, for instance, was a factor motivating the early US enthusiasm for a multilateral negotiation in services.

34. See the discussion in Sampson (1989) for further detail on the motives behind these negotiations.

35. For more detail on U.S. National Study on Services, see USITC (1984), appendix Q.

property, the investment agreement will be more limited, and any services agreement will be some distance from providing concrete disciplines in the key sectoral areas. Efforts to broaden the coverage of the trading system to deal with nongoods flows therefore have perhaps not been wholly successful. Attempts to negotiate new and broad frameworks of rules have proved more difficult than many expected. The application to key sectors of rules that might have emerged unearthed new and unanticipated problems. And the crossovers to other negotiating groups that supposedly were to have generated progress did not materialize.

But at the same time, this experience does not suggest that attempts to remove barriers to nongoods flows should cease. Indeed, the annual value of international financial transactions (including foreign direct investment) is substantially larger than that of international trade flows, and though current estimates only provide an approximation, international flows of services seem to be growing more rapidly than goods flows.[36] The issue, therefore, is what can be done in the 1990s to accelerate new liberalization in these areas.

One possible approach is the use of a more flexible and less rule-bound approach of trying to relax existing regulatory constraints rather than first seeking to agree on systems of general rules and principles. Because of the complexity of existing regulatory arrangements, the approach would be to identify constraints to trade and negotiate directly on ways of removing them rather than to try to agree on broad principles to which existing barriers are meant to conform through multilateral negotiation.

Air transportation is an illustration of this. Since 1944, international air transportation between cities in different countries has been regulated by a series of air services agreements, largely negotiated according to the Chicago Convention and registered with the International Civil Aviation Organization (ICAO).[37] These are time-limited, bilaterally negotiated agreements between national governments and usually involve an exchange of routes between national carriers from each of the countries. The agreements usually cover which airlines will service the routes, the capacity for each airline, and the potential for carriers from other countries to participate in the routes. Much effort goes into making the agreements balanced and mutually advantageous. Thus, for instance, in a bilateral India-Germany negotiation, India might allow Lufthansa to fly into Delhi in return for Air India being given permission to fly into Frankfurt.

---

36. According to GATT *International Trade '89–90* (Geneva: GATT, 1990, vol. 2), export volume expanded by 7 percent in 1989 while world trade in commercial services (transportation, tourism, banking, insurance, other professional services) increased by 9 percent (GATT 1990b, 87).

37. For the history of the development of air transportation regulation, see Doganis (1985). Findlay (1990) also gives an excellent summary of how this sector works.

But such negotiations are often slow, cumbersome, extremely complicated, and not very flexible once completed. Other negotiating issues frequently arise, such as fifth-freedom rights (the right to pick up passengers for transit to other countries), to which the other countries involved in the transaction must agree. Cabotage (the right to pick up passengers for flights to other cities—e.g., flights from Delhi to Frankfurt and on to Hamburg) is a further contentious issue.[38] Of increasing importance are access to computerized reservation systems and baggage handling.

The point is that, even within this complex bilateral framework of treaty arrangements and independent of any multilateral negotiation on broad principles of services trade, a concerted effort at liberalizing existing arrangements rather than first laying down a general system of rules for all agreements in all service sectors, may yield more concrete results.[39] For instance, some degree of additional liberalization might be possible if the bilateral system of treaties allowed foreign carriers to purchase routes from national governments instead of simply encouraging their own governments to trade routes for other routes from foreign governments. Thus, by allowing cash to be exchanged internationally for routes rather than relying on route-for-route exchanges, more liberalization might well result.

This is just one illustration of how new liberalization in nongoods trade might work. But, working within the existing institutional and regulatory framework sector by sector, the aim would be to identify ways of relaxing constraints to speed liberalization. This would stand in contrast to the top-down approach used in the Uruguay Round of trying first to agree on international principles and then attempting to determine whether existing practices are compatible with these principles. An approach of the type suggested here could also be pursued alongside efforts to achieve wider framework agreements.

Keeping the Global Economy Open

A further key challenge to the trading system beyond the Uruguay Round will be how to maintain the relative openness to trade that remains part of the wider System.T despite the growth of System.D. The fear is that a gradual closing of access could occur, driven by large-power trade conflict and an increasingly rule-inconsistent trade environment.

---

38. Cabotage rights are rarely granted. See Doganis (1985) for more detail.

39. However, see the discussion of the multilateral liberalization option in civil aviation in *The Avmark Aviation Economist*, August 1990, 4–7. Findlay (1990) also discusses how GATT principles might apply to the aviation sector.

Scenarios for a Closed System

The notion of "closing" applied to the trading system is usually taken to refer to erection of new trade barriers. New barriers are feared because it is believed they will reduce trade volumes and with them, the benefits from trade enjoyed by producers and consumers in different countries. The present concern is that if the poor macro performance of the early 1990s persists and lowered expectations begin to pervade the system, the remaining commitment to an open system may further erode. This could further accelerate system closing, which could generate income reductions and even deeper reductions in trade. While such a scenario seems unlikely to unfold at the same pace as it did in the 1930s, the recurrence of the pattern of trade and income reductions, with trade reductions larger than income reductions in proportional terms, is feared.

Perhaps the most serious form of system closing that could occur in the 1990s would be an outbreak of new retaliatory trade conflicts. The European Community could impose measures against the United States, the US could retaliate with measures of its own, the EC would counterretaliate, and so on. Such a scenario becomes more serious for economic performance the broader the product coverage of such retaliatory measures.[40]

In the 1980s, EC-US trade conflicts (such as over EC enlargement, or in the citrus-pasta war) involved retaliation that was largely confined to narrow product groups and usually involved only a single round of retaliatory trade actions before bilateral conciliation occurred. Though limited, retaliation in the 1980s was more confrontational than in the 1970s. The concern in the 1990s is that with a weak outcome to the Uruguay Round and more bilateral conflict in the offing—hormones, meat inspection, Airbus subsidies, further possible EC enlargement (*Financial Times*, December 7, 1990, 2)—trade conflicts will accelerate, culminating in retaliatory episodes even more serious than those in the past.

Ten or even twenty years ago, such a scenario would not be totally dismissed as far-fetched, although in its extreme form it remains in my view somewhat implausible. The Community and the United States have in the past recognized their clear joint interest in mediating trade disputes and will no doubt continue to do so. Also, as suggested above, the scenario of increased retaliatory tit-for-tat trade barriers, depicted as a revisitation of the 1930s, is based on a factually inaccurate portrayal of events of the period.

A less extreme scenario of what new system closing could entail in the 1990s focuses more on the economically harmful consequences of the

---

40. An example would be across-the-board import surcharges under Article 12 of the GATT. For instance, the US suspension of the Bretton Woods system in 1971 was accompanied by a 10 percent surcharge.

threat of increased barriers. This may be either barriers that it is feared might be introduced or the presence of systems of administered trade barriers,[41] whose introduction is conditional upon various criteria (dumping, subsidy, injury, etc.). The prospect of barriers can have effects similar to actual barrier introductions, since producers in exporting countries become more reluctant to invest and trade if they foresee greater barriers. Indeed, uncertainty over the size of future barriers can be even more damaging to trade if exporters come to view investment in export businesses as a no-win but risky proposition—i.e., they face barriers if they are successful and no barriers only if they are unsuccessful.

Administered (or contingent) trade barriers result from legal processes that allow domestic producers to request that barriers be introduced based on alleged harm to them (of injury, and from subsidy or dumping). Tribunals investigate these allegations, making decisions and eventually imposing remedies, if any.[42] Seemingly frivolous petitions may be initiated to harass foreign competition, and legal process in these areas may begin to stretch the outer limits of the original intent of the trade remedy laws when enacted. This uncertainty as to the outcome from petitions for remedy amplifies the threat to exporters of future barriers.[43] Furthermore, interim duties may be imposed pending a final decision, with no compensation paid to the importer if they are not upheld. These harassment effects are analogous to those emanating from threats of barriers. And as the system closes in this way, the willingness to explore the development of new trading patterns recedes, and trade growth falters.

Thus, this scenario for further closing focuses on threats of new barriers, with corresponding implications for new investment activity. New, visible trade barriers could emerge from a round of large-power trade conflicts and could serve to close the system, or the threat of new barriers could erode the commitment of exporters. Either way, closing occurs.

But perhaps the most plausible scenario is that a number of adverse developments, each of seemingly limited consequence, prove cumulatively disastrous for the trading system. These might include continuing and spreading sectoral derogations, threats of new barriers emerging from large-power conflicts, new mechanisms being found for the application of barriers on a contingent basis, escalation and emulation in the use of

---

41. See the discussion of administered US trade barriers in Anderson and Rugman (1989).

42. See also Grinols (1989, 512) for discussion of the various US trade remedy procedures. He notes the increasing trend toward greater activity under Section 301 and reports "more than $4.25 billion of trade in mid-1988 was subject to possible sanctions depending on the resolutions." By way of comparison, he notes the retaliation against Japanese failure to fully implement the semiconductor agreement only amounted to $300 million. Finger and Murray (1990) also describe the sequence and time limits of US procedures.

43. Messerlin (1989, 573) reports that even the threat of antidumping actions has had the effect of reducing exports to the European Community.

unilateral measures,[44] and the trade-depressing and protection-enhancing effects of a drawn-out recession in the early 1990s.

Under this scenario, each of these factors reinforces the others to accentuate the degree of market closing involved. Recession increases the risk and severity of sectoral derogations, which in turn make recovery from recession more difficult. Threats of unilateralism add to threats of major-power conflict, which in turn more strongly legitimize threatened unilateral actions. The downturn in trade from all the above factors puts more pressure on firms to seek remedy from contingent protection, which in turn reinforces the other factors.

Fending Off System Closing

While one can perhaps take such a scenario to extremes and overplay both the risks and the potential barrier increases that could result, the fact remains that trade in the 1990s is likely to take place in a world facing uncertain trade barriers, and one with the major powers reevaluating their trading relationships.

Given these risks, it seems reasonable to ask what steps could be taken to maintain today's relative openness. As emphasized above, the trading system of the 1990s will likely differ from that of past experience in important ways: the move from unipolarity (i.e., the hegemonic status of the United States) toward a three-power world (the European Community, the United States, and Japan); the effective end of the Cold War and the removal of the strategic underpinnings of the trading system; the progressive weakening of the GATT and System.M as a focal point, eroding the perceived joint benefits of collaborative activity; and the increasing rapidity of change in the system and the potentially larger adjustment problems associated with this.

The central idea behind the Uruguay Round was to strengthen System.M. Reform of the system's institutional structure was always seen as a key element. The approach was to try to reverse existing derogations in System.D, strengthen the rules of System.M where possible, and extend the rules of System.M to new areas such as services. The aim was to generate stronger trade rules with more effective enforcement and to reverse System.M erosion. In this way, it was hoped, the relative openness of the trading system would be protected and even enhanced.

Some, such as Jackson (1989 and 1990), advocated the establishment of a new institutional framework overseeing international trade arrangements, the World Trade Organization (WTO), as a central part of this process. Others suggested a strengthening of the institution of the GATT

---

44. In 1986 the European Community enacted its own version of Section 301–style unilateralism. See the discussion in Grinols (1989).

itself:[45] a stronger secretariat with powers to investigate and collect evidence of violations of GATT obligations, even to initiate enforcement proceedings against countries. These ideas are similar in spirit to those already embodied in the Trade Policy Review Mechanism emanating from the Montreal Mid-Term Review in the Uruguay Round. They seek to go substantially further in strengthening the investigative and other powers of the GATT Secretariat.

While acknowledging the potential benefits of such an approach, I question whether strong political consensus exists in enough countries for such major institutional reform to be agreed upon and implemented quickly. Many countries remain unwilling to submit to strong investigative scrutiny, and even fewer would be willing to comply with rulings of international bodies on the appropriateness of internal policies.

Also, while they could benefit from strengthened rules in System.M, developing countries remain concerned that a strengthened institutional structure covering the present global trade organizations could be used to enforce their compliance with policy objectives set in developed countries. Many of these countries would be reluctant to grant an international tribunal or quasi-judicial process powers to investigate their internal policies and in this way surrender autonomy over policy to an agency they would see as similar to the World Bank and the International Monetary Fund. Thus, strengthening multilateral trade arrangements by giving more powers to global trade institutions, while perhaps globally desirable, may be unrealistic as the main approach through which further system closing can be prevented.

New Trilateral Leadership

This being the case, my argument is that other complementary approaches may need to be explored, perhaps focusing on new trilateral arrangements between the major trading powers and more large-power leadership in the system. The idea would be to encourage joint action on trade issues from the European Community, the United States, and Japan so as to help keep the system open.[46] These powers clearly have a strong mutual interest in a well-functioning trading system, an interest that minimizes trade conflict and lessens the possibility of trade wars. Active management on their part could go some distance toward achieving these goals.

What I would see in such an arrangement would be a system of jointly agreed trade disciplines, which would also be GATT-consistent and ca-

---

45. For example, see Hufbauer (1989), Camps with Gwin (1981), Atlantic Council (1976). For further detail on suggested institutional reform, see Hamilton and Whalley (forthcoming).

46. See also Jones (1989), who recommends the negotiation of a formal agreement between at least these three powers to eliminate the use of discriminatory trade restrictions against each other.

pable of strengthening both System.M and System.T. Instead of waiting for the launch and outcome of a further round of GATT negotiations beyond the Uruguay Round, the three major powers in the system could begin immediately to develop a trilateral framework for trade and put in place mechanisms to defuse future trade conflicts.

Simply because such an approach does not fit directly within the framework of System.M does not, in my view, provide a reason to discount it. This approach might involve a gradation of measures, varying in strength depending upon how far the three powers would be willing to go in their joint commitments. Such an approach might begin with a firm statement by Japan, the United States, and the European Community on the need to strengthen trilateral trade arrangements so as to minimize the risk of major-power trade conflict and to do so in a GATT-compatible manner. An endorsement of this approach by other GATT contracting parties, if obtainable, would help take these commitments further through more concrete three-way arrangements.

One possibility might be to enlarge the scope of the GATT's TPRM as it applies to the three large powers. The three powers could, for instance, jointly support a continuous effort to monitor their bilateral trade flows, their barriers against each other as well as emerging conflicts and market situations. In effect, the mechanism would act as an early warning system on large-power trade disputes. This could be done by committing more resources to the GATT Secretariat for a more actively investigative three-power process than is currently embodied in the TPRM. Early identification of emerging problems in this way could prove helpful in defusing new trade conflicts.

A subsequent step might be jointly agreed rules to contain and limit any retaliation of large powers against each other. These rules could explicitly apply to trade disputes that spill out beyond the normal GATT process. Thus, the European Community, the United States, and Japan (or pairs in separate bilateral agreements) might agree that any retaliation be confined to the broad product category involved in the dispute (such as agriculture). They might agree to place on all retaliation an upper bound on the value of trade affected by the dispute. They might agree that after one round of retaliation each, they automatically move to some form of conciliation. They might also agree on a cooling-off period (say, six months) between rounds of retaliation and counterretaliation. The idea would be to contain and limit the potential wider damage to the trading system, System.T, through unconstrained retaliation—an attempt to establish a cooperative arrangement in the mutual interest of all three powers, replacing potentially destructive noncooperative behavior.[47]

---

47. See the discussion in Abbott (1985, 525–30), which illustrates the consequences of bilateral disputes involving retaliation and counterretaliation measures using a game-theory framework. See also Conybeare (1987).

Yet another step might be for joint trilateral commitments to be made that either forgo the use of certain GATT benefits, such as Article 12 balance of payments measures in response to import surges from each other, or if this were regarded as too extreme a step, to a cooling-off period on any use of such measures. This could be for a year, pending notification of intent. In some cases, the cooling off might allow underlying macro imbalances to right themselves and give rise to exploration of other ways of approaching outstanding trade problems.

Potential events such as oil prices shocks or a further worsening of the US trade deficit could result in one or more of the three larger trading regions using trade-restricting escape-clause measures under GATT Article 12. The use of a temporary across-the-board import surcharge of, say, 25 percent by the United States or the European Community following a sharp and rapid deterioration in their trade balances could result in major difficulty for the trading system, with the possibility of countermeasures by other large powers and global turmoil.[48] Jointly negotiated trilateral agreements in this area could help defuse such threats.

Opportunities exist for major-power agreements to fend off trade conflicts on other fronts. For instance, in the late 1980s the regions on occasion applied bilateral pressure to a smaller trading region to gain a concession covering areas outside GATT (such as intellectual property) on a non-MFN basis. When these concessions were made in a discriminatory manner, the other large powers would then request the same concession, generating further trade conflict.

One such case involved US threats against Korea in the late 1980s. The United States threatened to graduate Korea from the Generalized System of Preferences (GSP) unless intellectual property arrangements in Korea shifted away from process toward product patents. The concessions Korea made were applied only to the United States. This subsequently induced the European Community to also threaten Korea with GSP graduation unless these benefits were also fully extended to the Community. When Korea subsequently did not do this, the Community graduated Korea.[49]

Another possible avenue for large-power trade agreement would be to ensure that concessions requested of smaller trading partners would always be fully MFN, with the benefits fully extended to all other trading partners. This would help relieve large-power tensions in the system.

The three large powers could go even further and consider implementing arrangements that would freeze problem situations where they are now. They could, for instance, commit themselves to no new bilateral

---

48. In response to the mounting bilateral imbalances the United States faced in the early 1980s, a number of surcharge bills were introduced in the US Congress in 1985. For further discussion, see Rousslang and Suomela (1985).

49. For further discussion and examples of bilateral pressures, see Whalley (1989a).

negotiation of a comprehensive form for an agreed period, pending developments in the GATT and on other fronts. This would help relieve further pressures in the system: suspicion in the United States of exclusion from Europe 1992, concerns in Japan and the European Community of exclusions from US-Canada-Mexico arrangements, and possible confusion in the United States and Europe over Japanese intentions toward the Association of Southeast Asian Nations (ASEAN).

All of these are examples of possible concrete measures and agreements beyond existing GATT obligations. If the large powers were to adopt them, there would be more active leadership in the trading system, and the large powers would be acting cooperatively to strengthen the system.[50] Such a three-power trade framework could also coexist alongside Group of Seven discussions on international financial issues: exchange rates, debt issues, and interest rates. Major-power leadership in these areas has been accepted for a longer period, as in the Plaza Agreement of 1985, the Louvre Accord of 1987, and in other forums on exchange rate and other financial issues.[51] Factoring in such aspects of the wider relationship between the three major powers seems to provide an opportunity for building the more integrated financial-trade approach to international economic policymaking that so many have suggested over the years.

The obvious weakness of this approach is that such an arrangement might establish collusion between the large trading powers, an outcome that smaller countries would fear.[52] At the same time, it might lead to even more fragmentation of the trading system into three large trading areas, with satellite, or client, trading partners attached to each of the large powers.[53]

These are concerns, but at the same time, the stresses that may emerge in the trading system in the 1990s suggest that there is value in actively

---

50. See also the discussion in Bergsten, Davignon, and Miyazaki (1986), which also stresses the need for trilateral systemic cooperation.

51. For further discussion, see Bergsten (1990) and Funabashi (1988).

52. Bryant and Hodgkinson (1989, 7) note, "In practice a judgment has to be made about which is the greater danger: that in the absence of cooperation between governments, international interaction will work to the detriment of public policy . . . or, alternatively, that collusion between governments will work against the public interest." In their view, "cooperation between governments, particularly democratic governments, can be plausibly expected to further the collective interests of their people."

53. It is unclear what the best arrangements are for smaller countries: On the one hand, they could benefit if large countries engaged in retaliatory trade wars one with the other, since if they were not subject to the retaliatory measures, they would gain from the trade diversion. On the other hand, a collapse in trade by the major powers could generate a global recession of major consequence, and one in which smaller countries would suffer more than proportionately, as they are more trade-dependent.

exploring this option. A single multilateral framework for trade (System.M) in which all countries are thought to be of equal importance to the system and one in which all countries negotiate simultaneously, may not meet be sufficient to fend off trade conflicts between the large powers. These could adversely harm the trade interests of all countries in the system.

Indeed, rather than fragmenting the multilateral system, pursuit of this approach may strengthen it by generating new GATT-consistent arrangements in which the large powers would make commitments one with another that go beyond their existing multilateral obligations and eventually strengthen commitment to the GATT focal point. GATT compatibility, therefore, is an important ingredient in this approach, building stronger disciplines atop the present multilateral framework.[54]

The New Regionalism and Post-Uruguay Round System

While the need to improve access and maintain openness in the trading system is widely agreed upon, regionalism poses a special challenge for the trading system beyond the Uruguay Round. How best to approach it is uncertain since it is unclear whether, on balance, further regionalism is good or bad for system performance. Exclusionary trade deals raise the vista of Viner-style trade diversion,[55] and fears currently abound of a global gravitation toward three large trading blocs locked in trade conflict. But at the same time, further regional trade deals in System.R could be a main source for liberalizing in System.T if System.M yields little new liberalization. The challenge then, is to find ways to promote the positive elements of any further regionalism that might enter the system while mitigating negative effects.

The Content of the New Regionalism

The difficulties in concluding the Uruguay Round in the midst of seemingly accelerating regional trade liberalization (US-Canada, Europe 1992,

---

54. We would also see the involvement of other parties as a possibility but not a necessity. Such involvement would tend to weaken and slow down the three-country active management process advocated here, but it may be that an observer to such three-country discussions, jointly nominated by the other GATT members, might help, especially in facilitating information flows.

55. See Viner (1950) for a classic consideration of the benefits and dangers of customs unions and free trade areas.

US-Mexico-Canada)[56] have heightened speculation that the global trading system might move further toward regional trade blocs. Under this scenario, future multilateral negotiation comes to an end, and what remains of System.M progressively erodes. In frustration, the major powers each further develop networks of regional arrangements with neighboring countries that were already in place at the end of the 1980s: EC-Lomé-EFTA, US-Canada-Mexico, Japan-ASEAN. They also enter new and more extensive arrangements with other regional partners—US–Latin American, EC-Eastern Europe, Japan with Australia, New Zealand, and Korea— and over time further enlarge their involvement in regional schemes. At some point, these regional arrangements become so important and the multilateral system so weak that trade blocs replace the multilateral system: System.R dominates System.M.

It is the smaller countries, so it is argued, that have actively sought many of the new regional arrangements because they feared the loss of secure access to export markets in a weakening multilateral world and were attracted to the idea of firming up their access arrangements with their largest trading partner—a form of safe haven or insurance agreement aimed to prevent exclusion from their largest markets.[57] Larger countries have been attracted to these arrangements because, in a bilateral large-small country negotiation, the large country typically has the negotiating advantage. In addition, they have seen the prospect of new regional arrangements as putting pressure on the other large powers to negotiate multilaterally.

If the forces propelling regional arrangements continue in the 1990s, smaller countries could become even more trade-dependent on their larger neighboring trading partners, which in turn could negotiate bilateral arrangements with their smaller partners. What Wonnacott (1990) has termed a "hub and spoke" structure may emerge within System.R and, along with it, an increased potential for trade tensions between the three major powers.

Thus the fear in the 1990s is that both large and small countries may increasingly see their interests as lying in the negotiation of new regional, rather than multilateral, trade arrangements. This could destabilize the multilateral system if countries feel driven into regional arrangements because of escalating concerns over an ever-weakening multilateral system. Each step by each country serves to weaken System.M, which in turn accelerates the drift toward stronger regional trading blocs.

---

56. The recent volume by Hufbauer and Schott (1992) presents a comprehensive discussion of issues in North American trade. Also see Primo Braga (1992), and Whalley (1992).

57. This was one of the key arguments made in Canada for negotiating a bilateral trade agreement with the United States; see the Final Report of the Macdonald Commission (Government of Canada 1985, vol. 1).

Evaluating the New Regionalism

Despite current concerns about regional trade blocs in the 1990s, it is not clear whether more regional trade arrangements would be good or bad for the overall performance of the trading system. One can argue that if GATT rounds are stymied by a lowest common denominator outcome and the cumbersome nature of the multilateral process, more rapid progress toward liberalization may be achieved regionally rather than multilaterally. Indeed, if the multilateral route is blocked, regionalism can even be defended as the preferred route to further global trade growth in the '90s. The negatives are not only that trade diversion can occur and smaller countries' negotiating authority be weakened, but that new regional arrangements could prove to be the catalyst that eventually destroys whatever multilateral rules and disciplines remain.

Regionalism also cannot be regarded as uniformly good or bad for all countries in the system. For the smaller countries, regional trade arrangements have many undesirable features. There is the risk of being excluded from bilaterally negotiated arrangements involving other large powers. In many cases, the large country with which they finish negotiating will have more negotiating leverage, thus putting the smaller country in the position of having to accept whatever terms are offered. Being pressured to make further concessions after the initial negotiation, under a threat of withdrawal of benefits, is a further concern.

On the other hand, smaller countries have been attracted to such arrangements as a form of insurance that guarantees access to their most important large-country market, even if their large-country partner erects barriers against the rest of the world and there is a worldwide increase in protectionism. Indeed, one can argue that the most vocal demanders of the new regional arrangements negotiated in the mid to late 1980s were the smaller, not the larger, countries: Canada in the US-Canada agreement, and Mexico in the initial framework agreement with the United States and now in wider North American Free Trade Agreement (NAFTA) negotiations.

One can also argue that the prospect of regionalism historically has been an impetus to further multilateral negotiation, with the United States seeking trade deals with the emerging European Community in the 1960s rather than with separate European states.[58] This argument may have less force in the 1990s than previously since in the Uruguay Round concerns over regional fragmentation have served to complicate rather than speed negotiations.[59] Nonetheless, the point serves to further muddy the waters

---

58. See the discussion in Dam (1970), Evans (1971), and Preeg (1970).

59. Throughout the round, the accusation was that the major players were preoccupied with regional interests and were not paying enough attention to the round. For the United States

over whether movement toward trading blocs is good or bad for system performance.

Concerns over accelerating regionalism also have to be tempered by the observation that regionalism has long been present in both global trade patterns and negotiated arrangements. With a weakened multilateral process, especially if there is a weak outcome to the Uruguay Round, it is natural that countries should seek to deal directly (i.e., bilaterally) with their largest trading partners, rather than indirectly in a multilateral forum.[60] And while new regionalism risks further weakening the rules and disciplines in System.M, if the trading system is only generating limited new trade liberalization, it is not at all clear that fresh regional arrangements are detrimental to system performance. Hence, the possibility that the trading system will gravitate more toward regional trade blocs in the 1990s has to be approached dispassionately, recognizing the conflicting arguments. It is not clear whether this will happen, whether the trade impacts will be significant if it occurs, or whether it will be good or bad for system performance.

Origins of Regionalism

Regional trade arrangements have long been present, not just in the postwar global economy but in the interwar and prewar economies as well. Indeed, in most economic systems, domestic and international, key players typically seek some form of accommodation among their competing interests, frequently as an exclusionary device. This was true of the colonial trading systems, it remained true of the large-power dominated trading systems of the late 19th century, and it continued into the early years of the 20th century.

These regional arrangements include the formation of the European Economic Community in 1957, the near-simultaneous formation of the European Free Trade Association, the bilateral arrangements between Canada and the United States under the Auto Pact of 1965 and the 1988 Free Trade Agreement, and more recently other initiatives, including Community enlargement, an EC-EFTA negotiation, Canada-US-Mexico negotiations, and others.

---

it was the Canada-US Free Trade Agreement, and toward the end of the round, the US-Mexico discussions. For the European Community there was 1992, EC-EFTA and EC-Eastern Europe. At one point an "Eminent Persons Group" of prominent political and business leaders was set up to help give the talks a higher profile in the major countries (*Financial Times*, 7 April 1990, 2).

60. This was a further argument made by the Canadian Macdonald Commission in Canada in the mid-1980s in favor of direct bilateral negotiations with the United States. Why negotiate simultaneously with over 100 contracting parties in Geneva when 75 to 80 percent of your trade is with only one of these?

Many arrangements between countries other than those involved in US and EC regional arrangements have also evolved.[61] These usually attract less attention because the trade covered by them has been relatively small. They include the Latin American Free Trade Association of 1960, the Central American Common Market of 1960, and the East African Common Market of the same period. More recent examples are the Chile-Mexico Bilateral Trade Agreement concluded last year, and the new Chile-Venezuela bilateral arrangement. In the UN Conference on Trade and Development (UNCTAD), a negotiation on trade preferences among developing countries, the Generalized System of Trade Preferences (GSTP), continues.[62]

While many or most of these smaller-country arrangements have subsequently broken down, they serve to emphasize that, despite GATT, postwar regional arrangements have been a central feature of the development and evolution of the trading system rather than the exception to it. Indeed, Japan remains the only major country that is not a participant in some form of explicit regional trade arrangement. Even so, Japan has an investment and trade arrangement with the ASEAN countries and may be poised to move further in a regional direction in the 1990s.

Thus, while the GATT system of rules and disciplines has tried to deal with trade issues multilaterally, in the postwar years, regionalism has nonetheless grown continuously. Article 24 of the GATT sets out the conditions under which contracting parties are allowed to establish free trade areas with other contracting parties, but it has only been weakly applied. Of the more than 60 preferential trade agreements referred to GATT under Article 24 since 1947, none has been ruled in violation of GATT. Individual objections are common and strongly held (such as the United Kingdom's objections to the Common Agricultural Policy of the European Community in 1957), but collective disapproval has not occurred with any agreement notified to the GATT.[63]

Moreover, because for the smaller countries in the system the majority of their trade is typically with one of the larger powers, their trade patterns indicate why they seek bilateral, instead of or as well as, multilateral trade arrangements. Over 70 percent of Canada's trade is with the United States, as is Mexico's. In Europe, the largest trading partner for the European Community is the EFTA countries, who in turn have trade shares with

---

61. See Stoeckel et al. (1990, 24) for a detailed listing of trading arrangements, as well as Schott (1989, appendix A), which lists all preferential trade agreement notified to the GATT.

62. See the cautionary discussion of the GSTP scheme in Hudec (1989). He argues that negotiating preferences in a regime of unbound tariffs (as most developing-country tariffs are) is virtually doomed to failure. More details on the GSTP scheme can be found in Hamza (1987).

63. See the discussion of Article 24 consultations in Hart (1987).

the Community comparable to those of Canada and Mexico with the United States. Inter-Asian trade is growing more rapidly than trade between Pacific countries and other regions, and for such countries as Taiwan and Korea, their US and EC trade shares have been falling in recent years, and their trade with other Asian economies has been rising. For now, the Pacific is less regionalized than Europe or North America because there are other regional subpowers besides Japan, such as Korea, Taiwan, and the ASEAN countries. There are also significant historical impediments to be overcome before countries can enter into wide-ranging trade agreements.[64]

It is, perhaps, too easy to overestimate the potential for further regional arrangements in the 1990s to further fragment the trading system. The European Community, along with its free trade arrangements with EFTA, already covers most inter-European trade. New or further arrangements with bordering regions or countries (Turkey, North Africa, East Europe/former Soviet republics) may occur, but they are likely to account for a large fraction of European trade. Intensification of existing arrangements in Europe may also occur in the 1990s, but they are unlikely to focus more on financial and capital market issues than on trade. By negotiating with Canada and Mexico, the United States will have negotiated bilaterally with its first and third largest trading partners. Even negotiating with all the Latin American countries named in the Enterprise for the Americas Initiative does not add that much, and what is added is dominated by Brazil. It is in Asia where there have been the fewest and weakest regional arrangements thus far; larger potential may exist through the acceleration of the limited integration of ASEAN countries, extension of the Japan-ASEAN arrangement, and the beginnings of deals involving Japan, Australia, New Zealand, and Korea.

An especially dramatic development would be the elevation of one-sided US-Japan negotiations of the 1980s into a meaningful two-way negotiation leading to a broad-ranging bilateral trade pact.[65] An indecisive outcome to the Uruguay Round, for which European intransigence was blamed, could perhaps lead to some US-Japan arrangement a few years hence. Unlike the other possible arrangements touched on above, this

---

64. Discussion of an Asia-Pacific trading bloc dates back as far as 30 years. For further discussion, see Zerby (1990). With the Uruguay Round suspended, members of the East Asian Economic Grouping met in early 1991 to consider forming a formal regional free-trade agreement. This group (proposed by Malaysia) could include 10 members: ASEAN (6), Hong Kong, Japan, Korea, and Taiwan (*Financial Times*, 6 February 1991, 8).

65. After the successful conclusion of the Canada-US Free Trade Agreement, the United States seriously looked at the feasibility of concluding FTAs with a number of other trade partners, including Japan, Taiwan, Korea, and ASEAN. The USITC (1989) stressed the first priority was the multilateral approach and a successful conclusion to the Uruguay Round, but if the round did not provide adequate results, perhaps a series of FTAs would be the way to go. See also USITC (1988).

would have potentially large impacts on global trade flows and also would change the balance of power from a tripolar system into something closer to a bipolar system, with the US and Japan at one pole and the Community at the other.

Even before one considers concerns over a possible movement toward trading blocs, one has to remember the point made earlier: regionalism has been in the trading system for many decades. Current concerns, now so openly expressed, over fragmentation into regional trading blocs may fade when viewed against both this postwar history and today's actual trading patterns. The issues, then, are the extent to which prospective regional arrangements represent a marked acceleration in existing trends and whether this is good or bad.

Global Policy Responses

Whether rapid movement toward regional trade blocs is likely in the 1990s, especially in the event of continued slow progress in the Uruguay Round, is a topic that arouses considerable passion. The fear that the trading system is going regional is a fear of the intensification of existing regional trade arrangements as much as a fear of proliferation of more agreements, especially exclusionary ones. Hence, concerns over regionalism in the 1990s reflect increases in the coverage of countries in regional schemes where agreements already operate and increases in product coverage, services and investment provisions, and other instruments of trade protection.

The issue is what to do about the prospect of an acceleration in regionalism. Should it be resisted on the grounds it could eventually lead to the demise of remaining multilateral disciplines? Should it be encouraged on the grounds it facilitates new liberalization across one of the more potentially dynamic trade linkages in the system and helps keep global trade growth alive in the face of a slowing multilateral progress? If it is to be encouraged, should it be within a framework of rules that seeks to harness positive elements and control the negative ones?

In my view, the desirability or otherwise of large-power regionalism in the trading system depends both on its conduct and its intent. If such arrangements are pursued to pressure other large powers to negotiate multilaterally, or to indicate loss of interest in the multilateral process, then they are more aggressive in intent. If instead they are pursued as vehicles to generate new growth in trade flows, provide new disciplines in areas not covered by GATT that could subsequently be made multilateral, and perhaps accompany a trilateral trade management framework of the type outlined above, then they are more complementary to present system objectives.

Clearly, recent accelerating regional trends in part reflect both of these intentions, as well as some degree of frustration with the multilateral GATT process of System.M. That this acceleration has occurred during an ongoing GATT round is unusual; a round is usually sufficient to restrain countries from moving too far from the principles of the multilateral system. With a weak outcome to the Uruguay Round and a sense of failure of the multilateral process, the forces pushing countries in a bilateral direction could become considerably stronger.

A growing portion of global international trade is intrabloc rather than interbloc—that is, trade within Europe, within North America or the Western Hemisphere, and within the Pacific. As such, regional trade arrangements that concentrate on further liberalizing these components may be attractive, since they are focused on the dynamic and more rapidly growing portion of the world economy. Also, small countries want the relative safety of an "insurance policy" agreement with their largest trade partners, and other small countries are rushing forward to beat the queue.

Large countries see frustration with the multilateral process, a lineup of smaller countries wanting to negotiate with them, and the prospect of successful bilateral negotiation, which they also see as a way of pressuring other larger powers multilaterally. But as exclusionary agreements begin to be negotiated, the rush to be in at least one of these becomes a stampede, and surprisingly quickly, the trading system can experience further fragmentation along regional lines.

Hence, with the potential acceleration of regional arrangements, the focus naturally falls on the policy options. One approach is simply to encourage regionalism for the reasons stated above: frustration with the multilateral process and the chance that bilateral negotiation will reignite multilateral negotiations. On the other hand, there is the argument that regional negotiations will lead to a weaker set of multilateral trade institutions and globally produce exclusionary and inefficient regional trade arrangements.

The GATT, through its weakly applied Article 24, implicitly recognizes this dilemma—that is, that regionalism can have both good and bad effects. Article 24 tries to constrain regional trade agreements by requiring them to cover all trade (no product-specific exclusionary deals) and insisting that no barriers should be raised against third parties. One route may be to enlarge on this same approach of rule-constrained regionalism, perhaps within the trilateral framework I set out above.

Insurance-type regional trade agreements need not involve any Article 24 incompatibility since no barriers to third countries are raised at the point the agreement is struck. Perhaps one way forward is for other trilateral players to monitor such arrangements and seek to broaden their country coverage. This is especially the case where bilateral arrangements deal with nontraditional areas in which no multilateral disciplines apply (energy policy, for instance). Also, unusual agreements (the Japan-ASEAN agreement) could stand more careful scrutiny from other trilateral powers.

As I suggest above, the 1990s may witness a trading system that progressively devolves toward two sets of disciplines: multilateral disciplines dominated by large-power negotiations between American, European, and Pacific groupings led by the United States, the European Community, and Japan; and a second tier of regional arrangements that apply to trade between dominant and smaller powers whose trade is largely with one of the former. These will also show great variety due to the differences in bilateral structures.

Regionalism will likely continue to be approached from a wide range of reactions, from the rabid hostility of a committed multilateralist, to passionate embrace, to acceptance of it as part of an emerging two-tier structure. Under any of these reactions, the challenge will be to harness any dynamic, trade-liberalizing elements and weaken the trade-exclusionary and erosion-accelerating features.

Principles and Institutions in a Postround Trading System

This paper emphasizes how over the postwar years the trading system has become a patchwork quilt of arrangements that deviate to varying degrees from the basic principles laid down in the 1940s. Thus, the central contention of this paper is that, beyond the Uruguay Round, efforts to improve the trading system's contribution to global economic performance should focus as much on trade management within the established framework as on the restoration of basic principles. It is nonetheless the case that the trading system of today for now remains a GATT-based system onto which derogations and elaborations are grafted.

The current trading system represents a global heritage from the 1940s. And as I have emphasized, the main concerns post-Uruguay Round, when and if it concludes, are to continue to open markets worldwide while preventing return to the trade retaliation of the 1930s and, out of these, the military consequences of World War II. In the postwar years, the focus of much global trade negotiation has been on either tariff cutting or on reestablishing the consistency and application of the original GATT disciplines within the trading system through repeated trade negotiating rounds. The Uruguay Round has been more substantively about system strengthening in this sense than any previous GATT round.

But in my opinion, the underlying goals that characterize the system have changed since the 1940s. While nondiscrimination and multilateralism are clearly viewed neither as undesirable nor inconsequential, they are increasingly viewed as indirect and oblique objectives for the system relative to the deeper objective of improving global economic performance. Today's goals, therefore, are in my view more explicitly economic and more performance-oriented than were the goals of the 1940s, influenced as they were by recent memories of catastrophic world war and the need for strong security arrangements. This is not to deny the economic content of multilateralism, which attempted to limit the trade-diverting negative consequences of regional trade arrangements. But improving global resource allocation, attaining higher GDP growth, increasing global trade growth, and minimizing the risks of global trade wars all seem to be more directly performance-oriented goals toward which the trading system of today aspires.

As a result, the argument implicit in this paper is that new principles for a postround trading system would, in all likelihood, represent an improvement on the current institutional arrangements manifest in the GATT. At the same time, the present trading system is so far from these original principles that, realistically, trade management within this system rather than the restoration of original system goals seems the issue. I say this because the GATT, after all, is a contract between national governments. The GATT is not an explicit commitment to achieve free trade but instead a regulation of the way in which governments use trade-restricting instruments. In many instances, this can involve regulation of trade as much as free trade itself.

Free trade, I argue, is more directly identified with the access goals set out in the introduction of this paper: the freedom for individuals and corporations to buy goods and services from abroad without any impediments at or beyond the national border, the right of individuals to sell goods and services into foreign markets without impediment, and the right of free mobility of factors of production. These access goals are, of course, often equated with the principles of the GATT, but such central GATT principles as nondiscrimination and national treatment are only indirect mechanisms for improving access and hence moving toward these goals.

This paper suggests evaluating global trade performance in the post-Uruguay Round period as relative to these access goals, with improvement gauged on success in achieving them. Part of the postround process I suggest is to broaden the mechanisms through which improvements in access arrangements are achieved. The reciprocity approaches implicit in GATT negotiating rounds, while helpful, represent only one method of moving toward these access goals. Indeed, in the mid to late 1980s, the more dramatic improvements in access have come from unilateral liberalization in the developing countries, more so than in reciprocity-driven liberalization through exchanges of concessions. Under access goals, there are many ways to achieve improvements in system performance: reciprocity negotiations, support for constituencies in favor of freer trade, support for unilateral trade liberalization, and others. The trading system in the post-Uruguay Round years will, no doubt, become increasingly more complex. As this paper argues, the challenge is to manage the system in ways that improve its performance.

References

Abbott, K. W. 1985. "The Trading Nation's Dilemma: The Functions of the Law of International Trade." *Harvard International Law Journal* 26 (Spring): 501–32.

Anderson, A., and A. Rugman. 1991. "A Review of the Dispute Settlement Process Under the Canada-US Free Trade Agreement and the GATT." Working Paper, University of Toronto.

Atlantic Council of the United States. 1976. *GATT Plus—A Proposal for Trade Reform*. New York: Praeger Publications Inc.

Bergsten, C. F. 1990. "From Cold War to Trade War? Toward a Tripolar World Economy." *World Economic Spectrum*, Washington, D.C.

Bergsten, C. F., and William R. Cline. 1985. *The United States–Japan Economic Problem*. Washington: Institute for International Economics.

Bergsten, C. F., E. Davignon, and I. Miyazaki. 1986. *Conditions for Partnership in International Economic Management*. New York: The Trilateral Commission.

Bhagwati, J. 1987. "Trade in Services and the Multilateral Trade Negotiations." *The World Bank Economic Review* 1, no. 4: 549–70.

Brand, R. 1990."Private Parties and GATT Dispute Resolution: Implications of the Panel Report on Section 337 of the US Tariff Act of 1930." *Journal of World Trade* 24, no. 3: 5–30.

Bryant, R.C., and E. Hodgkinson. 1989. "Problems of International Cooperation." In R. C. Cooper et al., eds., *Can Nations Agree? Issues in International Economic Cooperation*. Washington: The Brookings Institution.

Camps, M., and W. Diebold, Jr. 1986. *The New Multilateralism*. New York: Council on Foreign Relations.

Camps, M., with C. Gwin. 1981. *Collective Management: The Reform of Global Economic Organizations*. New York: McGraw-Hill Book Co.

Clarete, R. 1989. "The Recent Phillipine Trade Liberalization: Can the Multilateral Trade System Sustain It?" In J. Whalley, ed., *Developing Countries and the Global Trading System, vol. 2*. London: The Macmillan Company.

Commission of the European Communities. 1989a. "The EC's 1992 Strategy: Market Integration and Economic Growth." Brussels.

Commission of the European Communities. 1989b. "1992 and Beyond." Brussels.

Congressional Quarterly Inc. 1984. *US Policy Since 1945*. Washington, DC.

Conybeare, John A. C. 1987. *Trade Wars: The Theory and Practice of International Commercial Rivalry*. New York: Columbia University Press.

Dam, K. W. 1970. *The GATT: Law and International Economic Organization*. Chicago: The University of Chicago Press.

de la Torre, Augusto, and Margaret R. Kelly. 1992. *Regional Trade Arrangements*. Washington: International Monetary Fund.

Destler, M., and J. Odell. 1987. *Anti-Protection: Changing Forces in United States Trade Politics*. Washington: Institute for International Economics.

Destler, M., and H. Sato. 1982. *Coping with U.S.-Japanese Economic Conflicts*. Lexington, MA: Lexington Books, D.C. Heath and Company.

Diebold, W. Jr., and H. Stalson. 1983. "Negotiating Issues in International Services Transactions." In W. R. Cline, ed., *Trade Policy in the 1980s*. Washington: Institute for International Economics.

Doganis, R. 1985. *Flying Off Course—The Economics of International Airlines*. London: George Allen and Unwin.

Dornbusch, R. 1990. "The SII Talks are a Joke." *The International Economy* (February): 47–99.

Erzan, R., K. Kuwahara, S. Marchese, and R. Vossenaar. 1989. "The Profile of Protection in Developing Countries." *UNCTAD Review* vol. 1, no.1, 29–50.

European Community. 1989. *EEC Competition Policy in the Single Market*. Luxembourg: Office for Official Publications of the European Communities.

Evans, J. W. 1971. *The Kennedy Round in American Trade Policy*. Cambridge, MA: Harvard University Press.

Findlay, C. 1990. "Services Sector Liberalization: Problems and Prospects for Aviation Arrangements." In H. E. English, ed., *Pacific Initiatives in Global Trade*. Institute for Research on Public Policy for PECC. Halifax, Nova Scotia: 235–44.

Finger, J. M., and S. Laird. 1987. "Protection in Developed and Developing Countries: An Overview." *Journal of World Trade Law* (December): 9–23.

Finger, J. M., and T. Murray. 1990. "Policing Unfair Imports: The U.S. Example." World Bank Working Paper Series 401. Washington: The World Bank.

Funabashi, Y. 1988. *Managing the Dollar: From the Plaza to the Louvre*. Washington: Institute for International Economics.

General Agreement on Tariffs and Trade. 1984. *GATT Activities in 1983*. Geneva: GATT.

General Agreement on Tariffs and Trade. 1985a. *Trade Policies for a Better Future*. Geneva: GATT.

General Agreement on Tariffs and Trade. 1985b. *GATT Activities in 1984*. Geneva: GATT.

General Agreement on Tariffs and Trade. 1990a. *International Trade '89-90* 2. Geneva: GATT.

General Agreement on Tariffs and Trade. 1990b. *Focus 76*. Geneva: GATT.

Government of Canada. 1985. Final Report of the Macdonald Commission, vol. 1.

Graham, E. M., and P. Krugman. 1990. *Foreign Direct Investment in the United States*. Washington: Institute for International Economics.

Grinols, E. 1989. "Procedural Protectionism: The American Trade Bill and the New Interventionist Mode." *Weltwirtschaftliches Archiv* (Review of World Economics) 125, no. 3, 501–21.

Guisinger, S. 1987. "Investment Related to Trade." In J. M. Finger and A. Olechowski, eds., *The Uruguay Round: A Handbook on the Multilateral Trade Negotiations*. Washington: The World Bank.

Hamilton, C., and J. Whalley. N.d. *The Future of the World Trading System*. Manuscript prepared for the Institute for International Economics, Washington, D.C. Forthcoming.

Hamilton, C. B. 1989. "The Political Economy of Transient 'New' Protectionism." *Weltwirtschaftliches Archiv* (Review of World Economics), 125, no. 3, 522–40.

Hamza, M. A. 1987. "Guidebook for the GSTP: The Global System of Trade Preferences Among Developing Countries—Origins, Dimensions, Negotiations and Prospects." Geneva: UNCTAD.

Hart, M. M. 1987. "GATT Article XXIV and Canada-United States Trade Negotiations." *Review of International Business Law* (December): 317–55.

Hudec, Robert E. 1989. "The Structure of South-South Trade Preferences in the 1988 GSTP Agreement: Learning to Say MFMFN." In J. Whalley, ed., *Developing Countries and the Global Trading System* vol. 1, 210–37. London: The Macmillan Press.

Hufbauer, G. 1989. "Beyond GATT." *Foreign Policy* 77 (Winter 1989-90): 64-76.

Hufbauer, G., and J. J. Schott. 1985. *Trading for Growth*. POLICY ANALYSIS IN INTERNATIONAL ECONOMICS 11. Washington: Institute for International Economics.

Hufbauer, G. C., and J. J. Schott. 1992. *North American Free Trade, Issues and Recommendations*. Washington: Institute for International Economics.

International Monetary Fund. 1988. *Issues and Developments in International Trade Policy*. Occasional Paper 63. Washington: IMF.

Jackson, J. H. 1969. *World Trade and the Law of GATT*. Indianapolis: Bobbs-Merrill.

Jackson, J. H. 1989. *The World Trading System*. Cambridge, MA: The MIT Press.

Jackson, J. H. 1990. *Restructuring the GATT System*. Chatham House for the Royal Institute of International Affairs. London.

Japan Echo. 1990. "Tackling the Impediments to Trade." XVII, no. 3 (Autumn): 6–33.

Jones, K. 1989. "Voluntary Export Restraint: Political Economy, History and the Role of the GATT." *Journal of World Trade Law* 23, no. 3, 125–40.

Julius, D. 1990. *Global Companies and Public Policy*. London: Royal Institute of International Affairs.

Lincoln, E. 1990. *Japan's Unequal Trade*. Washington: The Brookings Institution.

Low, P. 1990. *The United States Trade Policy and the Future of the Multilateral Trading System*. 20th Century Fund. Forthcoming.

Low, P. 1992. Minisymposium on "Trade and Environment." In Low, ed., *The World Economy* 15, no.1 (January): 101–71.

McCullough, R. 1988. "United States-Japan Economic Relations." In R. E. Baldwin, ed., *Trade Policy Issues and Empirical Analysis*. Chicago: University of Chicago Press.

McMillan, J. 1991. *Dango: Japan's Price-Fixing Conspiracies*. San Diego, CA: Graduate School of International Relations and Pacific Studies, University of California.

Messerlin, P. 1989. "The E.C. Antidumping Regulations: A First Economic Appraisal, 1980-85." *Weltwirtschaftliches Archiv* (Review of the World Economics) 125, no. 3, 563–87.

Messerlin, P. 1990. "The Antidumping Regulations of the European Community: the 'Privatization' of Administered Protection." In M. Trebilcock and R. York, eds., *Fair Exchange: Reforming Trade Remedy Laws*. Toronto: C. D. Howe Institute.

Nguyen, Trien T., Carlo Perroni, and Randall Wigle. 1991. "The Value of a Uruguay Round Success." *The World Economy* 14, no.4 (December): 359–74.

Noland, M. 1990. *Pacific Basin Developing Countries*. Washington: Institute for International Economics.

Preeg, E. 1970. *Traders and Diplomats*. Washington: The Brookings Institution.

Primo Braga, Carlos Alberto. 1992. "NAFTA and the Rest of the World." Draft paper presented at the Brookings Institution conference "NAFTA: An Assessment of the Research." Washington, 9–10 April.

Qureshi, A. 1990. "The New GATT Trade Policy Review Mechanism: An Exercise in Transparency or 'Enforcement'?" *Journal of World Trade* 24, no. 3, 146–60.

Rousslang, D. J., and J. W. Suomela. 1985. "The Trade Effects of a U.S. Import Surcharge." *Journal of World Trade Law* 19, no. 5: 441–50.

Sampson, G. 1989. "Developing Countries and the Liberalization of Trade in Services." In J. Whalley, ed., *Developing Countries and the Global Trading System*. London: The Macmillan Press.

Schott, J. J. 1989. *Free Trade Areas and U.S. Trade Policy*. Washington: Institute for International Economics.

Schott, J. J. 1991. "Trading Blocs and the World Trading System." *The World Economy* 14, no.1 (March): 1–17.

Srinivasan, T. N., Ian Wooton, and John Whalley. N.d. "Measuring the Effects of Regionalism on Trade and Welfare." In R. Blackhurst and K. Anderson, eds., *Regionalism in World Economy*. Forthcoming.

Stalson, H. 1985. *U.S. Service Exports and Foreign Barriers: An Agenda for Negotiation*. Washington: National Planning Association.

Stoeckel, A., D. Pearce, and G. Banks. 1990. *Western Trade Blocs*. Canberra, Australia: Centre for International Economics.

Trebilcock, M., and R. York. 1990. *Fair Exchange: Reforming Trade Remedy Laws*. Toronto: C.D. Howe Institute.

Tumlir, J. 1987. "International Trade Regimes and Private Property Rights." *Contemporary Policy Issues* 5, no. 2: 1–15.

Uekusa, M. 1987. "Industrial Organization." In K. Yamamura and Y. Yasuba, eds., *The Political Economy of Japan* 1. Stanford, CA: Stanford University Press.

United Nations Conference on Trade and Development. 1988. "Protectionism and Structural Adjustment." TD/B/1160. Geneva: UNCTAD.

US International Trade Commission. 1984. *Annual Report of the President of the United States on the Trade Agreements Program.* 27th Issue (1983), Washington: USITC.

US International Trade Commission. 1986. *Annual Report of the President of the United States on the Trade Agreements Program.* 28th Issue (1984-85), Washington: USITC.

US International Trade Commission. 1988. "The Pros and Cons of Initiating Negotiations with Japan to Explore the Possibility of a U.S.-Japan Free Trade Area Agreement." Report to the Senate Committee on Finance, Washington, DC.

US International Trade Commission. 1989. "The Pros and Cons of Entering on Free Trade Area Agreements with Taiwan, the Republic of Korea, over ASEAN or the Pacific Rim Region in General." Report to the Senate Committee on Finance, Washington, DC.

US International Trade Commission. 1990. *Operation of the Trade Agreements Program 41.* Report 1989. Washington, DC.

Viner, J. 1950. *The Customs Union Issue.* Lancaster, PA: Carnegie Endowment for International Peace.

Whalley, J. 1989a. "Developing Countries and the New Bilateralism." Paper prepared for a project on Trade Issues in Development, North-South Institute, Ottawa.

Whalley, J. 1989b. *The Uruguay Round and Beyond, The Final Report from the Ford Foundation-supported Project on Developing Countries and the Global Trading System.* London: The Macmillan Press Ltd.

Whalley, J. 1992. "Regional Trade Arrangements in North America: CUSTA and NAFTA." Paper prepared for a World Bank conference, "New Dimensions in Regional Integration" held in Washington, DC, 2-3 April.

Wolf, M. 1986. "Timing and Sequencing of Trade Liberalization in Developing Countries." *Asian Development Review* 4, no. 2: 1-24.

Wonnacott, R. 1990. "U.S. Hub-and Spoke Bilaterals and the Multilateral Trading System." *Commentary.* Scarborough, Ontario: D.D. Howe Institute and McGraw-Hill Ryerson Ltd.

Zerby, J. 1990. *Prospects for Trading Blocs in the Asia-Pacific Region.* Montreal: Centre for International Business Studies, University of Montreal.

3

Globalism and Regionalism: Complements or Competitors?

SOOGIL YOUNG

In the wake of the formation of the European Community (EC) in 1958, the 1960s saw a surge of regional trade liberalization agreements around the world and particularly among developing countries in the form of regional integration arrangements (RIAs) such as free trade agreements (FTAs) or customs unions (Bhagwati 1992). Of the RIAs that were created during this period, the EC and the European Free Trade Association (EFTA) have remained the most active and successful in achieving their objectives. Nearly all others have proved to be failures. There were also proposals for developed countries such as the North Atlantic Free Trade Area and Pacific Free Trade Area, but none has materialized.

The 1980s, however, saw a revival of regionalism in the wake of the EC's launching of its internal market program, and the trend has been continuing in the 1990s. As a result, as of early 1992 there were about 34 actual RIAs and 17 prospective ones.[1] The existing ones include seven that have been founded during the last five years. The first of the seven was the US-Canada FTA (1988).

Soogil Young is Senior Fellow and Director of the Korea Development Institute's Industry and Trade Department and is Vice-Chairman of the Presidential Commission on the 21st Century, Korea. The author would like to express his gratitude to Hugh Patrick, Mohamed Ariff, Marc Noland, and other participants in the PAFTAD conference for their valuable comments on the first version of the paper. He also acknowledges Seongyun Kang's able research assistance.

1. See de la Torre and Kelly (1992) for lists of regional integration arrangements. The authors list 19 prospective RIAs, including East Asian Economic Caucus (EAEC) and Asia Pacific Economic Cooperation (APEC). The latter two which will be discussed later, however, should not have been counted as RIAs by themselves.

Asia has been an exception in the formation of RIAs. Especially conspicuous is the fact that the highly trade-dependent economies of East Asia have never belonged to an RIA in their modern histories, except those in Southeast Asia. In this region, the Association of Southeast Asian Nations (ASEAN) unsuccessfully tried to set up a preferential tariff arrangement among its members in the late 1970s and is now making a second attempt (*The Economist*, 24 October 1992). In January 1992 it decided to launch an ASEAN Free Trade Area (AFTA) a year later.

The proliferation of RIAs suggests the picture of a highly fragmented global economy and causes concern that global trade may shrink as a result. This raises an intriguing question: does regionalism contribute to or interfere with the growth of global trade?

The impact of regionalism on global trade has always been highly controversial. As if to demonstrate this, there recently has been a flurry of inspiring papers on this issue, and most authors have concluded that new regional arrangements will serve as "building blocks" for an integrated global system unless the Uruguay Round fails to reach a successful conclusion (Lawrence 1991; Schott 1991 and 1992b; Krugman 1991b; Summers 1992; de Melo, Panagariya, and Rodrik 1992).[2]

From the viewpoint of East Asians who depend heavily on trade for their economic dynamism and feel that they have been left out without a bloc of their own, this is a comforting view but hardly a convincing one. In fact, their concern over new regionalism has been growing, and this is kindling their interest in a trading bloc of their own. It was out of this interest that Mahathir Mohamad, the Malaysian Prime Minister, proposed the formation of an East Asian Economic Group (EAEG) in 1990, right after the breakdown of the Brussels Ministerial on the Uruguay Round. Not having been warmly received, the proposal was later modified into that of an East Asian Economic Caucus (EAEC). With the launching of the North American Free Trade Agreement (NAFTA) negotiations, however, an East Asian trading bloc has come under serious consideration in many capitals in the region.

Against this background, this paper examines the implications of new regionalism for global trade from the standpoint of East Asia, with focus on the role East Asia may play in the evolution of the global trading system. Section 1 analyzes the implications of new regionalism for East Asia, with the conclusion that whether regionalism will contribute to growth of global trade depends on the strength of the multilateral trading system. Section 2 reviews the prospects of the multilateral trading system, deriving a rather pessimistic conclusion. Section 3 discusses whether the East Asian economies themselves should or are likely to form or join a

---

2. Bhagwati (1992) seems to disagree. See World Bank (1992) for a broad spectrum of views on this issue.

trading bloc. Section 4 concludes the paper with discussions of the role East Asia may play in the promotion of globalism.

New Regionalism as Viewed by East Asia

An important clue for understanding the global impact of new regionalism is the fact that the new RIAs are coalescing around either the European Community or the United States and thus constitute a trend toward the emergence of two giant trade blocs. One would be the European bloc, encompassing the whole Europe, and the other, the Western Hemisphere bloc encompassing the two American continents.

Renewed European integration began with the "deepening" of Europe through the internal market program.[3] This deepening will continue as the EC makes progress toward European Monetary Union. Deepening will be accompanied by "widening," which will begin in 1993 as the EC and seven member states of the EFTA join to form the European Economic Area (EEA). Within the EEA, there will be free movement of labor, services, capital, and nonagricultural goods. Also, countries in Eastern and Southern Europe are negotiating special association agreements with the EC and the EFTA to establish free trade areas. In addition, some of the EFTA countries have already applied for the EC membership, and many other non-EC European countries have also expressed their wish to become full members of the EC.

In the Western Hemisphere, the US-Canada FTA is expected to be formally extended in the NAFTA in 1993 to include Mexico.[4] In a parallel development, five RIAs, including the Mercosur common market among Brazil, Argentina, Paraguay, and Uruguay became effective in Latin America during 1990–91, and numerous other arrangements are being discussed at the moment. In this way, subregional integration is progressing rapidly in Latin America.

In June 1990 the United States proposed the Enterprise for the Americas Initiative (EAI), offering a vision of the Western Hemisphere FTA. The EAI has been received rather enthusiastically by the Latin American countries. The United States has already received requests for FTA negotiations from Chile and a few other Latin American countries. According to Schott (1992b), countries other than Chile are not yet ready for FTAs with an industrial country. Still, it appears that integration of North and South America may be well in progress before the end of the century.

---

3. The subsequent explanations on Europe are drawn from Hindley and Messerlin (1993).

4. See Schott (1992b) for a detailed discussion of the current integration process in the Western Hemisphere.

Table 1 Share of world trade by region, 1970 and 1990
(percentages)

	1970	1990
East Asia	10.4	20.5
Japan	6.2	8.4
Asian NIEs	2.1	7.6
ASEAN-4[a]	1.5	2.5
China	0.5	2.0
Australasia	2.1	1.5
North America	19.5	16.0
US	13.7	11.4
Canada	5.4	3.8
Mexico	0.4	0.9
South America	5.4	3.8
EEA	44.3	46.1
EC	37.9	39.7
EFTA	6.4	6.5
Rest of world	18.2	13.0

ASEAN = Association of Southeast Asian Nations
NIE = newly industrializing economies
EEA = European Economic Area
EFTA = European Free Trade Association
a. Singapore was included in Asian NIEs, rather than in ASEAN.

Source: IMF, *Direction of Trade Yearbook*, 1970 & 1990.

These blocs are bound to have a profound impact. Table 1 shows that the countries that will make up the European bloc accounted for about half of world trade in 1990. In the same year, the Western Hemisphere accounted for 20 percent of world trade. The two poles, the EC and the United States, accounted for 40 percent and 11 percent of world trade, respectively. The NAFTA countries' share was 16 percent. In contrast, East Asia accounted for 21 percent of world trade, Japan alone accounting for 8 percent.

Regional integration in Europe and the Western Hemisphere presents both opportunities and risks to East Asia. So long as external trade barriers of the regional countries remain unchanged, these RIAs are expected to boost economic growth in each region and stimulate external trade. But there are distinct possibilities that external barriers of these regions may be raised during integration and as a consequence of it.

There are several factors in RIAs that will contribute to acceleration of economic growth (Viner 1950; Lipsey 1960; Balassa 1962; Baldwin 1989). One is the static trade creation effect of integration. Provided that trade creation outweighs any possible trade diversion, there will be net efficiency gains due to greater specialization. Second, RIAs will give rise to economies of scale in production due to effective enlargements of the market size. Third, RIAs will enhance competition among the participating economies, reducing X-inefficiencies, and accelerating technological innovation. Fourth, all the efficiency gains will not only raise productivity

Table 2 Interregional trade intensity index,[a] 1990

	East Asia	Austral-asia	North America	South America	EC	EFTA
East Asia	2.29	1.55	1.62	0.47	0.41	0.34
Australasia	2.61	7.45	0.71	0.36	0.36	0.34
North America	1.34	1.44	1.92	2.82	0.52	0.41
South America	0.51	0.29	2.22	3.93	0.58	0.38
EC	0.33	0.58	0.44	0.49	1.53	1.60
EFTA	0.39	0.64	0.46	0.44	1.46	2.11

a. Defined as the ratio of the partner's share in the reporting country's total exports over the partner's share in the world's total imports.

Sources: Australia National University, Trade Tape; International Monetary Fund, Direction of Trade Yearbook, 1991.

but also stimulate investment, thereby raising the medium-term growth rate of the economies (Baldwin 1989). Fifth, the stimulation of investment will be further strengthened by improvement in investor confidence.

In the cases of both Europe and the Western Hemisphere, the economic growth effect is expected to be substantial. Apart from the above-mentioned general consequences, there are three facts that ensure this outcome.

First, the countries belonging to each bloc are mostly natural trade partners to each other, so trade diversion due to RIAs, if any, is not likely to be large (Krugman 1991b; Summers 1992). The natural trade partnership is in turn due to geographic proximity and is reflected in the high intraregional trade intensity of each region. As shown in table 2, trade intensity in North America, South America, the EC, and the EFTA, as well as between North and South America on the one hand, and between the EC and the EFTA on the other, is very high in each case, exceeding unity with a substantial or large margin.

Second, the economic growth effect of RIAs is expected to be substantial also because the economic size of the emerging bloc is very large. The larger the size of an economic area, the larger the potential scope for the internal division of labor (Balassa 1961). Third, in most cases, these RIAs have been or will be accompanied by many domestic reforms that will ensure large efficiency gains. For example, EC '92 is a package of internal reforms rather than preferential arrangements. Also, for the NAFTA, Mexico will have to undertake fundamental policy reforms over the next several years to promote economic restructuring. The same is expected of other Latin American countries that will promote the establishment of FTAs with the United States under the EAI (Schott 1992b).

The accelerated economic growth in the respective regions is bound to increase external trade so long as the external barriers of each region are not raised. Therefore, in order to determine whether new regionalism will contribute to increases in global trade, one has to determine whether regional integration will be followed by a rise or fall in protection in these regions. This is a matter that in turn depends on the strength of multilateral trading discipline. On this matter, the present multilateral trading system based on the General Agreement on Tariffs and Trade (GATT) scores rather poorly, as will be explained.

The GATT system has many loopholes and has proved to be particularly incapable of curbing the proliferation of discriminatory protection in the form of so-called gray-area measures and contingency protection.[5] The former, especially voluntary export restraints (VERs), was probably the most prominent form of nontariff barrier during the early 1980s. Of an even greater and increasing importance today for controlling trade and investment flows is contingency protection, which takes the form of unilateral actions against unfair trade practices such as dumping and export subsidies.

Hindley and Messerlin (1993) cite two ways in which contingent protection, especially the antidumping mechanism, may be, and has been, used as an instrument of protection. First, it is discriminatory by design and leads to high protection in the form of nontariff barriers. Second, the threat of contingent protection may be used to introduce protection under other instruments. It is frequently used as a means of introducing or maintaining VERs or other gray-area measures. The problem with contingent protection is that it is highly susceptible to abuse, and the relevant GATT codes are ineffective in regulating it. The abuse of contingency protection is hidden in its technical details. The EC has a proven record of actively using its antidumping mechanism for this purpose (Hindley 1988 and 1989; Messerlin 1989). The United States has also been a leading user of the antidumping mechanism, raising allegations of protectionist abuse.

Hindley and Messerlin (1993) argue that the perceived threat to outsiders of the EC's contingent protection in the form of antidumping action is so strong that a major advantage of full EC membership to the would-be members such as the EFTA countries and other European neighbors is that it provides insurance against this protection. Baldwin (1993) argues that an important motivation for Canada to negotiate an FTA with the United States was to bring US contingency protection against Canadian goods and services under tighter discipline.

In the presence of such loopholes in the multilateral trading system, as emphasized by Bhagwati (1992), the pressure of increased internal competition among members of RIAs that arises during integration is highly likely to spill over in the form of higher trade barriers against goods, services, and investment from nonmember countries. The trade barriers against nonmember countries need not take the form of gray-area measures and contingency protection. There are "holes and loopholes" in

5. See Baldwin (1993) for a comprehensive analysis of the problems of the GATT system.

RIAs that may impede both external and internal trade, and the area most susceptible to abuse is rules of origin (Hoekman and Leidy 1993; Palmeter 1993). The rules of origin can be designed—twisted and made complex—as an effective trade barrier against nonmember countries, especially in the case of FTAs, and this seems to have happened already to a significant degree in the case of the NAFTA.[6]

The fact that integration in both Europe and the Western Hemisphere will involve FTAs between developed countries and developing as well as newly marketizing countries strongly suggests the possibility of increased protection against the East Asian developing economies in such products as footwear, textiles and clothing, consumer electronics, steel, and automobiles, areas in which protectionism is already strong. Should this be allowed to happen, regional integration in Europe or in the Western Hemisphere will be trade-diverting—at least with respect to the East Asian economies (Young 1993).

There is thus a strong likelihood that new regionalism will be competing with globalism unless multilateral trading discipline is tightened. This highlights an important general point: the emergence of regionalism does not dispense with the need for multilateralism. Regionalism needs a well-functioning multilateral trading system in order to complement globalism (Bhagwati 1992). Accordingly, the relevant question now is whether the multilateral trading system will be strengthened. Section 2 addresses this question.

The Future of the Multilateral Trading System

The question of whether the multilateral trading system can be strengthened may be rephrased to ask whether main participants in international trading—the United States, the EC, Japan, and the developing countries of East Asia—will cooperate to strengthen the system. Rephrasing the question in this way makes it immediately clear that the prospect for a stronger multilateral trading system is less than bright. The very fact that the EC and the United States themselves are the driving forces for new regionalism reveals their faltering support for the multilateral trading system.

Indeed, it is mainly this faltering support on the part of the two big powers that has prompted other countries in the respective regions to seek RIAs with their big neighbors. To many of them, the primary role

---

6. Schott (1992c) reports that, in the case of industry-specific rules of origin in the NAFTA, traditional "transformation tests. . .now have been encumbered by complex value-added tests and/or arcane requirements that products not be contaminated by key components sourced abroad. The latter tests are particularly susceptible to political manipulation by customs officials."

of RIAs is to provide safe havens in case the multilateral trading system collapses (Srinivasan, Whalley, and Wooton 1993). In contrast, the East Asian countries have so far demonstrated their reluctance to form a regionwide trade bloc.

The EC's and the United States' faltering support for multilateralism is a clear indication of their failing confidence in multilateralism as well as their dissatisfaction with the GATT system as it has been operating so far. In the case of the EC, an additional explanation is that the EC has all along been preoccupied with its internal integration.

A number of problems with the GATT system as viewed by the Western industrial countries explain this dissatisfaction (Baldwin 1993). The problem that is taken most seriously is these countries' sense that multilateralism has failed to provide a level playing field. This grievance arises at two levels. For one thing, they have been unhappy with the fact that developing countries have failed to offer them reciprocal market access by refusing to give up special and differential treatment. For another, the Western industrial countries believe that Japan and other East Asian countries have been engaging in unfair trade, by subsidizing and dumping exports on the one hand, and by impeding foreigners' access to domestic markets with various nontariff barriers on the other.

This perception of Japan and other East Asian developing economies as unfair traders has been a major reason for the EC's and the United States' shift to new regionalism. The same perception has also been encouraging the EC and the United States to target contingency protection and gray-area measures against the East Asian exporters (Baldwin 1993). Particularly, the United States has also pursued aggressive unilateralism against these exporters.[7]

It should be noted at this point that aggressive unilateralism has been as much a threat as contingency protection to the multilateral trading system. Because aggressive unilateralism may extract trade-diverting concessions from trade partners, it poisons the atmosphere for trade policy cooperation and undermines confidence in multilateralism. It may also lead to a trade war (Bhagwati 1991).

While the Western industrial countries' view that multilateralism has failed to curb unfair traders such as Japan and some other East Asian economies is certainly a major explanation for their dissatisfaction with

---

7. Bhagwati (1991) defines aggressive unilateralism by the United States as imposition of the country's unilaterally defined view of unfair trade practices on others. Specifically, he refers to the use of the Section 301 and "Super 301" provisions of the American trade legislation as revised in the 1988 act to demand negotiations from specified countries on practices that the United States finds unacceptable, regardless of whether thy are proscribed by GATT or another treaty, and to seek their abolition on a tight time schedule set by the United States, using tariff retaliation by the United States if necessary. The United States has targeted its aggressive unilateralism at foreign trade and investment barriers as well as foreign infringement of the US intellectual property rights. See Bhagwati (1991, 48).

multilateralism, there is another factor, a more fundamental one, which undoubtedly has reinforced this dissatisfaction. It is the exposure to inexorable competition from East Asia's dynamic exporters that multilateralism forces on the domestic industries of these countries.

The remarkable export performance of the East Asian economies for the last three decades or so has been well documented. As table 1 shows, East Asia's share of world exports, due to extremely rapid export growth, doubled from 10 percent in 1970 to 21 percent in 1990. Most of the gain in East Asia's export share has been realized by developing economies, and the Asian newly industrializing economies (NIEs) in particular. Such a rapid growth of exports, nearly all of which have been manufactured products, is bound to have been highly disruptive to the importing Western industrial countries. Thus, with the extremely rapid growth of exports of low-cost manufactured products during the last three decades, the East Asian economies have been imposing a tremendous burden of adjustment on these Western industrial countries.

Facing limits to flexibility at home, these countries have not been able to make the necessary adjustment, and this failure has given rise to "Euroscelerosis" and the US Rust Belt. Viewed from this perspective, contingency protection as well as VERs have been playing the role of blunting the competition from the East Asian manufacturers. And by the same token, the EC and the United States, as well as other countries, have come to view multilateralism more as a threat than a catalyst for improved efficiency, and they see great value in regionalism as a new competitive strategy.

Unless there is a serious adverse turn of events for the East Asian economies, however, all indications are that their export dynamism is likely to continue with the same vigor as before and well into the 21st century, and the Western industrial countries' adjustment difficulties are unlikely to go away. If anything, the competitive pressure from East Asia may even increase with the accelerated industrial dynamism of China and the Southeast Asian economies. Thus, the Japan Center for Economic Research (1992) forecasts that East Asia's share of world exports will increase from 21 percent in 1990 to 27 percent in 2000 and to 31 percent in 2010.

This implies that the rest of the world, especially the EC and the United States, will continue to need both regionalism and discriminatory protection to enhance the competitiveness of their own industries and also to blunt the tremendous import competition from the East Asian industries. The increase in East Asia's share of world exports will come in no small part at the expense of those of the United States and the EC as well as their regional partners and is bound to pose serious threats to the industries in these regions.

It is then no wonder that the Uruguay Round, even when it is concluded successfully, is unlikely to strengthen the multilateral trading system in a fundamental way in regard to its problems of concern here. A successful Uruguay Round is expected to liberalize trade in agriculture, textiles, and services.[8] It will also include market-opening measures such as tariff cuts and removal of quota restrictions in regard to other goods. There will be an agreement on trade-related investment measures as well as one on standards of intellectual property protection. There will also be new rules on antidumping measures, subsidies and countervailing measures, emergency import control measures, and many nontariff measures. Finally, a successful Uruguay Round will include three major institutional agreements: first, for the strengthening of the dispute-settlement procedure; second, for the formalization of the Trade Policy Review Mechanism, which has been introduced on a provisional basis; and third, for the establishment of a new Multilateral Trade Organization.

The Uruguay Round package is thus expected to be comprehensive in the scope of coverage. But comprehensiveness is not the same thing as effectiveness. Expectations are that, even with a successful conclusion, the Uruguay Round will fail to make genuine progress in many areas (Wolf 1991). For example, the liberalization of trade in textiles and services is unlikely to be extensive. High tariffs are not expected to be cut very much, and many quantitative restrictions will remain more or less intact. Gray-area measures are also likely to remain unscathed. In addition, the Uruguay Round will not do much to discipline contingency protection, especially antidumping actions (Hindley and Messerlin 1993). Furthermore, the Uruguay Round will fail to constrain the use of aggressive unilateralism by such large countries as the United States and possibly the EC.

Thus, it is expected that a successful Uruguay Round will make important progress in some areas but not all. It will not do much to curb the proliferation of discriminatory protections such as VERs and contingency protection, as well as aggressive unilateralism. It has been argued already that, so long as East Asian export of manufactured goods continues at present strength, there is probably not much hope for a strengthened multilateral trading system, as far as the discipline to govern interregional trade is concerned.

This is not to say that the multilateral trading system will only continue to be weakened. Trading blocs need multilateral rules in general, weak or strong, to govern interbloc trade. This will induce major traders to come to multilateral trade negotiations. They may not be able to agree to tighten multilateral rules covering existing issues, but they will at least be able to agree to extend multilateral rules to cover new issues. This is essentially what is expected out of the Uruguay Round, for example.

---

8. The present description of the prospective Uruguay Round package is based on GATT (1992).

It is often suggested that a "GATT-plus" agreement may be reached among a subset of like-minded members of the GATT to strengthen the multilateral trading system by establishing a high level of GATT discipline and responsibilities (Baldwin 1993). The agreement could take advantage of the desire of some countries to establish stricter trading rules by establishing RIAs with other like-minded countries. The agreement would be open to all members of the GATT at any time, except that it would involve both greater responsibilities and additional privileges. The present analysis, however, indicates that a GATT-plus involving both key East Asian economies and such Western industrial powers as the United States and the EC may not be realistic.

The discussions of the section so far suggest that the multilateral discipline to govern interregional trade is likely to weaken further, driving a wedge between regions.[9] The most serious rupture may arise between East Asia, on the one hand, and Europe and the Western Hemisphere, on the other hand, although there will also continue to be trade frictions between the latter two.

An argument of this section has been that the EC and the United States have shifted to new regionalism because they wanted to supplement multilateralism with regionalism. If the East Asian economies find that multilateralism does not function well for them, should they not also supplement it with an RIA of their own? Will this be a desirable situation to East Asia? Does East Asia need an FTA or a customs union of its own? This is the question to be discussed in section 3.

An East Asian Trading Bloc?

An East Asian trading bloc is an idea with considerable appeal. Its potential merit rests in the fact that, despite the unilateral trade-liberalizing measures the regional countries have undertaken since the early 1980s, although to varying degrees, these countries still maintain many trade barriers. These barriers are not limited to border measures such as tariffs and import restrictions. Many instruments of industrial policy in such forms as industrial subsidies and assistance, as well as restrictions of competition, effectively serve as trade barriers. In some countries such as Japan, there are also structural barriers, such as closed distribution channels and inward-oriented business practices.[10] In principle, an East Asian trading bloc should remove all these barriers for intraregional trade.

---

9. See Preeg (1975) and Bergsten (1990) for scenarios of the development of a tripolar global economy.

10. In this regard, in comparison with other East Asian economies, Japan seems to be extreme. See various contributions in Krugman (1991a) as well as Noland (1993) on Japan's trade barriers.

When these barriers are removed for intraregional trade, trade diversion is likely to be substantial, but far more substantial will be trade creation. Accordingly, economic growth in East Asia is likely to be further stimulated.

This is so because many of the trade barriers have been erected especially against other East Asian countries for the purpose of protecting domestic industries, infant or declining, from the competing industries of other regional countries in order to pursue industrial policy objectives or to pursue "dynamic" comparative advantage.[11] These barriers, in turn, have had the effect of impeding the market-led integration of the regional economies.[12]

In principle, an East Asian trading bloc could stimulate intraregional, intraindustry trade by removing these barriers. In doing so, it would also have the critical effect of mitigating the acute adjustment pressure that East Asia has been imposing on the rest of the world. A unique feature of East Asia's development is the similarity of the pattern of industrialization between individual economies in the region. Similar patterns of industrialization in East Asia have, in turn, aggravated the adjustment difficulties of the Western industrial countries.

The similarity in the pattern of industrialization arises from the East Asian economies' similar industrial development strategies, which have contributed to the development of the regional economies. These economies are increasingly competitive with each other rather than complementary (Petri 1992). Under this pattern of development, the regional economies have had to look to outside markets, rather than each other, for new export opportunities. For this reason, the East Asian economies have developed a strong extraregional orientation in their exporting (table 3), and in this way, they have been intensifying the adjustment pressure on the rest of the world as well as trade frictions with industrial countries outside the region.

The adjustment problem of the Western industrial countries has been worsening as the Asian league of industrializing economies has been increasing its membership in a cascading pattern and Japan and other leading members have kept advancing.[13] This cascading pattern of industrial development means that East Asia's market penetration has been spreading to an ever-wider range of products, from the most traditional to the increasingly more sophisticated (Anderson 1991), leaving little

---

11. This situation may be illustrated with Korea's import-diversification system, which keeps designated Japanese products out of the Korean market.

12. Saxonhouse (1992) reports empirical results showing considerable segregation of the East Asian markets.

13. The pattern of East Asia's industrialization has another name: the flying wild-geese pattern of development (Park 1989).

Table 3   Direction of export by region, 1990 (percentages)

Reporter	East Asia	Austral- asia	North America	South America	EC	EFTA
			Partner			
East Asia	39.4	2.2	28.9	1.8	16.3	2.2
Australasia	45.0	10.8	12.7	1.4	14.4	2.2
North America	23.0	2.1	34.4	10.8	20.8	2.7
South America	8.8	0.4	39.8	15.0	23.1	2.4
EC	5.6	0.8	7.9	1.9	60.6	10.3
EFTA	6.8	0.9	8.1	1.7	57.8	13.6

Source: International Monetary Fund, *Direction of Trade Yearbook,* 1991.

room for Western industrial countries to make intraindustrial adjustments in manufacturing. In this way, these countries' problem has persisted.

There is another aspect to East Asia's trading that has exacerbated this problem, again fueling interregional trade frictions: the trilateral pattern of trading under which the developing East Asian economies, especially the NIEs, rely heavily on Japan for imports of capital and intermediate goods while exporting mainly outside the region. This pattern has been aggravating the problem of trade imbalances, which the United States and the EC have vis-à-vis Japan (Yoo 1990; Young 1993). Undoubtedly, the chronic trade deficits of these regions have been making industrial adjustment even more difficult. To the extent that it would stimulate intraregional trade, an East Asian trading bloc would ease the balance-of-payments problem.

Expansion of the intraregional market would make the East Asian economies less reliant on the extraregional markets and hence less vulnerable to discriminatory protection in these markets. In this way, an East Asian trading bloc could provide a safe haven to the regional economies and, for them, supplement the weakened multilateralism.

An East Asian trading bloc could also enhance the East Asian economies' bargaining leverage vis-à-vis the other blocs. Indeed, Saxon-house (1992), Krugman (1992), Summers (1992), and de Melo, Panagariya, and Rodrik (1992), all argue that a trade bloc will increase the bloc's bargaining power while improving its terms of trade and that the establishment of a countervailing trade bloc in the presence of other major ones could lead to global trade liberalization. Krugman (1992) and Summers (1992) further argue that the division of the world into large trading blocs may be conducive to global trade liberalization because it would help eliminate the free-rider problem and also because the interbloc trade negotiation may be an efficient way of reorganizing otherwise very complex multilateral trade negotiations. From this perspective, the tripolar division of the global economy into the European bloc, the Western Hemisphere bloc, and the East Asian bloc could contribute to global trade liberalization.

In evaluating the economic argument for an East Asian trading bloc, it should be noted that the argument is more for an Asia-Pacific bloc encompassing East Asia, North America, and Australasia, with a possible extension to Latin America, rather than for an East Asian trading bloc alone. The latter would only be a second best to the former.

Indeed, because of the existing intense trading relationship in the Asia-Pacific region, it can be considered already highly integrated. Considering the high values of the trade intensity index among the three subregions (table 2) and also that no RIA links the three, most of the economies belonging to this region may be considered to be natural trade partners. Accordingly, the East Asian trading bloc is likely to be considerably trade-diverting. Given the broad spectrum of goods in which the East Asian economies compete with North America, the East Asian trading bloc is likely to weaken the trade linkage between these two regions in particular. Conversely, an Asia-Pacific trade bloc is likely to be highly trade-creating, particularly because the most important region to be excluded, Europe, has generally very weak trade linkages with the economies in the Asia-Pacific region (table 2). Another important advantage of an Asia-Pacific trade bloc, or its expanded version including Latin America, is that, with a weight in world output and trade comparable to that of Europe, it can be a highly effective partner to Europe for negotiations of global trade liberalization.

This second-best nature of an East Asian trading bloc, then, raises a major reservation about it. As a corollary, an East Asian trading bloc is likely to provoke a strong reaction from North America and possibly even a trade war with the North American bloc, prompting it, if not the entire Western Hemisphere bloc, to erect retaliatory barriers against East Asia. Consequently, an East Asian trading bloc may not be feasible.[14] In this connection, an asymmetry between an East Asian bloc and the NAFTA should be noted. An East Asian bloc could be considerably trade-diverting for North America because the existing trade barriers in East Asia are considerably high. In contrast, the NAFTA in itself is not expected to be seriously trade-diverting because the pre-NAFTA trade barriers among members of the NAFTA are already very low (Schott 1992a).

The same point, however, validates the bargaining-leverage argument for an East Asian trading bloc. In other words, East Asian economies can use the threat to form an East Asian trading bloc as an important means of influencing the trade-policy behavior of the North American countries. Viewed from this perspective, the Malaysian proposal of EAEG, as well as the subsequent EAEC, by itself can be said to have served as a warning to the North American countries, and to the United States in particular.

---

14. The United States' hostile reaction to the Malaysian proposal for an EAEG seems to provide an indication of how it might react to an East Asian trading bloc.

For this reason, the Malaysian proposal should be seen as a highly significant development, and the East Asian countries should recognize value in it. For example, they can use the potential of an East Asian trading bloc to influence NAFTA, to deter the establishment of a Western Hemisphere FTA, or to force NAFTA to be opened to themselves.

The credibility of this threat can be questioned, however, because of two other problems of feasibility of an East Asian trading bloc. One is the problem of implementability. The other is the problem of weak political leadership.

An effective trading bloc in East Asia would require rather sweeping reforms of both trade and industrial policy in the cases of many of the developing economies and fundamental structural reforms in the case of Japan. A trading bloc may then be taken to mean the total surrender of industrial policy and thus be resisted by the affected developing economies. In the case of Japan, as the Structural Impediments Initiative (SII) discussions demonstrate, the requisite reforms may not be easy to implement, and the effectiveness and credibility of trade liberalization are likely to be questioned.

These considerations suggest that an East Asian trading bloc may not even be achievable, and that, even if implemented, it is unlikely to be effective. This conclusion is reinforced by consideration of the problem of political leadership. The experiences with the GATT system, as well as the cases of integration in Europe and the Western Hemisphere discussed here, demonstrate that it may not be possible to launch and maintain an effective trading arrangement, global or regional, in the absence of a strong hegemon. In East Asia, the strongest candidate for the hegemon is Japan. But Japan may not be able to become a strong and effective leader, despite its dominant influence as the main supplier of capital, technology, and important intermediate goods in the region. The fear that other regional economies may have about Japan's possible domination is an often-cited rationale (Young 1992). In addition, there are other contenders for political leadership in the region. One such contender is the ASEAN. Another is Korea. The third and most powerful challenger is China, which is predicted to challenge Japan's economic power within the next two decades (Perkins 1992).

There are two other, more immediate, problems that will constrain Japan's leadership role in the promotion and management of an East Asian trading bloc. One is credibility because of the problem of effective access to Japan's domestic market in pushing for regional trade liberalization. The other is Japan's relatively small weight as a trade partner to other regional economies. As table 4 shows, the Japanese market accounts for only 11 percent and 14 percent in the exports of the Asian NIEs and China, respectively. Japan accounts for a larger share in the combined exports of the ASEAN countries other than Singapore, but the share still does not exceed 25 percent. Other regional economies' relatively weak

Table 4 Direction of exports in East Asia, 1990 (percentages)

		Partner		
Reporter	Japan	Asian NIEs	ASEAN-4	China
Japan		19.7	7.7	2.1
Asian NIEs	11.5	12.4	8.2	8.3
ASEAN-4	24.4	22.0	4.2	2.1
China	14.1	43.0	2.7	

Source: International Monetary Fund, *Direction of Trade Yearbook*, 1991.

trade dependence on Japan is likely to weaken Japan's possible leadership role.

These analyses thus suggest that an East Asian trading bloc may not be a realistic idea.[15] Would an Asia-Pacific trade bloc be more realistic? Perhaps, but if so, not by a substantial degree. For one thing, whether in the context of an East Asian trading bloc or in the context of an Asia-Pacific trading bloc, East Asia's trade liberalization will suffer from the same problem of effectiveness. Also, while in the case of an East Asian trading bloc there may not be an effective leader, in the case of an Asia-Pacific trading bloc, the North American trade partners may not be interested in the idea itself, as they fear East Asian competition. The question then remains—how should East Asia cope with new regionalism? This is the issue to be taken up in the final section.

East Asia as a Globalist

Two giant trade blocs are emerging, encompassing Europe and the Western Hemisphere. The characteristics of these blocs are such that, despite some trade diversion, their formation is likely to be trade-creating for their extraregional trade partners so long as they do not raise external trade barriers. If the past trade-policy behaviors of the key regional countries are any indication, however, their external trade barriers are likely to be raised in sectors where they may experience acute adjustment difficulties, and the dynamic exporters of East Asia will be the main target. Trade barriers against these exporters may further be strengthened and the multilateral trading system further weakened as these exporters continue to grow rapidly, bringing the tremendous pressure of import competition to bear on the industries of the Western developed countries.

15. By the same token, the hypothesis ("The Yen Bloc," *The Economist*, 15 July 1989, and Dornbusch 1990) that there is an invisible trade bloc in East Asia dominated by Japan must be rejected. Frankel (1992) reports empirical work that rejects this hypothesis. If there is a Japan-dominated bloc in East Asia, which there seems to be (Petri 1992), it is not a trade bloc but a production bloc. I owe this point to Mohamed Ariff.

There is thus a legitimate concern that, because of the imperfection of the multilateral trading system, regionalism may undermine globalism in this way. The actual future of globalism will depend much on how dynamic exporters of East Asia, the ultimate source of the pressure for discriminatory protectionism, respond to regionalism in Europe and the Western Hemisphere.

They may attempt to bring the two regional blocs to agree to strengthen the multilateral trading system and to curb discriminatory protection, such as the abuse of contingency protection and gray-area measures, but it is unlikely to be successful. One thing they can do is seek an RIA of their own, whether in the form of an East Asian trade bloc or in the form of an Asia-Pacific trade bloc. Both can be conducive to economic dynamism of the participating economies, as well as to growth and liberalization of global trade, although an Asia-Pacific bloc will be superior to an East Asian trade bloc in a number of ways.

For the time being, however, neither bloc appears to be feasible because of political and structural difficulties accompanying genuine trade liberalization in East Asia. In addition, lack of effective political leadership on the part of East Asia will be a problem, as will the fact that North America may not welcome East Asia as partners for free trade. What should be the trade-policy agenda for East Asia under the circumstances?

First, the East Asian economies should continue to support and strengthen multilateralism. Multilateralism is necessary to discipline regionalism, and a weak multilateralism will be better than none. They should not only ensure that the Uruguay Round will be brought to a successful conclusion but also go beyond the Uruguay Round to organize new efforts to strengthen multilateralism. Given the strong outward-orientation of the North American economies and particularly the United States (table 3), East Asia will find North America to be relatively more responsive to these efforts than Europe.

Given the diverse membership of the GATT, however, another GATT round is unlikely to be any more effective than earlier ones, including the Uruguay Round, in tightening up multilateral disciplines such as nondiscrimination. Under such circumstances, East Asians may work with North Americans to promote a GATT-plus agreement among a subset of the like-minded members of the GATT, based on the conditional most-favored nation (MFN) principle (Baldwin 1993). The only form of a GATT-plus agreement that is compatible with the principles of the GATT—the foundation of the multilateral trading system—is an FTA (Snape, Adams, and Morgan 1992). Hufbauer (1989) has already proposed an OECD Free Trade and Investment Area (FTIA) to be promoted after the end of the Uruguay Round. Its core members will be the members of the OECD, but the membership will be open to all willing participants. While this proposal should be taken seriously, another possible, and probably more promising, form of a GATT-plus agreement that East Asia may promote is an Asia-Pacific FTA—an extended version of the NAFTA covering both North America and East Asia with an open accession clause without any geographic restriction on membership. This proposal takes advantage of the fact that the NAFTA contains a geographically nonspecific accession clause (Schott 1992a). This would offer a standing invitation to the EC and other European countries to join in global trade liberalization whenever they are ready. They may likely be eventually persuaded to join as the Asia-Pacific economies, and particularly the East Asian economies, continue to grow, with ever-increasing market size.

Difficulties in the promotion of multilateral trade liberalization, as well as a GATT-plus agreement such as an Asia-Pacific FTA, have been noted already. These difficulties, however, should not prevent the East Asian economies and others from trying. A major problem that may obstruct East Asia's efforts at enhancement of globalism is the regional countries' own unwillingness and failure to liberalize trade fully. It is up to the East Asians to remove this obstacle. East Asians themselves should accept the need to liberalize trade, as well as demonstrate their willingness and ability to do so by accelerating unilateral trade liberalization efforts in progress since the early 1980s (Drysdale and Garnaut 1993).

While trade liberalization will help, the East Asian economies should also make independent efforts to complement it in order to reduce reliance on the extraregional markets for the growth of their exports and economies. They need to promote intraregional, intraindustry trade by promoting functional integration through intraregional infrastructural investments and subregion-building (Young 1993; Drysdale and Garnaut 1993). With their continued growth, the East Asian economies should create new markets not only for themselves but for everybody, easing the burden of adjustment for others, thus addressing the ultimate source of global trade tensions.

In these and other efforts for global trade liberalization, the East Asian economies will need the United States and other countries in the Asia-Pacific region as partners. This is where APEC comes in. APEC should be used as the main forum in which matters for global trade liberalization are discussed, including the issue of macroeconomic adjustment and US-Japan frictions. APEC should be used as a source of discipline on the NAFTA as well as the AFTA. It is also where a GATT-plus arrangement, such as an Asia-Pacific RIA, should be discussed.

The EAEC proposal should not be disregarded. It should be kept on the table, as it has been. As long as it remains available as an option, it can enhance East Asia's leverage for influencing the trade-policy behaviors of the United States and other partners and to maintain discipline in NAFTA.

When checks and balances exist among major trading partners, regionalism need not compete with globalism: in fact, it will complement it. And it is the role of the East Asian economies to ensure that such checks and balances exist. As long as East Asia perseveres as a regional force for globalism, regionalism may serve as a complement to globalism.

References

Anderson, Kym. 1991. "Is an Asian-Pacific Trade Bloc Next?" *Journal of World Trade* 25, no. 4 (August): 27–40.
Balassa, Bela. 1962. *The Theory of Economic Integration*. London: George Allen & Unwin, Ltd.
Baldwin, Richard. 1989. "The Growth Effects of 1992." *Economic Policy* 9 (October).
Baldwin, Robert E. 1993."Adapting the GATT to a More Regionalised World: A Political Economy Perspective." In Kym Anderson and Richard Blockhurst, eds., *Regional Integration and the Global Trading System*. New York, London, Toronto, Sydney, Tokyo, and Singapore: Harvester Wheatsheaf.
Bergsten, C. Fred, 1990. "The World Economy After the Cold War." *Foreign Affairs* (Summer).
Bhagwati, Jagdish N. 1991. *The World Trading System at Risk*. Princeton, New Jersey: Princeton University Press.
Bhagwati, Jagdish N. 1992. *Regionalism and Multilateralism: An Overview*. Columbia University, Discussion Paper Series no. 603, April.
de la Torre, Augusto, and Margaret R. Kelly. 1992. "Regional Trade Arrangements." International Monetary Fund, Occasional Paper no. 93, March.
de Melo, Jaime, Arvind Panagariya, and Dani Rodrik. 1992. "Regional Integration: An Analytical and Empirical Overview." A paper prepared for The World Bank and CEPR Conference on New Dimensions in Regional Integration, Washington, DC (2–3 April).
Dornbusch, Rudiger W. 1990. "Policy Options for Freer Trade: The Case for Bilateralism." In Robert Z. Lawrence and Charles L. Schultze, eds., *An American Trade Strategy: Options for the 1990s*. Washington: The Brookings Institution.
Drysdale, Peter, and Ross Garnaut. 1989. "A Pacific Free Trade Area?" In Jeffrey J. Schott, ed., *Free Trade Areas and U.S. Trade Policy*. Washington: Institute for International Economics.
Drysdale, Peter, and Ross Garnaut. 1993. "The Pacific: An Application of a General Theory of Economic Integration." In Marcus Noland, ed., *Pacific Dynamism and the International Economic System*. Washington: Institute for International Economics.
Frankel, Jeffrey A. 1992. "Is Japan Creating a Yen Bloc in East Asia and the Pacific?" A paper prepared for NBER's Conference on the U.S. and Japan in Pacific Asia, held in Del Mar, CA (2–5 April).
General Agreement on Tariffs and Trade. 1992. *News of the Uruguay Round of Multilateral Trade Negotiations*, NUR 051, (10 November).
Hindley, Brian. 1988. "Dumping and the Far East Trade of the European Community." *The World Economy* (December).
Hindley, Brian. 1989. "The Design of Fortress Europe." *Financial Times*, 6 January.
Hindley, Brian, and Patrick Messerlin. 1993. "Contingent Protection and Regionalism." In Kym Anderson and Richard Blockhurst, eds., *Regional Integration and the Global Trading System*. New York, London, Toronto, Sydney, Tokyo, and Singapore: Harvester Wheatsheaf.
Hoekman, Bernard, and Michael P. Leidy. 1993. "Holes and Loopholes in Regional Trade Arrangements and the Multilateral Trading System." In Kym Anderson and Richard Blockhurst, eds., *Regional Integration and the Global Trading System*. New York, London, Toronto, Sydney, Tokyo, and Singapore: Harvester Wheatsheaf.
Hufbauer, Gary Clyde. 1989. *The Free Trade Debate: Reports of the Twentieth Century Fund Task Force on the Future of American Trade Policy*. New York: Priority Press Publications.
Japan Center for Economic Research. 1992. *The Coming Multipolar Economy: the World and Japan in 2010* (May).

Krugman, Paul., ed. 1991a. *Trade with Japan: Has the Door Opened Wider?* Chicago and London: The University of Chicago Press.

Krugman, Paul. 1991b. "Regional Blocs: the Good, the Bad and the Ugly." *The International Economy* (November/December).

Krugman, Paul. 1992. "Regionalism vs. Multilateralism: Analytical Notes." A paper prepared for the World Bank and CEPR Conference on New Dimensions in Regional Integration, Washington, D.C., 2–3 April.

Lawrence, Robert Z. 1991. "Scenarios for the World Trading System and their Implications for Developing Countries." OECD Technical Paper no. 47 (October).

Lipsey, R. G. 1960. "The Theory of Customs Unions: a General Survey." *The Economic Journal* 70 (September): 496–513.

Messerlin, Patrick A. 1989. "The EC Anti-Dumping Regulations: A First Economic Appraisal, 1980–1985." *Weltwirtschaftliches Archiv* 125.

Noland, Marcus. 1993. "Protectionism in Japan." *The Open Economies Review* 4: 67–81.

Palmeter, David. 1993. "Customs Unions and Free Trade Areas: Rules of Origin." In Kym Anderson and Richard Blockhurst, eds., *Regional Integration and the Global Trading System*. New York, London, Toronto, Sydney, Tokyo, and Singapore: Harvester Wheatsheaf.

Park, Yung Chul. 1989. "The Little Dragons and Structural Change in Pacific Asia." *The World Economy* 12, no. 2, (June): 125–61.

Perkins, Dwight H. 1992. "China's Economic Boom and the Integration of the Economies of East Asia." A paper prepared for the Korea Institute of Public Administration and the Economic Research Institute of the Daishin Group. Seoul.

Petri, Peter A. 1992. "The East Asian Trading Bloc: An Analytical History." Brandeis University, Working Paper no. 315.

Preeg, Ernest H. 1975. "Economic Blocs and the Multilateral System." In Theodore Geiger, John Volpe, and Ernest H. Preeg, eds., *North American Integration and Economic Blocs*. Trade Policy Research Centre Thames Essay No. 7.

Saxonhouse, Gary R. 1992. "Trading Blocs, Pacific Trade and the Pricing Strategies of East Asian Firms." A paper prepared for the World Bank and CEPR Conference on New Dimensions in Regional Integration, Washington, D.C., 2–3 April.

Schott, Jeffrey J. 1991. "Trading Blocs and the World Trading System." *The World Economy* 14, no. 1 (March): 1–17.

Schott, Jeffrey J. 1992a. "The North American Free Trade Agreement and Beyond." A statement prepared for the Subcommittees on Western Hemisphere Affairs and on International Economic Policy and Trade, Committee on Foreign Affairs, US House of Representatives, Washington, DC, 12 May.

Schott, Jeffrey J. 1992b. "Economic Integration in the Western Hemisphere: The Importance of Regionalism and Multilateralism." Institute for International Economics (July). Mimeo.

Schott, Jeffrey H. 1992c. "NAFTA: Highlights and Lowlights." Washington: Institute for International Economics. Mimeo (September).

Snape, Richard H., Jan Adams, and David Morgan. 1992. *Regional Trade Agreements: Part II, Options for Australia—Interim Report*, Monash University (June).

Srinivasan, T. N., John Whalley, and Ian Wooton. 1993. "Measuring the Effects of Regionalism on Trade and Welfare." In Kym Anderson and Richard Blockhurst, eds., *Regional Integration and the Global Trading System*. Harvester Wheatsheaf: New York, London, Toronto, Sydney, Tokyo, and Singapore.

Summers, Lawrence H. 1992. "Regionalism and the World Trading System." A paper prepared for the World Bank and CEPR Conference on New Dimensions in Regional Integration, Washington, D.C., 2–3 April.

Yoo, Jung-ho. 1990. "The Trilateral Trade Relation among the Asian NIEs, the U.S., and Japan." Korea Development Institute, Working Paper no. 9005 (April).

Young, Soogil. 1992. "Economic Development of East Asia: Its Impact on the Asia-Pacific." In *Which Direction is the Asia-Pacific Moving Towards: Intra-Pacific Economic Competitiveness and Cooperation, The Proceedings of Kyushu University International Symposium 1992.* Fukuoka, Japan: Kyushu University.

Young, Soogil. 1993. "East Asia as a Regional Force for Globalism." In Kym Anderson and Richard Blockhurst, eds., *Regional Integration and the Global Trading System.* New York, London, Toronto, Sydney, Tokyo, and Singapore: Harvester Wheatsheaf.

Viner, Jacob. 1950. *The Customs Union Issue.* New York: Carnegie Endowment for International Peace.

Wolf, Martin. 1991. "Pushing the Boulder Uphill: The Uruguay Round Crisis and the Future of the GATT." A paper prepared for the Royal Institute of International Affairs Conference on Uruguay Round Negotiations: Crisis and Response, held in London, 7–8 March.

World Bank. 1992. "Regionalism in trade is back—and here to stay." *Policy Research Bulletin* 3, no. 3 (May–July).

III

Regional Institutional Arrangements

4

The Existing Bloc Expanded?
The European Community, EFTA,
and Eastern Europe

PER MAGNUS WIJKMAN

During the 1990s the existing free trade area in Europe will both expand and become more cohesive in a complex process of multilayered change. The center of this bloc, the European Community, will grow geographically through the accession of additional countries (widening). The Community will also intensify cooperation in existing areas and expand cooperation to new areas (deepening). In short, the center will be transformed from an economic community of 12 countries to an economic, monetary, and political union of 16. At the same time, other states in Europe will become more closely associated with this center. Most of the states of the European Free Trade Association (EFTA) will be joined to the EC single market through the Agreement on the European Economic Area (EEA).[1] States in the east of Europe will be linked to both the EC and the EFTA countries through a web of bilateral free trade agreements for industrial goods.

Thus, there will emerge at the turn of the century a free trade area in industrial goods extending far to the east in continental Europe, and a single market for services, capital, and labor encompassing its western

Per Magnus Wijkman is Director of Economic Affairs at the EFTA Secretariat, Geneva, since 1988. He was previously Head of the Research Secretariat at the National Board of Trade, Stockholm. The views expressed are those of the author and do not necessarily reflect the views of the EFTA Secretariat or of EFTA states. The author thanks the PAFTAD conference discussants and participants, and Hannu von Hertzen, Sven Norberg, and Helen Wallace for comments.

1. Switzerland is not in a position to ratify the EEA Agreement following the negative outcome of the national referendum on 6 December 1992.

part. This remarkable achievement appears fairly certain now that most of the agreements are near ratification or conclusion. Much more uncertain than the geographic scope of these free trade areas is the pace at which widening and deepening of the center itself will proceed. The difficulties encountered in the national ratifications of the Maastricht Treaty have slowed down the pace and threaten the process itself. This makes it difficult to predict how open the European bloc will be, since the Community's external policies will depend on how enlargement proceeds.

For the outside world, this development poses two basic questions: what are the limits of Europe, and what are the limits of the Community in Europe? The answers to both these questions will determine how much the emergence of a regional bloc will discriminate against the Pacific-region countries, as any preferential trading arrangement inevitably must.

This paper begins by summarizing the deepening of the European Community prescribed in the Maastricht Treaty. It then reviews the Community's geographic expansion through accession and association, speculates on how these developments will affect internal decision making and the external policies of the enlarged Community, and, finally, draws some lessons from the European experience for the PAFTAD countries.

Expansion from Economic Community to Economic, Monetary, and Political Union

Since 1985 the European Community has been engaged in a dramatic process of revitalization and intensification. The first step was the EC's White Paper of 1985, a legislative program to achieve a single market without internal borders by 1 January 1993. With this program the Community will realize the so-called four freedoms—the free movement of goods, services, capital, and persons—set out in the Treaty of Rome that established the European Economic Community in 1956. Indispensable for the successful implementation of a single market is the Single European Act (SEA) of 1986, which extends the scope of majority voting in the Community.

The realization of the single market is in itself a major achievement even though it "only" implements principles already established. In addition, two intergovernmental conferences resulted, at the European Council in Maastricht in December 1991, in a Treaty on European Union, which involves major amendments of and additions to the Treaty of Rome that established the European Economic Community. The Treaty of Paris establishing the European Coal and Steel Community as well as the Treaty of Rome that established the European Atomic Energy Community are also amended, although not in the same major way. The Treaty on European Union expands the basic pillar formed by the European Economic Community and adds to it a second pillar on common foreign and security policy and a third pillar on justice and domestic affairs. Thus, the Maastricht Treaty can be seen as consisting of two major components: amendments to the three original treaties establishing the three European communities, and the addition of a new, political dimension involving foreign, security, and defense policies. The European Council agreed in Maastricht and at its Lisbon meeting in June 1992 that future negotiations for accession would be based on the Maastricht Treaty. It also called for a new intergovernmental conference in 1996 to consider institutional changes called for by future enlargements.

Strengthening the Community Pillar

The Currency Union

The centerpiece of the amendments to the Treaty of Rome is without a doubt the provisions calling for Economic and Monetary Union (EMU), seen by its advocates as a logical extension of the single market ("one market, one money"). Member states, having agreed to regard their economic policies as a matter of common concern, have set up a system of multilateral surveillance. On this basis, the amended treaty establishes a number of common institutions to implement a single currency, a single monetary policy, and a single exchange rate policy. The currency union will be established in three stages, which will take most of the 1990s to implement.

Stage I started on 1 July 1990 with the entry into force of the prohibition of all restrictions on capital movements within the Community and the introduction of multilateral surveillance of economic convergence. Stage II is scheduled to start on 1 January 1994 with *inter alia* the establishment of the European Monetary Institute (EMI). The EMI will assess whether individual countries fulfill the convergency criteria.[2] Once a majority of member states are judged by the EMI to qualify for economic and monetary union according to the convergency criteria, the council shall set the date for the beginning of stage III and the introduction of the ecu (European Currency Unit) as the single currency. If no date has been set for stage III by 31 December 1997, it will automatically start on 1 January 1999. The single currency can be introduced at the earliest in 1996 and at the latest on 1 January 1999. Member states that are judged not to fulfill

---

2. The convergency criteria are defined in terms of relative price stability, budget deficits, currency stability, and interest rate convergence. Although the criteria are quantitatively defined, considerable scope for judgmental assessment exists. See Qvigstad (1992).

the convergency criteria by then are considered to have a temporary derogation, and their situation will be reviewed again at least every two years. Thus, the single currency need not from the outset apply in all member countries. Monetary union allows the possibility for a "multi-speed" approach to a single currency. Thus, the monetary union also allows the possibility for a "variable geometry."[3]

In order to prepare for the introduction of a common currency some-time between 1996 and 1999, the Maastricht Treaty provides for the creation of appropriate Community monetary institutions. The EMI will prepare for the founding of a European Central Bank (ECB), which will replace it. On 1 July 1998 at the latest, a European Central Bank and a European System of Central Banks, consisting of the ECB and the national central banks, will be established.[4]

Introduction of a common currency, together with the establishment of the common monetary institutions, will be a major preoccupation for the member states and Community institutions during the decade. It is a step that is sure to have profound psychological and economic impacts. By the end of the decade, the same unit of account, means of payment, and store of value is likely to be used by a majority of member states. This is expected to lead to reduced costs for transactions between member states, stimulating intra-Community trade in goods, services, and financial and real assets. A single currency also means that participants will have given up the exchange rate as an instrument of economic policy with which to correct external imbalances. If nominal wage flexibility between regions is insufficient, the Community will experience greater labor mobility and/or will have to accommodate greater income transfers to offset the emergence of depressed regions.

National currencies, for many a symbol of national sovereignty, will have disappeared. EMU, by requiring member states to share sovereignty and by creating supranational institutions in the monetary field, consti-tutes a major step in the evolution of the Community. This step is unlikely to be delayed by the turmoil in European currency markets that developed in 1992. The arguments for—and against—a common currency stand unchanged. Developments in 1992 illustrated the difficulties in attaining that goal. In the future, more attention will have to be paid to the dynamics, as distinct from the comparative statics, of monetary union. As a result, greater emphasis is likely to be placed on multispeed approach.

---

3. In addition, the participation of Denmark and the United Kingdom in stage III is con-ditioned upon a referendum in the former and a government decision in the latter. For more about the possibility to opt out see "The Effect of Enlargement on Internal Decision Making" below.

4. Since monetary policy will be in the hands of the ECB while exchange rate policy will be in the hands of the council, major problems of policy consistency may arise.

Other Extensions of the Community Pillar

The Maastricht Treaty introduces the concept of union citizenship, which allows a citizen of one member state resident in another state to vote (and run for office) in elections there for local government and for the European Parliament. It also requires the embassy of one member state to assist the citizens of another member state in foreign countries where the latter has no representative. Community citizenship is also a symbol of the supranational element in the Maastricht Treaty.

The enforcement powers of Community institutions are strengthened. The EC Court of Justice and the council are empowered to assess fines on member states that do not comply with decisions of the court or with the criteria for government deficits in the third stage of EMU, respectively.

In addition, cooperation is gradually extended in the fields of social policy, education, culture, consumer protection, environment, and research and development, among others. The expansion of Community competence is reflected in the change in the name of the first pillar from European Economic Community to European Community.

Adding a Second Pillar: Common Foreign and Security Policy

The Maastricht Treaty states that the member states "shall define and implement a common foreign and security policy" (Article J.1.1). Cooperation in this field resembles intergovernmental cooperation. It is based on consensus decision making and provides little scope for the EC or for the European Parliament. The council may by consensus define a "common position," in which case member states are required to ensure that their national policies conform to this position. The council may also by consensus decide on "joint actions," which, once decided, bind member states' actions.[5]

The common foreign and security policy "shall include all questions related to the security of the Union, including the eventual framing of a common defence policy, which might in time lead to a common defence" (Article J.4.1). This is a statement of intent, and the practical modalities remain to be elaborated. The Western European Union (WEU), in which only nine EC member states participated, is termed an "integral part of the development of the Union" and is requested to "elaborate and implement decisions and actions of the Union which have defence implications" (Article J.4.2).[6] In declarations to the Maastricht Treaty, the nine

---

5. There is a possibility for majority voting in certain circumstances. Views differ on whether this would be frequent or exceptional.

6. Denmark, Greece, and Ireland did not participate in the WEU when the Maastricht Treaty was signed.

members of the WEU invite the three nonmembers to accede and state their wish to develop through the WEU "a common defence policy within the European Union, which might in time lead to a common defence."[7] As a means to stimulate development of a common defense policy, the council is invited to present a report to the European Council in 1996 evaluating the progress made and the experience gained.

The extent of cooperation in the second pillar is limited at present, but the Maastricht Treaty's evolutionary character suggests that significant progress toward common policies in this field may well be made during the 1990s. Applicant states are told that they will be required to accept the *acquis politique* (as this pillar is called, in distinction to the *acquis communautaire*) and should not expect to join the EC members that do not participate in the WEU.

Adding a Third Pillar: Judicial and Domestic Affairs

The Maastricht Treaty declares certain areas concerning, in particular, the movement of persons to be "matters of common interest": asylum policy, immigration, and other movements of nationals of third countries into the union, and rules and controls concerning the crossing of the external borders of member states. The emphasis is on cooperation (including police cooperation) in the control by member states of various criminal activities such as drug trafficking, fraud, terrorism, and unauthorized immigration, residence, and work by nationals of third countries (Article K.1). The union will have a common visa policy. The council is to decide which outside countries' citizens must have visas for travel to any member state. The decision is to be taken at first by consensus and as of 1 January 1996 by qualified majority vote. As in the second pillar, cooperation is of an intergovernmental kind based on consensus decision making, but of an evolutionary nature.

The Limits to Enlargement and the Need for Alternatives

The European Community now faces eight applications for membership and can expect more.[8] Czechoslovakia, Hungary, and Poland recorded

---

7. In November 1992 necessary steps were taken for Greece to become a full member, for Denmark and Ireland to become observers, and for Iceland, Norway, and Turkey to become associate members of the WEU.

8. The following countries have submitted formal applications for membership in the Community: Turkey (1987), Austria (July 1989), Cyprus (July 1990), Malta (July 1990), Sweden (July 1991), Finland (March 1992), Switzerland (May 1992), and Norway (November 1992). Iceland and Liechtenstein have until now declined to apply for EC membership.

their objective to become EC members in the preambles to the Europe Agreements, signed with the EC in December 1991.[9] Other countries have declared the same intention, albeit less formally. This poses a dilemma for the Community. On the one hand, enlargement is increasingly recognized as inevitable.[10] "Enlargement is a challenge which the Community cannot refuse," the Commission concluded in its report to the European Council in Lisbon in June 1992 (Commission of the European Communities 1992). On the other hand, a larger Community requires new working methods in order to remain effective. The Commission report formulates this dilemma succinctly: "the Community is attractive because it is seen to be effective; to proceed to enlargement in a way which reduces its effectiveness would be an error. . . . In that perspective [of a union of 20 or 30 members], how can we ensure that 'more' does not lead to 'less'?"[11]

In its report, the Commission solves this dilemma by proposing to make haste slowly. To enlarge the Community while preserving its effectiveness requires changes in Community institutions, and such changes require time. The existing institutional procedures can accommodate only a few new members.[12] The report singles out the EFTA countries as the first admittees. According to the conclusions of the EC Presidency in Lisbon, "The European Council agrees that this enlargement [with EFTA applicants] is possible on the basis of the institutional provisions contained in the Treaty of the Union." Additional members will have to await the implementation of the decisions of the intergovernmental conference to be held in 1996 concerning institutional aspects. In the meantime, alternatives to membership must be found for these other countries.

---

9. The preamble notes that "the final objective of Hungary [and Poland and Czechoslovakia] is to become a member of the community and that this association, in view of the parties, will help to achieve this objective."

10. Michalski and Wallace (1992) open their influential study with the categorical statement: "The EC is going to be enlarged; it is an illusion to believe any longer that there is anything optional about responding affirmatively to at least some of the pressing candidatures, both declared and potential."

11. The dilemma is echoed in the title of the report by the Centre for Economic Policy Research (1992): "Is Bigger Better? The Economics of EC Enlargement."

12. The importance of the institutional factor is illustrated by the case of German unification. The former German Democratic Republic (GDR) became part of the EC overnight. In economic terms its accession was like adding a 13th member with a population equivalent to that of all the Nordic EFTA countries combined (but with a GDP less than one-third of theirs). Since the East German Länder came in as part of an expanded Federal Republic of Germany, none of the awkward political questions—representation, new working methods—posed by enlargement were raised. See Spence (1991).

Partnership Before Membership

The Community originally proposed the EEA Agreement as a means to stave off membership applications from the EFTA countries. The EEA Agreement in fact provided a rapid transition to EC membership. The Commission Services in its report at Lisbon proposed (paragraph 35) creating a European Political Area (EPA) as a preparation for membership for the countries of Eastern Europe. However, the preparatory period is likely to prove much longer than in the case of the EFTA countries.

The European Economic Area

Signed in May 1992, the EEA Agreement was to have entered into force on 1 January 1993.[13] Its starting point was a proposal in January 1989 by EC President Jacques Delors to develop with the EFTA states a "new, more structured partnership with common decision making and administrative institutions." The proposal was welcomed by the EFTA countries. In terms of commodity trade they are already as integrated into the Community as the EC member states themselves—indeed, Switzerland and Austria trade more intensively with the Community than all but two EC states.[14] In the past, however, political constraints involving considerations of neutrality and sovereignty have prevented the EFTA countries from applying for EC membership. The EFTA was their preferred institution, with its consensus decision making, autonomy vis-à-vis third countries, and integration limited to free trade in industrial goods.

The EEA Agreement enables the EFTA states to participate in the EC single market without becoming EC members. Through the EEA Agreement, about two-thirds of the Community rules developed over the past 30 years will be incorporated into the national laws of the EFTA countries. These include the rules concerning free movement of industrial goods, services, capital, and persons and the relevant provisions on competition policy.[15]

However, the institutional provisions of the EEA Agreement give the EFTA countries limited participation in management of the existing *acquis*

---

13. This has been delayed until 1 July 1993 as a result of modifications to the agreement required by the nonparticipation of Switzerland following the negative outcome of the Swiss referendum on 6 December 1992.

14. Sixty percent of the EFTA countries' trade is with the Community, and 13 percent is with other EFTA countries. Thus, almost three-quarters of their trade is with other countries of the EEA.

15. In addition, the EFTA countries will participate in certain so-called horizontal policies (e.g., company law, statistics, consumer protection, and environment) and so-called flanking policies (e.g., research and development, education and training).

and development of new *acquis*.[16] The EFTA countries found their options reduced from a take-it-or-leave-it situation to a take-it situation. The possibility of exerting effective influence over legislation that ultimately would be binding on them could only be obtained by their becoming full members and acquiring voting rights in the Community. Thus, the EEA Agreement turned out to yield a result diametrically opposite to what it was originally intended to produce: it convinced most of the EFTA states that there is no better alternative to full Community membership.[17] Toward the end of the EEA negotiations, participants on both sides started to refer to the agreement as a "transitional arrangement"—transitional, that is, to EC membership.

The European Political Area

The EC has ruled out membership for the countries of Eastern Europe for at least a decade. During this time, the Europe Agreements will provide the principal framework for EC relations with these countries. To have to wait a decade for an uncertain membership may seriously jeopardize the prospects for economic stability and growth, given the unfavorable initial conditions in Eastern Europe. Failure to provide positive prospects now would expose the Community to at best an "unstable periphery of aggrieved dependents" (the felicitous phrase is from Michalski and Wallace 1992, 1) and at worst uncontained barbaric local conflicts on its eastern border.

For this reason, the Commission Services proposed the European Political Area as a means to intensify political relations now. The EPA is to allow the Eastern European countries to participate from the outset in European political institutions, albeit not necessarily with voting rights. Reference is made in the Commission's report to regular meetings at the level of heads of state and of government, in the framework either of the Council of Europe or of the European Council, and to various proposals for affiliate membership or associate status.[18] It would thus provide an immediate institutional anchoring while postponing full economic integration. Community rules, especially in the fields of agricul-

---

16. Early in the EEA negotiations, the EFTA countries were prepared to take over the existing EC *acquis* on the understanding that they would have a role in the shaping of a new *acquis*. With the agreement finally concluded, they found that if they did not take over also the new legislation prepared by the Community, the EC side could suspend related legislation previously taken over in the EEA Agreement (see Article 102 of the EEA Agreement).

17. It should also be mentioned that the political constraints that had prevented the neutral EFTA countries from applying for membership weakened after the fall of the Berlin Wall. As a result of the new political situation, the neutrals became disposed to submit applications for membership, and the Community became disposed to view such applications favorably.

18. Several such proposals have been made by Vice President Frans Andriessen of the Commission Services.

tural goods, services, movement of capital, and migration of persons, would be adopted only after the transition to market economies and higher standards of development had progressed. The EPA thus can be viewed as the opposite of the EEA Agreement, which requires the EFTA states to adopt the bulk of Community rules immediately but provides for very limited participation in Community institutions.

The Commission report is exceedingly vague in describing the institutional cooperation of the EPA. In its report from the Edinburgh Summit in December 1992, the Commission expanded on how to develop a structured institutional relationship in areas of common concern. Countries in Eastern Europe could, for instance, participate in meetings of the EC Council, Commission, or Parliament, or be given associate status in specific EC policy domains. The Europe Agreements could also be complemented by measures to create a Europe-wide free trade area, by investment protection schemes to encourage private investment flows, and by mobilizing financial instruments for infrastructure investments in trans-European networks in transport, telecommunications, and energy. Decisions will be taken at the Copenhagen Summit in June 1993 on these matters and on the Commission's proposal that the European Council confirm that it accepts the goal of eventual membership of the European Union for the countries of Central and Eastern Europe. It thus still remains to be seen if the "anticipated membership" to be provided through the EPA will be sufficiently positive to meet the acute needs of these countries.

On the Fast Track to Membership

The Commission report to Lisbon concludes (para. 31) that the accession of Austria, Finland, Sweden, and Switzerland "poses no insuperable problems of an economic nature" and "indeed would strengthen the Community." However, the question of neutrality and its compatibility with the common foreign and security policy is a particular concern.

The EC Presidency concluded in Lisbon that the European Council "considers that the EEA Agreement has paved the way for opening enlargement negotiations with a view to an early conclusion with EFTA countries seeking membership of the European Union." It noted that "negotiations on accession to the Union on the basis of the Treaty agreed in Maastricht can start as soon as the Community has terminated its negotiations on Own Resources and related issues in 1992."[19] The Council invited the relevant institutions to speed up the preparatory work needed to ensure rapid progress, including preparation before the European

---

19. This formulation does not require the ratification procedures for the Maastricht Treaty to have been completed before starting negotiations.

Council meeting in Edinburgh in December 1992 of the union's general negotiation framework. At Lisbon, the political will set the bureaucratic machinery in motion for geographic enlargement. At Edinburgh, the European Council agreed that enlargement negotiation would start with Austria, Sweden, and Finland at the beginning of 1993.

The Timetable for Accession

The stage is set for rapid accessions. The Commission has prepared opinions on the applicant EFTA countries at an accelerated tempo.[20] Negotiations with Austria, Sweden, and Finland started on 1 February 1993 and will, "to the extent possible, be conducted in parallel." The EFTA applicants foresee rapid negotiations, given that most of the spadework has been done through the EEA negotiations. Sweden, for instance, expects to conclude negotiations in time to present the result in 1994 to the spring and fall sessions of its Parliament, between which there is an intervening election.[21] Sweden could then enter the Community on 1 January 1995.[22] Finland is unlikely to be far behind, and Austria, as the first EFTA applicant, has an equally ambitious timetable.

The duration of the negotiations will be determined by the substantive difficulties that have to be solved in each case; these will differ from country to country. Entry of those EFTA countries that rapidly conclude the accession negotiations is likely to occur before 1 January 1996. Views differ within the Community as to whether the applicants should accede one by one as each country completes its negotiations, or whether they should be admitted in a group.

Costs and Benefits of Accession

Through the EEA Agreement, the EFTA countries will have made major adaptations required by EC membership already by 1995, when the majority of the transition periods contained in the EEA Agreement will have expired. EC membership will require the EFTA countries to make the following additional adjustments:

---

20. The Commission's opinion on Austria was presented in July 1991, that on Sweden in July 1992, and that on Finland in November 1992. In each case the time between submission of the application and presentation of the opinion was halved compared with the previous applicant. The Commission's opinion on Norway is expected in April 1993, when negotiations are likely to start.

21. The Swedish constitution requires that decisions of this nature be approved by two sessions of Parliament, between which an election has intervened.

22. This should be facilitated by the fact that most of the few transition periods that Sweden has in the EEA Agreement are two years or less. Hence, Sweden would already be applying all Community rules as called for in the EEA Agreement by 1995.

- adopt the common agricultural policy

- adopt the common fisheries policy

- adopt common policies vis-à-vis third countries (including in particular the common trade policy)

- participate in a binding arrangement for economic and monetary policy cooperation, and eventually in EMU

- harmonize taxation (including value-added and excise taxes)

- contribute to the cohesion funds.

Political benefits and economic costs for the EFTA countries The EFTA countries face major political benefits and uncertain economic gains from membership. Although the situation differs from country to country, in general EC membership provides few economic benefits for the EFTA countries beyond the major benefits already reaped through the EEA (see Baldwin 1992 for an extensive analysis). Estimates in the EFTA countries indicate that they will realize an increase of 5 percent to 10 percent of gross domestic product from the EEA, including the growth effect of endogenously induced capital formation. Membership, however, entails additional costs. The main ones are the required net financial contributions to the Community and adoption of the EC trade policy. The future annual net contribution by the EFTA countries combined has been estimated to be 3.5 billion ecu (Centre for Economic Policy Research 1992).

Upon accession, the EFTA countries will adopt the less liberal and less transparent trade policy of the Community. The increase in average tariff rates will be marginal, since the EFTA average tariff (3.0 percent) on industrial goods is close to the EC average (4.2 percent).[23] However, the averages hide significant adjustments in specific sectors, especially in Austria, where the variance is greatest. More important will be the cost of taking over the Community's system of contingent protectionism. In certain sectors this may lead to significant effects.

Economic benefits will arise in the short run from adopting the common agricultural policy, since the level of agricultural protection is higher in the EFTA countries than in the Community. However, being locked into the protective EC agricultural policy could in the longer run be viewed as a cost in countries, such as Sweden, that have already initiated a process of deregulating agriculture and exposing it to greater competition. In all the EFTA countries, agriculture is practiced under difficult climatic or

---

23. At the limits, industrial tariff rates in Austria will be reduced from the average 5.7 percent, and increased in Switzerland from the average 1.9 percent. See Herin (1986).

geographic conditions.[24] Participation in EMU would, by reducing interest costs, benefit those EFTA countries for which exchange rate changes have ceased to be an efficient adjustment mechanism.

The step from the EEA to EC membership thus probably involves net costs for most EFTA countries. Membership will be justified only if the political benefits of influence in the decision-making process outweigh the economic costs.

Economic Benefits and Political Costs for the Community

The opposite trade-off arises for the Community from EFTA country membership: important economic benefits and possible political costs. The anticipated net financial contributions of the EFTA countries provide an obvious attraction to a Community faced with budgetary problems. In addition, the EFTA countries that have applied for EC membership will remain good candidates in 1996 for the third stage of EMU if they continue present policies. One author (Qvigstad 1992) concludes, "Enlargement of the EC to include EFTA countries would thus increase the probability of an early introduction of a single currency." This assessment is not fundamentally changed by the turbulence that occurred on monetary markets in the second half of 1992. This turbulence should be viewed as a prolonged and painful process of appreciation of the deutsche mark rather than as a depreciation of the other currencies concerned.

Some EC member states fear that enlargement with EFTA states will entail political costs. They have expressed concern that neutral EFTA countries, once EC members, will make more difficult the development of a common foreign and security policy, including a common defense policy that might in time lead to a common defense. This view fails to recognize sufficiently both the specific circumstances of the neutral EFTA countries' policies and the radical change in the geopolitical context after 1989.[25] The dissolution of the Soviet Union and the Warsaw Pact has made the possibility of an armed conflict between the superpowers in Europe so remote that traditional policies of nonalignment and neutrality have been fundamentally reconsidered. The great threat to Europe's security now stems from local conflicts on its eastern border. This increases

---

24. Fisheries are a major activity in two of the EFTA countries, and considerations related to fisheries policies will be critical for any decision on membership.

25. In Sweden, following its experience in the Napoleonic wars, foreign and security policy has been based on the principle of nonalignment in peacetime in order to maintain neutrality in case of a war in Europe. The Treaty of Friendship, Security, and Assistance, concluded between Finland and the Soviet Union following the wars initiated by the latter's attack on Finland in 1939, has been repudiated. Switzerland's neutrality is the result of the international conference that followed the Napoleonic wars, while Austria's is the result of treaties that concluded the Allied occupation of Austria in 1955.

the need for regional collective security arrangements and peacekeeping operations, a role for which most EFTA countries are experienced.

The Side Track via Partnership

The restoration of effective national sovereignty in the countries of Eastern Europe after 1989 was accompanied by a rapid transition to parliamentary democracy and a market economy. The systemic fault line dividing Eastern and Western Europe throughout the postwar period disappeared, and aspects of the cultural, historic, and economic commonality that characterized Europe during the interwar and pre–World War I periods reemerged. One country after another expressed its determination to "return to Europe," as represented by the European Community. The Community exerted a strong attraction on the peoples of Eastern Europe, as evidenced by the dramatic pictures from East Berlin of demonstrators waving the EC flag. A free Europe wanted to be whole.

In its report to the European Council at Lisbon the Commission struck a broad perspective: "Enlargement. . . . can contribute to the unification of the whole of Europe. The Community has never been a closed club, and cannot now refuse the historic challenge to assume its continental responsibilities and contribute to the development of a political and economic order for the whole of Europe" (para. 5). However, when dealing with countries in Eastern Europe, the report adopts a tone of extreme caution and puts them on a side track in preparation for membership some time "well into the future" (para. 37).

In preparation for membership, the Commission advocates strengthening political cooperation on the basis of the existing Europe Agreements. After concluding such agreements with the three Central European countries in 1991, the Community concluded negotiations with Bulgaria and Romania on similar agreements in 1992. These will likely to go into effect in 1993. The Community has signed agreements on trade and cooperation with the Baltic republics and Albania. It is likely to do the same with some of the republics of the former Yugoslavia, if the situation there clarifies. It is unlikely that the Community will sign Europe Agreements with these countries in the near future, given the implicit endorsement of the membership objective that this implies.

Membership would require basic adjustments on both sides. The Eastern European countries still have to go through major adjustments to establish a functioning market economy and an administrative capacity sufficient to ensure compliance with Community rules. This does not constitute an argument against membership, but rather an argument for long transition periods. A more fundamental consideration concerns the relatively large size of most of the Eastern European countries. Czechoslovakia, Hungary, and Poland would together add 65 million people— roughly equal to the combined populations of Greece, Ireland, Portugal, and Spain—to the 342 million of the present 12-member Community.

Bulgaria and Romania would together add another 32 million. These are not marginal changes. While the case for EC membership can be argued more or less strongly for each individual country, it cannot be argued for several countries at the same time without implying a fundamentally changed Community system.

The most important adjustments required by the Community concern its system of income transfers, the common agricultural policy, and free movement of persons. Bulgaria, Czechoslovakia, Hungary, Poland, and Romania would qualify for large financial net transfers—estimated by the Centre for Economic Policy Research (1992, 72) at about 13 billion ecu annually—under the existing criteria of the structural and regional funds and agricultural policies. This is three to four times the probable net contribution of the EFTA countries (including Switzerland) as members, and about three times more than what the four southern EC members currently receive. Thus, EC membership would call for either larger contributions by existing EC members, redistribution of existing resources from south to east, or fundamental reform of the system itself.

The Community would have to reform the common agricultural policy if major agricultural producers such as Poland, Hungary, or Romania were to become members. Were these low-cost producers to enjoy the current level of agricultural protection, they would generate massive surpluses, which would have to be disposed of one way or another at high cost to taxpayers. Existing wage differentials between the Eastern European countries and their EC neighbors might give rise to significant net migration from east to west, perhaps leading the Community to limit the free movement of persons.

The size of the countries in Eastern Europe, the prejudicial effect of admitting any single one, and the complexity of the transition process facing each one stress the need for a time-consuming sequencing of accessions. This is a striking contrast to the EFTA countries, which are equivalent in population to Bulgaria and Romania combined, but have a combined national income exceeding that of the five largest Eastern countries combined and an economic system already highly integrated and compatible with that in the Community.[26]

In ten years, the situation will have changed, and the economic pressures to enlarge the Community eastward will be stronger than they are today. The economic center of gravity of the Community will have shifted to the east once living standards in eastern Germany have caught up with those in western Germany.[27] The increased economic weight of Germany

---

26. In 1989 the combined GNP of the EFTA countries, at purchasing power parities, was $534 billion, compared with $471 billion for Bulgaria, Czechoslovakia, Hungary, Poland, and Romania combined. See Wijkman (1992).

27. Germany's share of Community GDP would rise from 22.5 percent in 1989 to 27 percent after unification if the 16 million Germans in eastern Germany attain the same living standards as those in the west. See Wijkman (1992).

will stimulate trade with its eastern neighbors. The Czech Lands, Hungary, and Poland will become closely integrated with the Community—which will by then include neighboring Austria, Sweden, and Finland. A political factor favors the admission of Poland and the Czech Republic as EC members. An important driving force behind the creation of the European Coal and Steel Community and the EEC was the desire to achieve postwar reconciliation between Germany and Italy on the one hand, and France and the Benelux countries on the other, and make future wars impossible. The same logic of achieving reconciliation and ensuring peace through economic integration applies also in the East. After all, the invasion of Poland and Czechoslovakia by Hitler's Germany triggered the Second World War.

The Orphans of Europe—Cyprus, Malta, Turkey

Enlargement of the European Community beyond 16 members will require new working methods and institutional arrangements. Negotiations with additional countries could start at the earliest in 1997 after the EC intergovernmental conference. However, each country in this group poses specific problems that could delay membership further. The Commission report to Lisbon notes that Turkey would experience serious difficulties in taking on the obligations resulting from the Community's economic and social policies.[28] The European Council concludes that relations with Turkey should therefore be developed along the lines of the Association Agreement of 1960. Furthermore, the addition in Article F of the Maastricht Treaty of "respect for human rights" to the "eligibility criteria" has raised the entry threshold in a way that significantly reduces Turkey's prospects. It should also be noted that Turkey's large population, low per capita income, and large agricultural sector would combine to generate net transfers from the Community of about 8 billion ecu per year (Centre for Economic Policy Research 1992). Accession negotiations are not in prospect in this decade.

Membership for Cyprus will have to wait until the dispute between Greece and Turkey has been settled. Malta could accede if the question of how to treat micro-states in the enlarged Community is resolved by the intergovernmental conference in 1996 (Malta has roughly the same population as Luxembourg).

The Commission's report to the Council at Lisbon explicitly excludes from consideration the newly independent states of the former Soviet Union. With the exception of the Baltic republics, whose historical ties to the European core make them a special case, membership is not on the agenda even in a distant future.

---

28. An opinion on Turkey, which applied for membership in 1987, was presented in 1989.

The Future Union

The preceding discussion suggests that there will be three waves of accession: a first wave of EFTA countries around 1996, a second wave of smaller countries toward the end of the 1990s once the institutional reform of the Community has been accomplished, and a third wave of countries from Central and Eastern Europe after 2002, when the 10-year transition periods in the various Europe Agreements start to expire and after the start of the third stage of EMU.

The Pace of Enlargement

The Commission states in its report to the Lisbon Summit that the pace of enlargement must be adapted to the requirements of deepening: "The accession of new members will increase [the Community's] diversity and heterogeneity. But widening must not be at the expense of deepening. Enlargement must not be a dilution of the Community's achievements. On this point there should be absolute clarity, on the part of the member states and of the applicants." Clearly, it would be easier for the applicant countries and perhaps for some EC member countries if the Community were to widen without deepening, just as it would be easier for other members to deepen without widening. But the "acceleration of history" during the past three years makes some widening appear inevitable to many Community states, and acceptable to others if accompanied by deepening. This constellation of interests ensures that both processes will proceed simultaneously in the future—as they have in the past.[29] Indeed, the conclusions of the EC Presidency at the Edinburgh Summit explicitly linked widening and deepening by stating that the enlargement negotiations could only be concluded once the Maastricht Treaty had been ratified by all member states. Progress could, however, prove to be slower, more complex, and more risky than was thought a few years ago.

The Community now faces a major crisis in its drive to deepen, which threatens to paralyze it. Ratification of the Maastricht Treaty, the basis for the accession negotiations, has encountered unexpected difficulties. In a legal sense, the "no" in the Danish referendum on 6 June 1992 killed the Maastricht Treaty in its present form—all 12 states must ratify the treaty for it to enter into force. The French voted "yes" in the referendum on 20 September 1992 by such a narrow margin that it barely succeeded in keeping the treaty politically alive. Matters were further complicated when the United Kingdom postponed a definitive decision in the House of Commons until after a new Danish referendum, which will take place

---

29. The principle enunciated at the Hague Summit in 1969 was "achèvement, approfondissement, et élargissement"(completion, deepening, and widening).

on 18 May 1993. Even though Edinburgh found a way out of the Danish conundrum, it will require time to restore confidence. Continued progress will require utilizing whatever scope the Maastricht Treaty provides for differential solutions.

The Effect of Enlargement on Internal Decision Making

The process of simultaneous deepening and widening vastly complicates the internal decision making of the Community. Decision making on most new issues introduced through the second and third pillar will be by consensus. In a number of issues in the first pillar, there is a shift to majority voting (e.g., in EMU). At the same time, the number of decision-making procedures has multiplied, and the powers of the European Parliament have been expanded. The net effect, in addition to slowing down the decision-making process, is to increase the supranational element in it (de Schoutheete de Tervarent 1992).

Although the Maastricht Treaty expands the scope of majority voting, it also allows opting out. These phenomena are not unrelated. The move from consensus decisions to majority voting increases the pressure on a country that feels very strongly on an issue to try to opt out of the cooperation rather than risk finding itself in a minority position. The country might only agree to introduce majority decision making in a particular field if it can opt out. The Maastricht Treaty contains several important examples of provisions allowing for opting out.

EMU provides an example of *opting out ex post*. The United Kingdom and Denmark participate in EMU but have reserved for national institutions the right to determine when to enter stage III of EMU, even though the EMI should find that these countries fulfill the convergency criteria. A protocol to the treaty states that should the Danish government notify the European Council that it does not wish to participate in stage III, Denmark shall have an exemption until its government requests otherwise. Another protocol states that the United Kingdom "is not obliged or committed to move to the third stage of EMU without a separate decision to do so by its government and Parliament." The treaty also contains provisions allowing countries to enter stage III at different times, depending on when the EMI deems the convergency criteria are fulfilled (a multispeed approach to a common objective).

The protocol on social policy in the Maastricht Treaty provides an example of *opting out ex ante*. This protocol contains an extension of the provisions in the Treaty of Rome concerning social policy and labor market policy. It allows decisions concerning working conditions, equality of men and women, dialogue between management and labor information to workers, and consultation with them to be taken by qualified majority. The protocol is an agreement between 11 of the EC countries.

The United Kingdom is not a party to it and is not bound by any decisions the 11 might take. In this case, one country has placed itself outside a field of cooperation at the very outset.

The Western European Union provides a similar example of opting out at the outset. Through the Maastricht Treaty the WEU will become an "integral part of the development of the Union." However, only 9 of 12 EC states were members at the signing of the Maastricht Treaty, and the remainder are not under a legal obligation to join.

The Maastricht Treaty thus already contains important elements of variable geometry in addition to a multispeed approach to common objectives. This should provide sufficient flexibility to allow deepening and enlargement to proceed simultaneously.[30]

Enlargement and Community External Policies

The tremendous tasks involved in widening and deepening the Community will ensure that over the next ten years the Community will focus its energies and attention on itself and on relations with nonmember countries in Europe. The complexities of implementing the deepening provided for in the Maastricht Treaty are likely to be underestimated today. Introducing a common currency has major institutional and economic-political implications. Defining and implementing a common foreign and security policy, including the eventual framing of a common defense, means embarking on a new and difficult voyage. How to adapt EC institutions to an enlarged Community will not be decided overnight. These major undertakings can be expected to require concentrated efforts by Community institutions and member states' efforts for the rest of the decade.

These issues will overload decision-making systems and crowd out other issues on the Community agenda. The key bureaucrats in Brussels are surprisingly few, and the key units are dangerously understaffed. Hence, trade relations are likely to receive adequate attention only when problems reach crisis proportions, whether in trade negotiations in the

30. It is interesting to note the personal view of a former Director-General of the Commission's legal services: "Because existing Community law leaves considerable room for differentiation, there is much less need for the introduction of the "two speed" concept than is normally assumed. Even more important, however, are the complexities of any Treaty amendment intended to legalize this concept. The "threshold" for such an amendment is very high indeed. It seems, therefore, safe to assume that the "two speed" concept will never become the subject matter of a formal Treaty amendment. That does not mean, however, that the Community will never use de facto methods which might be very close to this concept, even while denying what it is doing. It will defend its actions on the basis of the existing possibilities of differentiation. Experience will finally show how wide these are" (Ehlermann 1984, 1292–93).

GATT or in bilateral relations with the United States and Japan. And in foreign policy issues the Community's difficulties in responding adequately—illustrated so tragically in the case of Yugoslavia—will remain for some time.

In the short run, enlargement is likely to have positive effects for the outside world. The entry of the EFTA countries, even though each of them is small, will influence Community decisions. By forming coalitions with like-minded members, these countries may contribute to more liberal and transparent trade policies, increased development assistance, and an opening to the east. However, enlargement to the east might have offsetting effects. In particular, the Community's tendencies toward restrictive trade policies will be strengthened, since the comparative advantage of these countries lies in land- and labor-intensive goods, where competition comes primarily from non-Community producers.

Increased regionalism will by necessity be one result of the economic reunification of Europe. It would be a grave mistake to view it as political isolationism and charge Europe with turning its back on its friends overseas. The historic process of European consolidation will require the patience, understanding, and cooperation of these old friends. Once it is achieved, the expanded bloc will emerge as a liberal, outward-looking continental market acting as an engine of growth in the world economy. Until then the Community will give priority to the construction of Europe. If forced to choose between this and multilateral considerations, it is likely to choose Europe.

Implications for the Pacific Basin Countries

The emergence of a preferential trading bloc encompassing most of continental Europe and the consolidation of the political and economic union at its center will have important impacts on the PAFTAD countries. Any preferential trading arrangement is inevitably discriminatory. Abolishing internal tariffs and quantitative restrictions improves the competitive advantage of insiders. The negative effect on outsiders can be mitigated or aggravated by an accompanying change in the external level of protection provided by tariffs and quotas.

The major impact on the Pacific Basin economies will probably arise through the regional free trade area rather than through changes in the external level of protection. Inclusion of the Eastern European countries in a European free trade area for industrial goods will, in the short run, give rise to increased competition in segments where many of the Pacific newly industrializing economies are specialized. Most of the Eastern European countries have low wage costs and a well-educated labor force—especially in the natural and engineering sciences. They are likely to be competitive in machine tools, motor vehicles, electronics, and computer components, especially if they can attract foreign direct investment and management skills. Thus, the Asia-Pacific countries are likely to encounter increased competition on the European market—in particular in the west. In the longer run this trade diversion may well be offset by increased growth in Europe—particularly in the east—following integration.

Accession of the EFTA countries is likely to raise marginally the average tariff protection of the EC. In the medium run, a Community of 16 might adopt more transparent—and therefore ultimately more liberal—policies than the EC 12. However, once the Eastern European countries become members, pressures for protectionism are likely to increase. Producer interests in these countries, which are competitive with the newly industrializing economies in Pacific Asia, will lobby for using Community policies of contingent protectionism to protect them.

An enlarged European bloc will reinforce the current global trend toward regionalism. A blossoming of regional trading arrangements will place the GATT in a new working environment. It will have to ensure that Article XXIV is observed. It will have to come to terms with a world where a few major players dominate trade policy discussions and make deals outside the GATT. It will have to prevent smaller participants from being marginalized when deals are struck in the GATT.

Should the Pacific Basin countries, finding themselves in such a situation, decide to form their own trading bloc, they may wish to recall some lessons from the European experience.[31] The first lesson concerns the importance of a closely knit trade web as a precondition for regional integration. Two countries are more likely to enter a preferential trade agreement the more they already trade with each other. Given the political economy of trade negotiations, the existence of export interests in each country lobbying for greater market access in the other country increases the prospect that the two countries will form a preferential trading area. The formation of EFTA, with the UK originally as the core country, and the European Community with Germany as the core country, can be explained in this way.[32] So can the linking of the two through the free trade agreements of 1972. They formed two groups of countries that traded intensively with each other, each group consisting of clusters of mutually dependent trade partners. The initial conditions for integration in the Pacific Basin are not as favorable as they were in Europe, since the share of intraregional trade is smaller and the web of trade flows is not as closely woven.

A second lesson, following from the first, is the dynamic effect of discrimination. The cost of remaining an outsider can be high if a country

---

31. This section draws on Wijkman and Lindström (1989).

32. The political constraint imposed by neutrality explains why Switzerland and Austria joined EFTA rather than the Community. See Wijkman (1990).

finds that its main competitors have negotiated preferential access to its major market. Such discrimination prompts outsiders to try to join preferential arrangements, too. Once started, preferential trading areas tend to grow. If a nucleus of countries creates a preferential trading area in one region, it is likely to attract additional members. Enlargement of the Community from 6 to 16 countries is a powerful example. Thus, small beginnings can lead further than grand designs.

A third lesson is that there must be a firm political commitment to integration. The European Community was not created to reduce tariffs but to make war impossible in Western Europe through fostering economic integration. Regional integration should attempt to liberalize trade not through a continuous negotiating process—the GATT is available for that—but through a predetermined timetable. Thus, a timetable for elimination of tariffs and quantitative restrictions must be agreed on at the outset of an integration scheme. The European experience was that liberalization occurred faster than the time tables prescribed.

A fourth lesson of European integration is the possibility of enlarging the geographic scope of integration through the use of variable geometry. Already in 1972 the signing of free trade agreements between the EFTA countries and the Community created a free trade area in industrial goods in Europe. Twenty years later the EFTA countries concluded the EEA Agreement with the Community, creating a free trade area in services, capital, and labor. With respect to all four freedoms, the EFTA countries and the Community kept their own external policies. Regional integration was achieved without applying a uniform model.

Finally, technical and financial support can be a powerful impetus to integration. The stimulus that the Marshall Plan gave to European integration may be the obvious example, but others exist. When Iceland joined the EFTA, which at that time did not extend free trade to fish, Iceland's main export, the Nordic countries set up an investment fund for Iceland. A similar fund was set up in 1975 for Portugal, which was the poorest EFTA country. The EEA Agreement could not be concluded until the EFTA side agreed to contribute to a "financial mechanism" for the southern EC states. Given the large disparities in per capita income levels in the Pacific Basin, a system providing significant financial support to the poorer countries in the region could well facilitate regional integration.

Conclusion

The unexpected and dramatic events in Eastern Europe following the fall of the Berlin Wall in November 1989 have completely transformed the European political scene. Almost overnight, democratic Europe has become wider, and the European Community has been thrust into the absolute center of that larger stage. At the same time, the political constraints that previously prevented the neutral EFTA countries from applying for EC membership have weakened. The negotiations on the European Economic Area convinced most EFTA states that there is no satisfactory alternative to full Community membership. Together, these developments drastically increased the pressures for geographic widening.

At the same time, the Community was surfing on a Europhoric wave toward completion of the internal market and on to even further deepening through the Maastricht Treaty. Since then, the unexpected complications in the ratification procedure reminded statesmen that ultimately it is popular support that determines how fast the deepening of the Community can proceed. The gap between the views of political leaders and the people in several member states initiated a period of introspection and self-doubt. The identity crisis that the Community is now experiencing could stop its deepening as well as its widening. This illustrates the need to proceed successively with widening and deepening and the dangers of making either one a precondition of the other.

Enlargement to the east confronts the Community with the choice of either major internal reforms or massive income transfers. To some extent this choice would be alleviated but not removed by the prior accession of the EFTA countries. The magnitude of the transfers involved recalls the Marshall Plan assistance Western Europe once received from the United States, and calls for a new cooperative effort. Expansion of the European bloc to the east, through accession or through free trade agreements, may lead to trade diversion elsewhere, and perhaps particularly in Pacific Asia. If successful, however, it will also lead to economic growth, whose effects are likely to swamp any initial trade diversion. It would therefore be shortsighted not to support the historic consolidation of the European region now taking place.

References

Baldwin, Richard E. 1992. "The Economic Logic of EFTA Countries Joining the EEA and the EC." *EFTA Occasional Paper* 41. Geneva: European Free Trade Association.

Centre for Economic Policy Research. 1992. *Third Annual Report on Monitoring European Integration: Is Bigger Better? The Economics of EC Enlargement.* London: CEPR.

Commission of the European Communities. 1992. Towards a Closer Association with the Countries of Central and Eastern Europe, 11–12 December.

Commission of the European Communities. 1992. "Europe and the Challenge of Enlargement." Brussels, 24 June.

Conclusions of the Presidency. 1992. European Council, Lisbon (26–27 June).

Ehlermann, Claus-Dieter. 1984. "How Flexible is Community Law? An Unusual Approach to the Concept of 'Two Speeds.'" *Michigan Law Review* 82, no. 5-6 (April-May).

Herin, Jan. 1986. "Rules of Origin and Differences between Tariff Levels in EFTA and in the EC." *EFTA Occasional Paper* 13. Geneva: European Free Trade Association.

Michalski, Anna, and Helen Wallace. 1992. "The Challenge of Enlargement." *RIIA Special Papers* 1. London: Royal Institute of International Affairs.

Qvigstad, Jan Fredrik. 1992. "Economic and Monetary Union (EMU): A Survey of the EMU and Empirical Evidence on Convergence for the EC and the EFTA Countries." *EFTA Occasional Paper* 36. Geneva: European Free Trade Association.

de Schoutheete de Tervarent, Philippe. 1992. "The Treaty of Maastricht and Its Significance for Third Countries." *Österreichische Zeitschrift für Politikwissenschaft* 92–3.

Spence, David. 1991. "Enlargement Without Accession: The EC's Response to German Unification." *RIIA Discussion Papers* 36. London: Royal Institute of International Affairs.

Wijkman, Per Magnus. 1990. "Patterns of Production and Trade in Western Europe." *EFTA Occasional Paper* 32. Geneva: European Free Trade Association.

Wijkman, Per Magnus. 1992. "Structural Change in European Production and Trade." Paper presented at the Symposium on "Europe into the Third Millenium: Leader or Laggard?" University of Exeter, United Kingdom.

Wijkman, Per Magnus, and Eva Sundkvist Lindström. 1989. "Pacific Basin Integration: A Step Towards Freer Trade." In John Nieuwenhuysen, ed., *Towards Freer Trade Between Nations*, 144–62. South Melbourne: Oxford University Press.

5

NAFTA and Pacific Partnership: Advancing Multilateralism?

H. EDWARD ENGLISH AND MURRAY G. SMITH

The prospect of a North American Free Trade Agreement (NAFTA) has raised concerns about a Fortress North America and with it significant trade and investment diversion. Many in the Asia-Pacific region are concerned that their present trade links with North America will be weakened, while protectionist interests in the United States are concerned that investment from outside North America will use Mexico as a back-door export platform to the United States.

Some of these concerns are a manifestation of a view that has emerged since 1945, following the construction of the postwar multilateral framework for economic relations that contributed so much to the years of growth that peaked in the 1960s with the full recovery of Europe and Japan. Economic growth was further sustained in the two decades that followed by the transfer of technology and global market access for those developing countries prepared and eager to exploit these opportunities. During this period there developed an attitude that regional approaches to trade liberalization were at best an inferior option to the multilateral GATT approach and could become the basis of trade conflicts. At the same time regional initiatives multiplied, the most spectacular being the European Community, the European Free Trade Association (EFTA), the deepening linkages between the Community and EFTA in the form of the European Economic Area (EEA), and the present tentative efforts to reintegrate the former CMEA economies (the former socialist member

H. Edward English is Professor of Economics, Carleton University, and Murray G. Smith is Director, Centre for Trade Policy and Law, Carleton University and University of Ottawa.

countries of the Council for Mutual Economic Assistance) into the world economy.

Dozens of other regional arrangements were also conceived, many involving groups of developing countries in Latin America and Africa. Most of these have been less significant engines of growth, partly because the majority of the trade of developing countries is with high-demand developed countries and partly because the developing countries' approach to regionalism was often inward-looking.

Gradually, and especially after regionalism became more common, multilateralism and regionalism came to be characterized as conflicting options. There were grounds for concern about the operation of both the GATT and some regional groups. The GATT was criticized because the rich countries that led it were inclined to reduce protection substantially and more quickly on goods they traded among themselves than on those supplied by less-developed countries. Some developing-country groups were content to maintain very high external barriers against the products of nonmembers, a practice that sometimes undermined movement toward a more efficient industry structure and performance within the group. However, regionalism within the European Community, with the exception of the agriculture sector, has been consistent with efficient industrial growth, and developing countries have gradually placed increased importance on competitive, export-oriented industry even when infant-industry protection remained in place.

In recent years, less protection-oriented or inward-looking regionalism has emerged in agreements between Canada and the United States and between Australia and New Zealand. However, with the emergence of the NAFTA, Asian countries have expressed greater concern about trade and investment diversion that could significantly affect sectors in which they are active as exporters or investors. In particular, they have singled out the textile and apparel and automotive sectors, and especially the restrictive nature of rules of origin in the agreement as sources of concern.

In dealing with these issues, we first present some historical and theoretical perspectives, then turn to a more detailed analysis of the relevant provisions of the NAFTA, and later to the implications for the GATT negotiations and Pacific economic cooperation in support of multilateralism.

Perspectives on Regional Economic Integration

When the concept of regional integration was given legal respectability in GATT Article XXIV, it was justified as an exception to the most-favored-nation (MFN) principle as a means of allowing small groups of countries to move more quickly to free trade than they could through multilateral action. Since the GATT had only 23 signatories at the outset, it was expected that the value of Article XXIV would be mainly to encourage developing countries to join while retaining infant-industry protection. The immediate challenge was to reduce the high levels of protection in the form of tariffs and quantitative restrictions built up during the 1930s and maintained into the postwar years.

Reconstructing countries in Europe found it convenient to use Article XXIV as part of their strategy for recovery at a time when they could not be fully competitive with North America. There was considerable debate about whether the appropriate vehicle was a customs union or a free trade area (see Balassa 1962, Curzon 1974, Lipsey 1970, Meade 1955). Encouraged through the Marshall Plan and the Organization for European Economic Cooperation, the original six members of the European Common Market moved toward the Treaty of Rome, which opened the door to achievement of a common market and even economic union. The political force that propelled this movement was the intense desire to preclude any recurrence of conflicts that had twice devastated Europe in the first half of this century. Other countries—Britain, the Nordic countries, Austria, Switzerland, and Portugal—pursued the EFTA route instead. While they shared the recognition of the benefits of economic integration, they wished to retain sovereignty—for example, in agriculture—and in some cases, neutrality. The results of European integration have been spectacular, but the circumstances were unique. Today the European Community is testing the willingness of its member states and public opinion to go further in the direction of economic and political union. With the end of the Cold War, some of the remaining EFTA countries are now seeking full membership in the European Community. Europe now faces the challenge of reintegrating the former CMEA economies. How this will unfold is difficult to predict, but Europe will be preoccupied for some years by the "widening versus deepening" debate—whether to give priority to bringing new members into the fold or to move toward full economic union and even common political institutions.

When developing countries in the postcolonial world responded to the opportunity presented by Article XXIV, as they have with dozens of schemes, their motivations were mixed, and the results even more so. In some instances—for example, in East Africa—they sought to preserve the convenience of common trade, monetary, and even fiscal union imposed on them by the colonial powers. In other cases, notably in Latin America (e.g., the Latin American Free Trade Area), they sought economic strength and bargaining power by retaining high levels of protection around a large regional market. All too often these regional initiatives foundered because of a lack of meaningful political commitment to economic integration and because of problems of macroeconomic instability, restrictive payments regimes and controlled exchange rates, and protectionist trade and investment policies.

By 1992 over 100 countries were participating in the GATT, most of them at various stages of development short of OECD status, and a substantial number of members and would-be members were moving for the first time toward much greater emphasis on the market economy. For some groups among these countries, Article XXIV has value for the reasons cited already, but this probably applies to more limited circumstances. These include groups of countries collectively encompassing a large enough market to contribute to efficient development, or, if smaller, to enable a collective strategy to benefit from access to world markets. For such groups to succeed it is probably necessary that the members of the group not vary greatly in economic size or in level of development. It is also clear from past experience that if such groups rely on continuing high levels of protection for the group or for important members, development leading to competitiveness in world markets will be much more difficult. The Association of Southeast Asian Nations (ASEAN) appears to have reached a point that accommodates these criteria, mainly through deregulation or liberalization of investment and trade restrictions, making them more equally competitive in world or regional markets.

What is also apparent, however, is that Article XXIV insufficiently accommodates all the various forms of regional initiative that may be beneficial to the global economic system. Most fundamentally, it calls for the substantial liberalization of trade through the removal of tariffs and other border measures among members while avoiding increases in barriers against nonmembers. Article XXIV thus seems to preclude regional action that can have the effect of liberalizing trade on a sectoral basis. It also presumes that national states will be participants in Article XXIV agreements.

The actions of governments in recent years indicate that other forms of regional cooperation are deemed to be complementary to, or if necessary substitutes for, GATT multilateral and Article XXIV methods. These other options include what we shall here label "subregionalism" and "superregionalism."

Subregionalism is cooperation that may include liberalization of trade in goods and services and factor movements between parts of countries. It is exemplified by the free trade zones along the China coast, led by that centered on Hong Kong; by the Batam-Singapore-Johor triangle, and by the maquiladoras and related arrangements along the US-Mexico border (see Chia and Lee, this volume). These arrangements are based on the proposition that to exploit the advantages of complementary endowments in such regions, and to enhance the commitment of larger and technologically less advanced countries to move toward fuller integration into the world economy or a larger regional economic group, such subregional groups can play an exemplary role. Have not maquiladoras contributed to the willingness of both Mexico and the United States to move toward a NAFTA?

Superregionalism is a newer concept (see Elek 1992 and Soesastro, this volume). It seems to be emerging as a way of accommodating the interests of larger groups of countries, at different stages of economic development, and/or of adjustment to an international mixed economy in which views on the complementary roles of markets and governments are converging. It is manifest both in the efforts of the European Community to define an appropriate relationship with its Eastern European neighbors, and one might add with its associated states in Africa, although the role of collective effort for them has been neglected in recent years. For the North American countries superregionalism has become a choice between the Enterprise for the Americas Initiative and Pacific partnership, now manifest in the institutions of the Pacific Economic Cooperation Council (PECC) and the Asia Pacific Economic Cooperation (APEC) ministerial-level meetings and supporting working groups. The former is a tripartite combination of business, academic, and government representatives seeking to develop consensus positions through task forces and fora. The APEC is now establishing a secretariat in Singapore, near that of PECC, which has been in existence since 1989. Both are fostering a concept of "open regionalism," which at least addresses the need for collective promotion of stronger initiatives toward freer flow of goods, services, capital, and technology among the Pacific Rim countries and through common positions in the deliberations of multilateral institutions. More ambitiously, the Pacific countries might contemplate specific liberalization arrangements among themselves, on either a conditional or an unconditional MFN basis.

The case for such superregionalism is that it is arguably a better option than relying exclusively on multilateral institutions or Article XXIV at a time when both are experiencing the understandable constraints of institutions designed for other times and different or more limited priorities. Are the interests of the NAFTA and its members better served by attempting to extend the NAFTA through deals with other Western Hemisphere countries, and perhaps selected Western Pacific countries, on an Article XXIV basis, or by an open regionalism approach as compatible as possible with the GATT, preferably promoting a stronger GATT?

Governments as well as individuals gravitate toward choices based on the search for optimum net benefits. In mixed economies, national and international, this normally leads to varying degrees of formal interdependence. Each nation now faces choices, not only of what level of integration best serves its purposes, but also what combination of multilateral options and various types of regional institutions arrangements is optimal. It is not a question of discarding older for newer options but of selecting appropriate combinations for the more complex realities of the 1990s. This paper will attempt to evaluate the NAFTA in relation to wider Pacific and global priorities in this context.

A Brief Review of NAFTA: Is it Compatible with Open Regionalism?

One striking feature of the NAFTA is that it is a regional integration arrangement encompassing countries with significant differences in per capita incomes. Although Mexico has special national sensitivities, which are reflected in NAFTA, such as the constitutional restrictions on foreign investment in the energy sector, Canada and the United States have their own national sensitivities, which are reflected in derogations from the general NAFTA provisions. There is no special and differential treatment for Mexico as a developing country. Thus, Mexican participation in the NAFTA is another major step in the dramatic liberalization of the Mexican economy since the mid-1980s. At the same time, although the differences in income levels raise anxieties and concerns about the labor adjustment implications in the United States and Canada, the NAFTA negotiations have moved on a very fast timetable, and Mexico will be relatively quickly integrated into the North American economy. In contrast to the EC approach of a full common market and fiscal transfers, the NAFTA approach of a conventional free trade area supplemented by investment, services, and carefully delimited temporary entry provisions instead of full labor mobility could prove more flexible in facilitating regional economic integration when countries have different income levels. Furthermore, the NAFTA includes a stronger commitment to foreign exchange rate convertibility, but there is no contemplation of anything analogous to the European Monetary System or currency union.

Some important issues were left unresolved in the NAFTA pending the outcome of the Uruguay Round of GATT negotiations, and the success or failure of the round will have much broader implications for the evolution of the NAFTA within North America and its potential extension to other countries. Clearly, the success or failure of the round, and the timing of its conclusion, will have important implications for the impact of the NAFTA on offshore trading partners and the multilateral system. It is noteworthy that the NAFTA goes beyond the Canada–US Free Trade Agreement (FTA) and anticipates the outcome of the Uruguay Round in incorporating an intellectual-property chapter based on the draft text submitted by GATT Director-General Arthur Dunkel. In addition, the NAFTA contains a number of new provisions relating to the interaction of trade and the environment. Moreover, environmental issues and human rights issues will attract considerable interest in the US Congress as implementation of the NAFTA proceeds. These issues are addressed below. What are the implications of the NAFTA if it is implemented on the basis of the negotiated text?

The *Wall Street Journal* has described the NAFTA as managed trade, not free trade. This section reviews selected key elements of the NAFTA and considers the broad question of whether the NAFTA promotes managed trade or freer trade, as well as the more conventional question: is NAFTA trade creating or trade diverting?

Rules of Origin and Border Measures

The proposed NAFTA will eventually eliminate tariffs and export duties among the three economies. In this respect the NAFTA would parallel the Canada–US FTA, but the timetable for tariff reductions between Mexico and the United States and between Mexico and Canada lags behind the present schedule of tariff reductions between Canada and the United States under the FTA. The rules of origin for the NAFTA differ from those in the FTA, most notably in the textiles and apparel sector, automotive products, and a few other areas.

Rules of origin are an essential element of any FTA. The valid purpose of rules of origin is to prevent trade and investment diversion when there are high and differentiated external trade barriers. However, restrictive rules of origin can frustrate the benefits of the removal of trade barriers.

The pressure for restrictive rules of origin is greater in industries characterized by significant nontariff barriers to trade. Moreover, rules of origin in themselves can become significant nontariff barriers to trade. Considerable effort was expended in order that the trilateral NAFTA have clear and transparent rules of origin, with the objective of minimizing compliance costs and administrative discretion. The existing Canada–US FTA utilizes primarily a change-of-tariff-classification criterion to determine substantial transformation. However, assembly activities have a 50 percent direct cost of manufacturing requirement, which may be subject to some degree of ambiguity in measurement and administration. Under the NAFTA, more products have rules of origin defined by changes in tariff headings, which makes the determination of origin more predictable. Although these rules of origin are detailed, offshore producers or North American operations sourcing offshore components can quickly determine whether a particular manufacturing activity meets the NAFTA rule of origin.

Many misgivings by other countries about the NAFTA negotiations were prompted by US proposals for more restrictive rules of origin in sectors such as textiles and apparel, automobiles, and computers. Protectionist groups in the United States sought to manipulate the rules of origin to restrict competition from Mexico and in some cases sought to claw back benefits under the Canada–US FTA as well as limit the opening of trade under the NAFTA. In the end, some of the more extreme proposals were discarded. In the case of computers, US multinationals appear to have belatedly realized that the proposed restrictive and cumbersome rules would be damaging to their own US operations in a technologically dynamic and globalized industry. Part of the solution to this issue was to agree to implement a low, common MFN tariff in the computer sector. The crass mercantilists inside and outside the US government lost this particular battle, but it appears there will be residual effects in the form of restrictive rules of origin for cathode ray tubes, televisions, and certain other electronic equipment.

The differences between the proposed NAFTA arrangements and the Canada–US FTA can be illustrated by reference to a particular industrial sector that was a central focus of concern during the trilateral negotiations, namely, the automotive sector. The United States pressed for a restrictive rule of origin for trade in automotive products. From a trade policy perspective it is puzzling why the United States, with a tariff of only 2.5 percent on automotive products currently, and an MFN tariff that could be even lower after completion of the Uruguay Round, would care very much about the rules of origin for automotive products. The potential incentives for trade diversion or trade deflection are extremely limited with such a low US tariff. (Of course, the situation is somewhat different with light trucks, which are subject to a 25 percent tariff as a result of the "chicken war" of the early 1960s.) However, the economic impact and political clout of the US automotive sector are such that the rules for this sector will receive great scrutiny in the Congress. Of course, the automotive sector is very important to the economies of Mexico and Canada as well.

The NAFTA negotiations over automotive rules of origin were influenced by trade disputes between Canada and the United States. Bilateral disputes over whether certain vehicle manufacturers are meeting the rules of origin under the FTA have important implications for the companies involved and will influence perceptions of third-country investors' perceptions of both the Canada–US FTA and the NAFTA.

Complicated technical issues are involved in the current bilateral disputes over whether vehicles manufactured by the General Motors–Suzuki joint venture in Canada and the Honda subsidiary in Ohio meet the rules of origin under the FTA. The key issue in each case is whether there is sufficient value added in Canada and the United States for the vehicles to qualify for duty-free trade under the FTA. Customs administration and legal interpretation of customs law are arcane issues, as was illustrated by a sudden ruling in the late 1970s that light trucks assembled in the United States were not transformed sufficiently to avoid paying the 25 percent US duty.

Rules of origin became a lightning rod for protectionism under the Canada–US FTA as well as in the NAFTA negotiations. There have been a number of bilateral disputes between Canada and the United States over the interpretation of the rules of origin in the FTA. For example, the controversial audit of Honda by the US Customs Service raises complicated issues. One of these is the "roll-up" problem. If a major component of an automobile, such as the engine, is manufactured in part overseas but still meets the FTA rule of origin, then all of the value of the engine, not just the domestic value added, counts toward the required 50 percent direct cost of manufacturing—the engine is "rolled up." On the other hand, if the engine is deemed *not* to meet the FTA rule of origin, then it is "rolled down," and only a small proportion of the value of the engine, which might be less than the domestic value added, is counted toward the direct cost of manufacturing. Roll-up versus roll-down is a key issue in the Honda dispute. Since engines machined and assembled by Honda in Ohio are not deemed to meet the FTA rules of origin, the Honda Civics assembled in Alliston, Ontario, containing those engines do not qualify for duty-free entry into the United States. As an illustration of the technical complexity of this issue, one of the problems is determining the non-arm's-length relationship between the Honda subsidiaries in the United States and Canada and the interpretation of the FTA by the US Customs Service.[1] The NAFTA seeks to resolve these technical problems for automobiles and to avoid the uncertainty of roll-up or roll-down through more detailed rules of origin, but the quid pro quo was tracing of the content and changes in the rules of origin requirements.

Some of the technical issues involved in automotive rules of origin were the subject of an arbitration panel under the Canada–US FTA. The binational panel convened under chapter 18 of the agreement ruled unanimously that Canada's interpretation permitting the deductibility of different types of interest charges was correct. However, many of the technical problems in the FTA rules of origin were addressed in the NAFTA negotiations. For example, in the NAFTA, alternatives to the controversial roll-up process are proposed, which it is claimed would be more easily administered by the governments. In addition, the NAFTA arrangements propose a new mechanism to develop common interpretations of rules of origin. This provision is aimed at limiting the scope for unilateral interpretation of the rules of origin by the national customs authorities. This appears to be a useful innovation, but it remains to be seen whether this mechanism and the proposed new definitions of rules of origin can stand the rigors of legalistic deconstructionism that dominates the US conduct of trade relations at the present time.

---

1. A bizarre aspect of the Honda ruling is that the substantial US value added in machining the engines was disallowed on the grounds of this intracompany transfer.

Mexico and Canada resisted restrictive rules of origin in the automotive sector, in part because of concerns about their impact on existing Japanese assembly plants and on new automotive investment by offshore firms. This issue and related issues about the Mexican automotive decree and duty drawback were among the most contentious issues in the negotiations.

The clarification of rules of origin to a net cost basis apparently offsets the choice of a higher content percentage requirement than the 50 percent direct cost of manufacturing in the Canada–US FTA, but what the actual equivalent percentage should be is debatable. Under the NAFTA the content requirement will stay at 50 percent for four years, rise to 56 percent for the next four years, and then remain at 62.5 percent. The final number is more restrictive than the existing requirements under the Canada–US FTA, notwithstanding the redefinition of rules of origin. In order to cushion the impact on new investment, new automotive production facilities qualify for a 50 percent content requirement for five years.

It is customary in free trade areas to eliminate duty drawbacks for exports qualifying for preferred access to the markets of free trade partners. Thus, duty drawbacks were scheduled to be eliminated by 1 January 1994 in the Canada-US FTA. For Canada, full duty drawback was extended for two years in the NAFTA. Mexico obtained a seven-year transition period, before full duty drawback benefits (or in-bond duty deferral arrangements) for the maquiladoras in Mexico disappear under the NAFTA. What is retained permanently is a device to eliminate double taxation—the lesser of the import duty or the drawback of the duty on imported inputs will be allowed to be remitted. Thus, goods not meeting the NAFTA rules of origin will continue to receive drawback, which removes a potential anomaly under the Canada–US FTA.

In addition to the rules of origin for preferential tariff access, the other key issue for border measures under the NAFTA will be the coverage of quotas and import licenses. In principle, all such quantitative restrictions should be eliminated, but there will be pressures to retain, at least for a considerable period, many of these restrictions. For example, Mexico is phasing out its import licensing and trade balancing requirements for the automotive sector over 10 years, but the phaseout favors the five existing automobile manufacturers in Mexico—the Big Three US manufacturers, Nissan, and Volkswagen. The stated rationale for this provision is that these companies have invested in Mexico on the basis of the previous policy regime and now must rationalize to meet competition. A further complexity in the automotive sector is that Mexican automotive factories qualify for rules of origin under Corporate Average Fuel Economy (CAFE) standards at the option of the manufacturer.

The issue of restrictive rules of origin and that of the retention of quantitative restrictions on imports are closely linked in other sectors. This is evident in the rules of origin in certain food industries, such as sugar-containing products, and in the textiles and apparel sector. Both Canada and the United States maintain extensive restraints on imports of textiles and clothing from low-cost countries (Smith and Bence 1989). As a result of protectionist pressures in the United States and related concerns about the potential for trade diversion involving apparel made from offshore fabrics, special, more restrictive rules of origin for apparel were included in the Canada–US FTA. Under the FTA, apparel had to meet a double transformation test: the fabric had to be woven and the garment manufactured in Canada or the United States to qualify for FTA treatment. Canadian apparel manufacturers who utilized fabrics from offshore sources complained and obtained substantial temporary tariff-rate quotas for exports of garments to the United States manufactured with offshore fabric.

The situation in the NAFTA is analogous, but even more complicated. Canada does not impose Multi-Fiber Arrangement (MFA) restraints on Mexico, presumably because competitive pressures are not intense, but the United States does impose extensive restraints on Mexican apparel exports. Responding to intense political pressures from textile and apparel producers concerned about lower-wage competition from Mexico, the United States proposed—and the NAFTA contains—triple transformation "yarn forward" and even quadruple transformation "fiber forward" rules of origin for textiles and apparel. (Cotton is protected by Section 22 import restrictions in the United States, which helped trigger the Multilateral Short-Term and later the Long-Term Arrangement for cotton textiles in the 1960s.)

These even more restrictive rules of origin for textiles and apparel in the NAFTA created anxiety for Canadian textile and apparel manufacturers. Since the United States does not apply MFA restrictions to Canada, since the FTA rules of origin were less restrictive, and since Canada already had temporary tariff-rate quotas for apparel manufactured with offshore fabric, the arrangement that was negotiated was a series of tariff-rate quotas with growth factors for Canadian exports of textiles and apparel. The Canadian textiles industry seems to be satisfied with this result, but the apparel industry has claimed catastrophe, although the grounds for the claim seem dubious since the industry has been expanding its exports to the US market.

The highly restrictive rules of origin in textiles and apparel are motivated by protectionist pressures in the United States, but they may inadvertently serve the valid purpose of limiting trade diversion at least in the short term. For the longer term, as the NAFTA internal barriers are reduced, investment diversion could become more of an issue as the restructuring of the textile and apparel industry within the North American market proceeds under the new regime. Liberalization of textiles and apparel trade on a multilateral basis in the Uruguay Round may increase short-term concerns about adjustment to import competition in the United

States and Canada but could also ease pressures for restrictive rules of origin for trilateral trade in this sector. Thus, these rules of origin in textiles and apparel ought to be revisited in the future, especially if the MFA is phased out as planned in the Uruguay Round.

The textile products sector is one where trade diversion is likely, because the United States and Canada maintain high trade barriers (both high MFN tariffs and restrictive MFA quota restraints against low-cost developing-country suppliers). In the short term the restrictive rules of origin cannot easily be avoided through investment. Southeast Asian and Chinese producers of such products are not major capital exporters, and the comparative advantage of Mexico in these products will be based on its relatively low wage rates in a North American context, combined with increased access to US capital and technology, making protection against Asian products more effective, even if trade barriers are somewhat reduced by the Uruguay Round. If the Uruguay Round reductions in multilateral barriers are not realized, however, the situation is much more problematic. A Pacific initiative for phasing out MFA quotas in the region might be explored, but this is an nth best option and would encounter strong resistance from US and Canadian producers.

Internal Measures and the Trade Laws

The negotiation of import quotas and trade laws is often linked to internal measures including subsidies, procurement preferences, and environmental regulations. Yet the asymmetries in the size and level of development of the three North American economies made it difficult to negotiate any restraints upon domestic policies. Mexicans and Canadians have often been extremely concerned about the threat to their sovereignty that could arise from US dominance. For its part the United States resists any restraints on its ability to take unilateral actions.

Subsidies

It proved impossible to agree on disciplines on either agricultural or nonagricultural subsidies in the Canada–US free trade negotiations, and it proved at least equally difficult to develop effective rules limiting the use of domestic subsidies when Mexico, with its much lower income levels and greater infrastructure needs, was added to the negotiations. As a result, the subsidy issues, both agricultural and nonagricultural, were referred to the Uruguay Round for resolution. However, it is curious that the NAFTA countries do not contemplate the possibility of refining these subsidy rules among themselves, because some of the provisions of the subsidy and countervailing duty text in the draft final act of the Uruguay Round proposed in December 1991 (the Dunkel text) impose stricter disciplines on subsidies by subnational governments—this could prove troublesome to federal countries such as the United States, Canada, and Mexico.

Antidumping Laws and Competition Policies

As with the countervailing duty laws, national antidumping laws are retained by each of the NAFTA partners. As was noted above, Mexico will amend its trade laws and procedures to make them similar to those of the United States and Canada. There is a chapter in the NAFTA dealing with monopolies and restrictive business practices. A working group is proposed to examine the antidumping laws and competition policies, but no deadline is proposed. Although the proposal of replacing antidumping laws with competition law remedies is virulently opposed by some business interests in the United States today, the prospects for negotiation of this approach could be much better five or ten years hence, as implementation of the NAFTA proceeds. The reason for some modest optimism on this score is that as rationalization of industries proceeds both in North America and globally, antidumping laws, which presume national firms and vertically integrated industries, become less and less relevant. If the NAFTA does evolve in this direction, however, the implications for third countries need to be carefully monitored because antidumping has become the chosen instrument in the European Community and the United States for enforcing managed trade.

The lack of any substantial progress on the trade laws, apart from elaboration of the FTA restraints upon the use of safeguards or emergency import measures on trade with NAFTA partners, will be perceived as a shortcoming of the NAFTA by many. However, this minimalist approach has one significant virtue. At least the three countries have avoided the EC route of common external antidumping and countervailing duty laws. Common external trade laws would increase the risk of managed trade substantially.

Environmental and Labor Measures

US and Canadian concerns about the cost-reducing effects of poorer conditions for workers, and lower effective standards applying to environmentally damaging industrial practices, have led to a call for remedy by Mexico's partners. Trade agreements by themselves are not likely to be an appropriate medium for arriving at measures to deal with these problems, and divisiveness could arise out of the problem of achieving agreement on the adequacy of remedies and the possible role of aid in financing improvements. In discussing these issues, Mexico will remind its North American trading partners that the NAFTA is not a European-style common market with free mobility of labor and significant fiscal transfers from high-income to low-income areas.

The two issues have rather different implications and may be handled differently. Lower labor costs as the result of inferior working conditions as well as lower productivity are primarily the consequence of lower labor skills and the weaker bargaining power of labor. While such conditions are influenced by the effectiveness of democratic political institutions, they are also influenced by population growth. The present age structure of the Mexican population implies rapid labor force growth in Mexico regardless of the policy regime. As Mexican President Carlos Salinas has emphasized, the opportunity for industrial growth in Mexico will raise both opportunity and income levels through expanded markets, investment, and productivity gains. This will provide an economic basis for improved social and environmental policies. These prospects are limited mainly by the rate of Mexico's population growth and the will to apply and enforce social and environmental regulations. To this extent the two issues are similar, but there are transboundary effects from environmental degradation, and there are broader issues about the relationship between international trade and environmental agreements.

Although at the outset the governments stated that environmental issues were being dealt with outside the trilateral free trade negotiations, the agreement contains a number of environment-related provisions. The preamble makes an explicit reference to sustainable development. There are proposals to include environmental experts in panels and to make certain environmental evidence is presented to panels. In response to concerns about environmental issues, there is a proposed obligation that derogation of environmental standards should not be used as an investment inducement or to defer plant closure. This provision does not impose mandatory contractual obligations, since the only requirement is intergovernmental consultation. However, this provision provides a vehicle for the proposed trilateral environment ministers council and the trilateral trade commission to address concerns about investment-inducement effects of relaxation of environmental measures and the effects on competitiveness of differences in environmental regulations. Since the NAFTA retains the Canada–US FTA provision permitting the parties to take bilateral disputes either to the GATT or to bodies established under the agreement, there may be implications for GATT dispute-settlement mechanisms, especially for cases involving environmental issues. At the option of the party subject to the complaint, the NAFTA takes precedence over the GATT on issues involving restrictions imposed on environmental grounds. Also, the NAFTA gives precedence to international environmental agreements: the Convention on International Trade in Endangered Species of Wild Fauna and Flora (CITES), the Montreal Protocol on Substances That Deplete the Ozone Layer, the Basel Convention on the Control of Transboundary Movements of Hazardous Wastes, and some bilateral environmental agreements. This approach raises some interesting issues about the relationship between international environmental agreements and trade agreements and the process of resolving trade disputes involving environmental factors.

These issues will receive continuing attention in the debate about the implementation of NAFTA in the three countries. Although the new US President Bill Clinton supports the NAFTA, these are the issues he identified as requiring further discussion as part of the implementation process.

Services, Investment, and Temporary Entry

In addition to establishing a free trade area for trade in goods, the NAFTA contains chapters covering cross-border trade in services, temporary entry for business and professional people, and investment. The services chapter follows a negative-list approach by covering all services with obligations for national treatment, for MFN treatment, and governing regulatory requirements for establishment, licensing, and certification, unless the service is explicitly excluded or specific derogations for particular policy measures are registered in country annexes. There are separate chapters governing telecommunications and financial services. Services such as land transportation and specialty air transportation are covered by the NAFTA although they were not covered by the Canada–US FTA.

The investment chapter follows an approach analogous to the services chapter by requiring derogations to be registered in country schedules or annexes. In contrast to the Canada–US FTA, which grandfathered all existing derogations from the services and investment obligations, the requirement to list derogations provides more transparency and predictability for firms operating within the NAFTA. One of the innovative and intriguing aspects of the NAFTA is its establishment of an investor-state private arbitral mechanism that provides firms operating in the NAFTA the opportunity to obtain financial compensation through international arbitration if a government contravenes investment obligations or obligations about the conduct of monopolies and state enterprises.

The temporary entry chapter covers business visitors, traders and investors, intracompany management transfers, and professionals. The chapter builds on a similar chapter in the Canada–US FTA, but the United States imposes a quantitative limit on the number of Mexican professionals who may gain temporary visas.

Dispute Settlement

Chapter 19 of the Canada–US FTA set up a binational appeal mechanism, which can replace existing judicial review by the domestic courts of final decisions by the national administrative agencies. It also set up a review mechanism to monitor changes in antidumping and countervailing duty laws as they apply to the partner country. The objective of these dispute-settlement procedures is to provide a more timely appeal mechanism than is available through the courts and to provide joint scrutiny of the decisions taken by the administrative authorities in both countries (Steger 1988, Coffield 1988, Dearden 1988, Horlick and Valentine 1988). Although the softwood lumber dispute influenced the free trade negotiations and the resulting agreement, the understanding on softwood lumber negotiated between Canada and the United States in late 1986 after the preliminary determination by the US Department of Commerce was not affected by the FTA. Thus, the issue of stumpage subsidies remained to be resolved either through future negotiations on subsidies or through the dispute-settlement processes under the agreement. Now that Canada has terminated the softwood lumber memorandum of understanding and the United States has initiated a countervailing duty case against softwood lumber, the application of the dispute-settlement processes to this difficult set of issues will be tested.

The free trade negotiations were, however, able to resolve some contentious subsidy issues in other sectors. In the automotive sector, the issue of Canada's export-based duty remission mechanism was resolved in a way that served both Canadian and US objectives, while avoiding a potential US countervailing duty action, which would have been very disruptive to bilateral trade.[2]

The influence of US protectionist pressures was evident in the softwood lumber dispute. Although various congressional bills directed against softwood lumber imports did not become law, a change in the interpretation of US countervailing duty law by the US Commerce Department in the 1986 case resulted in a negotiated settlement whereby Canada imposed a 15 percent export tax on lumber shipped to the United States (Percy and Yoder 1987). The bitter conflict over softwood lumber shaped official attitudes on both sides during the free trade negotiations and influenced the agreement that emerged. In effect, the Canada–US FTA seeks to prevent the recurrence of a situation like that in this case, where the administrative interpretation of the trade laws was perceived by Canadians as being altered in response to protectionist pressures. Just as the 1986 dispute shaped Canadian attitudes to the Canada–US free trade negotiations, the outcome of the 1991–93 softwood lumber countervailing duty case will influence Canadian and also US attitudes to the dispute-settlement processes for the trade laws in the NAFTA. Furthermore, the outcome of the 1991–93 case could influence the implementation of the NAFTA.

There were difficulties in generalizing the review mechanisms governing the trade laws under FTA chapter 19 on a trilateral basis in the

---

2. For an analysis of the implications of the automotive provisions of the FTA see Paul Wonnacott (1988).

NAFTA. Although there are technical differences, Canadian and US trade laws and administrative procedures for antidumping and countervailing duties are remarkably similar. It is more difficult to apply the Canada–US agreement's review mechanism for decisions involving antidumping and countervailing duties to a third country, Mexico, whose domestic trade laws and administrative procedures differ substantially from those of the United States and Canada. To respond to this concern, Mexico has agreed to implement trade laws and procedures similar to those of the other two countries. In addition, it is difficult to involve Mexico in this type of judicial review, because the Mexican legal system does not have the same basic concepts of administrative law and judicial review as the Canadian and US legal systems. The proposed NAFTA arrangement does extend the chapter 19 mechanism to Mexico, but it introduces a new special committee process, which can be triggered if a country fails to initiate a binational panel or to implement the panel results.

Impact on the Global Trading System

There is a debate between those who take the view that there is a constructive and creative tension between regional economic integration and multilateral liberalization, and those who take the opposite view that regional integration efforts can be corrosive and even cancerous to the multilateral system. This is a question on which economists, who broadly share a consensus about the benefits of trade liberalization, have divergent views. The NAFTA will create a large trading area, and it cannot but have repercussions for the global trading system. Concluding the NAFTA could stimulate trade liberalization either through progress in resolving the outstanding issues in the Uruguay Round, through competitive regionalism in Europe or Asia, or through the accesssion of more countries to the NAFTA. For the longer term, the NAFTA raises some issues that clearly need to be addressed on the multilateral agenda.

The complicated and customized structure of the NAFTA means that accession by other countries will not necessarily be straightforward. It appears that each accession will have to be negotiated on a case-by-case basis and ratified by the legislatures of all the parties.

Linkages to the Uruguay Round

The uncertainties about the outcome of the Uruguay Round after the impasse at the 1990 Brussels ministerial meeting, which required the US administration to request extension of negotiating authority, and the failure to break this impasse at the July 1992 Munich economic summit before expiration of this authority, complicate the intra–North American arrangements as well as creating potential problems for fourth countries in their trade and investment relations with the NAFTA members. From the very beginning of the NAFTA negotiations, it appeared that there was a vague consensus among the three countries that it would be very convenient if the most difficult issues—agricultural subsidies and trade barriers, textiles trade restrictions, trade rules for subsidies and counter-vailing and antidumping duties, government procurement practices, and rules for intellectual property—were resolved through the multilateral process. Of course, the precise interaction between the NAFTA arrange-ment and the Uruguay Round agenda varies from issue to issue. Although the impasse in the multilateral negotiations reinforces interest in regional trading arrangements, the failure to deal with these more difficult issues, as well as more prosaic issues such as multilateral tariff reductions, has made the substantive negotiations among the United States, Mexico, and Canada more difficult. And a continuing impasse will complicate the evolution of the NAFTA and make its impact on the multilateral system more problematic.

The agricultural trade and subsidy issues illustrate some of the diffi-culties for the NAFTA negotiators arising from the impasse in the Uru-guay Round. Much of Mexico's remaining import licenses and most of the Canadian and US quotas are concentrated in the agricultural sector. The delays in achieving a meaningful outcome to the Uruguay Round negotiations on agricultural subsidies and trade barriers have set the parameters for the trilateral negotiations. This is not a new problem. Neither the United States nor Canada was prepared to reduce domestic agricultural subsidies in the Canada-US free trade negotiations because of concerns about the impact of EC and Japanese agricultural policies. For its part, Mexico was reluctant to dismantle its restrictions on imports of corn, grains, and lentils because millions of small Mexican farmers depend upon these products.

Closing the NAFTA deal before the Uruguay Round concluded posed a particularly serious problem for Canada on agriculture, because Canada remains politically committed to its Uruguay Round position of seeking to preserve and to extend import quotas for supply-managed products under Article XI of the GATT. Thus, Canada was preoccupied with pre-serving the exceptions for these import quotas contained in the Canada–US FTA. As a result, the agricultural arrangements in the NAFTA consist of three bilateral agreements.

The Mexico–US bilateral agreement provides for replacement of import quotas and licenses with tariff-rate quotas, to be eliminated over a 10- or 15-year time frame. Mexico's import restrictions on corn and dry beans and US restrictions on sugar and orange juice are subject to a 15-year phaseout. The Canada-Mexico chapter is analogous, except that dairy, poultry, and eggs are excluded. Thus, apart from Canada's idiosyncrasies, the market access elements of the NAFTA on agricultural products are remarkably comprehensive. However, the obligations on domestic support and export subsidies appear to be merely hortatory, except in that they incorporate the GATT obligations that are to be part of the conclusion of the Uruguay Round.

The situation on subsidies and countervailing duties in the NAFTA is analogous to that on agricultural subsidies. The NAFTA proposes to implement the Dunkel text on subsidies and countervailing duties at the end of the Uruguay Round and abandons the effort to develop subsidy and countervailing duty rules, which was mandated in the Canada–US FTA. Certainly the Dunkel text offers a useful basis for introducing subsidy disciplines, both in the form of prohibitions of export subsidies and in giving some effect to the serious prejudice obligations under the GATT.[3] Politically, a Uruguay Round deal involving Europe and Japan has the potential muscle to get changes in countervailing duty laws and subsidy disciplines through the Congress, while the NAFTA does not.

However, it is curious that the NAFTA countries do not contemplate the possibility that they might wish to improve or refine the rules for subsidies and countervailing duties among themselves either at the end of the Uruguay Round or subsequently. An unusual aspect of the Dunkel text on subsidies is that it imposes tighter disciplines on the use of subsidies by subnational governments than it does on their use by national governments. As three federal nations, the NAFTA countries might find it in their interest to modify this provision among themselves. Perhaps the NAFTA negotiators are being shrewd and anticipate that the imposition of greater discipline on subnational governments, which is in the Dunkel text as a result of EC insistence, will be modified now that the Maastricht Treaty faces some hurdles.

Government procurement is another example of where the Uruguay Round could go further than the NAFTA because of the attraction of the opening of the European and Japanese markets. There will be a substantial procurement package in the NAFTA, with more extensive coverage than that under the Canada–US FTA, which is linked to the GATT procurement code. In addition to the entities covered under the GATT code, the United States under the NAFTA will include purchases by entities such as the US Army Corps of Engineers, and Canada will cover the purchases of departments such as transportation and fisheries. This substantial procurement package was achieved because Mexico has agreed to cover procurement by entities such as Pemex (the state oil company) and CFE (the electric power generation commission), as well as direct government purchases. Once again, the success or failure of the Uruguay Round will

---

3. The GATT itself permits the use of domestic subsidies unless they are causing "serious prejudice" to the interest of a trading partner (Article XVI), but these obligations are merely hortatory and have never been effectively applied.

determine the extent to which preferential access is developed within North America.

The interaction between the NAFTA and the Uruguay Round with respect to intellectual property rules is intriguing. In essence, the three countries have adopted the Dunkel text on intellectual property, but the rights and obligations will apply only among the three countries unless the Uruguay Round is also implemented by January 1994.

Challenges for Asia-Pacific Cooperation

As of this writing the most probable final outcomes of the Uruguay Round are moderate though comprehensive success, or (less likely) failure. Neither outcome is likely to be viewed as exhausting the scope for further initiatives at either the multilateral or the regional level. However, it is clear that failure would have much greater consequences for global and regional economic relations and for political harmony as well. Failure, whether it comes from an early French rejection of the US–EC oilseeds compromise or from rejection of the full Uruguay Round package, will mean substantial problems for European unity in the form prescribed in the Maastricht Treaty, and a preoccupation for some time to come with the form and content of relationships with the remaining EFTA countries and Eastern Europe. Failure could also come from protectionist pressures and concerns pressed by environmental groups, which in conjunction with the transition to a new US administration could delay the conclusion of the round beyond 2 March 1993 and necessitate a renewal of negotiating authority from the Congress.

The reaction of the NAFTA members and Western Pacific partners could be to rely on strengthening regional trade positions. This could take a reactive form, such as a joint decision of the Cairns Group of agricultural exporters, a majority of which are Pacific Rim countries, or by the APEC group, to take subsidy-countervail action against subsidized agricultural exports by the European Community. Alternatively, trade and investment undertakings might be explored, either through bilateral agreements of the hub-and-spoke variety with individual NAFTA partners (Mexico already has embarked on this process with some other Latin American countries), through accession to the NAFTA by other Western Hemisphere or Western Pacific countries, or by APEC collectively. A comprehensive approach is much to be preferred, since trans-Pacific bilateral agreements, such as potential deals involving links with Australia and New Zealand, could restore interest in an East Asian economic arrangement that would feel justified in matching the NAFTA in perceived exclusiveness.

If the Uruguay Round is a substantial success, then the next steps may come at a slower pace. Reactive regionalism would be less likely, and hemispheric and trans-Pacific relations would be affected by the pace of economic recovery in the United States, and by the form and priority of trade and related policies adopted by the new US administration, particularly as these relate to Japan and China.

The choice between the extension of the NAFTA through individual accession and a superregional approach as a response to Pacific concerns will not be settled soon, especially given the arrival of a new US administration. One thing is clear, however. The broad or comprehensive application of GATT Article XXIV to the Pacific region is not feasible. Some Latin American and Caribbean countries and possibly two or three Western Pacific economies might achieve accession to NAFTA; even this would take considerable time from a basically domestic US agenda. In any case this is a highly unlikely outcome for Japan and China. President Clinton will be more likely to resist the pressures from those congressional Democrats most antipathetic to improving relations with the leading East Asian countries by approaching Pacific economic relations with a strategy of superregionalism, by seeking an alliance with Asians that encourages liberal solutions to trade and other economic problems that Europe also will find it difficult to resist and will also strengthen multilateral institutions.

Conclusion

The broad answer to the question of whether the NAFTA is managed trade or free trade is that it can be a significant step toward a new form of regional initiative in economic relations between countries at different stages of development that accommodates more fully the role of trade in goods, services, and technology, assisted by appropriate foreign and domestic investment policies. By itself, the NAFTA will achieve significant internal liberalization, but the broader repercussions for the rest of the world depend on the outcome of the Uruguay Round and the subsequent behavior of the NAFTA countries.

The NAFTA gets full marks for elimination of duties and quantitative restrictions, but the quid pro quo was restrictive rules of origin in some sectors. Some of the rules of origin are byzantine in their complexity, but the serious issues are concentrated in the textiles and apparel and automotive sectors. For textiles and apparel, the rules are very restrictive, but this is as much an issue among the NAFTA partners as for other countries, especially if MFA quotas are phased out. The complex arrangements in the automotive sector do not make a summary assessment easy, but one can conclude that investment diversion or restriction is the major concern, with potential effects primarily within the NAFTA region. The restrictive automotive rules of origin, especially after 2002, are a matter of concern, notwithstanding the removal of some of the uncertainties arising from the curious interpretation of the rules of origin by the US Customs Service in the Honda case. It is important to remember that the NAFTA was negotiated during a prolonged slump in the North American automotive sector. One may hope that the restructuring of the North American automotive industry will restore confidence in its ability to meet international competition in the 21st century.

A successful conclusion to the Uruguay Round will enhance the prospects for achieving deeper liberalization of trade within the NAFTA and can also reduce the potential for trade and investment diversion. It is in the interest of all three North American countries to avoid any tendency toward a Fortress North America and to stimulate trade and investment flows across the Pacific and globally. All the APEC countries must be prepared to make the conclusion of the Uruguay Round as comprehensive as possible.

The NAFTA should avoid any serious shift to managed trade because it reduces trade barriers among the partners without raising conventional trade barriers against other countries. Agreements under Article XXIV, especially when they involve a large market and countries already heavily involved in trade among themselves, are expected to be trade creating. But the NAFTA will certainly be watched closely by other GATT members, and clarification of the criteria governing free trade areas could help to ensure that practices such as duty drawbacks are not used indefinitely as means of favoring regional producers over exporters from nonmember countries. Fortunately, the NAFTA has not chosen to adopt common antidumping and countervailing duty laws, which have been a motor of managed trade in the European Community and the United States.

Accession of other countries to the NAFTA will be on a case-by-case basis, with Chile being one of the few early prospects. Since the accession of other Latin American and Western Pacific countries would probably offer little prospect for comprehensive participation, and deals involving Japan and China are least likely, the best strategy for the NAFTA partners is to encourage open regionalism through such new institutions as APEC. Given the common interest of the Pacific countries in preserving and enhancing the effectiveness of trade and investment as engines of development, initiatives to deal with conventional and less conventional trade barriers, either through new multilateral rounds, or where appropriate through regional example, can ensure that the momentum to liberal global solutions is maintained. Such initiatives can be particularly effective if agreement between Japan and the United States is achieved in the process, and if the interests of such varied economies as those of China, the Northeast Asian NIEs, Southeast Asia, and Australia and New Zealand are accommodated. Europeans must not be permitted the political luxury of representing the proposals supported by a market close to twice the size of their own as being purely American inventions. As for the newest issues, such as the reconciliation of environmental and trade concerns, and of trade and competition policies and practices, these seem particularly appropriate areas for the search for prior consensus in the Pacific, where the variety of practice is well matched by a motivation to achieve more convergent policies.

References

Balassa, B. 1962. *The Theory of Economic Integration*. London: Allen and Unwin.

Chia Siow Yue and Lee Tsao Yuan. 1993. "Subregional Economic Zones: A New Motive Force in Asia-Pacific Development." In M. Noland, ed., *Pacific Dynamism and the International Economic System*. Washington: Institute for International Economics.

Coffield, Shirley A. 1988. "Dispute Settlement Provisions on Antidumping and Countervailing Duty Cases in the Canada–U.S. Free Trade Agreement." In Donald M. McRae and Debra P. Steger, eds., *Understanding the Free Trade Agreement*, 73–84. Halifax: Institute for Research on Public Policy.

Curzon, Victoria. 1974. *The Essentials of Economic Integration: Lessons of EFTA Experiences*. London: Macmillan.

Dearden, Richard G. 1988. "Antidumping and Countervailing Duty Provisions: Judicial Review by Binational Panels." In Donald M. McRae and Debra P. Steger, eds., *Understanding the Free Trade Agreement*, 85–102. Halifax: Institute for Research on Public Policy.

Diebold, William, Jr., ed. 1988. *Bilateralism, Multilateralism and Canada in U.S. Trade Policy*. Cambridge, MA: Ballinger.

El-Agraa, Ali M. 1982. *International Economic Integration*. New York: St. Martin's Press.

Elek, Andrew. 1992. *Pacific Economic Co-operation: Policy Choices for the 1990s, Asian-Pacific Economic Literature*. Canberra: Australian National University Press.

Horlick, Gary N., and Debra A. Valentine. 1988. "Improvements in Trade Remedy Law and Procedures Under the Canada–U.S. Free Trade Agreement." In Donald M. McRae and Debra P. Steger, eds., *Understanding the Free Trade Agreement*, 103–28. Halifax: Institute for Research on Public Policy.

Hufbauer, Gary Clyde, and Jeffrey J. Schott. 1992. *North American Free Trade: Issues and Recommendations*. Washington: Institute for International Economics.

Lipsey, Richard. 1970. *The Theory of Customs Unions: A General Equilibrium Analysis*. London: Weidenfeld and Nicolson.

Lipsey, Richard. 1990. *Canada at the U.S.–Mexico Free Trade Dance: Wallflower or Partner?* Toronto: C. D. Howe Institute.

Lipsey, Richard, and K. Lancaster. 1956. "The General Theory of Second Best." *Review of Economics Studies* 20 (1), no. 63: 11–32.

Lipsey, Richard, and Murray G. Smith. 1989. "The Canada–U.S. Free Trade Agreement: Special Case or Wave of the Future?" In Jeffrey J. Schott, ed., *Free Trade Areas and U.S. Trade Policy*, 317–35. Washington: Institute for International Economics.

Long, Olivier. 1985. *Law and its Limitations in the GATT Multilateral Trade System*. Dordrecht: Martinus Nijhoff.

McRae, Donald M., and Debra P. Steger, eds. 1988. *Understanding the Free Trade Agreement*. Halifax: Institute for Research on Public Policy.

Meade, J. E. 1955. *The Theory of Customs Unions*. Amsterdam: North-Holland.

Percy, Michael, and Christian Yoder. 1987. *The Softwood Lumber Dispute and Canada–U.S. Trade in Natural Resources*. Halifax: Institute for Research on Public Policy.

Smith, Murray G., and Jean-François Bence. 1989. "Tariff Equivalents for Bilateral Export Restraints on Canada's Textile and Apparel Trade: Analytical Issues, Measurement

Methodologies, and Selected Estimates." Paper prepared for the Canadian International Trade Tribunal. Ottawa: Institute for Research on Public Policy (September).

Soesastro, Hadi. 1993. "Implications of the Post–Cold War Politico-Security Environment of the Pacific Economy." In M. Noland, ed., *Pacific Dynamism and the International Economic System*. Washington: Institute for International Economics.

Steger, Debra P. 1988. "Dispute Settlement Mechanisms of the Canada U.S. Free Trade Agreement: Comparison with the Existing System." In Donald M. McRae and Debra P. Steger, eds., *Understanding the Free Trade Agreement*, 49–72. Halifax: Institute for Research on Public Policy.

Wonnacott, Paul. 1988. "The Auto Sector." In Jeffrey J. Schott and Murray G. Smith, eds., *The Canada–United States Free Trade Agreement: The Global Impact*, 101–09. Washington: Institute for International Economics, and Halifax: Institute for Research on Public Policy.

6

The Pacific: An Application of a General Theory of Economic Integration

PETER DRYSDALE AND ROSS GARNAUT

The rapid expansion of intraregional trade within East Asia and in the wider Asia-Pacific region has been one of the defining characteristics of East Asian economic dynamism in recent decades. This paper seeks to explain the nature of intraregional economic integration in East Asia and the Pacific, and to draw implications for the future of the international trading system and for the place of East Asia and the Pacific in it.

East Asia's share of world trade expanded from 13.7 percent in 1980 to 19.3 per cent in 1990, rising from a bit less than North America's share (15.0 percent) to somewhat more (16.6 percent). The share of world trade of the economies in the Asia Pacific Economic Cooperation (APEC) group rose from 30.1 percent to 37.4 percent over the same period.[1] Our own projections see the East Asian share of world trade rising to 33.1 percent at the end of the century, and the APEC share to 48.7 percent (Drysdale and Garnaut 1992).

The major part of East Asian and APEC trade expansion over recent years has been with partners in the Asia-Pacific region. Intra–East Asian trade increased from around 30 percent of the East Asian total in 1970 to around 40 percent in 1990 (table 1). Intra-APEC trade expanded from

Peter Drysdale is Director, Australia-Japan Research Centre and is Professor of Economics, as is Ross Garnaut, at Australian National University. The authors are grateful for excellent research assistance provided by Yiping Huang and Ligang Song and for the support of the Australia-Japan Research Centre and the PAFTAD Conference in undertaking this project.

1. East Asia includes China, Japan, Hong Kong, Korea, Taiwan, Brunei, Indonesia, Malaysia, Philippines, Singapore, and Thailand. The Asia Pacific Economic Cooperation (APEC) group additionally includes Canada, the United States, Australia, and New Zealand.

Table 1 Asia Pacific and world bilateral trade flows, 1970 and 1990 (percentages of total)

	Western Pacific	Australasia	East Asia	North America	Asia Pacific	Western Europe	European Community	Rest of world
1970								
Western Pacific								
Exports	34.99	3.63	31.36	27.88	62.85	18.18	13.64	18.97
Imports	34.09	6.51	27.58	26.52	60.62	18.39	13.90	20.99
Australasia								
Exports	39.06	5.93	33.13	16.33	55.39	27.54	26.38	17.07
Imports	22.92	5.84	17.08	26.98	49.91	39.61	29.35	10.48
East Asia								
Exports	34.22	3.19	31.02	30.04	64.26	16.41	10.27	19.33
Imports	36.10	6.63	29.47	26.44	62.54	14.58	11.13	22.88
North America								
Exports	16.17	2.25	13.92	32.50	48.67	28.61	27.42	22.72
Imports	19.53	1.88	17.65	38.31	57.84	24.02	19.42	18.14
Asia Pacific								
Exports	*23.52*	*2.79*	*20.73*	*30.69*	*54.21*	*24.53*	*22.04*	*21.26*
Imports	*25.57*	*3.80*	*21.77*	*33.42*	*58.99*	*21.68*	*17.13*	*19.33*
Western Europe								
Exports	4.81	1.47	3.35	9.31	14.13	66.75	53.85	19.12
Imports	4.79	1.34	3.45	12.30	17.09	61.90	50.97	21.01
European Community								
Exports	4.97	1.57	3.41	9.63	14.61	66.24	53.10	19.15
Imports	5.00	1.54	3.46	13.19	18.19	59.62	50.24	22.19
Rest of World								
Exports	21.83	1.16	20.67	17.64	39.47	40.41	38.64	20.12
Imports	8.89	0.79	8.10	31.19	40.08	37.93	32.96	21.99
World								
Exports	12.53	1.76	10.77	16.98	29.51	47.04	40.59	23.45
Imports	12.40	2.11	10.29	20.11	32.50	43.97	36.19	23.53

1990

Western Pacific								
Exports	42.71	2.63	40.08	27.55	70.26	18.48	19.93	11.26
Imports	47.35	4.39	42.96	21.17	68.52	16.58	16.11	14.90
Australasia								
Exports	57.12	7.25	49.87	12.44	69.56	15.83	15.11	14.61
Imports	42.54	7.29	35.25	23.15	65.68	27.61	21.53	6.70
East Asia								
Exports	41.67	2.30	39.37	28.65	70.32	18.67	16.24	11.02
Imports	47.76	4.14	43.62	21.00	68.76	15.64	14.12	15.60
North America								
Exports	24.50	2.02	22.48	33.98	58.48	23.34	20.55	18.18
Imports	34.81	1.03	33.78	27.49	62.30	20.93	17.18	16.77
Asia Pacific								
Exports	*35.23*	*2.38*	*32.85*	*30.19*	*65.43*	*20.47*	*17.97*	*14.10*
Imports	*40.95*	*2.67*	*38.27*	*24.39*	*65.34*	*18.80*	*15.97*	*15.85*
Western Europe								
Exports	6.70	0.77	5.93	7.90	14.60	71.66	55.24	13.73
Imports	9.77	0.64	9.12	8.00	17.77	68.99	67.38	13.24
European Community								
Exports	5.99	0.69	5.29	7.29	13.27	66.19	55.77	20.54
Imports	8.21	0.52	7.69	7.27	15.47	59.96	51.18	24.57
Rest of World								
Exports	17.68	0.65	17.03	18.55	36.23	35.22	32.29	28.55
Imports	13.65	1.36	12.29	13.98	27.63	35.89	33.59	36.49
World								
Exports	19.06	1.35	17.71	17.89	36.95	46.79	37.71	16.25
Imports	22.50	1.55	20.95	15.39	37.89	43.78	42.84	18.33

Source: The Australian National University, International Economic Databank, compiled from United Nations, International Monetary Fund, and national statistics.

around 56 percent of the Asia-Pacific total in 1970 to around 65 percent in 1990. By 1990, intraregional trade accounted for substantially more of East Asian than of North American total trade, and the intraregional share of Asia-Pacific trade was almost as large as the (rising) share of Western European trade.

At a time of focus on the role of discriminatory trade expansion in the European Community and in the North American Free Trade Area (NAFTA), there is loose talk of the emergence of regional trading blocs in the world. This, together with the increased commitment to regional discrimination in Europe and North America, has generated some discussion of a regional discriminatory bloc within East Asia itself.[2]

This chapter begins by outlining some key features of the unusual model of regional trade expansion that is developing among the Asia-Pacific economies. The second section discusses the distinctive features of East Asia and Pacific trade expansion, evaluating the concepts of "market" and "institutional" or "discriminatory" integration that have emerged in the literature. Next, the range of barriers or resistances to trade is discussed, including but extending far beyond official barriers, the reduction of which leads to increased "economic integration" and gains from trade. Several means of measuring the effects of "trade resistances" on patterns of trade are discussed in the fourth section, and data are presented on three measures of the effects of trade resistances in the Asia-Pacific region: import shares (from various sources) of GDP, intensity indexes, and intraindustry trade indexes. The concluding section assesses the prospects for the "Pacific model" of nondiscriminatory open regionalism, the entrenchment and extension of which can help to preserve the regional and world benefits of established patterns of rapid growth and structural change, in an era of discriminatory integration in the Americas.

The Asia-Pacific Trade Model

East Asian and Asia-Pacific regional trade expansion is very different in nature from that which is currently emerging in North America and from what has been established and is continuing to develop in Europe. There has been no economically important trade-expanding discrimination in East Asia: trade preferences within the ASEAN region so far have had trivial effects, although the 1991 commitment by the ASEAN heads of government to move toward an ASEAN Free Trade Agreement (AFTA)

---

2. See, for example, the original proposals for an East Asia Economic Group by Malaysian Prime Minister D. S. Mahathir bin Mohamed. The decision by the ASEAN heads of government to move toward an ASEAN Free Trade Area (AFTA) followed a period of pessimism about Uruguay Round outcomes in late 1991.

will have future significance. The two most rapidly expanding intra–East Asian bilateral trading relationships over the past several years, those between mainland China and Taiwan, and between China and the Republic of Korea, have developed around and despite discriminatory restrictions on bilateral trade. Trade discrimination in Australia–New Zealand and North America has been associated with relatively small parts of the total Asia-Pacific trade expansion.

East Asian and Asia-Pacific trade expansion has nevertheless been associated with reductions in barriers to international, including intraregional, trade. All the Western Pacific member economies of APEC except Hong Kong and Singapore have substantially reduced official border restrictions over the past decade, and especially since the mid-1980s. Hong Kong and Singapore have, throughout the period under discussion, been the world's most important examples of free trading economies. There has been major import liberalization in Japan, Korea, Taiwan, mainland China, Thailand, Malaysia, Indonesia, Australia, and New Zealand. Political weakness has meant slower progress in the Philippines, although recent official commitments are impressive. Trade liberalization has been mostly nondiscriminatory and unilateral, and sometimes influenced by the multilateral disciplines of the General Agreement on Tariffs and Trade (GATT). The main exceptions, sometimes temporary, have favored the United States, following pressure from that country to reduce bilateral trade imbalances. Even more important has been the reduction of nonofficial barriers to trade of many kinds, as part of the process of deep integration into the international economy.

The new model of regional and international trade expansion that has developed in the Asia-Pacific region, and especially in the Western Pacific economies, is consistent with the spirit of the GATT as it was conceived in the 1940s and as it developed in the early postwar decades. Three crucial features distinguish Asia-Pacific trade expansion and take it beyond the GATT's constitution, rules, and practice, and beyond the GATT's framework for the encouragement of regional trade expansion under Article XXIV.

The first distinguishing feature derives from the fact that GATT negotiations in practice have assumed that liberalization is a concession, the withholding of which has value for a member country. The trade negotiations "game" therefore has elements of the prisoner's dilemma, in which, in the absence of deliberate communication and cooperation, the most unfavorable outcome for each participating country is the one that occurs. In contrast, the trade expansion game that has emerged in the Western Pacific can be characterized as "prisoner's delight." Observation of the highly beneficial effect of one country's liberalization on its own trade expansion has led each Western Pacific economy to calculate that, whatever policies others follow, it will benefit more from keeping its own borders open to trade than from protection. Each country's liberalization in its own interest has increased the benefits that trading partners receive from their own liberalization. This prisoner's delight game consists of a series of movements toward sets of trade policies that are more favorable for all countries. There are gaps and exceptions (notably in East Asian agriculture), reflecting the domestic political economy of industry policy in most of these economies. It is in these excepted areas that outside pressure plays an important role in each individual country's trade liberalization, so far most effectively through multilateral negotiations and other fora of the GATT, and sometimes in bilateral negotiations influenced by GATT disciplines.

The payoffs from unilateral trade liberalization that generate the prisoner's delight are recognizable as the outcomes predicted by standard trade theory. What is new in East Asia and the Western Pacific is that close observation in neighboring country after neighboring country that trade liberalization enhances economic performance has changed political perceptions of the payoff matrix. Any perceived disadvantages in changes in income distribution associated with trade liberalization are judged by the political process to be less important than the gains for the nation as a whole—helped along by the obviously favorable effects on the incomes of the relatively poor of labor-intensive manufactured export expansion in labor-abundant economies.

Second, Asia-Pacific trade expansion has not been associated with substantial discrimination in trade policy. Official barriers have not been lower for intraregional than for extraregional trade expansion.

Third, the East Asian and Pacific experience demonstrates powerfully the importance of nonofficial barriers to trade, and the role that their reduction plays in trade expansion and economic development.

Market Integration and Discriminatory Integration

Analysis of the unusual character of Asia-Pacific trade expansion has been advancing over the past quarter century, not least within this conference series and among people associated with it. It is, however, only in the past few years, when the United States and the European Community have been seeking to understand and respond to an East Asian presence of obviously large proportions in the international economy, that many trans-Atlantic mainstream economists have turned their attention to the character of Asia-Pacific trade expansion. Much of the recent American and trans-Atlantic discussion of East Asian and Asia-Pacific trade expansion has made little use of the insights that have emerged from a quarter century of analysis of the different trade phenomenon across the Pacific.

Cooper (1974) was one of the first to draw attention to the various origins of regional trade expansion with his identification of "market integration" around institutional and legal barriers to trade, involving capital movements and other forms of economic interchange. In contrast to this form of integration, economic integration in Europe has flourished within the institutional arrangements of the European Community. European institutional integration discriminates against economies outside the region: the removal of internal barriers to trade has been accompanied by the maintenance of external barriers, while others, such as those affecting agricultural trade, have become a greater encumbrance to global trade growth.

The terms "market integration" and "institutional integration" have been useful in drawing attention to the difference between European and Asia-Pacific economic integration. But they are misleading to the extent that they are interpreted literally. The emergence of new institutions—to a considerable extent private but increasingly intergovernmental—to reduce the costs of trade expansion has been important in the Asia-Pacific region. Meanwhile the important role of integrative institutions embodying large elements of official discrimination in Europe and now North America has not excluded market pressures from playing a major role in trade expansion in those areas (Milner 1991, 7).

On balance, we have found it useful to retain Cooper's term "market integration" for the case where the initiative has remained primarily with enterprises acting separately from state decisions, and where official encouragement of regional integration does not include major elements of trade discrimination. We prefer the term "discriminatory integration" to "institutional integration" for arrangements of the EC and NAFTA kind.

A General Theory of Economic Integration

We define "economic integration" as movement toward one price for any single piece of merchandise, service, or factor of production. The global economy is, in this sense, considerably dis-integrated. The price for an undifferentiated item may vary greatly between a store on 49th Street and another on 120th Street in New York, between a market in East Java and another in North Sumatra, or between Tokyo and Paris.

Dis-integration persists because of barriers, or resistances, to trade. We define resistances to trade as phenomena that prevent or retard the immediate movement of commodities in response to price differentials.

One line of literature that has developed out of analysis of the Asia-Pacific experience distinguishes two basic types of resistances: objective and subjective. (For background to the discussion in this and subsequent paragraphs see Garnaut 1972, Drysdale and Garnaut 1982, and Drysdale 1988).

Trade Resistances and Economic Integration

Objective resistances can be overcome by firms only at some objectively determined minimum cost. They comprise principally transport, communications, and other costs of overcoming distance, and official barriers to trade (principally protection).

Subjective resistances comprise a range of social, psychological, and institutional factors that cause prices to vary across geographic space by larger margins than can be explained by the necessary costs of overcoming objective resistances. Subjective resistances derive from perceptions of risk and uncertainty about property rights and valuations at various stages of trade transactions, from imperfection in the information available to firms, and from the processes through which firms engaged in trade make decisions that affect the volume, geographic direction, or commodity composition of trade.

Johnson (1968) suggested a slightly different categorization of the same phenomena, distinguishing "geographic distance and the transport cost of overcoming it," "differences of political and legal systems, culture and language that differentiate nations from one another as market areas," and "protection." We think that it is more useful analytically to see Johnson's second category as factors affecting the costs of overcoming subjective resistances to trade, rather than as separate resistances in themselves.

Resistances are present in all economic transactions, whether domestic or international. They are commonly, although far from universally, lower within than between countries. This difference is one of the factors distinguishing international from interregional trade. There are, however, important exceptions to the common pattern. Regional price disparities within some large, weakly integrated economies (say, Indonesia and China) can exceed disparities, at least for many commodities, between major cities exposed to trade between countries (Arndt and Sundrum 1975). Border trade occurs between adjacent regions of two countries when the cost of overcoming intranational resistances exceeds the cost of overcoming international resistances.

The costs of overcoming various resistances vary across bilateral trading relationships. The divergences from the law of one price associated with resistances to international trade are typically very large. Among objective resistances, while official barriers have received the most consideration in public discussion and the literature, these are probably less important than transport costs today, at least in relation to imports of most manufactured goods into advanced industrial economies. There are exceptions, of which restrictions on the import of textiles and clothing into the OECD countries are the most important.

There is some evidence to suggest that subjective resistance can be quantitatively more important than objective resistances (Garnaut 1972).

Sung (1992) underlines the importance of these considerations in his discussion of the large and increasing role that Hong Kong is playing in China's trade—a role that contributes a major part of Hong Kong's raison d'etre today. Interestingly, Hong Kong's role in the China trade has expanded as China has opened to the outside world, despite reductions in resistances to direct trade between established enterprises in China and in the rest of the world (Sung 1992). The resolution of this paradox can be found in the effect of China's internationalization in increasing the range of firms and commodities participating in foreign trade, and therefore the transaction costs in dealing with them.

The costs of overcoming various types of resistance to bilateral trade, objective and subjective, are closely interrelated. Economies of scale affect the cost of overcoming all except official resistances: objective transport and communications costs up to quite large levels of bilateral trade, and subjective resistance of all kinds. There are externalities stemming from one firm's investment to reduce the cost of overcoming resistances to trade: investment in the organization of a new pattern of transport or communication will reduce costs for other firms in the bilateral trading relationship; and investment in information to support a new pattern of trade provides information to others—including through observation of the resulting trade expansion itself.

These two characteristics of the costs of overcoming resistances to trade together introduce a conservative bias and stability in bilateral trade patterns. They increase the time lags in the adjustment of trade patterns to new relative cost relationships, which in any case would be long as the time needed for enterprises to search for information, process that information, and respond to it. They cause trade expansion associated with reduction in one type of resistance to trade, to reduce the cost of overcoming all other resistances to trade. And they demonstrate the importance of institutions, private or public, from the internally integrated multinational enterprise to mechanisms to enforce contracts in international trade, in determining the costs of overcoming resistances to trade.

Resistances and Trade Discrimination

The cost of overcoming trade resistances has not been treated systematically in the theory of international trade. Subjective resistances make a cameo appearance in the theory of the product cycle (Vernon 1966), but disappear without influencing the whole corpus of theory.

The exceptions are the theory of protection (Corden 1971, 1974) and the theory of customs unions (Lipsey 1960; Vanek 1965), which analyze the impact of official barriers to trade that are, respectively, uniform and differentiated across countries. Insights from the theories of protection and of customs unions are of considerable value in understanding the impact of resistances more generally on trade and welfare.

"Multilateral" reductions in resistances to a country's international trade unambiguously expand the welfare of the country itself and the rest of the world. However, reductions in resistances in some bilateral relationships but not in others may raise or lower the welfare of countries involved in the resulting bilateral trade expansion, depending on the balance of trade creation and trade diversion. Such differentiated reductions in resistances in some bilateral trading relationships unambiguously reduce trade with and the welfare of countries in the rest of the world outside the trade-expanding bilateral relationships, unless the income-increasing effects of trade creation are very large compared with other economic effects.

There may be a shift of trade from established channels resulting from reduction in subjective resistances to trade, resulting from private firms' investment in information about opportunities in a new bilateral trading relationship, or in building business relationships to support a new pattern of bilateral trade. In the case of subjective resistances, however, the new knowledge of superior gains from trade with a new partner is more likely to be analogous to the removal of trade discrimination against the new partner than to classical trade diversion. Trade may, indeed, be diverted from old channels to new. It could be trade diversion in the classic sense, for example, if the investment in information and business ties with the new partner is associated with an absolute decline in effort in maintaining the old relationships. It is more likely, however, that the switch will divert trade from a less profitable to a more profitable partner, in the case in which the initiative lies with nonstate businesses rather than governments. The latter is not classic trade diversion and has different economic effects.

Let us illustrate the point with one example of considerable contemporary significance. As Taiwan enterprises have put more effort into trade and investment with mainland China in recent years, they have perforce devoted less managerial time to identifying and exploiting business ties in the rest of the world. This may have increased absolutely resistances to trade between Taiwan and (parts of) the rest of the world, especially when economies of scale in overcoming resistances to bilateral trade are taken into account. But even if it has not, the reduction of resistances to trade between Taiwan and mainland China, in, say, labor-intensive electronic components, will have had some effect in diverting trade in these components from other bilateral relationships. This tends to reduce welfare in the rest of the world, unless income growth associated with trade creation in Taiwan and China makes these two economies much larger participants in trade with the world as a whole.

Such a change in the pattern of subjective resistances is more likely to raise the welfare of the new trading partners, Taiwan and mainland China, than is a discriminatory reduction in official barriers. It is therefore more likely to be associated with a preponderance of classic trade creation over trade diversion, a net increase in the economic welfare of the bilateral trading partners, and welfare gains for the world as a whole and the rest of the world.

The discussion in the preceding paragraphs of trade diversion and trade creation associated with the reductions in resistances in some but not all bilateral trading relationships exemplifies a general difference between differential reduction in official and other resistances to trade. Reductions in other resistances result from independent firms' search for lower-cost and more profitable patterns of trade. While the reduction in the gap between minimum possible and actual transport costs may divert trade from old relationships, it is unlikely to divert trade from lower-cost to higher-cost sources and destinations. Unlike discriminatory reduction in official barriers, it is highly unlikely to reduce welfare in the trading partners experiencing trade expansion or in the world as a whole, although it may still reduce welfare in the rest of the world outside the trading partners.

The presence of externalities in investment to reduce subjective resistances to trade, and to bring transport and communications costs closer to their objective minima, introduces the possibility of economically efficient roles of government, quite separate from those associated with the imposition of official barriers to trade. These are the roles of governments in providing public goods that are relevant to the efficient operation of an international market: improving transport and communications infrastructures, including through regulatory regimes; reducing perceptions of risk in international contracts; and disseminating information on profitable trade opportunities (Garnaut 1993). The impact of these roles of government on trade and welfare is best analyzed in a framework analogous to that applied to independent enterprises' efforts to reduce the cost of resistances, rather than that developed in the pure theory of customs unions for analysis of differentiated reduction in official barriers.

In this section we have articulated elements of a general theory of economic integration. Within this theory, dis-integration is the normal condition of interregional and international trade in goods and services. The reduction of resistances takes investment and time and is affected by the whole range of cultural, linguistic, legal, and other factors that affect the cost of trade transactions. Much of the dynamism in Asia-Pacific trade expansion derives from the progressive reduction of subjective and objective but nonofficial resistances to trade. The process has been driven by independent enterprises' search for more profitable patterns of trade, sometimes assisted by provision by governments of public goods that affect the operation of private markets.

The general theory of economic integration brings out the crucial distinction between reductions in resistances in some trading relationships through a process of official discrimination, on the one hand, and reductions in resistances through a process of market and nondiscriminatory integration, on the other. Discriminatory integration blocks the economic processes of search for more profitable patterns of trade.

Where discrimination favors trading relationships that would in any case, through market processes, be large relative to the partner countries' total trade, the chances of economic loss in the partner countries and the world as a whole are correspondingly reduced. These conditions reduce the magnitude of economic loss in the rest of the world.

Working against a presumption that discrimination in favor of trade between naturally close states will not reduce world welfare, Krugman (1991, 1992) makes this point but takes it too far. Summers (1991) asserts a similar point more strongly, and does not attempt to justify his strong arguments in support of discriminatory liberalization. The reality that "optimal" patterns of trade are different across commodities, however, increases the costs of general official discrimination in bilateral trading relationships, for the bilateral partners and the rest of the world. The presence of economies of scale and externalities in overcoming many resistances compounds the effect of trade discrimination in promoting welfare-reducing trade. Discriminatory official barriers block the role of market pressures in reducing trade resistances in new trading relationships when changing economic circumstances and opportunities justify the effort.

Measuring the Effects of Resistances

The recent focus in the United States on Japanese official and subjective barriers to trade has spawned myriad attempts to measure these resistances and their impact on trade (Krugman 1991). The recent literature also uses various statistical measures and indicators of the tendency towards regionalization of world trade. Much of this recent search for measures and indicators suffers from being developed for the particular dispute of the day, and from being too thinly rooted in analysis of the general phenomenon of resistances to trade. Here we discuss some of the more useful indicators before applying them to analysis of trade patterns in the Asia-Pacific region.

Trade shares of output and expenditure are weak indicators of openness to foreign trade. It is well-known that a country's trade share is influenced strongly by its economic size (by various measures) and the skewedness of its patterns of relative costs of production of goods and services. Importantly (and this is less discussed in the literature), it is also influenced by whether there are large opportunities for trade with the particular economies from which the country is separated by low resistances to bilateral trade. Deviations from a trend line linking these variables to trade shares could, in principle, be used as a measure of resistance to trade, or of openness. However, the prodigious number of relevant variables, and the limited number of national economies to observe, removes the prospect of statistical precision.

The influence of economic size on trade shares can be reduced if we focus on countries of similar size, or amalgamate economies into regions of similar size. We do this in the next subsection, to compare the openness and changes in openness over time in Western Europe, North America, and East Asia.

A different type of indicator is required to measure tendencies in the regionalization of world trade. Some authors cite growing intraregional trade shares in drawing attention to the dangers of regionalism or, in the case of East Asia, as evidence of the emergence of some trading bloc within the region. But we learn little from observation of the share of intraregional trade in total trade: if, holding the number of countries in each region constant, the home region represents a large proportion of world trade, then the regional trade share will be high, even if resistances to intraregional trade are not particularly low (Frankel 1992, 10); and a region's share of world trade is increased arbitrarily if the region is divided into more countries. The share of intraregional trade in a region's total trade is therefore a quite inadequate measure of regional trade bias.

The arbitrary influence of the size of the region on regional trade shares is removed by the use of intensity-of-trade indexes. The intensity index compares the size of a bilateral or regional trade relationship with what it would be if there were no variation in trade shares across bilateral trading relationships. A finer and more precise version of the intensity index, for the purposes of assessing the influence of variations in resistances on bilateral and interregional trade flows, is the trade bias index, which allows systematically for the effects of trade on intensity of greater or less complementarity in the commodity composition (Drysdale 1988).[3]

---

3. The intensity index (I_{ij}) is defined for country i's exports to country j as the share of i's exports going to $j(X_{ij}/X_i)$ relative to the share of j's imports (M_j) in world trade (T). That is:

$$I_{ij} = (X_{ij}/X_i)/(M_j/T).$$

The complementarity and bias indexes (C_{ij} and B_{ij}) for country i's exports to country j are as follows:

$$C_{ij} = \left(\frac{X^{k_i}}{X_j} \frac{T}{T^k} \frac{M^{k_j}}{M_j} \right)$$

$$B_{ij} = X_{ijk} \left(\frac{T^k}{X^{k_i} M^{k_j}} \right)$$

where k refers to individual (SITC three-digit) commodities. Note that the intensity index, I_{ij}, is the product of C_{ij} and B_{ij} and that, on average, across all of a country's (or region's) bilateral trades, these indexes have a value of one.

A less direct indication of the extent of resistances to bilateral trade is provided by the intraindustry trade index.[4] It is most useful as an indicator of resistances to trade among countries of similar and relatively high per capita income, and relatively strongly specialized in export of manufactured goods. It is useful because the gains from intraindustry trade are typically low relative to the value added that is traded, so that substantial resistances wipe out the gains and deter trade. It is an indicator of the levels of total resistances to international trade, including objective resistances other than protection. It is not, therefore, directly a measure either of the extent of policy barriers or of culturally based resistances, unless one is able to control the effects of objective transport and communications costs.

Intraindustry relative to interindustry trade is less important in an economy where relative production costs across industries are very different from the rest of the world, including regions such as East Asia where resource endowments are highly skewed. It is strongly influenced by the costs of transport and communications, and so tends to be deterred by isolation from economies that, in their relative cost structures, provide opportunities for intraindustry trade. Used with care, however, the intraindustry trade index does provide some guidance on the costs of overcoming resistances to trade in various bilateral relationships, and on their changes over time.

Import Shares of GDP

If one looks simply at import shares of GDP, East Asia is a touch less open than the world as a whole, and North America is considerably less open. These two Asia-Pacific regions roughly doubled their import share of GDP in the 1970s and experienced a further small increase in the 1980s. The world as a whole experienced a large increase in the 1970s and none in the 1980s. In contrast, the import share of the European Community's output rose reasonably strongly through both decades.

As discussed above, this ratio is a poor indicator of openness. It takes no account of the effects of regional size on opportunities for profitable

---

4. The intraindustry trade index (IIT_{ij}) used here is based on Grubel-Lloyd formula (1975) and is defined as:

$$IIT_{ij} = 1 - \frac{k \mid X_{ijk} - M_{ijk} \mid}{k (X_{ijk} + M_{ijk})}$$

where X_{ij} and M_{ij} are total exports and imports of country i's trade in commodity k with country j, $k = 1, \ldots k$ for all manufactured commodities (SITC 5-8) and $k = 1, \ldots T$ for total commodities (at the SITC 3-digit level). For the overall indexes of intraindustry trade of both manufactured commodities and total commodities (reported in table 6), j represents the rest of the world to which country i trades.

international trade, nor of the artificial impact of the separation of a region into varying numbers of countries on the extent of intraregional and therefore total international trade.

North America, the European Community, and East Asia are now, or at least are now becoming, of similar economic size. The "number of countries" factor is thus a more important influence on the trade shares of output across the three regions. In 1970 intraregional trade represented three times the proportion of output in the European Community (9 percent) as in East Asia (3 percent), and almost five times the proportion of output in North America (less than 2 percent). By 1990, the intraregional trade share of output had grown much more strongly in East Asia (to over 7 percent, as many developing countries in the region joined Japan as significant players in world trade) and the European Community (to 17 percent) than in North America (still less than 3 percent).

We can abstract from the arbitrary impact of intraregional boundaries by focusing on the extraregional import share of GDP as our first, crude measure of openness, or low resistances to international trade. The extraregional import shares of output are similar in East Asia and the European Community, having risen moderately through the 1970s, and having given up some of that ground in the 1980s. The North American ratios are much lower, but grew proportionally more in the 1970s, and expanded a little in the 1980s.

Is North America less open to foreign trade than are the other major economic regions of the world? East Asia's resource endowment is more skewed (toward abundance of labor in the early stages of development and scarcity of natural resources at all times), and this tends to generate high import ratios, independently of the extent of resistances to international trade. Extraregional primary commodities imports represent a much higher proportion of East Asian (and EC) than of North American output. A focus on the extent of extraregional primary imports goes some way to explaining the deceleration of growth in import shares in the 1980s in East Asia (and the Community) but not North America: changes in primary commodity (especially oil) prices boosted import ratios in the 1970s and reduced them in the 1980s.

Table 2 presents data on the share of extraregional imports of manufactured goods (Standard International Trade Classifications [SITC] 5 to 9) in GDP for the three major regions and several individual countries. The rates are similar in the three regions. The skewedness of East Asia's resource endowments militates against high import ratios for manufactured goods, and so tends to depress the "economic" import ratio. Conversely, the fact that East Asian GDP as conventionally measured, although rapidly increasing, remains somewhat smaller than EC or North American GDP, may raise by a small margin the "economic" scale of extraregional trade.

Table 2 Imports of manufactured goods from various sources as a share of importing countries' GDPs, 1970, 1980, and 1990[a] (percentages)

	East Asia	Japan	North America	United States	Canada	Australia	New Zealand	European Community	Germany	Extraregional world[b]	World
East Asia											
1970	1.65	1.23	1.2	1.13	0.07	0.1	0.01	1.12	0.41	3	4.65
1980	3.24	2.01	1.74	1.64	0.1	0.12	0.03	1.31	0.49	3.92	7.16
1990	5.62	2.2	2.17	2.06	0.11	0.16	0.02	1.96	0.71	5.37	10.98
Japan											
1970	0.23		1.22	1.15	0.07	0.06	0.01	0.69	0.29	2.58	2.81
1980	0.6		1.09	1.02	0.07	0.06	0.02	0.64	0.22	2.37	2.97
1990	1.09		1.22	1.16	0.06	0.07	0.02	1.08	0.4	2.97	4.06
North America											
1970	0.78	0.57	1.47	0.76	0.71	0.02	0	0.88	0.31	1.9	3.48
1980	1.98	1.18	2.03	1.13	0.9	0.04	0.01	1.27	0.44	3.77	6.11
1990	3.48	1.77	2.41	1.17	1.24	0.05	0.01	1.66	0.55	5.77	8.82
United States											
1970	0.78	0.56	0.77		0.77	0.02	0	0.82	0.3	1.81	2.7
1980	2.03	1.21	0.99		0.99	0.04	0.01	1.23	0.44	3.79	5.11
1990	3.56	1.8	1.37		1.37	0.05	0.01	1.63	0.55	3.8	7.85
Canada											
1970	0.82	0.63	9.77	9.77		0.01	0	1.62	0.4	2.93	12.73
1980	1.43	0.88	12.56	12.56		0.03	0	1.6	0.44	3.57	16.25
1990	2.72	1.48	12.08	12.08		0.05	0.01	1.86	0.58	5.47	17.92

Australia										
1970	1.81	1.48	3.12	2.8	0.33		0.17	4.07	0.82	9.83	10
1980	3.38	2.27	2.96	2.73	0.23		0.3	2.84	0.79	10.12	10.42
1990	4.39	2.57	3.43	3.22	0.21		0.37	2.98	0.9	11.91	12.28
New Zealand										
1970	2.38	1.91	2.76	2.18	0.58	3.26		6.83	0.82	12.75	16.01
1980	4.56	3.66	3.58	3.18	0.4	3.22		4.97	0.93	14.33	17.56
1990	5.44	3.56	4.11	3.77	0.34	3.81		4.17	1.04	15.53	19.34
European Community										
1970	0.41	0.27	1.5	1.3	0.2	0.03	0	6.83	2.15	2.87	10.88
1980	1.12	0.62	1.54	1.43	0.11	0.04	0	8.93	2.55	3.73	14.29
1990	2.41	1.25	1.96	1.83	0.12	0.04	0.01	13.69	3.9	5.9	22.02
Germany										
1970	0.43	0.27	1.31	1.21	0.1	0.02	0	5.95		2.53	9.89
1980	1.36	0.69	1.27	1.19	0.07	0.02	0	7.56		3.7	13.33
1990	3.21	1.68	1.75	1.65	0.1	0.04	0	11.49		6.63	21.71
World										
1970	0.86	0.63	1.6	1.22	0.39	0.05	0.01	3.56	1.18		7.44
1980	1.98	1.25	1.97	1.62	0.35	0.06	0.01	5.09	1.61		11.28
1990	3.55	1.7	2.26	1.78	0.49	0.08	0.02	6.3	2.02		14.51

a. Manufactured goods include Standard International Trade Classifications 5 through 9.

b. Data exclude Europe from European Community and Germany; the Americas from the United States and Canada; East Asia from East Asia and Japan; and Australia and New Zealand from Australia and New Zealand.

Source: Calculations performed at the Australian National University using the International Economic Databank, compiled from United Nations, International Monetary Fund, and national statistics.

Each region's import ratio is an average of diverse experience in several countries. The diversity in manufactured import shares of GDP is greatest in East Asia, where Japan's ratio is well below that of the region's developing countries. Japan's ratio now is also well below that of the major economies in North America and Europe (the United States and Germany, respectively). The skewedness of Japan's resource endowment, with relative abundance of capital accompanying relative scarcity of natural resources, has a more powerful effect on Japan's than on the poorer East Asian economies' comparative advantage in manufactured goods. In 1970, when Japan was still in the process of catching up with North Atlantic capital endowment and output per capita, its extraregional manufactured import ratio was higher than that of the United States and Germany's. These data for the largest economies in each of these regions are notable for the strong growth in extraregional manufactured goods import ratios in Germany and the United States over the past two decades.

The number of variables affecting "economic" import ratios is so large, and the number of country observations so small, that we must take care in using the crude data in table 2 as an indicator of the extent of resistances to foreign trade. But, as a first guess, we can draw three rough conclusions. First, there are, on this evidence, no obvious differences in the contemporary openness to extraregional trade of Europe, East Asia, and North America. Second, resistances to extraregional trade seem to have declined markedly over the past two decades when intraregional trade was growing strongly. That means that if trade diversion through official discrimination was rising in Europe through the 1970s and 1980s, its impact on trade patterns was less powerful than the dynamic process of market integration that was continuing through these periods. Third, and with all the cautions of the preceding paragraphs, Japan's resistances to international trade may now be moderately larger than those of Germany and the United States.

Trade Intensities and Trade Bias

Table 3 sets out the intensity of regional and world trade in 1970 and 1990 for the same country groups whose trade shares are recorded in table 1. The table reveals high average trade intensities among the Asia-Pacific economies, alongside high average trade intensities among the economies of the European Community and Western Europe generally. Average trade intensities are also high among the Western Pacific and East Asian economies. Within the Asia-Pacific economy, trade intensities have generally fallen over the last twenty years, while in Western Europe they have generally risen.

It is noteworthy that, while East Asian trade intensities with Europe rose slightly from a low base over this period, trade intensities between

Table 3 Indexes of trade intensity for major trading regions, 1970 and 1990

	Western Pacific	Australasia	East Asia	North America	Asia Pacific	Western Europe	European Community	Rest of world
1970								
Western Pacific	2.79	2.06	2.91	1.64	2.13	0.39	0.34	0.81
Australasia	3.12	3.37	3.08	0.96	1.88	0.59	0.65	0.73
East Asia	2.73	1.81	2.88	1.77	2.18	0.35	0.25	0.82
North America	1.29	1.28	1.29	1.91	1.65	0.61	0.68	0.97
Asia Pacific	1.88	1.59	1.92	1.81	1.84	0.52	0.54	0.91
Western Europe	0.38	0.83	0.31	0.55	0.48	1.42	1.33	0.82
European Community	0.40	0.89	0.32	0.57	0.50	1.41	1.31	0.82
Rest of world	1.74	0.66	1.92	1.04	1.34	0.86	0.95	0.86
1990								
Western Pacific	2.24	1.95	2.26	1.54	1.90	0.39	0.53	0.69
Australasia	3.00	5.37	2.82	0.70	1.88	0.34	0.40	0.90
East Asia	2.19	1.70	2.22	1.60	1.90	0.40	0.43	0.68
North America	1.29	1.50	1.27	1.90	1.58	0.50	0.54	1.12
Asia Pacific	1.85	1.76	1.86	1.69	1.77	0.44	0.48	0.87
Western Europe	0.35	0.57	0.33	0.44	0.40	1.53	1.46	0.84
European Community	0.31	0.51	0.30	0.41	0.36	1.41	1.48	1.26
Rest of world	0.93	0.48	0.96	1.04	0.98	0.75	0.86	1.76

Source: Calculations performed at the Australian National University using the International Economic Databank, compiled from United Nations, International Monetary Fund, and national statistics.

Australasia and Europe and between North America and Europe fell noticeably.

High trade intensities among the Asia-Pacific economies are in part a product of higher trade intensities among the countries of Europe. One contributor to both phenomena is discrimination in European trade and economic policies, including the deterrents to European purchases from efficient suppliers of agricultural commodities.

East Asian trade has not only become more important to the East Asian economies themselves (Saxonhouse 1992). It has also become more important to North America, Europe, and Australasia. This is largely the result of East Asia's rapidly increasing weight in the world economy and world trade, and also reflects the globalization of East Asian trade. As table 3 shows, the intensity of the East Asian economies' trade with each other has actually declined over the last two decades, from an index value of 2.88 in 1970 to 2.22 in 1990.

Table 4 reports indexes of trade intensity among 15 individual Asia-Pacific economies in 1970 and 1990. The data show that the intensity of trade among Asia-Pacific economies is by no means uniform, although it is commonly high. The mean trade intensity in 1970 was 2.16, and by 1990 it had fallen to 1.84. In 1970, 50 percent of the intensity coefficients were above unity; that proportion had grown to 58 percent by 1990. The net effect of changes in Asia-Pacific trade relations over the past two decades has been to reduce the variation across Asia-Pacific trade intensities, and gradually to produce a more fully integrated trading community. The variance in trade intensities among the Asia-Pacific economies in 1970 was 19.03, but by 1990 it had fallen to 7.76. The Asia-Pacific economies are steadily developing more intensive trade ties with all countries in the region, not just the few partners with whom in the earlier period they had especially deep trade relations.

There is declining intensity in what had been the closest trading relationships, with the exceptions of the United States–Canada and Australia–New Zealand (both supported by trade discrimination) and China–Hong Kong (where low subjective variances had more powerful effects after the withdrawal of some official barriers). Asia-Pacific trade intensities still contain more variation than EC intensities (Drysdale 1988, 89), but this is steadily changing as resistances to trade fall across a wider range of trade flows within the region. Canada and Mexico stand out as economies that are weakly integrated with the Asia-Pacific economy as a whole, although they have very intense trade relationships with the United States.

Analysis of trade intensities in East Asia and the Pacific is elaborated in Drysdale (1988, especially chapter 4), where it is demonstrated that the changes in the pattern of trade intensity among Asia-Pacific economies between the 1960s and the 1980s resulted primarily from high trade biases or low relative resistances to trade, and not significantly from complementarity in trade among regional partners. In recent studies, Anderson (1992) and Anderson and Norheim (1992) replicate Drysdale's results and, in the latter study, positing stability in complementarities in Asia-Pacific trade, attribute variation in trade intensities to bias in regional trade.

In fact, there was a small increase in complementarities in Asia-Pacific trade relationships between 1970 and 1990, slightly offsetting a fall in regional trade bias. Trade intensity is the product of complementarity and bias in trade flows. Table 5 reveals that the mean trade bias index in 1970 was 3.0, and by 1990 it had fallen to 1.8. As with trade intensities, Asia-Pacific trade bias indexes became more uniform over time. The variance in trade bias indexes among the 15 individual Asia-Pacific economies was 78.7 in 1970, but by 1990 it had fallen to 8.5.

While the rapid expansion in import shares of output suggest a reduction in resistances to Asia-Pacific trade with the world, the falls over time in trade bias suggest larger falls in extraregional than intraregional trade resistances.

Growth in Intraindustry Trade

Intraindustry trade has become popular as another measure of international economic integration in studies of Japan's openness to international trade (Lawrence 1987, Krugman 1991). Low levels of intraindustry trade and trade in manufactured goods relative to GDP have been cited as evidence of the closed nature of Japan's markets to international transactions (Lawrence 1987).[5]

We discussed earlier how distance and relative resource adjustments can be expected to affect intraindustry trade. Other studies have also attempted to incorporate the distance variable into the analysis of intraindustry trade variations (Lawrence 1987, Balassa 1986). If transportation and communication technologies and factors affecting their application in domestic and international transactions do not change significantly over some time period, changes in the pattern of intraindustry trade can provide some measure of changes in the level and structure of international economic integration.

Tables 6 and 7 provide information about trends in intraindustry trade in all commodities and manufactures, respectively, for the Asia-Pacific economies in 1970, 1980, and 1990. These data reveal a generally rising trend in intraindustry trade for all 15 economies over the 20-year period,

---

5. It has become popular to invoke the unique institutional characteristics of the Japanese economy as an explanator of Japan's trade patterns in general and the closed nature of Japan's markets to international transactions in particular. The Japanese *keiretsu* (affiliated companies) are prominent in this discussion. However, the argument is by no means settled. Two recent studies, one by Noland (1993) and one by Sheard (1992), illustrate the difference in analytic approaches to this issue.

Table 4 Trade intensities for 15 individual Asia-Pacific economies, 1970 and 1990

	Australia	New Zealand	Japan	Korea	India	Malaysia	Philip-pines	Singa-pore	Thailand	China	Hong Kong	Taiwan	United States	Canada	Mexico
1970[a]															
Australia		14.28	5.01	0.43	1.21	3.15	2.45	2.91	1.98	4.67	1.95	0.84	0.99	0.65	0.32
New Zealand	5.80		1.77	0.38	0.18	1.35	1.13	1.28	1.04	0.58	0.47	0.20	1.25	0.73	0.28
Japan	2.10	1.51		6.27	0.72	1.74	5.18	2.63	5.65	4.90	3.54	3.62	2.33	0.64	0.53
Korea	0.24	0.19	5.27		0.08	0.32	0.29	1.60	1.50	0.00	3.27	0.87	3.58	0.52	0.50
India	1.19	0.99	2.68	0.26		1.62	0.21	1.33	1.00	0.00	1.08	0.16	1.06	0.41	0.60
Malaysia	1.61	1.28	3.52	4.03	0.53		3.99	27.06	2.20	2.25	1.27	1.35	1.02	0.44	0.33
Philippines	0.32	0.30	7.71	4.68	0.11	0.06		0.86	0.78	0.00	1.30	1.93	3.24	0.08	0.00
Singapore	2.32	1.12	1.41	1.09	0.88	44.31	0.60		8.06	2.44	4.00	0.84	0.83	0.26	0.37
Thailand	0.37	0.25	4.92	0.39	0.98	11.88	0.24	8.66		0.00	7.71	5.08	1.05	0.03	0.01
China	1.48	0.77	2.58	0.00	0.00	8.32	0.00	8.35	0.00		25.21	0.00	0.00	0.24	0.00
Hong Kong	2.01	2.13	1.37	1.03	0.09	2.81	1.48	5.12	2.47	0.73		1.02	2.81	0.63	0.29
Taiwan	1.02	0.15	2.88	3.00	0.04	1.76	2.60	3.13	4.44	0.00	9.64		3.09	0.81	0.07
United States	1.44	0.74	1.82	2.01	1.65	0.29	1.75	0.61	0.78	0.00	0.84	1.12		4.25	3.95
Canada	0.80	0.65	0.86	0.16	1.03	0.17	0.39	0.08	0.11	1.36	0.12	0.11	4.70		0.60
Mexico	0.16	0.09	1.00	0.02	0.08	0.02	0.14	0.01	0.12	0.00	0.11	0.22	4.45	0.21	

1990[b]

	Australia	New Zealand	Japan	Korea	India	Malaysia	Philippines	Singapore	Thailand	China	Hong Kong	Taiwan	United States	Canada	Mexico
Australia		19.49	4.75	2.94	1.80	2.37	2.13	2.63	1.21	1.39	1.03	2.55	0.71	0.45	0.18
New Zealand	16.38		2.52	2.35	1.09	2.38	2.26	0.77	0.98	0.58	0.63	1.45	0.91	0.47	1.07
Japan	2.03	1.64		3.18	0.86	2.47	2.10	2.13	3.39	1.22	1.84	3.41	2.06	0.63	0.64
Korea	1.47	1.01	3.30		1.24	1.34	1.95	1.52	1.51	0.00	2.37	1.32	2.16	0.87	0.67
India	1.10	0.73	1.70	0.55		1.21	0.51	1.10	1.65	0.13	1.33	0.48	1.26	0.29	0.30
Malaysia	1.48	0.93	2.42	2.54	2.46		3.38	13.79	3.93	1.26	1.35	1.94	1.16	0.22	0.17
Philippines	1.05	0.46	3.16	1.56	0.04	2.11		1.77	2.16	0.46	1.73	1.90	2.61	0.43	0.90
Singapore	2.24	1.61	1.40	1.24	3.22	17.85	3.26		7.52	0.92	2.80	1.10	1.33	0.25	0.13
Thailand	1.45	0.74	2.77	0.97	0.45	3.47	1.88	4.46		0.75	1.95	1.11	1.56	0.38	0.30
China	0.77	0.37	2.22	0.00	0.47	0.79	0.77	1.74	1.42		16.27	1.12	0.72	0.24	0.12
Hong Kong	1.35	0.75	0.91	1.29	0.57	0.96	2.67	1.93	1.48	14.98		1.76	1.66	0.53	0.29
Taiwan	2.07	1.39	2.18	0.95	0.50	1.42	2.98	1.80	1.88	3.45	2.10		2.50	0.76	0.39
United States	1.69	1.03	1.70	1.75	0.83	1.02	1.38	1.06	0.74	0.64	0.64	1.71		5.22	5.32
Canada	0.49	0.41	0.84	0.51	0.29	0.21	0.33	0.15	0.35	0.59	0.19	0.48	4.85		0.31
Mexico	0.17	0.18	0.85	0.09	0.18	0.30	0.10	0.06	0.15	0.20	0.10	0.39	4.98	0.69	

a. Mean = 2.1578095; standard deviation = 4.3724398; variance = 19.027191.
b. Mean = 1.8426667; standard deviation = 2.7817394; variance = 7.7612261.

Source: Calculations performed at the Australian National University using the International Economic Databank, based on the United Nations, International Monetary Fund, and national statistics.

Table 5 Index of trade bias for 15 individual Asia-Pacific economies, 1970 and 1990

	Australia	New Zealand	Japan	Korea	India	Malaysia	Philippines	Singapore	Thailand	China	Hong Kong	Taiwan	United States	Canada	Mexico
1970[a]															
Australia		16.9	1.67	0.84	3.29	2.89	3.7	3.66	2.8	12.59	1.89	2.05	0.87	1.04	0.83
New Zealand	16.64		1.27	0.48	0.69	2.33	1.98	1.99	1.56	6.65	0.54	0.6	1.59	1.89	0.57
Japan	1.63	1.1		4.95	3.21		4.68	2.28	4.19	4.11	2.93	4.18	2.01	0.57	0.51
Korea	0.3	3.59	3.24		3.09	0.59	2.25	1.81	2.56		2.25	5.14	2.45	0.8	0.29
India	3.03	0.12	1.49	1.17			6.19	5.19	0.12	0.02	2.52	1.85	0.9	0.02	
Malaysia	2.04	1.36	0.96	2.39	7.35		4.77	5.19	4.04	0.82	2.78	2.12	0.68	0.65	0.6
Philippines	0.91	0.97	1.49	2.05	3.95			1.71	2.98		3.35	3.42	2.76	0.13	0.61
Singapore	2.12	0.98	0.62	1.51			0.85		6.6		3.75	1.82	0.62	0.6	0.83
Thailand	1.06	3.23	2.41	2.34	119.03	12.84	2.1	3.61		1.22	12.06	9.36	1.09	0.28	19.26
China	1.41	0.83	2.74	0.0		6.33		5.8	0.04		12.36		0.0	0.41	0.17
Hong Kong	1.7	2.77	1.28	0.6	3.61		2.39	2.37	2.03	5.13		4.58	2.02	0.79	0.44
Taiwan	0.91	0.97	3.83	6.22	9.59	2.07		1.71	2.98		6.09		2.26	0.99	0.16
United States	1.05	0.62	1.25	1.66	1.3	0.3	1.7	0.65	0.55	2.77	1.09	1.03		3.09	3.09
Canada	0.72	0.68	0.43	0.33	0.43	0.18	0.44	0.11	0.12		0.23	0.35	3.13		0.62
Mexico	0.36	0.21	0.64	0.07	0.01	0.16	0.31	0.15	0.47		0.31	0.89	3.79	0.34	

1990[b]

Australia	27.54	24.69	1.46	1.6	4.97	2.93	3.05	1.71	1.08	2.19	1.38	1.3	0.65	0.56	0.38
New Zealand	1.67	1.3	1.39	1.67	3.33	3.24	2.93	1.03	1.26	1.22	0.83	1.1	1.33	0.8	1.1
Japan	1.28	0.74		2.93	2.34	1.88	2.17	1.58	2.76	1.39	1.78	2.95	1.74	0.6	0.88
Korea	1.77	1.22	3.67		2.91	1.17	1.91	1.2	1.6		1.22	1.18	1.72	0.86	1.12
India	1.64	1.06	1.81	1.33		2.03	3.8	2.29	0.98	2.42	0.93	1.47	0.68	0.25	0.70
Malaysia	1.24	0.72	1.21	1.4	2.04			7.9	3.01		1.18	1.32	0.9	0.37	0.24
Philippines	1.64	1.17	2.16	1.33	1.9			1.52	1.6		0.95	1.49	2.2	0.66	0.2
Singapore	1.63		0.93	0.78		10.98	3.16		6.09	1.01	2.0	2.24	1.04	0.24	0.16
Thailand	1.16		2.16	1.23	1.82	3.4	2.61	3.85		1.00	1.11	1.47	1.38	0.47	0.61
China	1.31	0.55	1.66		2.02			1.4	2.09		6.51		1.01	0.54	0.6
Hong Kong	1.5	0.75	0.82	0.67	1.85	1.08	2.65	1.52	1.34	11.19		2.16	1.64	0.82	0.41
Taiwan	1.27	0.99	2.36	1.0	3.0	1.97	3.03	1.57	2.27		2.86		1.91	0.7	0.62
United States	0.44	0.78	1.45	1.3	0.62	0.81	1.46	0.87	0.6	0.76	0.63	1.34		4.46	6.49
Canada	0.24	0.37	0.63	0.44	0.33	0.26	0.45	0.16	0.32	0.84	0.22	0.29	3.61		0.61
Mexico		0.16	0.36	0.13	0.13	0.06	0.08	0.08	0.07	0.33	0.16		2.68	0.19	

a. Mean = 3.0366495; standard deviation = 8.8924168; variance = 78.667473.
b. Mean = 1.8456186; standard deviation = 2.9236399; variance = 8.5036102.

Source: Calculations performed at the Australian National University using the International Economic Databank, based on the United Nations, International Monetary Fund, and national statistics.

Table 6   Indexes of intraindustry trade in all commodities for 15 Asia-Pacific economies, 1970, 1980, and 1990

Country	1970		1980		1990	
	Index	Rank	Index	Rank	Index	Rank
China	0.14	11	0.22	11	0.38	10
Hong Kong	0.31	4	0.41	4	0.47	5
Taiwan	0.31	5	0.33	7	0.48	4
Korea	0.17	10	0.35	6	0.44	7
Japan	0.24	7	0.22	12	0.32	12
Indonesia	0.07	15	0.15	15	0.21	15
Malaysia	0.19	9	0.30	8	0.46	6
Philippines	0.08	14	0.30	9	0.39	8
Singapore	0.54	2	0.52	2	0.65	1
Thailand	0.10	13	0.22	13	0.36	11
Mexico	0.27	6	0.36	5	0.38	9
Canada	0.56	1	0.53	1	0.64	2
United States	0.49	3	0.46	3	0.63	3
Australia	0.22	8	0.24	10	0.31	13
New Zealand	0.12	12	0.17	14	0.27	14

a. Indexes are calculated for intraindustry trade at the Standard International Trade Classification three-digit level.

Source: Calculations performed at the Australian National University using the International Economic Databank from United Nations and national statistics.

with the exception of Australia in manufactures from 1980 to 1990. The rise in intraindustry trade for all commodities is nonmonotonic for Japan, Singapore, and Canada: their indexes fell in 1980 before rising in 1990; similarly, the manufactures intraindustry trade index is nonmonotonic for Taiwan, Japan, Indonesia, Canada, and Australia. However, the mean index of intraindustry trade for these economies in all commodity trade rose from 0.25 to 0.43, and the mean index for manufactured goods trade rose from 0.28 to 0.46. Asia-Pacific economies, on this measure, have become more deeply integrated with the international economy over these years.

Since high trade intensity is, like high levels of intraindustry trade, associated with relatively low resistances to trade, it is not unexpected that there has been some correlation between the growth of intraindustry trade among the Asia-Pacific economies and strong intensities in trade within the region.[6]

Table 7 sets out indexes of intraindustry trade in manufactured goods for trade among the Asia-Pacific economies in 1970 and 1990. All these countries, with the exception of Australia, have experienced growth in overall intraindustry trade in manufactured goods over this period. Significantly, even for Australia, intraindustry trade has generally risen for

---

6. In 1970 the correlation between trade intensity and intraindustry trade among the 15 Asia-Pacific economies was 0.038; it rose steadily to 0.116 in 1980 and was 0.129 in 1990.

Table 7 Indexes of intraindustry trade in manufactures for 15 Asia-Pacific economies, 1970, 1980, and 1990

Country	1970 Index	1970 Rank	1980 Index	1980 Rank	1990 Index	1990 Rank
China	0.19	10	0.28	10	0.40	10
Hong Kong	0.33	5	0.46	4	0.50	5
Taiwan	0.36	4	0.35	8	0.49	6
Korea	0.19	9	0.39	5	0.48	7
Japan	0.33	6	0.27	11	0.36	12
Indonesia	0.14	12	0.08	15	0.19	15
Malaysia	0.13	13	0.37	6	0.58	4
Philippines	0.07	14	0.17	14	0.42	9
Singapore	0.44	3	0.65	1	0.71	1
Thailand	0.05	15	0.24	13	0.39	11
Mexico	0.29	7	0.36	7	0.48	8
Canada	0.63	1	0.62	2	0.68	3
United States	0.57	2	0.62	3	0.69	2
Australia	0.28	8	0.29	9	0.26	14
New Zealand	0.16	11	0.27	12	0.32	13

a. Manufactures include Standard International Trade Classifications 5 through 8.

Source: Calculations performed at the Australian National University using the International Economic Databank, from United Nations and national statistics.

trade flows within the region. The country patterns of intraindustry trade growth are of particular interest. Intraindustry trade within North America, among the East Asian economies, within Australasia, and between Australasia and Southeast Asia has grown more strongly than intraindustry trade more generally. Casual inspection of table 7 gives a powerful impression of steadily falling resistances to trade in the Asia-Pacific economy over these two decades.

At first sight, this evidence of falling intraregional trade resistances might seem to contradict the evidence in tables 4 and 5 of rising intraregional relative to extraregional resistances. It does not. Taken together, tables 4 to 7 indicate falling resistances to all international trade, but larger falls in resistances to extraregional trade, and higher absolute levels of resistances to extraregional trade at the end of the period.

The impression of steadily falling intraregional trade resistances is confirmed by closer analysis of intraindustry trade in the Asia-Pacific economy. A recent study by Fukasaku (1992) explores the role of intraindustry trade in the economic integration of, and determinants of, intraindustry trade among, the Western Pacific economies. He concludes that greater similarities in demand and production structures and lower transport costs between trade partners within the region are associated strongly with higher levels of intraindustry trade. Here we extend Fukasaku's analysis to include intraindustry trade flows among all the Asia-Pacific economies (table 8) and compare the strength of factors affecting intraindustry trade within the whole region in 1980 and 1990.

Table 8   Determinants of Asia-Pacific intraindustry trade, 1980–90

Independent variable[a]	1980	1990
Constant	0.43**	0.73**
	(3.98)[b]	(7.78)
RPC	−0.002*	−0.0015*
	(−1.44)	(−1.81)
RFE	−0.007**	−0.005**
	(−2.17)	(−2.20)
DIS(LOG)	−0.023*	−0.054**
	(−1.92)	(−5.16)
DUM 1	0.012	0.016
	(0.125)	(0.20)
DUM 2	0.31**	0.177*
	(2.53)	(1.69)
DUM 3	0.14*	0.25**
	(1.31)	(2.68)
DUM 4	0.05*	0.032
	(1.15)	(0.82)
R-squared	0.17	0.36
F-values	5.54	15.38

* = statistically significant at the 10 percent level; ** = statistically significant at the 5 percent level

a. See text for explanation of variable names.

b. Numbers in parentheses are *t*-statistics.

Source: Calculations performed at the Australian National University using the International Economic Databank, from United Nations and national statistics.

Following the line of discussion in previous sections, we hypothesize that bilateral levels of intraindustry trade will be:

■ negatively correlated with differences in per capita incomes, similarity in which represents similarities in demand patterns;

■ negatively correlated with differences in relative factor endowments;

■ negatively correlated with average relative distance from other trading partners, representing objective trade resistances;

■ positively correlated with the existence of common borders with trading partners (for which a dummy variable is introduced);

■ positively correlated with participation in a discriminatory regional trade arrangement (dummy variables are introduced for participation in ASEAN, the Australia–New Zealand Closer Economic Relations [CER] arrangement, and the Canada-US Free Trade Area).

Balassa and Bauwens (1988) use a similar model in testing for influences in intraindustry trade.

Hence, the basic model of intraindustry trade flows (IIT_{ij}) is shown as:

$$IIT_{ij} = F(RPC_{ij}, RFE_{ij}, DIS_{ij}, DUMS) + U_{ij}$$

where RPC is relative differences in per capita income, defined as the absolute difference in per capita income divided by the average per capita income of the two trading partners; RFE is relative differences in factor endowments, defined as the relative difference in the share of primary products in total merchandise exports; DIS is an index of distance between trading partners (distances[7] were taken mainly from the 1982 *George Philips Universal Atlas*); and $DUMS$ represents the following dummy variables: *DUM 1* is for trade between countries with a common border (e.g., China–Hong Kong, United States–Mexico; the variable is set equal to 1 if countries i and j share a border); *DUM 2* represents participation in the Canada-US free trade arrangement; *DUM 3* is for the ANZ CER arrangement between Australia and New Zealand; *DUM 4* is for ASEAN; and U_{ij} is the disturbance term. Table 8 reports the results of estimations from these data for the Asia-Pacific economies in both 1980 and 1990.

Estimates of the coefficients of independent variables included in the regression analysis all have the expected signs, and all variables except the dummy variables for ASEAN and US–Canada border trade are statistically significant in 1990. When the sample was expanded to include European countries, similar analysis of this larger sample (not reported here) strengthened the explanatory power of all independent variables. A notable feature of the result for the Asia-Pacific economies, however, is the steady increase in the importance of the specific independent variables in determining patterns of intraindustry trade over time.

The place of Japan in Asia-Pacific intraindustry trade has particular interest. In his study, Fukasaku (1992) included a dummy variable for trade with Japan to test whether Japan had a negative effect on intraindustry trade levels. While the coefficient for the Japan dummy in his study has the correct sign, the results are statistically insignificant. Between 1980 and 1990, Japan's intraindustry trade with the world at large rose somewhat. But the intraindustry trade index for Japan of 0.36 in 1990 is low compared with indexes of 0.69 for the United States, 0.68 for Canada, and higher indexes for Mexico and all other East Asian economies except Indonesia. Subtracting intra–North American trade reduces the Canadian index to 0.41 and the United States index to 0.61, similar to Canada and somewhat higher than Australia of the 1980s (0.31). Australia, more than Japan, has high relative isolation from potential trade

---

7. Distances are from capital to capital. In those cases where figures are not available, calculations are made according to the shipping distances between main ports from *World Map*, China Map-Making Publishing House, 1990.

and skewed relative resource endowments. Like Japan, Australia is becoming less isolated as the center of gravity of the world economy moves toward the Western Pacific. The Australian outlier was once easily explained by high Australian protection. Following substantial trade liberalization and internationalization through the 1980s, the Australian case stands as evidence of the power of relative geographic isolation and skewed resource endowments in deterring intraindustry trade.

Table 7 reveals that there was a marked increase in Japan's intraindustry trade with the Asia-Pacific economies—especially with other East Asian economies, less so for North America—between 1970 and 1990. In the earlier period extreme differences in relative factor endowments dominated intraindustry patterns of trade for Japan. These developments over the last decade are reflected in the regression results in table 8, as income growth within the region and growing similarity of per capita income level and demand patterns among proximate traders in East Asia was associated with higher levels of intraindustry trade between Japan and its East Asian neighbors as well as among the East Asian economies more generally.

The Prospects for the Pacific Model

The Pacific model of economic integration has contributed substantially to the dynamism of the Asia-Pacific economies in recent decades. Its main elements include the Western Pacific economies' unilateral and multilateral trade liberalization, encouraged by the "prisoner's delight" trade policy game that has emerged since the mid-1980s. It is built upon market integration, with resistances to trade being reduced by enterprises' successful search for and investment in more profitable patterns of trade. It has been associated with rapid expansion of both extraregional and intraregional trade, the latter being quantitatively larger because East Asia has been expanding its share in world production and trade, and not through trade discrimination.

What are the prospects for continued gains from trade expansion within the Pacific model of regional integration? The logic of the "prisoner's delight" remains powerful. The reduction of resistances to trade through market processes still has great momentum, currently most powerfully around the borders of the People's Republic of China (and on a smaller scale, Vietnam). The beneficent processes of market integration are likely to continue unless the intrusion of new official barriers to extraregional trade from outside the Western Pacific destabilizes the political economy of regional trade policy.

We judge the odds to favor the continuation of market integration in the Asia-Pacific region. Success will, however, require careful management of two interrelated challenges: from the implementation of the North

American Free Trade Agreement, and from international reaction to disappointing outcomes from the Uruguay Round.

We accept that it is highly probable that the United States will proceed with the NAFTA, and subsequently with the negotiation of similar arrangements within the Enterprise for the Americas Initiative, aimed at liberalizing trade "from the Yukon to Tierra del Fuego." It will be a central challenge to post-NAFTA trade strategy to hold the United States to its announced policy to reduce intra-American trade barriers without raising protection against the rest of the world, in an environment that will contain pressures and temptations to raise barriers.

This vast exercise in discriminatory integration will be the main trade policy preoccupation of the US administration through the first half of the 1990s and beyond. Despite the small scale of most of the economies south of Mexico, the implementation of the Enterprise for the Americas Initiative will place significant pressure for structural change on the United States and Canada at a time of historically low rates of growth in economic output.

The diversion of administrative talent and congressional time, energy, and political will to the pan-American exercise will inevitably limit the capacity for American initiative in multilateral, regional, and non-American bilateral trade policy reform. The rest of the world—or those parts of it that are interested in preserving and extending the postwar system of relatively liberal, multilateral trade—will have to build strategic responses around the need to economize on a scarce and valuable commodity: American trade liberalization initiative.

These post-NAFTA strategic responses will be played out in an environment of significantly diminished intellectual and political commitment in the United States to free and multilateral trade. This diminished commitment had its origins in American political responses to the international economic problems of the 1980s—which themselves principally derived from errors in domestic macroeconomic policy, but were associated politically with the economic success of Japan and other East Asian economies. It has been entrenched by disappointment with the difficulties of achieving a satisfactory outcome in the Uruguay Round, by the inability of the Japanese government to share political leadership in an area of huge shared interests, and by the unwillingness of the EC leadership to share responsibility for the completion of an agreement that has been substantially negotiated.

In the new environment of diminished intellectual commitment to liberal trade, preferential trade has become an acceptable strategy (Bhagwati 1992). We expect that the pan-American initiatives will be successful politically, despite the strains of structural adjustment out of labor-intensive activities that will accompany them in North America. They will support and extend the recent shift to outward-oriented development strategies in Mexico, Chile, Brazil, Argentina, and elsewhere on the South

American continent. The emergence of Latin America from the debt-ridden stagnation of the 1980s will be seen politically as an important vindication of regionally oriented and preferential trade policies. Expanded US exports and investment south of the Rio Grande, modest though it will be in comparison with total US trade and economic activity, will enhance the aura of success.

Meanwhile, there will have been no diminution of trade tensions across the Pacific, especially with Japan and China, but also with other dynamic East Asian economies. Presuming that there is no early, decisive action to correct North American fiscal imbalances, the return of economic growth will be accompanied by the reemergence of large current account deficits, exacerbated by sluggish growth in Japan in the period immediately ahead. The bilateral deficits with East Asia will again be identified as a principal cause. The diversion of American focus away from the trans-Pacific economic relationships to the Americas (and Eastern Europe) will sustain the misperception of the 1980s and early 1990s that East Asian barriers to trade are the root cause of bilateral deficits. Trade diversion to higher-cost American sources of at least some goods and services will diminish to some extent the competitiveness of US suppliers in East Asian markets. The same trade diversion will, without any deliberate action in the Western Pacific, enhance the competitiveness of East Asian producers in each other's markets. The inevitable consequence will be some further intensification of regional trade within East Asia and the Western Pacific—again, quite independently of deliberate policy action. This, we think, is the dangerous environment in which Australasia and the East Asian economies will need to formulate post-NAFTA trade strategies in relation to the Americas.

The environment for liberal trade in the United States is likely to be diminished through this period by complications in the political economy of European unity. The accommodation of the restructuring of the Eastern European and Russian economies and recent steps toward European monetary union place pressure on European unity and capacity for adjustment. Europe can be expected to place low value on reducing trade barriers to the rest of the world.

Despite their relative decline, North American markets remain important to internationally oriented growth in East Asia and the Western Pacific. We consider the first Asia-Pacific trade objective in the post-NAFTA environment to be reduction of the risk of American economic integration being accompanied by increased barriers at the border to non-American imports. Our view is that this objective is best secured by directing the powerful pressures now promoting regional integration to the cause of multilateral liberalization.

Post-NAFTA options will be shaped significantly by the outcome of the Uruguay Round, which must finally emerge during 1993. There are now only two options: agreement on the substantial but limited package that came together in the months preceding the 1992 G-7 meeting, or no agreement at all.

Even a limited agreement would represent a substantial strengthening of the multilateral system: the extension of GATT disciplines to agriculture, textiles, and a range of services that have become much more important in international trade in recent years, and significant progress in reducing residual barriers to manufacturing trade in the OECD, Korea, and some other developing countries. It would be well worth having. But the modesty of the outcome on some of the issues that emerged in the Uruguay Round, including European and East Asian agriculture, is likely to generate disappointment in the United States. No agreement at all—not a likely outcome, but possible—would be the trigger for comprehensive disillusionment with the GATT–based system in the United States.

Agreement in the Uruguay Round would strengthen US commitment to implement intra-American integration without raising external barriers. This would be no safeguard against discrimination, especially given the ease with which discrimination is now introduced through nontariff measures (Bhagwati 1992). The strengthened GATT disciplines would, however, provide a first line of defense against the raising of barriers to imports from the rest of the world. The Western Pacific economies could seek to build further upon their liberalization given the reality of recent, substantial success.

Without agreement in Geneva, there would be a requirement to engage the United States urgently in discussions aimed at building confidence in an alternative framework for liberal trade, supporting the old disciplines to the greatest extent possible, and going beyond them where practicable.

Each Western Pacific economy will have its own bilateral trade policy agenda with the United States after the conclusion of the round. But now, unlike in previous periods as recent as the mid-1980s, each recognizes that its interests in continued favorable access to neighboring regional markets is quantitatively larger than its trade interests in the Americas. Each must weigh the effects of destabilization of the liberal trading environment in East Asia and the Western Pacific, and the favorable environment it provides for extending market integration in the region, against the possibility of negotiating bilaterally favorable access to the Americas.

There has been some recent discussion of extending NAFTA into the Western Pacific—of allowing some Western Pacific economies to "dock on" to North American free trade. This is not a viable or useful strategy, for reasons that vary from economy to economy.

Japan, at the center of trade expansion in the Western Pacific in recent decades, and less dependent on intraregional trade simply because it cannot trade internationally with itself, comes closest to being more heavily dependent on trans-Pacific than Western Pacific trade.

The economic incentive for seeking to negotiate bilaterally, perhaps toward a free trade area, would be strongest for Japan. Our judgment is that Japan is likely to remain strongly aware of its interests in nondiscriminatory trade expansion within East Asia and the Western Pacific. Heightening US tensions, reflected in rising American barriers against Japanese exports, perhaps in the aftermath of Uruguay Round failure, would be more likely to diminish Japanese inhibition about the discriminatory expansion of East Asian trade than to trigger negotiation of bilateral free trade with the United States. Nor would these circumstances be favorable for initiation of bilateral negotiations by the United States. More likely, Japanese interest would quicken in Asia-Pacific free trade, within the context of APEC. There would be considerable Japanese resistance to regional liberalization with discrimination against the rest of the world, given Japanese sensitivity to its increasing worldwide economic interests.

For the United States to invite some Western Pacific states to "dock on" to NAFTA, but to exclude Japan, would invite tension and dangerous confrontation, increasing incipient support for East Asian discriminatory regionalism, including initiatives between Japan and China.

China, with its growth closely linked to export expansion and now integrated inextricably with Hong Kong and Taiwanese trading interests, would be threatened more immediately than Japan by tendencies to post-NAFTA protectionism in the Americas. Subject to annual reviews of its most-favored-nation status by the United States since the 1989 Tiananmen Square massacre, and with its trading relationship with the United States overhung by political considerations, China needs the security of GATT membership and disciplines. Impressive recent progress on price and trade reform is removing the trade-related reasons for China's exclusion from GATT membership. But the political dimension of China's trading relationship with the United States has become more complex and difficult with the diminution of its strategic importance since the collapse of the Soviet Union, the diminution of presidential power over the past year, and the possibility of a change to a president with a less acute awareness of the role of liberal foreign trade in long-term economic and political liberalization in China. China may have an opportunity to press its claims for GATT membership in the aftermath of agreement in the Uruguay Round, given its current preparedness to negotiate a range of market access issues in the context of GATT membership (Drysdale and Elek 1992). It is unlikely to be able to secure its trading interests in the United States in the aftermath of Uruguay Round failure. In either case, it is inconceivable that a political basis could be established for Sino-American bilateral free trade in the foreseeable future.

The ASEAN group, experiencing less political and trade tension with the United States, and like the United States currently committed to discriminatory regional trade liberalization (through the ASEAN Free

Trade Area), is the least unlikely East Asian candidate for bilateral free trade with the Americas. But even in ASEAN, such a development would run counter to increasing recognition of wider East Asian economic interests. The trans-Pacific trade tensions of recent years have been greatest with Japan and China, and to a lesser extent with Taiwan and Korea. But they have strong echoes in ASEAN, for example in the persistent Malaysian support for a form of East Asian economic cooperation that would have no place for the English-speaking countries of the Northeast or Southwest Pacific.

Australia and New Zealand have the least economic interest among the Western Pacific economies in discriminatory free trade with the Americas (Anderson 1992). But in an uncertain world—and particularly in the post–NAFTA world of trans-Pacific tension that could follow failure in the Uruguay Round—the political and cultural tug of membership of an extended pan-American free trade area, if it were ever offered, would not be negligible. In considering discriminatory free trade with the Americas, Australia would be choosing between its economic and geostrategic interests on the one hand, and old cultural and political affinities of undoubted continuing importance to Australians. To choose discriminatory trade with America in these circumstances, without first having entered parallel arrangements with Indonesia or ASEAN, and without the ASEAN countries having announced a similar choice, would be seen in East Asia as a decision to avoid being part of the emerging, dynamic international pluralism of the Western Pacific. An Australian choice along these lines would exacerbate and encourage a cultural and racial interpretation of wider trans-Pacific tensions. It could deepen and entrench the fracture that has recently become important in trans-Pacific economic and political relations.

In our judgment, the Asia-Pacific region's interests in conserving as much as possible of the Asia-Pacific model of open trade would be undermined by the extension of NAFTA-style discrimination on a bilateral basis to any single countries in the Western Pacific. The particular objections introduced in the preceding paragraphs would not hold for extension of NAFTA-type arrangements to all APEC members. Australia and New Zealand would not cut themselves off from critical economic and geostrategic interests in East Asia, nor ASEAN from strengthening perceptions of an East Asian destiny.

But most of the problems of a discriminatory Asia-Pacific free trade area that we identified four years ago (Drysdale and Garnaut 1989) would still be present. There is no political basis now in Sino-American relations for such intimate integration—indeed there is somewhat less basis than there was four years ago, although the economic conditions are more favorable now. The exclusion of Vietnam and Russia would be felt more heavily than in 1989. We must now recognize Vietnam's cooperation with APEC members in the Cambodian settlement, and the new Vietnamese commitment to internationally oriented growth. The circumstances of Russia—the rapid expansion of trade across the Chinese border and the strong Korean interest—make its discriminatory exclusion more difficult. Vietnam may be able to meet the conditions of NAFTA-style integration within the foreseeable future, although the political relationship with the United States could not yet support its inclusion. Russia would not be able to meet the economic conditions in the foreseeable future.

The discriminatory exclusion of India and the rest of South Asia from trade and specialization with the dynamic Asia-Pacific economies would be felt more keenly now than ever. Economic success in China has left South Asia as the world's largest (although not least tractable) development problem. The Indian government is seeking to implement substantial external and domestic liberalization, within the constraints of a democratic polity. The collapse of the Soviet Union has removed a Cold War taint in relations with the West, and there has been some easing of political tensions with China. There is no Asia-Pacific interest in putting barriers in the way of Indian trade expansion.

In the aftermath of failure in the Uruguay Round, there would be some Asia-Pacific sentiment in favor of punishing the European Community. But would any substantial Asia-Pacific interest be served by formation of an Asia-Pacific bloc along NAFTA lines that discriminated against Europe—at a time when Western Europe is grappling with the accommodation of political change in its formerly communist neighbors, and straining at domestic economic integration? We think not. The Asia-Pacific interest is in building conditions within which Europe will recognize its own interest in liberal multilateral trade, not in entrenching the barriers that have been placed in the way of Europe's economic relations with the rest of the world.

Our survey of the constraints, the possibilities, and the interests of the Asia-Pacific economies leads us back to the point we reached four years ago. The first objective must be a conservative one: to stop new, official trade barriers getting in the way of the powerful processes of market integration that have been at work in the region in recent decades. The reduction of subjective resistances would be enhanced in the aftermath of the Uruguay Round by trade liberalization among the member economies of the APEC forum. But the crucial steps can be taken on a multilateral basis, without any element of NAFTA-style discrimination. This can occur alongside the implementation of the Enterprise for the Americas Initiative, reducing its risks for the Americas and the Western Pacific, reducing its costs, and delivering substantial benefits. The sensible path ahead, therefore, is to provide opportunities to "dock on" to APEC—to intensify cooperation among the APEC countries, and to ensure that newly opening economies have nondiscriminatory access to expanding markets within APEC.

In the aftermath of agreement at Geneva, regional governments could do much to enhance the processes of market integration through improvement in public goods supporting international transactions within the Pacific. The first steps have been identified in the APEC context: facilitation of business information flows and communications; harmonization of some aspects of standards, measures, and commercial law; and so on (Elek 1992a). Other steps could aim to reduce resistances through the provision of a wider range of public goods to support the international market: measures to reduce uncertainty about future market access (arising from resort to arbitrary and discriminatory measures to deal with losses of market share); to loosen physical bottlenecks (ranging from harbors to telecommunications, and affecting the most rapidly growing parts of the region, including China, Indonesia, and Thailand); and to diminish differences in domestic rules and legislation (including divergent standards relating to safety, quality, and environmental matters and different approaches to commercial legislation affecting trade and investment). This should soon be augmented by agreement on a package of nondiscriminatory trade liberalization measures to reduce official barriers on a sectoral basis, covering sectors in which APEC members have major interests, and in which it is judged that Uruguay Round outcomes can be taken further. Progress is more likely if the issues can be broken down into discrete and well-defined components on each of which there is strong support from a number of APEC members (Elek 1992a, 6).

Early candidates for sectoral agreements among APEC members to liberalize trade on a nondiscriminatory basis could include steel, grain, textiles, and civil aviation. China and the ASEAN countries would be encouraged to enter Uruguay Round–style understandings on steel trade liberalization by the prospect of easier flows of direct investment and capital in the context of greater confidence in the market environment (Drysdale 1992). China and Taiwan, which are not parties to the Uruguay Round, could be drawn into sectoral understandings, in the context of APEC support for their GATT membership. APEC understandings on insurance against market instability might encourage commitment to agricultural internationalization in China and ASEAN (Garnaut and Ma 1992).

It would be even more important to take early, more comprehensive and decisive steps on sectoral trade liberalization in the aftermath of failure in the Uruguay Round. The first priority would be to implement on a multilateral basis, but through regional agreement, as many as possible of the commitments to trade liberalization in key sectors that had been negotiated prior to the failure of the negotiations. Textiles—especially the phasing out of the Multi-Fiber Arrangement in North America—would need to be an early target. So would metals, including steel—bringing in APEC members who did not participate in this component of the multilateral negotiations.

Parts of the American political and administrative leadership would recognize the value of upholding and strengthening trans-Pacific links as NAFTA is implemented and extended. They provide the political base upon which APEC liberalization must be built.

The building of support for nondiscriminatory, APEC-based liberalization may make it necessary to limit European free-riding on multilateral liberalization in some commodities—perhaps agriculture. The whole framework of open regionalism would fail unless this were limited to exclusion of export subsidies through measures that are the regional equivalent of national antidumping. Any more, and measures of this kind would entrench the European-Pacific trade tensions and divisions that they were designed partially to avoid.

Active participation in APEC-based liberalization itself would help to sustain outward-looking American interests at a time when the Enterprise for the Americas Initiative was diverting American eyes away from the Western Pacific. It would hold out some prospect of securing the conservative goal of strengthening the US commitment not to raise trade barriers against third parties. At best, it could in itself become a substantial agent of expanding Asia-Pacific trade and economic welfare.

Conclusions

Our growing understanding of the Asia-Pacific model tells us that the process of reducing subjective and nonofficial barriers generates large gains in trade and welfare, and that there are still large potential gains from the continuation of the process in the Western Pacific economies.

At best, governments can assist market integration through improvement of public goods that support the international market, and through unilateral and multilateral reductions in official barriers. These conditions have been present in the Western Pacific, and their presence in more countries and relationships has encouraged others to join the process.

At worst, increases in protection and official trade discrimination can cut across the beneficent processes of market integration, not least because of the interrelationships between the costs of overcoming various resistances, and because of economies of scale in overcoming resistances. But we can take comfort from the reduction of resistances to trade between major regions through the 1970s and 1980s and the strong expansion of extraregional trade, despite the proliferation of protective and discriminatory measures in Europe and North America. The NAFTA will not seriously set back Asia-Pacific trade expansion and economic dynamism, despite its trade discrimination, if it avoids increases in barriers to Western

Pacific trade. The securing of restraint in NAFTA extraregional trade policy is the first, reasonable, and realistic objective of APEC trade diplomacy in the period ahead.

It happens that this first objective is best encouraged by APEC members, including the United States, going further to enhance the process of market integration in the Asia-Pacific region, through measures to expand the provision of public goods to reduce resistances in the international market, and through nondiscriminatory sectoral liberalization. In these ways, the current pressures toward regionalism in the international economy can be brought to the support of strengthening the liberal international trade system.

References

Anderson, Kym. 1992. "Europe 1992 and the Western Pacific Economies." *Economic Journal* 101 (November).

Anderson, Kym, and Hege Norheim. 1992. "Is World Trade Becoming More Regionalized?" Geneva: General Agreement on Tariffs and Trade, Secretariat.

Arndt, H. W., and R. M. Sundrum. 1975. "Regional Price Disparities." *Bulletin of Indonesian Economic Studies* 11, no. 2 (July).

Balassa, Bela. 1986. "Japan's Trade Policies." *Weltwirtschaftliches Archiv* 122, no. 4.

Balassa, Bela, and Luc Bauwens. 1988. *Changing Trade Patterns in Manufactured Goods: An Economic Investigation.* Amsterdam: North-Holland.

Bhagwati, Jagdish. 1992. "Regionalism vs. Multilaterism: An Overview." Paper presented at the World Bank–CPER Conference on New Dimensions in Regional Integration, Washington (2–3 April).

Cooper, Richard. 1974. "Worldwide Versus Regional Integration: Is There an Optimal Size of the Integrated Area?" *Yale Economic Growth Center Discussion Paper* 220 (November).

Corden, W. M. 1971. *Protection.* Oxford: The Clarendon Press.

Corden, W. M. 1974. *Trade Policy and Economic Welfare.* Oxford: The Clarendon Press.

Drysdale, Peter. 1988. *International Economic Pluralism: Economic Policy in East Asia and the Pacific.* New York: Columbia University Press, and Sydney: Allen and Unwin.

Drysdale, Peter. 1991. "Open Regionalism: A Key to East Asia's Economic Future." *Pacific Economic Papers* 197. Canberra: Australia-Japan Research Centre, Australian National University. (July).

Drysdale, Peter, and Andrew Elek. 1992. "China and the International Trading System." *Pacific Economic Papers* 214. Canberra: Australia-Japan Research Centre, Australian National University (December).

Drysdale, Peter, and Ross Garnaut. 1982. "Trade Intensities and the Analysis of Bilateral Trade Flows in a Many-Country World." *Hitotsubashi Journal of Economics* 22, no. 2 (February).

Drysdale, Peter, and Ross Garnaut. 1989. "A Pacific Free Trade Area?" In Jeffrey J. Schott, ed., *More Free Trade Areas?* POLICY ANALYSIS IN INTERNATIONAL ECONOMICS 27. Washington: Institute of International Economics.

Drysdale, Peter, and Ross Garnaut. 1992. "NAFTA and the Pacific Region: Strategic Responses." Paper presented at the Conference on the Implications of the North American Free Trade Agreement, Adelaide University (July).

Elek, Andrew. 1992a. "Pacific Economic Cooperation: Policy Choices for the 1990s." *Asia Pacific Economic Literature* 6, no. 1 (May).

Elek, Andrew. 1992b. "Trade Policy Options for the Asia Pacific Region in the 1990s: The Potential of Open Regionalism." *American Economic Review: Papers and Proceedings* 82, no. 2 (May).

Finger, Michael J. 1992. "GATT's Influence on Regional Trade Arrangements." Paper presented at the World Bank–CPER Conference on New Dimensions in Regional Integration, Washington (2–3 April).

Frankel, Jeffrey A. 1991. "Is a Yen Bloc Forming in Pacific Asia?" In R. O'Brien, ed., *Finance and the International Economy: The AMEX Bank Review Prize Essays*. Oxford: Oxford University Press.

Frankel, Jeffrey A. 1992. "Is Japan Creating a Yen Bloc in East Asia and the Pacific?" Paper presented at the NBER Conference on Japan and the US in Pacific Asia, Del Mar, CA (3–5 April).

Fukasaku, Kiichiro. 1992. "Economic Regionalism and Intra-Industry Trade: Pacific Asia Perspectives." *OECD Development Centre: Technical Papers* 53. Paris (February).

Garnaut, Ross. 1972. *Australian Trade With Southeast Asia: A Study of Resistances to Bilateral Trade Flows*. Doctoral thesis. Canberra: Australian National University.

Garnaut, Ross. 1993. "The Market and the State in Economic Development: Applications to the International System." *Singapore Economic Review* 36, no. 2 (March): 13–26.

Garnaut, Ross, and Guonan Ma. 1992. "China's Grain Economy." Canberra: Australian Government Publishing Service.

Grubel, Herbert G., and P. J. Lloyd. 1975. *Intra-Industry Trade: The Theory and Measurement of International Trade in Differential Products*. London: Macmillan.

Irwin, Douglas A. 1992. "Multilateral and Bilateral Trade Policies in the World Trading System: An Historical Perspective." Paper presented at the World Bank–CPER Conference on New Dimensions in Regional Integration, Washington (2–3 April).

James, William E., and Robert McCleary. 1992. "The U.S. Response to Increasing Regionalism: A Pacific Perspective." In Michael G. Plummer and William E. James, eds., *Europe and Asia in the 1990s*.

Kojima, Kiyoshi. 1975. "Japan and the Future of World Trade Policy." In C. Fred Bergsten, ed., *Toward a New World Trade Policy: The Maidenhead Papers*. Lexington Books.

Krugman, Paul. 1991. "The Move to Free Trade Zones." *Federal Reserve Bank of Kansas Review* (December).

Krugman, Paul. 1992. "Regionalism vs. Multilateralism: Analytical Notes." Paper presented at the World Bank–CPER Conference on Regional Integration, Washington (2–3 April).

Lawrence, Robert. 1987. "Imports in Japan: Closed Markets or Closed Minds?" *Brookings Papers on Economic Activity* 2.

Lawrence, Robert. 1991. "How Open is Japan?" In Paul Krugman, ed., *Trade with Japan: Has the Door Opened Wider*? Chicago: University of Chicago Press.

Lincoln, Edward J. 1990. *Japan's Unequal Trade*. Washington: The Brookings Institution.

Lipsey, R. G. 1960. "The Theory of Customs Unions: A General Theory." *The Economic Journal* 70, no. 279.

Milner, Helen. 1991. "A Three Bloc Trading System." Paper presented at the IPSA Conference, Buenos Aires, Argentina (20–25 July).

Nogues, Julio, and Rosalinda Quintanilla. 1992. "Latin America's Integration and the Multilateral Trading System." Paper presented at the World Bank–CPER Conference on New Dimensions in Regional Integration, Washington (2–3 April).

Noland, Marcus. 1993. "Protectionism in Japan." *The Open Economies Review* 4: 67–81.

Odagiri, Hiroyuki. 1992. *Growth Through Competition, Competition Through Growth, Strategic Management and the Economy in Japan*. Oxford: Clarendon Press.

Pacific Basin Economic Council. 1992. *North American Free Trade: Implications for International Business*. San Francisco: PBEC Secretariat.

Petri, Peter. 1991. "Japanese Trade in Transition: Hypotheses and Recent Evidence." In Paul Krugman, ed., *Trade with Japan: Has the Door Opened Wider*? Chicago: University of Chicago Press.

Saxonhouse, Gary. 1992. "Trading Blocs, Pacific Trade and Pricing Strategies of East Asian Firms." Paper presented at the World Bank–CPER Conference on New Dimensions in Regional Integration, Washington (2–3 April).

Sheard, Paul. 1992. "Keiretsu and Closedness of the Japanese Market: An Economic Appraisal." *Discussion Paper* 273. The Institute of Social and Economic Research, Osaka University (June).

Summers, Lawrence H. 1991. "Regionalism and the World Trading System." Paper presented at the Jackson Hole Conference on Free Trade Areas, Federal Reserve Bank of Kansas City (August).

Sung Yun-Wing. 1992. "The Economic Integration of Hong Kong, Taiwan and South Korea with the mainland of China." In Ross Garnaut and Liu Guoguang, eds., *Economic Reform and Internationalization: China and the Pacific Region*. Sydney: Allen and Unwin.

Vanek, J. 1965. *General Equilibrium of International Discrimination: The Care of Customs Unions*. Cambridge, MA: Harvard University Press.

Vernon, R. 1966. "International Investment and International Trade in the Product Cycle." *Quarterly Journal of Economics* 79 (May).

Vollrath, Thomas L. 1991. "A Theoretical Evaluation of Alternative Trade Intensity Measures of Revealed Comparative Advantage." *Weltwirtschaftliches Archiv* 127.

Whalley, John. 1992. "Regional Trade Arrangements in North America: CUSTA and NAFTA." Paper presented at the World Bank–CPER Conference on New Dimensions in Regional Integration, Washington (2–3 April).

Winters, Alan. 1992. "The European Community: A Case of Successful Integration?" Paper presented at the World Bank–CPER Conference on New Dimensions in Regional Integration, Washington (2–3 April).

7

Subregional Economic Zones: A New Motive Force in Asia-Pacific Development

CHIA SIOW YUE AND LEE TSAO YUAN

The economic dynamism of the Asia-Pacific region has been fueled by both investment and trade flows. Recent trends in both of these flows are leading to the growing integration of the economies of the region.

There have been two successive waves of foreign direct investment (FDI) in the Asia-Pacific region in recent decades. The first wave began in the 1960s and was led by multinational corporations from the developed countries, first the United States and Western Europe and later Japan, seeking low-cost export platforms, access to domestic markets protected by import substitution policies, and access to the abundant natural resources of Southeast Asia. The bulk of this investment went to the Asian newly industrializing economies (NIEs) and the resource-rich countries of the Association of Southeast Asian Nations (ASEAN). With the Plaza Agreement of September 1985 and the sharp rise of the yen, as well as the growing threat of protectionist measures directed at Japan's industrial exports, Japanese outward investment surged. The investments of Japanese firms in the Asian NIEs and ASEAN were largely cost-motivated, while those in North America and Western Europe were largely market-motivated.

The second wave of FDI emanated from the Asian NIEs in more recent years (Chia 1992). This surge of investment went to the ASEAN region, mainly in search of low-cost export platforms; the driving factors were rapidly rising production costs in the NIEs in the wake of labor and land

Chia Siow Yue is Associate Professor of Economics, National University of Singapore, and Lee Tsao Yuan is Deputy Director, The Institute Policy Studies, Singapore.

shortages, as well as appreciating currencies. These countries, particularly South Korea and Taiwan, also invested in North America and Western Europe in order to secure access to these huge markets as well as to their technology. Investments in ASEAN were attracted by the sharply improved investment climate, particularly in Indonesia, Malaysia, and Thailand, where extensive economic reforms were aimed at trade and investment liberalization, deregulation, and privatization. The investment wave has now spread further, to China and Vietnam as well as to South Asia, as these countries one by one are embarking on market-oriented liberalization. Investors from the ASEAN countries are also increasingly involved in this outreach.

This paper examines one manifestation of the intensified intraregional investment flows and the accompanying trade flows in the Asia-Pacific region, namely, the phenomenon of subregional economic zones (SREZs). After outlining the conceptual framework underlying this phenomenon, case studies of two established SREZs—the Singapore-Johor-Riau Growth Triangle and the Hong Kong–South China–Taiwan SREZ—are presented. The concluding section discusses the broader issues of the effects and implications of and prospects for SREZs in the Asia-Pacific region.

Conceptual Framework

The Emerging Phenomenon of Subregional Economic Zones

Various forms of economic integration and cooperative groupings have emerged or are being planned in the Asia-Pacific region (table 1). In terms of geographical scope, the two largest are the Asia Pacific Economic Cooperation (APEC), a pan-Asia-Pacific intergovernmental forum, and the East Asian Economic Caucus (EAEC), a proposed intergovernmental consultative caucus comprising only the East Asian economies. The next tier comprises arrangements among groups of neighboring countries, ranging from formal arrangements such as the three free trade areas: the North American Free Trade Area (NAFTA) comprising the United States, Canada, and Mexico; the ASEAN Free Trade Area (AFTA), and the Closer Economic Relations (CER) group, comprising Australia and New Zealand.

A third, newly emerging category of economic grouping is that of subregional economic zones. Like the groupings already mentioned, SREZs transcend political boundaries, but unlike them, SREZs do not always involve entire national economies. Instead, each SREZ involves only the border areas of at least one of the economies involved. For example, the Greater South China (GSC) Economic Zone comprises the economies of Hong Kong, Macau, and Taiwan but only two of the coastal provinces of southern China—Guangdong and Fujian (figure 1). The

Table 1 Cooperative economic groupings in Asia

Economic grouping	Date formed	Basis	No. of countries	Component countries or areas
Panregional groupings				
Asia Pacific Economic Cooperation (APEC)	1989	Intergovernmental forum	15	ASEAN, United States, Canada, Australia, New Zealand, Japan, South Korea, Hong Kong, China
East Asian Economic Caucus (EAEC)		Concept phase	?	East and Southeast Asia
Northeast Asia				
Greater South China Economic Zone		Private-sector activity	3	Coastal South China, Hong Kong, Taiwan
Yellow Sea Economic Zone		Private-sector activity	3	Northern China, Japan, South Korea
Japan Sea Economic Zone		Private-sector activity	5	Japan, East Russia, Northeast China, South Korea, North Korea
Tumen River Delta Area		Concept phase	5	East Russia, China, Mongolia, South Korea, North Korea
Southeast Asia				
ASEAN	1967	Trade preferences	6	Brunei, Indonesia, Malaysia, Philippines, Singapore, Thailand
SIJORI Growth Triangle	c. 1989	Private-sector activity	3	Singapore, Johor (Malaysia), Riau (Indonesia)
Northern Growth Triangle		Concept phase	3	West Indonesia, Northern Malaysia, South Thailand
Baht or (Tonkin-Mekong) Economic Zone		Private-sector activity	4	Yunnan (China), Vietnam, Laos, Northeast Thailand

Source: Adapted from Japan External Trade Organization (JETRO), *White Paper on International Trade, 1991* (October).

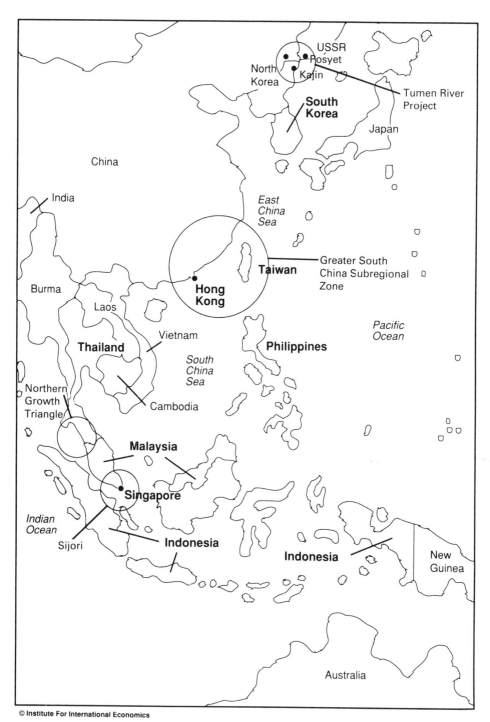

Figure 1. Subregional economic zones in Asia

Singapore-Johor-Riau Growth Triangle comprises Singapore, the state of Johor in peninsular Malaysia, and the Riau province in Indonesia. In addition to these two already-established SREZs, four others are on the drawing board: the Northern Growth Triangle, involving southern Thailand, northwestern Malaysia, and western Sumatra; the Tumen River Delta Area project, involving eastern Russia, China, Mongolia, and South and North Korea; the Yellow Sea Economic Zone, involving Japan, South Korea, and northern China; and the Japan Sea Economic Zone, involving Japan, eastern Russia, northeastern China, and South and North Korea.

At this early stage in the formation of SREZs, their conceptualization is necessarily deductive—that is, generalizations about them are made from observation of real-world occurrences. The following paragraphs therefore first provide an overview of these SREZs. An attempt at conceptualization follows.

Growth Triangles in Southeast Asia

In ASEAN, the growth triangle concept has caught interest in recent years. The idea of an economic zone linking Singapore and adjacent areas in Malaysia and Indonesia was officially proposed in December 1989 by Singapore's then–Deputy Prime Minister Goh Chok Tong, as a new form of subregional economic cooperation in ASEAN through cooperation in investment rather than through trade. There was concern over the slow pace of trade cooperation and trade liberalization and the difficulty of always having to achieve consensus among the six member countries of ASEAN. Various names have been given to the growth triangle that has since developed in the area: SIJORI (coined by Indonesian Minister B. J. Habibie), the Johor-Singapore-Riau (JSR) Growth Triangle (popular in Singapore), and Nusa Tiga, which means "three areas" and was coined by Chief Minister Muhyiddin of Johor. There has been official endorsement of increased cooperation at the highest levels of all three governments, but there is as yet no formal trilateral agreement. There are only two formal documents, signed by Singapore and Indonesia and not directly related to the growth triangle as a whole, outlining Singapore's role in the development of the Riau province and Indonesia's undertaking to supply water to Singapore as well as guaranteeing investments in Indonesia. SIJORI is discussed further in the next section.

Following the success of SIJORI, there are proposals for more growth triangles within ASEAN. Of these, the furthest advanced is the Malaysian proposal for a Northern Growth Triangle (NGT) encompassing the contiguous subregions of northwest Malaysia (4 states), southern Thailand (14 provinces), and western Indonesia (2 provinces in Sumatra), to jointly develop infrastructure, natural resources, and industries (Salleh 1992).

The NGT covers an area of 230,000 square kilometers, with an estimated population of 26 million.

The industrial development of the NGT is more problematic than in the case of SIJORI, for a number of reasons. First, while SIJORI is distinguished by the economic complementarity of Singapore and Johor and Singapore and Riau, such complementarity is less evident in the NGT. It is difficult to identify an area in the NGT that could play Singapore's role as growth pole, with substantial cross-border spillovers. The most developed area in the NGT is Penang, the growth pole of northern peninsular Malaysia. However, any metropolitan spillover effects from Penang are more likely to occur within the political boundaries of Malaysia. The same goes for the provinces of Indonesia and Thailand involved in the proposal. Second, geographical proximity needs to be supported by infrastructure capable of facilitating economic linkages. The infrastructure linking the three areas of the NGT is limited, and capital for its development is not readily available within the NGT. Third, the institutional arrangements for the NGT would be more complicated than for SIJORI, as they involve not only three central governments, but also 20 provincial and state governments in Indonesia, Malaysia, and Thailand. Finally, there are greater political and security sensitivities in the NGT areas than in SIJORI, since the centrifugal pull of subregional development may reactivate latent separatist sentiments in the border areas of the three countries. However, there is potential for joint development of tourism and agro-business in the NGT.

The growth triangle concept is one means of accelerating ASEAN regional economic cooperation through resource pooling, since efforts at regional trade liberalization have hitherto met with limited success. At its Fourth Summit in Singapore in January 1992, ASEAN finally agreed to form a free trade area, within a time frame of 15 years. The growth triangle approach was endorsed as a parallel and supportive mechanism of regional economic cooperation. There is also the possible emergence of a Baht Economic Zone in Indochina, with Thailand (whose currency is the baht) as the hub.

Subregional Economic Zones in Northeast Asia

For decades, ideological and strategic conflicts restricted economic linkages between the countries of Northeast Asia. In the last decade, however, these barriers have come tumbling down, and cross-border economic activities have intensified, particularly between Hong Kong and China's southern coastal province of Guangdong, and between Taiwan and China's province of Fujian across the Taiwan Straits. Various schemes of regional economic integration and cooperation have also been proposed, encompassing the former Soviet Far East, northeastern China, Mongolia, the Korean peninsula, and Japan.

The economic subregion of GSC encompasses the contiguous economies of Hong Kong–Macau, Taiwan, and China's southern coastal provinces of Guangdong and Fujian. Close economic linkages already exist between Hong Kong–Macau and Guangdong, and similar ties are developing between Taiwan and Guangdong and Fujian. Unlike SIJORI, where the economic integration process was partly government-led, and the institutional structure has been formalized by meetings of political leaders and bilateral treaties (between Indonesia and Singapore), the economic integration of GSC has been more market-driven, although the policy framework in facilitating economic linkages is also crucial.

The economic restructuring of Hong Kong and the creation of special economic zones (SEZs) in China have precipitated the economic integration of Hong Kong and the Pearl River Delta in Guangdong province. This process has been continuing for over a decade, and the pace has quickened in the early 1990s. Despite the absence of political and diplomatic relations, economic linkages are also increasingly being forged between Taiwan and the Chinese provinces of Guangdong and Fujian. The high level of integration already achieved is evident from the bilateral trade and investment statistics. Much of the trade, investment, and tourist flows between the two countries is channeled through Hong Kong.

Political developments and economic imperatives are behind many of the proposals in recent years for economic cooperation and integration involving subsets of the Russian Far East, Mongolia, northeastern China, the Korean peninsula, and Japan. First, political relations in Northeast Asia have changed markedly for the better. Hostilities have ceased and some countries have normalized relations. Even North and South Korea have begun high-level dialogues. Thus the political climate for economic cooperation has improved markedly. Second, there is economic complementarity between parts of Northeast Asia. Japan and South Korea have abundant capital and industrial technology but lack natural resources and find labor in increasingly short supply. The Russian Far East and Mongolia meanwhile are rich in natural resources but have sparse populations and, together with North Korea, lack capital and technology. Northeastern China has abundant labor and natural resources but lacks capital. Nonetheless, Northeast Asia still faces formidable obstacles to economic cooperation, arising from still-unresolved historical disputes, the lack of diplomatic relations between some countries, and continuing differences in political and economic systems.

The most advanced of the proposals for economic cooperation of Northeast Asia involves the Tumen River Delta Area (TRDA), which covers contiguous areas of the Russian Far East, northeastern China, and North Korea; essentially the subregion stretches from Posyet in Russia to Hunchun in China and Rajin in North Korea (see figure 1). The proposal calls for the massive development of infrastructure and transportation networks in the subregion to facilitate resource exploitation, trade, and industrial development. Russia, China, and North Korea have already established economic zones in the parts of this subregion lying within their own borders. Proponents of the scheme to integrate these national economic zones argue that the TRDA has tremendous potential for development, but that a cooperative effort is required for its realization (Koo 1991). First, the subregion lies strategically between Japan and Europe. The transcontinental railway, with the construction of a land bridge, will provide a more efficient transportation link between the two developed regions, with the potential to divert trade flows away from the more circuitous southward sea route from Japan to Europe. The development of transportation networks and easier access to seaports in the TRDA will also facilitate regional maritime trade among the participating areas. Second, the TRDA has abundant natural resources and labor and is geographically proximate to industrialized Japan and South Korea with their abundant capital resources, managerial know-how, advanced technology, and large markets. The TRDA is expected to become a transportation hub and an industrial center in the coming decades, and a new driving force for the economic development of Northeast Asia.

The United Nations Development Programme (UNDP) is sponsoring meetings between interested parties and funding feasibility studies of the TRDA project. There are two major difficulties facing the scheme. First, it requires an investment of $30 billion[1] over a period of 20 years for infrastructural development. Financing of this enormous investment is beyond the resources of the participating countries. Japan is the most likely major source of funds, but so far Japan is lukewarm to the scheme. Second, the participating countries have not reached agreement on the form that cooperation should take, and creating the technical and operational mechanism for joint infrastructural development will pose a huge challenge.

Driving Forces in SREZs

One can, from the above overview, identify five driving forces behind the emergence of SREZs, which may be present with varying degrees of importance in different SREZs.

Economic Complementarity

SREZs are formed by geographically contiguous areas separated by political boundaries. The development of intense economic linkages between

---

1. Dollar amounts are stated in US dollars except where noted otherwise.

such areas depends on the existence of economic complementarity. Such complementarity in turn arises from different levels of economic development and different resource endowments. On the one hand, there is usually a fairly developed urbanized area with a strong manufacturing sector and financial, commercial, transportation, and information technology capabilities and skilled personnel; with economic growth, there emerge problems of labor shortage and land scarcity, and rising labor and real estate costs. Meanwhile, across the border, there exists a complementary economy that is less developed, where incomes are lower than in the urban core, and where there is still a plentiful supply of labor and land.

These differences in levels of development and in resource endowment give rise to factor price differences, which prevail because border restrictions prevent the free movement of labor and capital. An SREZ is established when barriers to such cross-border flows are reduced or removed, enabling investments to take advantage of the existing economic complementarity. The entire SREZ becomes borderless to investment as capital becomes mobile. However, some restrictions to labor flow continue to exist, preserving cross-border wage differentials.

Economic complementarity as a key driving force in SREZs cannot be underestimated. This factor, among others, explains why both GSC and SIJORI only began to materialize in the late 1970s. Before then, neither Hong Kong, nor Taiwan, nor Singapore was at a sufficiently advanced level of economic development to cause significant relocation of labor-intensive production processes.

Geographical Proximity

Foreign investment has occurred, and continues to occur, in countries that are not neighbors. For example, Hong Kong investments began to relocate to Southeast Asia as early as the 1970s, even before they moved into southern China. But in addition to economic complementarity, one other major reason why Singapore companies choose to relocate in Johor and Batam and Hong Kong companies in Guangdong instead of many other, more distant locations with plentiful supplies of labor and land is that of geographical proximity. Geographical proximity is an important consideration when there is a competitive need to minimize transaction and information costs and remains so even in the face of revolutionary changes in transportation and telecommunication technology. Although modern technology does offer effective communication at great distances, there is no perfect substitute for face-to-face interaction. Proximity also reduces transportation time, a positive factor when the market is constantly changing and delivery schedules are tight. In the case of SIJORI, geographical proximity to Singapore is cited as an important factor for locating in Johor or Batam; travel to and from these areas is convenient, and the round trip can be done in a single day, so that executives and their families can be domiciled comfortably in Singapore. Similarly, for managers and professionals in Hong Kong, a return trip to Guangdong can be made within a day (Lee 1992a).

There is, in addition, a technological reason. The introduction of flexible production systems in manufacturing has made spatial proximity important, and thus promoted the reemergence of regional economies, for various reasons: to facilitate just-in-time inventory between vertically nonintegrated production units; to develop a production culture, that is, to produce innovations from the shop floor to management; to provide a wide base of support, that is, many suppliers and workers to allow for fluctuations in market demand; and to provide access to cheap labor and avoid interruptions to production distribution schedules caused by civil strife, labor militancy, and even traffic jams (Tan 1992). Regional production systems are more effective if anchored to transportation, telecommunications, and information hubs such as Hong Kong and Singapore, since they facilitate coordination and minimize transaction costs.

Geographically proximate areas often, but not always, have similar languages and cultures, with family and kinship ties that minimize information costs and create interpersonal bonding and business trust. Thus, there is a strong bond of kinship and culture between the Cantonese-speaking people of Hong Kong and Guangdong, and between the Fujianese-speaking people of Taiwan and Fujian. For SIJORI, the cultural bonding is between Singaporeans and Malaysians, and there is some evidence of the Chinese ethnic connection in Singapore-Indonesian joint ventures.

The Policy Framework, Political and Economic

As outlined earlier, there have been dramatic political developments in Northeast Asia. These have removed or reduced conflicts and tensions and the barriers to cross-border trade and investment flows. In both Northeast and Southeast Asia, governments face the imperatives of economic development and are more prepared to cooperate to improve their investment climate through economic liberalization, infrastructural development, improvements in industrial efficiency, and access to markets.

The relaxation of rules governing foreign investment has been instrumental in increasing the mobility of capital across borders. The opening up of China since the late 1970s and the establishment of special economic zones, and the allowance of 100 percent foreign ownership for export-oriented companies under certain conditions, first in Malaysia and then for the Batam Economic Zone, constitute another important explanation for the timing of the spillover of investments from Hong Kong and

Singapore across their borders. The emergence of SREZs has therefore to be seen in the perspective of the unilateral trade and investment liberalization moves of China, Malaysia, and Indonesia.

Infrastructure

Geographical proximity is an economic advantage only if the transportation and telecommunications network is reasonably well developed. The role of the government is not necessarily confined to facilitating cross-border flows of investment, finance, labor, and goods through reduction or removal of regulations and restrictions. Government may also be actively involved in the provision of industrial infrastructure (for example, industrial estates), tourism parks, transport and telecommunications, and public utilities. Where huge infrastructural investments are involved, as in the case of the TRDA, intergovernmental cooperation is essential. A basic condition is that the governments either pool their financial resources for joint infrastructural development, or appeal to Japan and/or to regional and international institutions such as the Asian Development Bank and the World Bank for financial help.

Market Access

Unlike a free trade area, the attraction in some SREZs is not preferential access to the domestic or subregional market, but the creation of efficient production and distribution systems that are competitive internationally. As such, the SREZ is critically dependent on access to world markets, especially those in developed countries with purchasing power.

A Categorization of SREZs

A categorization of different types of SREZs can be determined, depending on the relative importance of each of the various driving forces mentioned above.

Metropolitan Spillover into the Hinterland

This category of SREZs is essentially a growth pole–spillover phenomenon in a transnational context. The driving forces here are economic complementarity, geographical proximity, and a policy framework more favorable to foreign investment in the less developed countries. Economic complementarity is what motivates the cross-border movement of capital, after an initial change in the policy framework in favor of foreign capital. Geographical proximity comes into its own as an economic factor that lowers transaction costs, but also because of cultural and kinship factors.

McGee and MacLeod (1992) term this concept the "extended metropolis region," while Scalapino (1992) calls them "natural economic territories."

Within this category, further differences exist between those SREZs that are market-driven and those that have a greater degree of specific government facilitation or political motivation other than a general relaxation of investment rules. The GSC SREZ falls into the market-driven category, as the main actors are the business firms themselves. The Singapore-Johor link of SIJORI is similarly market-driven, with relatively little government participation. On the other hand, government has had greater involvement with the Singapore-Batam link of SIJORI. Not only have there been investment and water agreements signed between Indonesia and Singapore, but two investment missions to Northeast Asia to promote SIJORI have been organized with ministerial participation. The Batam Industrial Park, the first industrial estate to be built on Batam, is jointly owned and managed by an Indonesian conglomerate as well as two Singapore government–linked companies.

Metropolitan spillovers are primarily investment-driven. At the moment, both GSC and SIJORI are export platforms, or the equivalent of transnational export processing zones, for exporting to other countries. However, the market potential of the SREZ itself as well as the countries whose areas are involved in the SREZ could increase. Foreign companies operating in southern China, for example, also anticipate greater access to the Chinese market.

Joint Development of Natural Resources and Infrastructure

Countries may cooperate in SREZs in order to minimize disputes over ownership and utilization of a common resource such as a major river, and to exploit the economies of agglomeration. These considerations underlie the multicountry cooperation in the development of the Mekong River in Southeast Asia in the 1960s and early 1970s, and the proposed multicountry cooperation in the development of the Tumen River Delta. This second category of SREZ is therefore driven less by economic complementarity than the first.

Common Geopolitical Interests and Geographical Proximity

Common geopolitical interests and geographical proximity can lead to a coming together of countries and parts of countries, not only to exploit economies of scale and agglomeration, but to ensure faster economic growth and greater economic security in a second-best world of emerging trading blocs. This is part of the rationale for the proposals to create a Yellow Sea Economic Zone and a Japan Sea Economic Zone. Such zones have the potential to develop into free trade areas.

Comparisons of SREZs with EPZs and FTAs

The two existing SREZs in the Asia-Pacific region are both of the metro-politan spillover type. In the comparison of an SREZ with an export processing zone (EPZ) or special economic zone and a free trade area (FTA), the SREZ will refer to the first category of extended metropolitan spillovers.

The EPZ is a special geographical area within a country that has been earmarked for special treatment by government policy, generally targeted at foreign investors and for the promotion of export-oriented industrial-ization. There are usually political, financial, and economic reasons why it is not possible to remove import tariffs and provide infrastructure and industrial facilities on a nationwide basis. A typical EPZ has the following features:

- It is a special customs area where tariffs in effect elsewhere in the economy are waived. EPZ enterprises are thus able to import interme-diate inputs at world prices or pay low import tariffs only. Tariffs and taxes usually apply on domestic sales outside the zone.

- Foreign investors in the zone are usually given preferential treatment over investors in the rest of the country, with 100 percent equity own-ership generally allowed and with zero or minimal restrictions on repatriation of profits and foreign-exchange availability for import re-quirements.

- The bureaucratic regulations and requirements for investment approval and implementation are usually simplified.

- The government usually provides infrastructure and industrial facili-ties.

The SREZ has the same objectives and policy framework as an EPZ, as they are both export platforms targeted to attract foreign investments. They differ, however, in two respects. First, the SREZ is transnational, involving subsets of different national economies, while the EPZ is a subset of the national economy. As a result, the distributional issues associated with SREZs are more complex than those of EPZs (see the concluding section of this paper). Second, the SREZ combines the re-sources of advanced and less advanced economies, integrating the avail-ability of capital, technology, and human resources with the availability of land, natural resources, and labor. Such a combination of resource endowments is generally not available elsewhere and makes the SREZ a much more attractive investment location than the EPZ.

FTAs are more formal institutionalized arrangements that involve na-tional entities. SREZs usually involve contiguous parts of countries, except for the city-economies of Hong Kong and Singapore. FTAs focus on trade liberalization and the enlargement of the domestic market, while SREZs focus on economic complementarity to promote private-sector investments. As such, SREZs are less likely to be perceived as zero-sum games, since domestic enterprises are not threatened by more competitive enterprises from partner countries. Since the SREZ is obviously not a protectionist trading bloc, it is also more acceptable to other countries. The SREZ is also an easier form of economic integration to achieve than an FTA, which involves protracted negotiations because of its more formal nature. Both FTAs and SREZs improve competitiveness through exploitation of economies of scale and agglomeration.

The Singapore-Johor-Riau Growth Triangle

SIJORI has an area of 20,000 square kilometers and a population of 5 million (table 2). Annual per capita GDPs in the constituent areas ranged from over $3,000 in Johor and possibly less than $1,000 in Batam to nearly $13,000 in Singapore. There are concerted trilateral efforts to promote SIJORI, particularly the Singapore-Johor and Singapore-Riau links. SIJORI remains mainly a bilateral rather than a trilateral arrangement, with Singapore as the growth pole. In that sense, the term "triangle" is a misnomer. The Johor-Riau side of the triangle is the least developed, and the economic linkages between Johor and Riau remain limited, because the two areas appear to be more competitive in resources than complementary, and factor price differentials in land and labor appear insufficient to induce investment flows.

Until recent years, economic linkages in SIJORI were limited. A common history and geographical proximity led to strong economic linkages between Singapore and Johor. However, with the separate political development of Malaysia and Singapore since the mid-1960s, economic ties were gradually eroded. Nonetheless, movements of people and goods remained at a high level, in spite of immigration restrictions on both sides and the Malaysian government's desire to reduce the amount of external trade routed via Singapore. In spite of their geographical proximity, Singapore had negligible economic linkages with the islands of Riau province, because of separate political histories, the Indonesian government's restriction on foreign investment, and the relatively underdeveloped infrastructure in Riau. Economic linkages in SIJORI have increased significantly since the mid-1980s.

Rationale for SIJORI

The economic rationale for the promotion of SIJORI is that it makes possible the joint development of the subregion, capitalizing on the

Table 2   Basic indicators for the SIJORI Growth Triangle and the Greater South China Subregional Zone

	SIJORI			
Indicator	Johor	Singapore	Riau	Total
Area (square kilometers)	18,914	639	3,300[a]	22,853
Population (millions)	2.2[b]	2.8[c]	0.1[c,d]	5.1
GDP (million of US dollars)[e]	4,300[b]	34,600[b]	45[d,f]	38,945[g]
Per capita GDP (US dollars)	3,594[b]	12,940[b]	500[d,f]	
Growth rate of GDP (percentages)	9.0[c]	6.7[c]	n.a.	

	Greater South China Subregional Zone			
Indicator	Hong Kong	Guangdong	Taiwan	Total
Area (square kilometers)	1,075	180,000	36,000	217,075
Population (millions)	5.7[b]	62.5[b]	20.4[b]	88.6
GDP (billions of US dollars)[e]	59.7[b]	30.8[b]	157.0[b]	247.55
Per capita GDP (US dollars)	14,150[c]	493[b]	7,761[b]	
Growth rate of GDP (percentages)	3.9[c]	12.2[b]	7.3[c]	

n.a. = not available
a. Includes only Batam, Bintan, Bulan, Singkep, Rempang, Galang, and Barelang.
b. 1990.
c. 1991.
d. Batam only.
e. At current prices.
f. 1988.
g. Figure is approximate.

Sources: Johor State Economic Development Corporation, Johor Investment Guide 1991; Department of Statistics, Yearbook of Statistics Singapore 1991; World Bank, World Development Report 1992; Sakura Institute of Research, Pacific Business and Industries, vol. II, 1992; Asiaweek, 31 July 1992, 57; Guangdong Yearbook 1991; Guangdong Statistics Yearbook 1991; Batam Industrial Development Authority, Development Data up to December 1991; Malaysian Industrial Development Authority, Statistics on the Manufacturing Sector in Malaysia, 1985–1990; Mari Pangestu, "An Indonesian Perspective," in Lee Tsao Yuan, Growth Triangle: The Johor-Singapore-Riau Experience, 75–116 (Singapore: Institute of Southeast Asian Studies and Institute of Policy Studies, 1991).

resource complementarity and geographic proximity of the three component areas.

SIJORI offers the investor the whole range of business requirements: land, infrastructure, workers, and skills. However, economic complementarity can only be exploited when there is a favorable political and policy environment and available infrastructure to facilitate the movement of goods, people, and capital.

Political Commitment and Policy Changes

It may be argued that SIJORI has been proposed largely in response to market forces, and that official cooperation has merely facilitated the already-growing economic linkages undertaken by the private sector.

While this may be true of Singapore-Johor, official policy was decisive in promoting the Singapore-Riau side of the triangle, where market forces were weak.

SIJORI would not be what it is today without political commitment at the highest levels. The Indonesian Minister of State for Research and Technology, B. J. Habibie, who has responsibility for the development of Batam Island, first discussed the concept of interlinked development of the area with then–Singapore Prime Minister Lee Kuan Yew in 1979. He proposed that, like balloons, Singapore and other economies of the area could only continue to expand without bursting by being linked to each other. He further proposed an arrangement similar to those that link the Benelux countries, with free entry and exit of people, goods, and services (Habibie 1992). This idea of interlinked development between Singapore and Batam took 10 years to reach fruition. In October 1989, the development of Batam was discussed at a meeting between Indonesia's President Suharto and Lee Kuan Yew. This was crucial to the subsequent relaxation of Indonesian regulations governing foreign direct investment on Batam, and the growth in economic relations. In June 1990, when Suharto visited Malaysia, both heads of government endorsed the growth triangle concept.

Policy changes by Indonesia to attract investments to Batam include the following:

- 100 percent foreign equity ownership is allowed for the first five years, after which there must be a 5 percent divestment; no further divestment is required if the company is 100 percent export-oriented (this condition is different from other parts of Indonesia, where divestment must reach at least 51 percent within 15 years);

- investment applications can be processed in Batam itself rather than at the Investment Board (BKPM) in Jakarta;

- the private sector is allowed to set up industrial estates in Indonesia; this relaxation of the rules led to the establishment of the Batam Industrial Park as a joint venture between the Indonesian private sector and Singapore state organizations and enterprises.

These major policy changes, and the strong support of the Singapore government, were instrumental in overcoming the earlier reluctance of Singaporean investors and foreign multinationals based in Singapore, and led to a surge in Singapore investments in Batam, which had earlier been designated as a duty-free zone. For example, the Japanese multinational firm Sumitomo was the first to commit itself to becoming a tenant in the Batam Industrial Park and cited the urging of the Singapore government as one important reason for the investment move (Lee 1992b). Two high-level Indonesia-Singapore joint investment promotion missions were also organized to promote investment opportunities available in Batam (and Bintan): the first traveled to Osaka in December 1990, and the second to Hong Kong, South Korea, and Taiwan in September 1991.

In August 1990, Singapore and Indonesia signed two bilateral agreements providing the framework for the joint development of Riau. The Agreement on Economic Cooperation in the Framework of the Development of the Riau Province is an enlargement of the Batam Economic Cooperation Agreement of 1980. The Agreement on the Promotion and Protection of Investments supplements the ASEAN Investment Guarantee Agreement. A third bilateral agreement in June 1991 provided for the joint development by Indonesia and Singapore of water resources in Riau, under which Singapore is guaranteed water supply from the Riau island of Bintan for at least 50 years. A joint committee at the ministerial level was set up to coordinate development efforts in Riau. There are ongoing efforts to coordinate and harmonize regulations and procedures. One example is cooperation on immigration procedures, which has helped to streamline commuting between Singapore and Batam; computerized processing of immigration procedures through the use of smart cards (plastic cards containing information on a microprocessor) was introduced in October 1991.

Although Malaysia's Prime Minister Mahathir had endorsed the growth triangle concept, Malaysian federal support for Johor's participation is not as enthusiastic as Indonesian central government support for Riau has been. However, the Johor state (provincial) government is a strong advocate of promoting bilateral Johor-Singapore economic linkages. Johor has benefited from its proximity to Singapore as well as from the Malaysian relaxation of foreign investment rules and regulations in recent years. Johor also has an EPZ at Pasir Gudang, which enables the duty-free importation of raw materials and intermediate inputs used in export production.

Economic Complementarity

SIJORI as an integrated subregion is more attractive to investors than its separate parts. Each of SIJORI's three nodes has specific comparative advantages. Singapore's advantage lies in its managerial and professional expertise and its well-developed financial, transportation, and telecommunications infrastructure. Riau and Johor can offer land and labor at lower cost than can Singapore. Together they can produce a competitive business environment. However, while economic complementarity in the Singapore-Johor and Singapore-Riau sides of the Growth Triangle is obvious, that between Johor and Riau is less apparent, and helps to explain why this side of the triangle remains relatively less developed.

Participation in SIJORI will help Singapore achieve the following objectives: economic restructuring; becoming a high-value-added service economy and a hub city; promoting the regionalization and internationalization of Singaporean enterprises; providing leisure areas in proximity; achieving a secure water supply; and helping promote the economic advancement of the ASEAN region out of enlightened self-interest.

Singapore's per capita GNP reached $13,240 in 1991 after a quarter century of rapid economic growth. The city-state, with its resident population of 2.7 million and a miniscule land area of 639 square kilometers, is faced with labor and land shortages, rising wages, and rising real estate costs. There are obvious limits to the importation of foreign workers before they pose a political and social problem. The relocation of labor-intensive industries and processes and land-intensive activities to Johor and Riau will enable the Singapore economy to shift to new areas of comparative advantage in high-value-added manufacturing and service activities, and to become a regional hub for trade, finance, transportation, telecommunications, and information, and the regional headquarters of multinational corporations. SIJORI enables multinationals based in Singapore to relocate their labor-intensive manufacturing processes outside of Singapore while remaining within the region; Singapore benefits from the retention in Singapore of the service functions attached to those industries, such as management, finance, marketing, communication, and transport.

The Singapore economy has become a net capital exporter. Hitherto this exportation of capital has mainly taken the form of government portfolio investment, usually in developed countries. Increasingly, the large state enterprises and private companies are being urged to move into the international marketplace with the aim of promoting homegrown multinationals. Small and medium-sized Singapore enterprises are also encouraged to invest offshore to overcome factor scarcities in Singapore and to secure markets. Johor and Riau represent opportunities for Singapore's state enterprises and banks to internationalize their activities and for small and medium-sized enterprises to expand offshore to gain experience for eventual internationalization.

The rising affluence of Singapore has led to a growing demand for leisure and recreational facilities in close proximity to the city-state. The strength of the Singapore dollar vis-à-vis the Malaysian ringgit provided an added attraction for Singapore tourist spending in Johor. With the tourism boom in Southeast Asia, Singapore, as the transportation hub of the region, has become an increasingly important tourism gateway for Johor. Both Johor and Riau are developing leisure and tourist facilities to attract Singaporeans, foreigners based in Singapore, and the tourist traffic through Singapore.

Singapore is critically dependent on Johor for its water supply, and this vulnerability has been highlighted whenever bilateral relations with Malaysia reach an ebb. Economic cooperation with Johor through SIJORI

Table 3 Costs of land and labor in Johor, Singapore, and Batam, 1989

	Land (US dollars per square meter)	Labor (US dollars per month)		
		Unskilled	Semi-skilled	Skilled
Johor	4.08	150	220	400
Singapore	4.25	350	420	600
Batam	2.3	90	140	200

Source: Richard I. Mann, ed., *BATAM: Step-by-Step Guide for Investors* (Toronto: Gateway, 1990), 50.

has as a major objective the improvement of bilateral relations. However, it is anticipated that because of Johor's own growing needs as well as the needs of other Malaysian states for water, Singapore cannot continue to depend on Johor water for its growing future needs. Thus, to ensure an adequate supply of water for the future, Singapore entered into an agreement with Indonesia to help develop the Riau islands.

Singapore also sees SIJORI as a vehicle to promote ASEAN regional economic cooperation and ensure Singapore's economic future. Progress in intra–ASEAN trade liberalization and industrial cooperation has been painfully slow. SIJORI enables more like-minded members of ASEAN to cooperate at a faster pace. Through the relocation to Johor and Riau of some of the activities of Singapore-based multinationals and Singapore-owned enterprises, and through joint missions to promote inward foreign investment, Singapore hopes to help promote investment and technology transfer in neighboring countries, in the firm belief that a more prosperous ASEAN will also mean a more peaceful and stable ASEAN.

Similarly, Johor and Riau also have motivations for cooperating within the growth triangle framework. Their policies are explicitly aimed at twinning their investment attractions with those of Singapore to take advantage of Singapore's infrastructure. Proximity to Singapore will enable investors in Batam and Johor to be more efficient and competitive in production and distribution. It is to be noted that there is no over-abundance of labor in Batam, and also more recently in Johor, and these two areas are dependent on immigration from other parts of Indonesia and Malaysia, respectively. The point of SIJORI is not so much that there is abundant cheap labor in these areas, but that labor is available near Singapore. In fact, given the limited supply of labor in Johor and Batam, investors from Singapore (both foreign multinationals and Singapore enterprises) are venturing beyond these two areas into the other Malaysian states north of Johor, and into the other Riau islands.

Table 3 shows relative land and labor costs in the constituent areas of SIJORI. There is no significant difference in land cost between Singapore and Johor, while the cost of land in Batam is much lower. Labor costs in Johor are about half to two-thirds those in Singapore, while labor costs in Batam are about half to two-thirds those in Johor. On the basis of land and labor costs alone, Batam would appear to be a more attractive investment location than Johor. In both areas real estate prices are rising rapidly in response to demand from Singapore investors. In 1990 some 85 percent of Singapore investment in Batam was in tourism and housing (Pangestu 1991).

Availability of Infrastructure

The provision of infrastructure and industrial facilities such as industrial estates facilitates private-sector investments. Johor has a relatively well developed infrastructure for industries, including port and airport facilities, industrial estates, and free trade zones. Government resources are able to provide for further infrastructural expansion. As such, Singapore's participation in infrastructural development is limited, except for the development of water supply and the proposed construction of a second causeway linking Johor with Singapore. In contrast, the Riau islands are much less developed than Johor, and the Indonesian government lacks adequate financial resources to allocate to Riau's development. Thus, two features were introduced for infrastructural development, namely, private-sector participation and joint ventures between countries. The largest joint infrastructural projects are the Batam Industrial Park (BIP) and the Bintan Integrated Development Project (BIDP). The BIP is a S$600 million, 500-hectare joint venture between an Indonesian conglomerate (the Salim group) and Singapore state enterprises. The BIP provides investors with a one-stop business center to minimize the formalities of setting up production. The BIDP is a joint venture between the Indonesian and Singapore private sectors to develop the Bintan Beach International Resort and the Bintan Industrial Estate. Work started in March 1991. The Bintan Beach International Resort will cover 19,000 hectares and cost S$3.5 billion to develop. The Bintan Industrial Estate is being developed along the same lines as Batam Industrial Park. It will complement BIP, which is intended for electronics-based industries, by providing facilities for light and medium industries, such as textiles and garments, woodwork, footwear, food processing and packaging, toy manufacturing, and electronics.

Impact

At the macroeconomic level, Singapore will benefit from the reduced pressure on land and labor, and these scarce resources can then be put to more productive use. Johor and Riau in turn will gain from the increased investment inflows, with their attendant positive effects on GDP and employment growth, as well as from the training, technology transfer, and export marketing expertise that normally accompany foreign direct investment. The land-abundant areas of Johor and Riau could also specialize in tourism and agrobusiness. At the microeconomic level, firms in the SREZ are able to rationalize their resources and production and distribution through vertical specialization and division of labor. For those firms engaged in manufacturing, labor-intensive processes could be located in areas with abundant labor resources, while activities requiring knowledge and skill inputs, such as engineering development, marketing, supply acquisition, and finance, as well as newer and more complex production lines, could be based in Singapore. Intra-subregional effects on Singapore and on Johor are not so large that structural adjustments can be attributed to the formation of the SREZ, as distinguished from other general factors affecting Singapore and Malaysia. It is otherwise for the Riau islands of Batam and Bintan.

Effect on Singapore

The impact of the SIJORI growth triangle on Singapore to date can be seen mainly in the outward investment and relocation of industries in Johor and Batam. Lee (1992a) reported two surveys that sought to determine the extent of relocation of labor-intensive activities from Singapore to the neighboring region. A survey in January 1992 by the Singapore Manufacturers' Association of its members, 270 of which responded, showed that 40 percent have either moved or intend to relocate part of their business to neighboring countries (not necessarily Johor and Riau) to cope with rising labor costs, although only 3.8 percent said they would relocate their entire operations. Other measures to cope with rising labor costs in Singapore were training, automation, and upgrading to higher-value-added activities; some businesses even contemplate abandoning manufacturing altogether. A second mail questionnaire survey, by Yeoh, et al. (1992), of 310 respondents showed that 47.7 percent already had offshore production facilities: 45.9 percent had facilities in Johor and 10.8 percent in Batam. Respondents who indicated plans to invest in Johor and Batam were mainly engaged in manufacturing, involving both expansion as well as relocation of certain processes. Although biases in responses may be expected, the survey results do point to significant relocation of labor-intensive activities offshore.

The extent of Singapore investments in Johor and Batam is shown in tables 4 and 5. Relocation of production facilities to Johor and Riau appears to have no significant impact on Singapore's industrial structure and employment. The manufacturing sector's share of GDP in 1988–91 remained at 27 percent to 28 percent, largely unchanged from the level of 1980–81. Likewise, the manufacturing sector's share of employment remained at 28 percent to 29 percent of the national total, and the absolute number employed in manufacturing has risen from under 300,000 in 1986 (a recession year) to nearly 430,000 in 1991.

Table 4   Johor: sources of foreign equity in approved projects, 1982–91 (millions of Malaysian dollars)

Country	1982	1983	1984	1985	1986	1987	1988	1989	1990	1991[a]
Indonesia							4.8	1.4	21.1	24.3
Philippines									13.0	
Thailand	0.3						10.2	0.3		
Hong Kong	0.0	1.1	2.4	3.2	6.4	6.5	19.1	36.3	74.0	65.6
South Korea		0.3	0.7				7.5	18.3	89.2	307.5
Singapore	4.8	9.2	22.1	17.6	42.6	41.7	101.9	131.5	406.9	294.5
Taiwan		0.5	1.1	5.5	0.7	54.4	98.3	98.9	212.4	395.7
Japan	0.3	1.4	9.9	2.9	28.5	43.6	49.8	282.7	507.7	221.1
United States	5.3	0.7	0.4		0.5	10.5	123.8	15.6	145.1	32.0
Europe[b]	36.2	0.6	8.0	2.1	1.0	6.2	65.2	92.1	111.4	54.7
Others[c]	5.3	18.6	26.5	19.2	22.3	36.8	77.0	8.6	36.8	722.9
Total	52.1	32.3	71.0	50.5	102.1	199.7	557.6	685.7	1,617.6	2,118.3

a. January to November.
b. Austria, Belgium, Denmark, France, Germany, Great Britain, Italy, Netherlands, Sweden, and Switzerland.
c. Includes Australia, Canada, China, India, New Zealand, Saudi Arabia, and Sri Lanka.

Source: Johor State Economic Development Corporation (JSEDC).

Trade linkages between Singapore and Johor and Riau have increased, but their magnitudes cannot be ascertained in the absence of published statistics.

Effect on Johor

Johor covers 19,000 square kilometers and has a population of 2.2 million. There is intensive movement of people and goods between Johor and Singapore, resulting in serious traffic congestion at the causeway linking the two areas during peak hours. Unfortunately there are no published statistics on the number of people and volume of goods moved across the causeway. A second causeway is being planned, and an extension of Singapore's mass rapid transit system into Johor has also been mooted.

Johor is now Malaysia's second most important industrial region and investment destination (after Selangor). Its share of approved foreign direct investment (FDI) in Malaysia has been rising, to 20 percent in 1989 (Kumar and Lee 1991). Table 4 shows a sharp jump in FDI to Johor after 1987. The main investors are from Japan and the Asian NIEs. Singapore is not the lead investor, although there was a quantum jump in investment approvals from Singapore in 1990. FDI in Johor is wide-based, ranging from proposed multibillion-dollar Taiwanese and Korean steel mills to small Singaporean textile and plastics factories.

The inward surge of FDI is rapidly transforming the physical landscape and the labor and property markets. Labor shortages have emerged in certain critical areas, and wages as well as land and property prices are rising rapidly. The increased investments as well as the surge of visitors

Table 5   Batam: stock of PMA investment, December 1991[a]

Country	Total investments		Total foreign companies	
	Millions of US dollars	Percentage of total	Number	Percentage of total
Singapore	531.8	50.5	51	51.0
United States	159.0	15.2	11	11.0
Japan	119.8	11.4	11	11.0
Hong Kong	88.7	8.4	5	5.0
Netherlands	35.6	3.4	6	6.0
Great Britain	31.5	3.0	5	5.0
France	24.0	2.1	2	2.0
Taiwan	18.8	1.8	1	1.0
Switzerland	16.3	1.5	1	1.0
Thailand	10.0	0.9	1	1.0
Bahamas	8.6	0.8	2	2.0
South Korea	4.0	0.4	2	2.0
Panama	3.0	0.3	1	1.0
Malaysia	3.7	0.3	1	1.0
Total	1,054.8	100.0	100	100.0

a. PMA refers to private limited companies with foreign equity. The investment figures are based on approvals; the level of realized investment is lower.

Source: Batam Industrial Development Authority, Development Data up to December 1991, 35.

from Singapore, taking advantage of the exchange rate and lower prices in Johor, have contributed to a sharp rise in retail prices and the cost of living of Johor residents.

Effect on Riau

To date, the biggest impact of SIJORI has been on the Riau islands. These islands have long been on the periphery of Indonesian development and are only now emerging as a possible major growth center. Linkages between Singapore and the Riau islands, particularly Batam, have grown rapidly in recent years. This is reflected in the growth of ferry services between Singapore and Riau islands; the widespread use of the Singapore currency for transactions in Batam; the development of a direct telephone link between Singapore and the Batam Industrial Park; and the introduction of smart cards for commuting between Singapore and Batam.

Development of Batam   Batam Island is part of Indonesia's Riau province and has an area of 415 square kilometers, two-thirds the size of Singapore, from which it is separated by only a 30- to 40-minute ferry ride. A 1970 presidential decree designated Batam as the logistics base for the Indonesian oil industry. In 1978 Batam was declared a duty-free zone. The Batam Industrial Development Authority (BIDA) is responsible for development of the island. Batam has been growing rapidly since 1988 in population, employment, GDP, tourism, trade, and shipping as a result of the foreign investment boom. The population has grown from 7,000 in the early 1970s to over 100,000. Employment grew from around 6,000 in the mid-1980s to nearly 23,000 in 1991. Workers are brought in from other parts of Indonesia, mainly Java, on a contract basis. Batam's GDP increased by 14 percent annually during 1988–90, much faster than the national average. Batam accounts for 3.5 percent of Riau GDP and 16 percent of its manufacturing sector. Exports from Batam increased 10-fold in five years: from $20.9 million in 1986 to $210.3 million in 1991. Tourist arrivals (mainly from and through Singapore) increased 10-fold from about 60,000 in 1985 to over 600,000 in 1991. Batam has surpassed Bali as the number-two tourist entry point in Indonesia after Jakarta (Pangestu 1991, Ahmad 1992).

Investment in Batam boomed following changes in Indonesian foreign investment policy and the establishment of the Batam Industrial Park. Data from BIDA show that by end-1991 total cumulative investments in Batam amounted to $3.3 billion, of which 19.2 percent is government investment in basic infrastructure; foreign investment accounts for 32.2 percent, domestic private investment 18.3 percent, and nonfacility investment 30.4 percent (nonfacility investment is investment made without prior application to the Indonesian Investment Coordinating Board, and which thus does not receive investment incentives). Most of the companies with nonfacility investment are small in scale or engaged in agriculture. Private-sector investments are concentrated in manufacturing (48.6 percent), followed by tourism and hotel development (17.1 percent) and real estate (18.5 percent). Within manufacturing, the electronics industry is the fastest growing. Investments in residential property and tourism facilities are targeted at the Singapore market. As table 5 shows, investments from Singapore (including multinationals based in Singapore) are the major source of FDI in Batam, accounting for over half the foreign companies. More than 90 percent of present Singapore investments in Batam were undertaken in 1989–91. Singapore's share of Batam FDI was $532 million or 50.5 percent, followed by the United States with 15.2 percent and Japan with 11.4 percent. Investments from Malaysia (including the Johor node of SIJORI) were negligible.

Development of Bintan and other Riau islands   Bintan island is located 42 kilometers, or less than an hour's ferry ride, from Singapore. It has a land area almost double that of Singapore and a population of 130,000. Bintan will be developed for industry and tourism as well as a water supply project to cater to the needs of Singapore and Bintan itself. The development cost is estimated at about $7 billion. The private sector is expected to participate heavily in these three basic infrastructure projects, with the Indonesian government undertaking the provision of infrastructure outside these project areas (Ahmad 1992).

For industrial development in Bintan, a Singapore-Indonesia joint venture with partners from the Indonesian private sector and Singapore's state-owned Jurong Town Corporation will develop a 4,000-hectare bonded industrial estate at Tanjung Uban at an estimated cost of $800 million. Construction is expected to be completed by 1995. The industries planned include aluminum processing, oil refining, downstream petroleum-based products, textiles, garments, electronics, wood-based products, metal components, and agro-based industry. Development of a tourist resort is being undertaken by a consortium of Indonesian and Singapore companies, with the intention of catering to both Singaporean and other foreign tourists. The resort will cover 23,000 hectares. The project is estimated to cost S$3 billion to S$5 billion. Work started in 1991 and will take 10 years to complete. The water supply project will cost about S$1 billion and involves construction of five dams and a water treatment plant. The project is designed to operate for 50 years and will produce 121 million gallons of water per day. A construction contract was signed in March 1992 between Singapore's Public Utilities Board and an Indonesian private-sector group. The entire project will take 15 years to complete.

There are also plans for the joint development with Singapore of the other Riau islands, particularly Bulan (where there are already pig and orchid farms) and Karimun (where a giant shipyard and oil processing center is being proposed).

The Greater South China Subregional Economic Zone

Factors Contributing to Economic Integration in Greater South China

Political Developments and Policy Changes

The GSC SREZ does not have the formal structure of the SIJORI Growth Triangle but is rather an example of economic integration through private-sector linkages. However, while factor complementarity may serve as the basic foundation of the region's economic integration, and geographical proximity and cultural affinity are facilitators, government policies are crucial in determining whether such economic linkages actually take place and to what extent. Taiwan has historically prohibited direct trade with and investment flows to and from China, and diplomatic and official commercial relations are still lacking. Restrictions at a lesser level exist between China and Hong Kong and will remain in place after China resumes sovereignty over Hong Kong in 1997, as the Sino-British Agreement guarantees that Hong Kong will remain a separate customs and currency area, and migration from China to Hong Kong will continue to be restricted.

China launched its open-door policy and economic reforms in 1978 and made moves to build closer links with Hong Kong and Taiwan. Special economic zones were established in the southern provinces of Guangdong and Fujian. Three such zones were set up in Guangdong: namely, Shenzhen and Zhuhai, adjacent to Hong Kong and Macau, respectively, and Shantou, which has close links to the overseas Chinese population. Xiamen, the only SEZ so far established in Fujian, faces Taiwan across the Taiwan Straits.

Officially, Hong Kong businesses do not receive more favorable treatment than other businesses in South China. In practice, however, geographical proximity and kinship ties confer certain significant advantages (Sung 1992). Hong Kong investors have been able to obtain favorable concessions from the Guangdong local authorities, and Hong Kong visitors to China require no visas. However, Hong Kong does not extend reciprocal favored treatment. Hong Kong maintains strict controls on visitors from China for fear of a flood of illegal immigrants. China, in cooperation with Hong Kong, also imposes strict controls on visits to Hong Kong. Still, an estimated 60,000 mainland Chinese are working in China-owned companies in Hong Kong (Sung 1992).

Taiwan, because of the rapid growth of its foreign-exchange reserves and the escalation in its labor costs in recent years, has carried out a policy of import liberalization and currency appreciation so as to reduce its increasingly and embarrassingly large trade surpluses. These developments have enabled Hong Kong to take advantage of its geographical location, excellent infrastructure, and communal and kinship ties to serve as middleman for trade and investment between Taiwan and China.

China does not regard Taiwan as a foreign country, and Taiwanese businesses enjoy special concessions in China over all other foreign businesses. In June 1980 China abolished all tariffs on imports of goods with Taiwan certificates of origin, on grounds that such trade constituted internal rather than external trade. This concession had to be modified when goods with fake Taiwan certificates of origin began to flood the Chinese market. Thus, in May 1981 China levied adjustment taxes on Taiwan goods; these were fixed at a level below the prevailing import tariffs. Import controls on goods of Taiwanese origin were also less stringent than those from other sources. In 1988 a China State Council decree also accorded Taiwanese investors preferential treatment; this included permission to develop land and a longer duration period before divestment of equity joint ventures. China's local authorities also tend to give Taiwanese investors more favorable treatment in terms of faster approval of investment applications and better support services (Sung 1992).

While China accords preferential treatment to Taiwan (as a reunification move), Taiwan defensively discriminates against China. No direct economic contact is allowed, as a result of which all trade and investment are conducted via third parties, usually via Hong Kong. Although import controls on Chinese products have been gradually liberalized since 1987, only 92 items of indirect imports were allowed by end-1990 (Sung 1992). The import of semi-manufactures from Taiwanese ventures in China for further processing or finishing in Taiwan is prohibited. These trade controls have led to rampant smuggling across the Taiwan Straits. The rapid growth of indirect bilateral trade and investment shows that political and bureaucratic restrictions have not been able to stifle economic exchange, particularly as Hong Kong is able to provide intermediation. Taiwan passed a landmark law in July 1992 paving the way for expanded economic and political links with China. The Statute for Relations across the Taiwan Straits authorizes the lifting of the decades-old bans on a wide range of contacts with China, including direct air and shipping links. The bans will be lifted gradually if China makes concessions, such as renouncing the use of force against Taiwan and halting efforts to isolate Taiwan diplomatically. The law allows direct air, shipping, and communications links with China. It also empowers Taiwan to import Chinese workers to ease the severe Taiwanese labor shortage. Taiwanese visiting China will be allowed a maximum stay of four years instead of the current two years, and travelers will be allowed to carry Chinese currency in and out of Taiwan (*Straits Times*, 17 July 1992).

Economic Complementarity

China's open-door policy and economic reforms have brought about tremendous economic opportunities for its Guangdong province, which is adjacent to Hong Kong and geographically close to Taiwan. Compared with Hong Kong, Guangdong has a massive land area. Its population of over 60 million far outnumbers those of Hong Kong and Taiwan combined, providing a large pool of cheap and trainable labor. Rapidly rising income levels and accumulated savings also make Guangdong a huge potential consumer market. Economic reforms in China have proceeded fastest in Guangdong, with an estimated 80 percent of commodity prices being market determined. On the other hand, Guangdong lacks the capital, technology, management, and marketing expertise for further and accelerated development. Guangdong's provincial and municipal governments have been highly successful in improving the investment climate for foreign business; their actions have included developing infrastructure and industrial facilities to alleviate bottlenecks in production and distribution.

Hong Kong is a commercial and financial center. It has an abundant supply of capital and expertise in management, marketing, and finance, as well as an excellent infrastructure for trade, telecommunications, and finance. However, sustained and rapid economic growth has led to shortages and escalating wages and land costs. There has been massive relocation of production facilities into the Pearl River Delta area of Guangdong. It is estimated that some 80 percent of Hong Kong manufacturers have relocated facilities to Guangdong, most of them outward processing arrangements. A 1991 survey by the Federation of Hong Kong Industries showed that more than 60 percent of respondents identified labor scarcity and escalating wages as the key impetus for moving into the Pearl River Delta (Tan 1992).

Taiwan has an ample supply of investment capital and the world's largest foreign reserves: over $90 billion as of mid-1992. Technical competence is rapidly improving, and Taiwan is producing increasingly sophisticated industrial products for the world market. However, like Hong Kong, it is plagued by rapidly rising costs of land and labor following a sustained period of rapid economic growth. Guangdong appeals as an attractive, low-cost production base for Taiwanese manufactures. Taiwanese investment in China is estimated to have reached $3 billion (Lin 1992).

Thus, these three geographically proximate areas exhibit a high degree of economic complementarity. In combination they have the key ingredients for sustained dynamic growth. Hong Kong and Taiwan will continue to relocate labor-intensive industries and processes to Guangdong and serve as sources of financial, marketing, and technological expertise as well as links to the rest of the world. Economic integration will enhance the competitiveness of all three components of GSC.

Differences in wages and in land and rental costs between Hong Kong and Guangdong are large. Different sources give different estimates. According to the Hong Kong Government Secretariat cited in Wong (1991), the manufacturing wage averaged HK$5,520 a month in Hong Kong in 1990, and less than 20 percent of that in the economic zones in Guangdong (table 6). Wages outside these zones would probably be much lower. Although the statistics are not strictly comparable, the figures in table 6 do indicate that wage costs in Guangdong are substantially lower than those in Johor and Batam.

Geographical and Cultural Proximity

Geographical and cultural proximity has facilitated the establishment of economic linkages between Hong Kong, Guangdong and Fujian provinces, and Taiwan. Hong Kong is only a half-hour train ride from Guangdong, and Taiwan faces Fujian province across the Taiwan Straits. Most of the Chinese population in Hong Kong and Taiwan can trace their roots to Guangdong and Fujian provinces, respectively. Communal and cultural ties, when combined with geographical proximity, can lower transaction and information costs dramatically and facilitate economic linkages between countries. The importance of kinship and communal ties among the overseas Chinese communities is well known and has led to an

Table 6 Costs of land and labor in Hong Kong and Guangdong, 1989

| | Flatted factory space | | Manufacturing wage rate per month |
	Rental price (per square meter per month)	Selling price (per square meter)	
Guangzhou Economic and Technological Development Zone	US$3.4 (approx. HK$27)	US$238–275 (approx. HK$1,856–2,145)	HK$1,000–1,200
Shenzhen Special Economic Zone	Rmb 10–20 (approx. HK$15–29)	Rmb 1,000 (approx. HK$1475)	HK$800
Dongguan	HK$10	n.a.	Rmb 500 (approx. HK$740)
Hong Kong	approx. HK$193	approx. $HK12,000	HK$5520

Source: John Wong, "Economic Integration of Hong Kong and Guangdong: Hong Kong's Outward Processing in China" *Internal Study Paper* 2 (Singapore: Institute of East Asian Political Economy, October 1991).

intricate and effective business network throughout Southeast Asia. In spite of political and bureaucratic barriers, economic networking among the Chinese communities of Hong Kong, Taiwan, and South China has been extensive and growing, much of it indirect and even illegal.

Impact

Intra-subregional Trade

Published statistics on the extent and pattern of Hong Kong–China and China–Taiwan bilateral trade can be very misleading because of the large volume of transshipment and entrepôt trade via Hong Kong and the extensive indirect and illegal trade between China and Taiwan.

Hong Kong–China Since the open-door policy was implemented in 1979, China has established numerous direct economic links with the rest of the world. Nevertheless, the middleman role of Hong Kong has become even more prominent because of the need for intermediation services with a proliferation of trading channels (Sung 1992) and an increasing share of China's merchandise trade is handled through Hong Kong. Table 7 shows that Hong Kong accounted for 44 percent of China's total exports and imports in 1991, the bulk of which represented entrepôt trade. Hong Kong is not only a crucial entrepôt but also a transshipment center for Chinese goods. The extent of transshipment is unrecorded by Hong Kong customs. Sung (1992) estimated that the total share of China's exports retained, reexported, transshipped, and intermediated by Hong Kong

Table 7 Hong Kong and China: bilateral trade, 1980–91

	Hong Kong trade statistics			China's trade with Hong Kong (millions of US dollars)			
	Domestic exports	Reexports	China's share of reexports	Exports to Hong Kong	Reexports via Hong Kong	Imports from Hong Kong	Hong Kong reexports to China
1980							
Millions of HK$	68,171	30,072	8.4				1,438
Percent of total	69.4	30.6	27.9				6.5
1981							
Millions of HK$	80,423	41,739	12.8	5,293	1,828	1,961	
Percent of total	65.8	34.2	30.7	24.1	8.3	8.9	
1982							
Millions of HK$	83,032	44,353	14.7				
Percent of total	65.2	34.8	33.1				
1983							
Millions of HK$	104,405	56,294	19.7	5,818	2,139	2,531	1,675
Percent of total	65.0	35.0	35.0	26.2	9.6	11.8	7.8
1984							
Millions of HK$	137,936	83,504	28.1	6,689	2,709	5,033	3,590
Percent of total	62.3	37.7	33.7	25.6	10.4	18.4	13.1
1985							
Millions of HK$	129,882	105,270	34.6	7,168	3,422	7,857	5,907
Percent of total	55.2	44.8	32.9	26.2	12.5	18.6	14

Year		Col 1	Col 2	Col 3	Col 4	Col 5	Col 6	Col 7
1986	Millions of HK$	153,983	122,546	51.6	9,778	5,045	7,550	5,241
	Percent of total	55.7	44.3	42.1	31.6	16.3	17.6	12.2
1987	Millions of HK$	195,254	182,780	84.3	13,762	8,052	11,290	7,716
	Percent of total	51.6	48.4	46.1	34.8	20.4	26.1	17.9
1988	Millions of HK$	217,664	275,405	131.3	18,269	12,690	17,030	12,157
	Percent of total	44.1	55.9	47.7	38.4	26.7	30.8	22.4
1989	Millions of HK$	224,104	346,405	188.3	21,916	17,323	18,816	13,268
	Percent of total	39.3	60.7	54.4	41.7	32.9	31.8	22.4
1990	Millions of HK$	225,876	413,999	240.4	26,650	22,287	20,305	14,219
	Percent of total	35.3	64.7	58.1	42.9	35.9	38.1	26.6
1991	Millions of HK$	231,045	534,841	315.7	13,536	11,524	11,774	8,685
	Percent of total	30.2	69.8	59.0	44.5	37.9	44	32.4

a. The 1991 figures for China's trade with Hong Kong represent only the first half of 1991. Percentage shares for China's trade with Hong Kong refer to China's total exports divided by imports. Exports to Hong Kong = reexports via Hong Kong + exports retained in Hong Kong (not shown).

Sources: Census and Statistics Department, Annual Digest of Statistics, various years; Census and Statistics Department, Monthly Digest of Statistics, August 1991. Nomura Research Institute, Asian Perspectives, December 1991, 31; Census and Statistics Department, 1991 Economic Background; Sung Yun-Wing, "Non-Institutional Economic Integration via Cultural Affinity: The Case of Mainland China, Taiwan and Hong Kong." Paper presented at the International Symposium on the Coordination of Chinese Economic Systems, organized by the Hong Kong Society of Asia and Pacific 21 Ltd., the Democracy Foundation (Taiwan), and the Centre for East-West Studies in Hong Kong, Hong Kong, January 1992.

amounted to 56 percent in 1990. Similarly, the total share of China's imports produced, reexported, transshipped, and intermediated by Hong Kong amounted to 49 percent.

In turn, China's impact on the level and pattern of Hong Kong's trade is substantial. In 1980 domestic exports accounted for 70 percent and reexports for 30 percent of Hong Kong total exports; in 1991 the shares were almost exactly reversed (table 7). China dominates Hong Kong's entrepôt trade; it was the source of 59 percent of such trade and the destination for 29 percent in 1991. An increasing share of Hong Kong's domestic exports are also China-bound, rising from 0.2 percent in 1978 to 23.5 percent in 1991 (Sung 1992). China and Hong Kong are each other's most important trading partners.

A large part of the growth in Hong Kong–China trade is bound up with the outward processing phenomenon, in which Hong Kong manufacturers contract or subcontract their production to Guangdong. This phenomenon came into prominence beginning in 1988. Data for the first three quarters of 1991 show that 77 percent of Hong Kong domestic exports, 49 percent of its reexports to China, and 66 percent of its imports from China were due to outward processing activities (Sung 1992). Hong Kong's Trade Development Council surveys of 1988 and 1991 show that, of total exports undertaken by the surveyed firms in Hong Kong, the share made in China rose from 35.8 percent to 57.6 percent, and the share made in Hong Kong fell from 35.8 percent to 22.1 percent; depending on product categories, the share sourced from China ranged from 53 percent to 92 percent. The effect of outward processing on Hong Kong trade is also evident in the declining share of miscellaneous manufactures (Standard International Trade Classification 8) in domestic exports and its rapid growth in reexports. The significance of outward processing for China is reflected in the fact that the share of total exports generated by processing imported raw materials in 1989 was 40 percent and rose further in 1990. Enterprises with foreign equity investment accounted for 7.9 percent of total China exports in 1989, but the share was much higher in Guangdong (28 percent). In 1991 Guangdong alone accounted for $13 billion in exports, or more than 20 percent of China's total exports.

Hong Kong earns a substantial value-added margin by acting as China's entrepôt. In 1990, 62 percent of Chinese exports to the United States were reexported through Hong Kong. Apart from merchandise, Hong Kong exports a wide range of services to China, but there are no reliable data on such transactions. Hong Kong visitors accounted for 66 percent of tourist arrivals and tourist expenditures in China in 1990. Travel to China by Hong Kong residents mushroomed from nearly 4 million visits in 1980 to more than 16 million visits in 1990 alone (Sung 1992). Hong Kong is also the foremost gateway for foreigners touring China.

China-Taiwan   As noted above, there is no direct trade between China and Taiwan. China allows some direct "minor" trade through designated coastal mainland ports, but Taiwan regards this as illegal. Indirect trade is conducted mainly through Hong Kong, and there is rampant smuggling across the Taiwan Straits. Sung (1992) noted that, besides direct smuggling, it is well-known that Taiwanese businessmen have illegally transshipped goods to China via Hong Kong on a large scale. Such goods are reported on the bill of lading as destined for Hong Kong when the cargo carriers exit Taiwan; but the shipment documents are switched in midvoyage and the goods transshipped via Hong Kong to China. The magnitude of such trade is indicated by the large discrepancies between Hong Kong and Taiwanese trade statistics on the countries' bilateral trade: in 1990, recorded Taiwanese exports to Hong Kong exceeded Hong Kong imports from Taiwan by $1 billion.

In 1990 indirect bilateral trade reached over $5 billion, the bulk being via Hong Kong (tables 8 and 9). In the first five months of 1992 indirect trade reached $2.8 billion, showing a growth rate of 33 percent (*Asian Wall Street Journal*, 27 July 1992). The trade remained largely one-sided, with $2.3 billion exported and only $0.5 billion imported by Taiwan. The tourist traffic between China and Taiwan is also largely one-way. Of the 950,000 Taiwanese visitors to China in 1990, 920,000 entered via Hong Kong (Sung 1992).

Intra-subregional Investment

Hong Kong–China   China's attempts to attract FDI since 1978 have attracted investments mainly from Hong Kong, Taiwan, and the ethnic Chinese communities in Southeast Asia. Investors from the United States, Japan, and other advanced countries have remained wary of China's political changes and its unfamiliar bureaucratic system. Investments from Western countries dropped sharply after the Tiananmen Square incident in June 1989, as China was chastised for its human rights violations. US cumulative investment in China was equivalent to only 37 percent of US investment in Hong Kong and only 0.6 percent of its total overseas investment by end-1990. Similarly, Japan's cumulative investment in China up to mid-1990 was only 29 percent of its investment in Hong Kong and only 0.9 percent of its total overseas investment (Sung 1992). However, recent indications are that Japan has accelerated the pace of its investments in China in a reassessment of China's political risk and investment climate.

Chinese statistics show that Hong Kong contracted investment in China in 1978–90 amounted to $26.5 billion, with only 52 percent, or $14 billion, utilized. The official statistics are gross overestimates, as they include investments by foreign multinationals based in Hong Kong, Taiwanese

Table 8 China: bilateral trade with Taiwan, 1988–91

	Exports to Taiwan			Imports from Taiwan		
	Indirect exports via Hong Kong	Direct exports	Total	Indirect imports via Hong Kong	Transhipment via Hong Kong	Total
1988						
Millions of US dollars	382			2,239	121	2,360
Percent of total	0.8			4.1	0.2	4.3
1989						
Millions of US dollars	470	93	563	2,896	697	3,593
Percent of total	0.9	0.2	1.1	4.9	1.2	6.1
1990						
Millions of US dollars	612	320	932	3,278	1,456	4,734
Percent of total	1.0	0.5	1.5	6.1	2.7	8.9
1991[a]						
Millions of US dollars	393	241	634	2,048	1,479	3,527
Percent of total	1.3	0.8	2.1	7.6	5.5	13.2

a. Percentage shares are those of China's exports or imports.

Source: Sung Yun-Wing. "Non-Institutional Economic Integration via Cultural Affinity: The Case of Mainland China, Taiwan and Hong Kong." Paper presented at the Conference on Regional Cooperation and Growth Triangles in ASEAN, organized by the National University of Singapore, Singapore, 23–24 April 1992.

Table 9 Taiwan: bilateral trade with China, 1988–91

	Exports to China			Imports from China		
	Indirect exports via Hong Kong	Transshipped via Hong Kong	Total	Indirect imports via Hong Kong	Direct imports	Total
1988						
Millions of US dollars	1,964	116	2,080	476		
Percent of total	3.2	0.2	3.4	1.0		
1989						
Millions of US dollars	2,540	642	3,210	587	97	684
Percent of total	3.4	1.0	4.8	1.1	0.2	1.3
1990						
Millions of US dollars	2,875	1,361	4,275	765	333	1,098
Percent of total	4.3	2.1	6.3	1.4	0.6	2.0
1991[a]						
Millions of US dollars	1,781	1,417	3,203	491	251	742
Percent of total	4.9	3.9	8.9	1.6	0.8	2.4

a. Percentage shares are those of China's exports or imports.

Source: Sung Yun-Wing. "Non-Institutional Economic Integration via Cultural Affinity: The Case of Mainland China, Taiwan and Hong Kong." Paper presented at the Conference on Regional Cooperation and Growth Triangles in ASEAN, organized by the National University of Singapore, Singapore, 23–24 April 1992.

investments via Hong Kong, and even Chinese investments made via Hong Kong to take advantage of Chinese foreign investment incentives. There is also evidence that Hong Kong investors often connive with local Chinese officials to overstate the value of their investments (Sung 1992). Hong Kong investments in Guangdong have become more diversified, from the initial small-scale, labor-intensive operations to more recent large-scale, infrastructural projects.

China has also been investing in Hong Kong, and these investments have grown sharply in recent years. Earlier Chinese business interests were mainly in banking, retail trade, warehousing, tourism, and shipping, but they have since diversified into manufacturing, construction, and real estate. Cumulative investment in Hong Kong is estimated to be around $10 billion, with 30 percent in manufacturing. On record there are about 400 Chinese state-owned enterprises operating in Hong Kong. Lin (1992) argues that this is a gross underestimate, as each state enterprise can set up a host of subsidiaries to evade China's control on foreign trade and foreign exchange. The actual number of Chinese firms could be as high as 5,000.

China-Taiwan   China has accorded preferential treatment to investments from Taiwan since 1988, but until 1991 Taiwan banned all investments in China. In 1991 the Taiwan government formally sanctioned indirect investment and officially asked firms with investments in China to register with the Ministry of Economic Affairs; more than 2,700 firms registered (Lin 1992).

Taiwanese investments in China have escalated in recent years. Official statistics show that during 1979–87 cumulative Taiwanese investments totaled only $100 million and were mainly in Fujian province. In 1988 alone, the amount jumped to $300 million, and in 1989 to $600 million, making a cumulative investment of $1 billion for 1979–89. The Chung Hua Institute for Economic Research has estimated that Taiwanese investment in China could have been as high as $3.7 billion by April 1991 (Lin 1992).

Investments in China accelerated in 1992. The bulk of Taiwanese investments in China are concentrated in Guangdong and Fujian provinces. Taiwanese investments initially went mostly to Fujian province, especially Xiamen because of kinship ties, but the investments quickly spread to the Pearl River Delta and the 14 coastal cities, especially Shanghai and Tianjin (Lin 1992). The sectoral distribution of investments shows concentrations in electronics, footwear, plastics, garments, umbrellas, and travel accessories, representing mostly Taiwan's sunset industries. However, more recent investments are larger and more inclined toward technology-intensive products such as chemicals, building materials, automobiles, and electronic products and components. There has also been diversification beyond manufacturing into real estate, finance, tourism, and even agriculture.

Taiwan still prohibits investments from China, although such investments are reported to have taken place, through overseas subsidiaries of Chinese firms (Sung 1992).

Effects on Hong Kong and Taiwan

The economic prosperity of Hong Kong is increasingly linked with that of China. The impact of China on the Hong Kong economy is twofold. First, the massive relocation of production facilities to Guangdong, mostly in the form of outward processing, has enabled Hong Kong to overcome its labor shortage and facilitated economic restructuring out of labor-intensive manufacturing toward higher-value-added manufacturing and service activities. Success in this economic restructuring is evident from Hong Kong statistics on GDP and employment. The share of manufacturing in GDP shrank from 22.5 percent in 1980 to 15.8 percent in 1990, while its share of private-sector employment fell from 49.3 percent to 31.3 percent (table 10). Manufacturing employment has even declined in absolute terms, from 900,000 in 1980 to less than 700,000 in 1991. With the shedding of low-end manufacturing operations, productivity has improved. Relocation of labor-intensive processes to low-cost Guangdong has enabled Hong Kong manufactures to remain competitive in international markets and increased the demand for Hong Kong's services, including entrepôt, shipping, insurance, and other business and financial services.

Second, Hong Kong resumed its historical role as the entrepôt of South China, and this led to a boom in its entrepôt trade. By 1988 Hong Kong's total reexports exceeded its total domestic exports. China's share of Hong Kong domestic exports jumped from 17.5 percent in 1988 to 21.2 percent in 1990. Outward processing is the main factor in the phenomenal growth of Hong Kong reexports and domestic exports to China. The importance of the China trade to Hong Kong's economy can be seen from estimates of the impact on Hong Kong should China lose its most-favored-nation status in the United States. The Hong Kong Director-General of Trade estimated that Hong Kong stands to lose up to HK$123 billion in overall trade, or 8 percent of Hong Kong's total trade, and as many as 60,000 jobs; it could also halve Hong Kong's GDP growth rate for 1992 from 5 percent to 2.5 percent (*South China Morning Post*, 14 March 1992). Hong Kong's loss would be felt in both reexport margins and in decreased profits from outward processing. According to Sung (1992), Hong Kong's loss could be as large as China's, because of the low value added from outward processing activities.

The impact of the GSC SREZ on Taiwan's economy is less dramatic than that on Hong Kong. The economic linkages have been indirect,

Table 10 Hong Kong: sectoral composition of employment and value added, 1980 and 1990

Sector	No. of persons engaged[a]		Value added[b] (millions of $HK)	
	1980	1990	1980	1990
Mining and quarrying	809	511	213	209
Percent of total	0.0	0.0	0.2	0.0
Manufacturing	907,463	715,597	30,549	88,825
Percent of total	49.3	31.3	22.5	15.8
Electricity and gas	9,312	11,481	1,703	12,623
Percent of total	0.5	0.5	1.3	2.2
Construction	90,498	69,138	8,570	30,730
Percent of total	4.9	3.0	6.3	5.5
Commerce	455,100	829,591	26,169	127,575
Percent of total	24.7	36.3	19.3	22.7
Transport, storage, and communication	77,272	132,792	9,645	49,504
Percent of total	4.2	5.8	7.1	8.8
Financial and business services	131,600	276,621	29,292	109,135
Percent of total	7.2	12.1	21.6	19.4
Community, social, and personal services	167,966	250,241	16,066	82,472
Percent of total	9.1	10.9	11.8	14.7
Other[c]			13,406	61,183
Percent of total			9.9	10.9
Total	1,840,111	2,286,061	135,613	562,256

a. Figures are those for the fourth quarter of the year.
b. Sectoral shares were computed based on factor cost without taking into consideration imputed bank service charges and import duties. Hence the percentages shown may differ from those found in the original source.
c. Includes agriculture and fishing and ownership premises.

Sources: Census and Statistics Department, *Estimates of Gross Domestic Product*, 1966 to 1991; *Annual Digest of Statistics*, various years; *Monthly Digest of Statistics*, August 1991.

started later, and were of smaller magnitude than those between Hong Kong and South China. The entrepôt role is also absent for Taiwan. Given the indirect nature of the economic linkages, the impact on the Taiwanese economy is not readily measurable. However, the surge of Taiwanese investment in China in recent years has raised security concerns for Taiwan as well as concerns about a possible hollowing out of Taiwanese industry. In July 1990 the Taiwanese government attempted to cool the China investment fever by improving the investment environment in Taiwan itself and by encouraging Taiwanese businesses to invest more in ASEAN. However, the July 1992 legislation sanctioning conditional direct contacts with China is likely to lead to a greater surge in investments in China.

Effect on Guangdong

Guangdong has received a disproportionately large share of China's FDI inflows by virtue of its three SEZs and its proximity to Hong Kong and

Taiwan. In recent years the province accounted for about 25 percent of total foreign capital inflows and about 35 percent to 40 percent of total FDI in China (Wong 1991). During 1979–89 contracted foreign investment amounted to $20.9 billion, with $10.3 billion utilized. Foreign investment received includes both FDI and foreign funds involved in outward processing operations. In 1990 foreign investment accounted for 54 percent of China's exports, of which outward processing accounted for 41 percent and FDI enterprises accounted for only 13 percent (Sung 1992).

Guangdong has become the richest and most dynamic province in China. Per capita GNP is estimated at $600, far above the national norm, and that of Shenzhen exceeds $1,000. The Pearl River Delta, which includes the Shenzhen and Zhuhai SEZs, is the engine of growth for the province. During 1979–89, Guangdong provincial GDP grew at an annual rate of 12.3 percent, compared with the national average of 9.0 percent. The manufacturing sector grew at 17.8 percent a year, and its share of GDP reached 42 percent in 1989. The share of state-owned enterprises declined to 38 percent by 1989. Over 80 percent of industrial output came from small and medium-sized enterprises. A 1991 survey by the Federation of Hong Kong Industries shows an estimated 3 million workers employed in Guangdong by Hong Kong firms. Wages in the sector that includes foreign-invested enterprises were 30 percent higher than the national norm in 1989, and grew at 14.5 percent a year in 1986–89 (Sung 1992).

There are indications that FDI is spreading from the southern and coastal zones toward the north and inland, where wage rates are considerably lower. And the success of the Guangdong model has encouraged China's political leadership to push forward with economic reforms and to replicate the Guangdong model in other parts of China.

Comparison of the SIJORI and greater south China SREZs It is useful to note the similarities and differences between SIJORI and GSC. The main similarity is that both these SREZs belong to the category of metropolitan spillover subregions, with some of the characteristics of a transnational export processing zone, and with geopolitical factors as important, but not overriding elements in their formation. The driving forces mentioned above—namely, economic complementarity, geographical proximity, infrastructure, political endorsement and intergovernmental cooperation, and export markets—are all present in both SREZs.

However, there are also a number of differences (Lee 1992a). First, GSC, and in particular Hong Kong–Guangdong, is larger and far more advanced in its economic integration than SIJORI. GSC has a much larger population (90 million excluding Fujian and about 120 million with it) and a much larger GDP than SIJORI. Economic integration of GSC began with China's economic reforms and open-door policy in 1978, and the process has accelerated since 1988. SIJORI took off later, although it is difficult to pinpoint the date. Companies in Singapore began relocating to Johor from the early 1980s on, and especially since 1987 when the labor market was tight. However, the Singapore-Riau connection took off only after 1988. The extent of Hong Kong and Taiwanese investments in Guangdong (and Fujian) is much greater than Singapore investments in Johor or Riau. The Hong Kong dollar is used as a transaction currency in Guangdong to a greater degree than the Singapore dollar is used in Johor or Riau. The Monetary Authority of Singapore actively discourages the regionalization of the Singapore dollar, as it could greatly exacerbate its volatility.

Second, there is a sharp difference in the level of government commitment and formal institutional framework. SIJORI shows formal government commitment to economic integration at the highest level, including the signing of bilateral treaties between Singapore and Indonesia. For GSC, the main impetus came from China's economic reforms, while Taiwan still disallows direct linkages with China. Third, there are sharp differences in political and historical relationships. The GSC incorporates different political and economic systems, but communal and cultural ties help overcome these institutional differences. For SIJORI, differences in political and economic systems are minor, but ethnic and cultural ties are also less important and are, in fact, a somewhat politically sensitive issue.

Fourth, there are differences in the types of investors and investments. While GSC investments in Guangdong and Fujian are dominated by indigenous private investors from Hong Kong and Taiwan, Singapore investments in Riau (but to a lesser extent in Johor) are dominated by Japanese, American, and European multinationals with operations in Singapore and by Singapore state enterprises. Initial investments in Guangdong have been largely concentrated on manufacturing and undertaken by small and medium-sized enterprises. Only more recently, as economic reforms have taken hold and political risks have been reduced, have Hong Kong and Taiwanese conglomerates and large enterprises ventured to invest in South China on a larger scale and diversified into infrastructure development and real estate. For SIJORI, investments in tourist and leisure facilities such as hotels and golf courses are important, while in GSC, tourism development lags behind manufacturing investments.

Effects, Implications, and Prospects

Effects and Implications of SREZs

The case studies of SIJORI and GSC in this paper have highlighted many effects and issues related to the emergence and development of subregional economic zones. Some of these are outlined below.

Growth, Employment, and Structural Change

There are many positive effects arising from the metropolitan spillover subregion version of the SREZ for its participating members. For the less developed areas of the SREZ there are the usual positive growth, employment, and technology transfer effects arising from accelerated inflows of foreign investment and increased domestic investment for infrastructural development and directly productive activities. The presence of export-oriented foreign investors and the ready availability of export infrastructure (finance, transportation, telecommunications, and trade networks) enable these areas with limited experience to have a jump start in export manufacturing. As the initial areas become more developed in terms of infrastructure, industry, and employment, the effects of economic development spread to an ever-widening zone, so that these areas themselves become secondary growth poles.

For the urban metropolis, outward investment, relocation of industries, and outward processing to the less developed areas facilitate the process of industrial restructuring toward higher-value-added manufacturing and service activities, with consequent improvements in resource allocation and gains in productivity. The Singapore and Hong Kong experiences suggest that there have been no major relocation costs or negative effects from the hollowing out of their industry. Instead, the high-value-added functions are retained or are attracted to the metropolis. At the same time outward investment to a geographically proximate area provides the domestic firms with the learning experience for eventual internationalization.

For the type of SREZ typified by the Tumen River Delta Area, where the basic rationale is joint development of infrastructure to attract investments from outside the SREZ to develop the subregion's resources, the economic gains from infrastructural development are obvious. However, such proposals face the severe problem of finding financing for the scale of investment required and ensuring attractive returns to such investments.

Political, Distributional, and Social Issues

The SREZ as a transnational phenomenon involves relations at multiple levels and different perceptions of the benefits and costs of participation. These may be differentiated into relations and effects between the central government and provinces not in the SREZ and the province in the SREZ and between participating areas and between economic and social groups within the SREZ.

Since an SREZ involves parts of different countries, there is the possibility of perceived conflicts of interest between the participating province and its central government and other provinces within the country. For example, there are already indications of unhappiness in some quarters in Malaysia and Indonesia over the perception that areas of these countries are coming "under the influence" of Singapore. In Malaysia, the economic advantage that Johor enjoys with SIJORI has introduced a new element in federal-provincial and interprovincial relations. In Jakarta, some have questioned the utility and equity of large government infrastructure expenditures on the Riau islands of Batam and Bintan, which are perceived to be benefiting only a small elite group, especially when there are strong contending claims for development funds in other parts of Indonesia. Some argue that the SREZ increases FDI in the Riau islands, but possibly at the expense of other parts of Indonesia, due to the investment diversion effect. However, this intracountry resource allocation issue is not peculiar to the SREZ, as it would also arise in a national EPZ. In China, the growing disparities in the level of development and standard of living between the southern coastal provinces of Guangdong and Fujian on the one hand and the northern and inland provinces on the other is also emerging as an issue. This has led China's leader, Deng Xiaoping, to launch an aggressive campaign to open up the interior to trade and foreign investment and to encourage the southern coastal provinces to act as models of development and engines of growth for the rest of China.

Relations between the more developed and less developed areas of an SREZ are akin to metropolis-hinterland or center-periphery relations within a single country. However, when the urban center and the hinterland are located in different countries, and where there are ethnic overtones, the political sensitivities are much greater. It would appear that the issue of adjustment costs and distribution is more sensitive in SIJORI than in GSC, even though the intensity of change and economic integration are greater in GSC. In the urban metropolis, adjustment costs have fallen on those workers who have lost their jobs with the relocation of industries; for unskilled workers of mature age, finding a new job can be difficult. Small and medium-sized enterprises also worry about loss of business when their multinational customers relocate offshore and they have difficulties in maintaining business links. For the rapidly expanding economies of Hong Kong and Singapore, such adjustments do not pose a serious political, social, and economic problem. In the less developed areas, on the other hand, there are social problems of massive immigration, particularly of young female workers. Infrastructural bottlenecks in housing and transportation could develop, and traffic congestion and environmental pollution could rise noticeably. Consumer groups in Johor have been vocal about some adverse effects of the Singapore connection, manifested in a higher cost of living, escalation in real estate values, traffic congestion, and a rise in socially undesirable activities. In Batam and Bintan there are issues of unfair compensation for community and private land acquired for infrastructural, industrial, tourism, and commercial development.

These political, social, and distributional issues arise as a result of accelerated economic growth within the SREZ. In order to ensure continuing economic integration and growth, the political economy of SREZs needs to be handled with care. Rapid economic growth and its attendant consequences for economic and social adjustments will always upset those who wish to maintain the status quo. Governments (and politicians) have a role to play in managing the political overtones, inasmuch as they have a role in liberalizing investment regulations and facilitating infrastructural development and hence the process of economic integration.

Prospects

Notwithstanding political sensitivities and distributional issues, the economic forces of complementarity, comparative advantage, and division of labor have led to the development of SREZs. What are the prospects for SIJORI and GSC for the remainder of the 1990s? What is the likely evolution of SREZs? To what extent are SREZs replicable elsewhere?

As both SIJORI and GSC evolve, their character will change. Both Johor and Batam are experiencing shortages of skilled workers, which are expected to worsen as investments in the pipeline come into commercial production. The fact of an emerging scarcity of labor is discouraging new investments in Johor. In Batam, industrial estates such as Batam Industrial Park are assisting investors in recruiting workers from Java and other parts of Indonesia. In Guangdong and Fujian, the labor pool is huge and can be readily augmented by migration from other parts of the country. Nonetheless, the present subregional division of labor cannot be sustained. There are limits to the relocation of "sunset" and "residual" industries from Singapore and Hong Kong to the less developed areas. And both Batam and Johor in SIJORI and coastal South China in GSC are pressing for more FDI with higher value added, skills, and technology. The Malaysian Minister of Trade and Industry, Datuk Seri Rafidah Aziz, recently reiterated that Malaysia had graduated out of the "cheap labour country club" and would like Singapore investors to look at Malaysia as a location for non-labor-intensive investments (*Straits Times*, 7 August 1992).

Investments in Johor and Riau and coastal South China are already diversifying away from labor-intensive industries. Newer investments include infrastructural projects, resource-based and tourism projects, and property development; these are not the labor-intensive and low-value-added investments that typify export platforms. For South China, investors are also anticipating further liberalization measures that will enable them to participate in the state enterprises being privatized.

There is also evidence that SREZs are extending beyond their original geographical boundaries. For example, the GSC first started with Hong

Kong and Shenzhen. As Shenzhen became more developed, costs rose, and investments spilled over into other parts of the Pearl River Delta and the rest of Guangdong province. Similarly, developments in the Indonesian part of SIJORI started with Batam but have since extended to other Riau islands such as Bintan, Bulan, and Karimun. And as Johor experiences labor shortages and rising property prices, investors have gone further north to Malacca and elsewhere. In other words, the initial "hinterlands" of SREZs could themselves develop into growth poles, generating spillover effects into ever-widening contiguous areas.

The replication of SREZs in the Asia-Pacific region is contingent on the presence of the same key factors that promoted their growth in SIJORI and GSC: namely, economic complementarity, geographical proximity, infrastructure availability, and government commitment to facilitate the cross-border movements of capital, people, and goods. The success of SIJORI has a demonstration effect and could encourage formation of other growth triangles in ASEAN, although not all of the proposed SREZs will have the same favorable conditions. The emergence of multiple and overlapping growth triangles may lead to their eventual merger under the umbrella of the ASEAN Free Trade Area. The success of GSC will encourage China to seek further SREZs for its huge country, possibly linking southwestern China with Thailand and Indochina, and northeastern China with the Korean peninsula.

With a growing number of countries in the Asia-Pacific region pursuing FDI to promote economic development, the intensified competition will lead to the formation of more SREZs to maximize attractions for investors. Geographic competition for FDI will increasingly take the form of competition among SREZs rather than among individual countries. There may be eventual specialization among SREZs as each seeks its own niche in the regional and international division of labor (Wong 1992).

Although they are currently export platforms, it is conceivable that, with rapid economic growth and newfound affluence, SREZs will also evolve into consumption centers, much like other metropolitan areas around the world. SREZs would then be a truly major motive force and engines of growth in the Asia Pacific.

References

Ahmad, Mubariq. 1992. "Economic Cooperation in the Southern Growth Triangle: An Indonesian Perspective." Paper presented at the Conference on Regional Cooperation and Growth Triangles in ASEAN, organized by the National University of Singapore, Singapore (23–24 April).

Batam Industrial Development Authority. 1992. *Development Data up to December 1991.*

Chia Siow Yue. 1992. "Trade and Investment in the Asia-Pacific." Paper presented at the Second Training Seminar on Monetary and Fiscal Policies, organized by the Asian Development Bank and the Institute for Fiscal and Monetary Policies, Tokyo (March).

Habibie, B. J. 1992. "Technology and the Singapore-Johor-Riau Growth Triangle." Speech delivered at the Tripartite Meeting and Seminar on Economic Development in the Growth Triangle and Its Environment Impact, Batam (8 May).

Koo Bon Hoo. 1991. "The Tumen River Area Development Program." Paper presented at the United Nations Chitose Forum on South-South Economic Cooperation with Particular Reference to Asia and the Pacific, organized by UNCTAD, Chitose (May).

Kumar, Sree, and Lee Tsao Yuan. 1991. "A Singapore Perspective." In Lee Tsao Yuan, ed., *Growth Triangle: The Johor-Singapore-Riau Experience*, 1–36. Singapore: Institute of Southeast Asian Studies and Institute of Policy Studies.

Lee Tsao Yuan. 1992a. "Regional Economic Zones in the Asia-Pacific: An Overview." Paper presented at the Conference on Regional Cooperation and Growth Triangles in ASEAN, organized by the National University of Singapore, Singapore (23–24 April).

Lee Tsao Yuan. 1992b. "Growth Triangles in ASEAN." *PITO Economic Briefs* 10. Honolulu: East-West Center.

Lin Tzong-Biau. 1992. "Economic Nexus Between the Two Sides of the Taiwan Straits, with Special Emphasis on Hong Kong's Role." Paper presented at the International Academic Conference on Outward Looking Strategy and Development of the Economy, Guangdong (June).

McGee, T. G., and Scott MacLeod. 1992. "Emerging Extended Metropolitan Regions in the Asian-Pacific Urban System: A Case Study of the Singapore-Johor-Riau Growth Triangle." Paper presented at the Workshop on the Asian Pacific Urban System: Towards the 21st Century, held at Chinese University of Hong Kong, Hong Kong (11–13 February).

Pangestu, Mari. 1991. "An Indonesian Perspective." In Lee Tsao Yuan, ed., *Growth Triangle: The Johor-Singapore-Riau Experience*, 75–116. Singapore: Institute of Southeast Asian Studies and Institute of Policy Studies.

Salleh, Ismail Muhd. 1992. "Economic Cooperation in the Northern Triangle." Paper presented at the Conference on Regional Cooperation and Growth Triangles in ASEAN, organized by the National University of Singapore, Singapore (23–24 April).

Scalapino, Robert A. 1992. "The United States and Asia: Future Prospects." *Foreign Affairs* Winter 1991–92: 19–40.

Sung Yun-Wing. 1992. "Non-Institutional Economic Integration via Cultural Affinity: The Case of Mainland China, Taiwan and Hong Kong." Paper presented at the International Symposium on the Coordination of Chinese Economic Systems, organized by the Hong Kong Society of Asia and Pacific 21 Ltd., the Democracy Foundation (Taiwan), and the Centre for East-West Studies in Hong Kong, Hong Kong, January.

Tan, Clifford. 1992. "Growth Triangles from Several Angles: A NIE Perspective Based Upon Hong Kong–Guangdong Industrialisation." Paper presented at the Conference on Regional Cooperation and Growth Triangles in ASEAN, organized by the National University of Singapore, Singapore (23–24 April).

Wong Poh Kam. 1992. "Economic Cooperation in the Southern Growth Triangle: A Long Term Perspective." Paper presented at the Conference on Regional Cooperation and Growth Triangles in ASEAN, organized by the National University of Singapore, Singapore (23–24 April).

Wong, John. 1991. "Economic Integration of Hong Kong and Guangdong: Hong Kong's Outward Processing in China." *Internal Study Paper* 2. Singapore: Institute of East Asian Political Economy (October).

Yeoh, Caroline, Lau Geok Theng, and G. Ray Funkhouser. 1992. "Summary Report: Business Trends in the Growth Triangle." Singapore: Faculty of Business Administration, National University of Singapore (mimeographed).

IV

Systemic Implications of Pacific Dynamism

8

Changing Patterns of Direct Investment and the Implications for Trade and Development

SHUJIRO URATA

The economies of the Asia-Pacific region have been outperforming the rest of the world in the economic growth race for the last few decades. In the 1950s and 1960s Japan achieved remarkable economic growth, while in the 1970s and 1980s the developing economies in the region, namely the Asian newly industrializing economies (the NIEs, hereafter), the Association of Southeast Asian Nations (ASEAN), and China, have shown impressively high growth performance. Favorable economic performance in recent years by these economies has not been achieved without difficulties, however. In the early 1980s a number of economies faced serious balance of payments problems, but with structural adjustment policies, most of the economies have overcome the problems and regained growth momentum.

Rapid export expansion contributed significantly to economic growth of the economies in the Asia Pacific, as export earnings enabled them to import important items for promoting economic development such as capital goods and foreign technology. Although foreign trade is still very important for these economies to maintain rapid growth, foreign direct investment (FDI) has come to play an important role in promoting economic development in the 1980s, especially in the second half of the decade. FDI can contribute to economic development in various ways, since FDI transfers not only financial resources, which would be used to expand production facilities, but also technology and management know-

Shujiro Urata is Associate Professor of Economics, School of Social Sciences, Waseda University. The author is grateful for the comments from Edward M. Graham, Somsak Tambunlertchai, Marc Noland, and other participants at the conference.

how, which would improve technical and managerial efficiency. More-over, it has been recognized that FDI promotes economic development by expanding marketing and information networks.

In light of the increasing importance of FDI in economic development in the Asia Pacific, we attempt to achieve two objectives in this paper. One is to examine the pattern of FDI in the Asia Pacific, and the other is to analyze the impact of FDI on the economic development of the countries in the Asia Pacific. In the final section of the paper, some concluding comments will be presented.

Changing Pattern of FDI in Asia

FDI in the world increased rapidly in the 1980s, and the rate of increase accelerated in the second half of the 1980s. Asia has been an active investor as well as an increasingly important recipient of FDI. In this section, we first examine the changes in the importance of Asia in world FDI. We then study the changing patterns of FDI in Asia closely by focusing separately on Japan, the NIEs, and ASEAN.

Rapid Increase of FDI in Asia

Table 1 shows the changing patterns of both outward and inward FDI for selected Asian countries and regions in the second half of the 1980s. As an investor, Japan and the NIEs increased their importance. Between 1985 and 1990, the magnitude of outward FDI for Japan and the NIEs increased 7.5-fold and 16.5-fold, respectively. As the rate of increase of outward FDI by Japan and by the NIEs each exceeded the corresponding rate for world outward FDI in the second half of the 1980s, their respective shares in world outward FDI increased from 11.1 and 0.7 percent in 1985 to 22.1 and 3.0 percent in 1990. In 1990 outward FDI by Japan and by the NIEs amounted, respectively, to $48.0 billion and $6.6 billion. In 1990 Japan was the world's largest investor, and it was followed by the United States ($33.4 billion), France ($24.2 billion), and Germany ($22.3 billion). In terms of cumulative outward FDI for the 1970–90 period, the United States is by far the largest investor at $421.5 billion, followed by the United Kingdom ($233.6 billion), and Japan ($201.4 billion).

As a recipient of FDI, the NIEs and ASEAN countries attracted substantial amounts of FDI in the second half of the 1980s, as the magnitude of inward FDI for these two regions increased, respectively, 4.3- and 5.7-fold during the period. Since the rate of world inward FDI increased more slowly—by 3.3 times over the 1985–90 period—the shares of the NIEs and ASEAN in world inward FDI increased from 3.3 and 2.5 percent, respectively, in 1985 to 4.3 percent each in 1990. As the relative share of

Table 1   Foreign direct investment in Asia

	1985				1987				1990			
	Out		In		Out		In		Out		In	
	Millions of dollars	Share of world total	Millions of dollars	Share of world total	Millions of dollars	Share of world total	Millions of dollars	Share of world total	Millions of dollars	Share of world total	Millions of dollars	Share of world total
Japan	6.4	11.1	0.6	1.2	19.5	14.3	1.2	1.1	48.0	22.1	1.8	1.1
NIEs	0.4	0.7	1.6	3.3	1.1	0.8	4.2	3.8	6.6	3.0	6.9	4.3
ASEAN	0.0	0.0	1.2	2.5	0.1	0.1	1.5	1.4	0.1	0.0	6.8	4.3
China	0.6	1.0	1.7	3.5	0.6	0.4	2.3	2.1	0.8	0.4	3.5	2.2
World	57.4	100.0	48.3	100.0	136.4	100.0	110.5	100.0	217.2	100.0	159.2	100.0

ASEAN = Association of Southeast Asian Nations
NIEs = Newly industrializing economies

Source: International Monetary Fund. *International Financial Statistics,* various issues, and *Statistical Yearbook of the Republic of China.* Executive Yuan, Republic of China, various issues.

developing countries in world inward FDI declined in the second half of the 1980s, the fact that the NIEs and ASEAN increased their respective shares in world inward FDI is particularly noteworthy.

Similar to other Asian countries, China was successful in attracting FDI in the second half of the 1980s, as the magnitude of inward FDI doubled in five years from $1.7 billion in 1985 to $3.5 billion in 1990. As an individual country in Asia, China is second only to Singapore in the magnitude of inward FDI.

It is to be noted that Japan's inward FDI is quite limited, not only in terms of absolute value, as shown in table 1, but also in relation to the size of its economy. According to one estimate, the ratio of stock of inward FDI to GNP at the end of 1989 was a mere 0.3 percent for Japan, while the corresponding ratios for the United States, United Kingdom (1988), and West Germany (1988) were, respectively, 7.7, 14.1, and 3.0 percent (Japan Development Bank 1991). A number of obstacles for undertaking FDI in Japan have been raised by foreign firms. Some of them are tough competition, high land prices, high wages, high demand by consumers, high material costs, government regulation, and difficulty in entering the keiretsu-dominated market (Japan Development Bank 1991). Costs of undertaking FDI in Japan rose with the yen appreciation. Although the obstacles noted above are pointed out by foreign investors, it is important to note that Japanese potential entrants to the existing markets also face most of these.

We noted above that in the second half of the 1980s Japan and the NIEs increased their position as FDI suppliers in the world while the NIEs, ASEAN, and China increased their position as FDI recipients among developing countries. In the next section, we examine the patterns of outward as well as inward FDI in Asia by focusing on Japan, the NIEs, and ASEAN.

FDI in Asia: Japan, NIEs, and ASEAN

Japan: An Active Foreign Direct Investor

Japanese FDI started to increase rapidly in 1986, and the rapid increase continued until 1989. The speed of the increase during the 1986–89 period was unprecedentedly high, as the average annual growth rate for the period was as high as 53.3 percent. In 1990 the magnitude of annual Japanese FDI declined from the previous year for the first time in eight years, and the declining trend continued in 1991.

Although the rapid increase of Japanese FDI was mainly led by FDI in nonmanufacturing sectors such as financial services and real estate in developed countries, Japanese FDI in Asia has been increasing significantly in various sectors, including manufacturing and nonmanufacturing. The magnitude of Japanese FDI in manufacturing in Asia on an annual basis increased from $460 million in 1985 to $3,068 million in 1990. The substantial appreciation of the yen in the mid-1980s led Japanese firms to undertake FDI in Asian countries, especially in the NIEs, to take advantage of low production costs. In 1987, however, Japanese firms started to shift the location of FDI from the NIEs to ASEAN countries, as the NIEs lost cost advantages because of rising wages and the appreciation of their currencies.[1] In addition, the fact that the NIEs were graduated from the US Generalized System of Preferences (GSP) scheme further reduced their attractiveness as a host to FDI.

The shift in Japanese manufacturing FDI from the NIEs to ASEAN can be seen clearly in table 2, where the cumulative FDI values are shown. Between 1985 and 1987, the value of Japanese manufacturing FDI to the NIEs was increased by $1.5 billion, significantly higher than that to the ASEAN countries at $0.9 billion. The situation changed drastically after 1987; over 1987–90, the value of Japanese manufacturing FDI in the NIEs rose $2.9 billion, substantially lower than the corresponding value for ASEAN, at $5.0 billion. It is also to be noted that Japanese manufacturing FDI to China increased significantly after 1987.

As for the sectoral distribution of Japanese FDI to Asia, the share of the nonmanufacturing sector is increasing in the NIEs. Within manufacturing, the electrical sector captured a large share, and moreover, its share increased significantly during the second half of the 1980s. The rate of increase was particularly notable for ASEAN and China. The share of the electrical sector in overall manufacturing FDI in cumulative value from 1951 in these respective groups of countries increased from 4.9 and 10.1 percent in 1985 to 20.6 and 35.8 percent in 1990. As the electrical sector increased its share, a number of sectors lost their shares. The textiles sector experienced a remarkable decline in the NIEs and ASEAN while the food sector lost its share in China. The decline in the share of textiles in Japanese FDI to the NIEs and ASEAN indicates that these countries lost a comparative advantage in labor-intensive production such as that in textiles because their factor endowments changed as a result of economic development. More specifically, with accumulation of physical and human capital, the capital-labor ratio increased rapidly in the NIEs and ASEAN, resulting in the loss of a comparative advantage in labor-intensive production. A similar argument may be made for the decline in the share of the food sector in Japanese manufacturing FDI in China.

The pattern of Japanese FDI observed above was realized by the interaction of supply-side factors in Japan and demand-side factors in the

---

1. MITI reports the results of survey indicating 39.5 percent of the surveyed Japanese firms investing in the NIEs said low wages were a motive behind FDI; the corresponding value for the firms investing in ASEAN was higher at 52.3 percent (*Statistics on Foreign Investment*, no. 4, 1991).

Table 2 Japanese FDI in Asia

	Amount (billions of dollars)		Share of manufacturing (percentages)								
	Total	Manu-facturing	Food	Textiles	Wood	Chemicals	Metals	Machinery	Elec Machinery	Trans Machinery	Other
World											
1985	83.7	24.4	4.5	8.5	4.6	16.3	21.3	8.1	15.4	13.8	7.5
1987	139.3	36.0	4.3	6.5	4.1	14.6	17.5	9.1	19.9	15.7	8.3
1990	310.8	81.6	5.0	4.9	3.6	13.4	12.6	9.7	24.9	13.3	12.4
NIEs											
1985	7.6	3.3	2.4	10.7	0.9	25.4	5.8	14.4	19.0	8.6	12.9
1987	11.7	4.8	3.4	7.9	0.7	22.4	6.2	13.0	23.2	9.9	13.3
1990	23.3	7.7	9.5	7.1	0.9	18.5	6.9	10.9	24.0	8.7	13.4
ASEAN											
1985	11.2	4.0	3.8	20.4	3.9	10.7	36.8	2.3	4.9	9.2	8.2
1987	12.8	4.9	4.7	17.1	3.5	9.8	35.3	3.0	7.7	10.2	8.8
1990	20.8	9.9	3.7	11.8	4.4	11.3	22.4	7.0	20.6	9.5	9.3
China											
1985	0.3	0.05	26.7	4.4	5.1	22.3	8.3	6.0	10.1	1.1	16.0
1987	1.7	1.0	15.0	4.8	2.8	15.1	9.5	5.3	36.3	0.4	10.7
1990	2.8	2.8	8.4	7.7	1.5	7.5	6.1	15.6	35.8	1.1	16.2

ASEAN = Association of Southeast Asian Nations
NIEs = Newly industrializing economies

Source: Ministry of Finance, Japan.

recipient countries.[2] As for the factors in Japan promoting Japanese FDI, the most important factor is the rapid and substantial yen appreciation, which reduced the international competitiveness of Japanese products by increasing the cost of production in Japan. To overcome the unfavorable situation, Japanese firms have adopted various strategies, including globalization, rationalization, and diversification. Globalization has been pursued not only through FDI but also through forming alliances with foreign firms. Alliances have taken forms such as technology tie-up, production cooperation, original equipment manufacturing (OEM), and others.

Rationalization is pursued to increase competitiveness by improving productive efficiency, and diversification is undertaken to increase profitability by upgrading the quality of the products and by moving into a new line of business where higher profitability may be realized. One of the important developments observed in the latter half of the 1980s was that a number of firms pursued these three strategies simultaneously in coherent fashion in order to facilitate industrial restructuring, in responding to drastic changes in their environment. Such a strategy was most apparent in the electrical industry. Take color television production, for example. A number of Japanese TV producers shifted their production of standard color TVs, such as small and medium-sized TVs, to the NIEs and to ASEAN, where production of such standardized TVs was efficiently performed with low-wage labor, while in Japan they concentrated on the production of high-quality TVs such as those capable of receiving satellite broadcasting and/or large-screen color TVs (Urata, 1991b).

Although there is no doubt that the significant yen appreciation precipitated globalization of Japanese firms, there were other factors at work. The "bubble economy" created by excessively expansionary monetary policy, which was conducted in order to deal mainly with recessionary pressures resulting from the yen appreciation, promoted domestic and foreign investment. Under the bubble economy, the prices of stocks and land in Japan skyrocketed, enabling firms with appreciated assets to obtain loans for investment. Another factor promoting Japanese FDI was the impetus that FDI undertaken by Japanese firms had in encouraging other Japanese firms to invest. There were two motivations leading to this reaction. One motivation was to keep up with the investing rival firms in business performance; the other was to follow the investing trading partners to maintain business. Furthermore, the overseas experiences accumulated by Japanese firms also contributed to rapid FDI in the latter half of the 1980s.

As a result of rapid increase in FDI by Japanese firms, overseas production by Japanese firms expanded rapidly. In manufacturing, the over-

---

2. Urata (1991a) discusses in some detail the factors that promoted FDI in the second half of the 1980s.

seas production ratio—defined as the ratio of overseas production to total (overseas and domestic) production—grew from 3.0 percent in 1985 to 5.7 percent in 1989 (MITI, *Statistics on Foreign Investment*, no. 4, 1991). Despite the notable increase, the overseas production ratio by Japanese manufacturing firms is still much lower than the corresponding ratio for the firms in other developed countries, as US and German firms recorded overseas production ratios of around 20 percent. Among the manufacturing subsectors, the overseas production ratio is particularly high for transport machinery and electrical machinery subsectors, for which the overseas production ratios in 1989 were 14.3 and 11.0 percent. The overseas production ratios for most sectors are likely to increase in the future, as FDI projects undertaken in the latter half of the 1980s will soon be fully operational.

The NIEs: Active Participants in Inward and Outward FDI

We already saw that inward as well as outward FDI for the NIEs increased significantly in the second half of the 1980s[3]. We also found that Japanese FDI in the NIEs increased during the period. The speed of increase as well as the magnitude of FDI from Japan to the NIEs was particularly notable in nonmanufacturing and the electrical industry in manufacturing. In this section, therefore, we examine the factors in the NIEs that attracted inward FDI first, and then turn to the discussion of their outward FDI.

The composition of inward FDI in the NIEs changed drastically in the second half of the 1980s. In total inward FDI, the share of nonmanufacturing, especially that of services, increased, and among the manufacturing subsectors, inward FDI shifted from labor-intensive subsectors to technology-intensive sectors. Various factors promoted inward FDI in nonmanufacturing in the NIEs. Demand for services increased as income levels grew with economic development. A typical example may be active FDI in commercial sectors—for example, retail services such as department stores and supermarkets—responding to increased consumer demand for a variety of products. Furthermore, deregulation and liberalization contributed to increasing inward FDI. For example, deregulation and liberalization in the insurance sector in Korea led to active FDI in that sector.

The shift in inward FDI in the NIEs toward technology-intensive sectors was attributable to the NIE governments' FDI promotion policies in high-technology sectors. Such policies were pursued because the NIEs felt a need to improve competitive advantage in high-tech sectors to compensate for their loss of comparative advantage in low-technology products to the ASEAN countries. To gain competitive advantage in high-tech

---

3. Among the NIEs, the patterns of FDI for Korea and Taiwan are analyzed, respectively, by Lee and Ramstetter (1991) and Schive and Tu (1991).

products, policymakers in the NIEs thought foreign technology was necessary, and they thought FDI would be an important means for importing technology.

Outward FDI has been actively undertaken by the NIEs since the mid-1980s, in particular by Taiwan. Destinations of outward FDI differ among the NIEs, but the shares of ASEAN and China have increased in recent years (table 3). The key factors in NIEs' outward FDI are similar to those observed for the rapid rise in Japanese FDI: a sharp increase in wages due to shortage of labor, appreciation of their currencies, and trade frictions with developed countries. As such, the sectors actively undertaking outward FDI are those losing a comparative advantage, such as toys, apparel, sporting goods, and other labor-intensive products, and those subject to trade frictions such as electronics.

There are some similarities as well as differences in the pattern of FDI by the NIEs and that by Japanese firms. One important similarity is the motive for FDI. In both cases, FDI was undertaken to promote industrial restructuring in these countries, which would lead to further economic growth. Indeed, outward FDI promotion policies have been adopted not only in Japan, but also in Korea, Taiwan, and Singapore. For example, the Export-Import Bank of Japan provides preferential loans for undertaking FDI. As for the differences, one may note the difference in the size of the firms undertaking FDI in Japan and in the NIEs, although there are substantial differences in this regard among the firms in the NIEs. In general, the NIEs' firms undertaking FDI are smaller than the Japanese counterparts, as reflected in the sectoral distribution of FDI in these two groups of countries. However, compared with US firms, the share of small and medium firms in total investing firms is significantly higher for Japan.

ASEAN: An Increasingly Attractive Recipient of FDI

It was shown earlier that inward FDI in ASEAN on a balance of payments basis increased remarkably toward the end of the 1980s.[4] The same observation may be made from the statistics on an approval basis (table 3). As a source of FDI in ASEAN, the NIEs expanded rapidly in importance. In 1990 Japan was the largest investor in Thailand, but in other ASEAN countries—Malaysia, Indonesia, and the Philippines—the NIEs were the largest investors. Even in Thailand, the amount of Japanese FDI was only slightly greater than that of NIEs.

We have already discussed the factors in investing countries—Japan and the NIEs—that led to active FDI in the ASEAN countries. As for the

---

4. Pangestu (1991) and Tambunlertchai and Ramstetter (1991) respectively examines the cases of FDI in Indonesia and Thailand.

Table 3 Inward foreign direct investment in ASEAN and China from Japan, NIEs, US, and the world, 1987–90

Recipient		Japan		NIEs		US		World
		Millions of dollars	Share of world total	Millions of dollars	Share of world total	Millions of dollars	Share of world total	Millions of dollars
Malaysia	1987	284	34.7	236	28.9	65	7.9	818
	1988	467	25.1	607	32.6	204	11.0	1863
	1989	993	31.1	1335	41.8	119	3.7	3194
	1990	657	28.5	1100	47.8	69	3.0	2302
Thailand	1987	965	36.6	501	19.0	172	6.5	2634
	1988	3045	48.7	1684	26.9	673	10.8	6249
	1989	3524	44.1	2011	25.2	550	6.9	7996
	1990	2706	33.7	2696	33.6	1091	13.6	8031
Philippines	1987	29	17.4	38	22.8	36	21.6	167
	1988	96	20.3	141	29.8	153	32.3	473
	1989	158	19.7	323	40.2	131	16.3	804
	1990	306	31.8	384	39.9	59	5.2	961
Indonesia	1987	532	36.5	172	11.8	73	5.0	1457
	1988	247	5.6	1588	36.0	672	15.2	4409
	1989	769	16.3	1197	25.4	348	7.4	4719
	1990	2241	25.6	2598	29.7	153	1.7	3750
China	1987	220	9.5	1620	70.0	263	11.4	2314
	1988	515	16.1	2123	66.5	236	7.4	3194
	1989	356	10.5	2162	63.7	284	8.4	3393
	1990	503	14.4	1963	56.3	456	13.1	3487

NIEs = Newly industrializing economies
Notes: For Malaysia and Indonesia, approval data for manufacturing, and for the Philippines and Indonesia, approval data for the whole sector, and for China, executed data.

Sources: Country Official Sources

factors in the ASEAN countries that attracted FDI, it is important to point out the change in trade and FDI policies from inward-oriented to outward-oriented ones. For example, in order to expand exports, export-processing zones where preferential tax treatment is applied to attract FDI have been established in ASEAN countries. The shift from the inward-looking policies to outward-looking ones such as export and FDI promotion policies by the ASEAN countries appears to have been prompted by the successful experiences of outward-oriented policies of the NIEs.

By sectors, the increase in FDI is noticeable in manufacturing, hotels, commerce, and other services. Although there are substantial differences among ASEAN countries, among manufacturing, the electrical and chemicals sectors attracted significant FDI in the ASEAN countries. In recent years, automobiles and automobile parts sectors are experiencing an increase in FDI. The increase of FDI in automobiles is mainly due to the increased demand for automobiles in ASEAN resulting from economic development. Since the automobile market in ASEAN is virtually closed to imports because of strict protection for foreign producers, FDI is the only means for serving the local market.

FDI and Economic Development

FDI transfers not only financial resources to the host country but also other factors of production such as technology and management know-how. In the host country, inflow of financial resources leads to construction of production facilities, which in turn increases employment and production, while inflow of foreign technology improves production and management efficiency. In addition, FDI helps the host country to build and expand various networks, including procurement and marketing networks, which promote economic development by enabling the host country to widen the scope of procurement sources and sales destinations. Furthermore, if FDI leads to export expansion or import reduction by substituting local production for imports, FDI increases the host country's foreign exchange earnings.

Against these favorable effects of FDI on the host country, unfavorable effects such as exploitation and domination of the host country by foreign firms have been suggested. In recent years, environmental issues related to FDI have received attention, as some foreign firms have been allegedly exporting pollution to the host countries. Despite the criticisms of FDI in some particular cases, host countries emphasize the favorable effects of FDI, as inflow of FDI contributes to their economic development. Indeed, a number of governments of Asian countries have adopted measures to promote inflow of FDI. In this section, we examine the impact of FDI inflow on the Asian host countries.

The Impact of FDI Inflow on Host Countries

The impact of FDI on host countries varies widely among Asian countries. For example, the ratios of FDI to domestic capital formation are quite different among the NIEs, ASEAN, and China. In 1990 Singapore and Malaysia recorded high ratios of 36.6 and 21.2 percent, respectively, while Korea registered a significantly lower ratio of 0.8 percent.[5] For other countries, the ratios are between 2.5 percent (Indonesia) and 8.3 percent (Thailand); the ratios for the remaining sample countries are Taiwan (3.8 percent), China (5.3 percent), and the Philippines (5.5 percent) (International Monetary Fund, *International Financial Statistics Yearbook 1991* and *Balance of Payments Statistics Yearbook 1991*). These differences in the importance of FDI in domestic capital formation among the countries are mainly attributable to the differences in the policies toward FDI in these countries. Singapore and Malaysia actively attracted FDI, while Korea limited FDI and relied on other means such as foreign borrowing and technology imports to obtain resources from foreign countries.

As for the impact of FDI on employment in host countries, table 4 shows the magnitude of employment at all foreign subsidiaries and at Japanese subsidiaries in the Asian countries. The largest number of workers employed by foreign firms in Asia was in the Philippines, with more than half a million workers working for foreign firms there. The Philippines is followed by Korea at 416,000. Even the smallest number of employment at foreign firms, which was recorded in Hong Kong (only in manufacturing), was greater than 100,000. For the sample Asian countries as a whole, as many as 2 million workers are employed by foreign firms.

Based on statistics from different sources (*Toyo Keizai* and *Kaigai Shinshutsu Kigyo Soran* 1989), we obtain information on employment at Japanese subsidiaries. In 1988 the number of workers at Japanese subsidiaries in Asia amounted to 797,000, of which 685,000, or 86 percent of the total are employed in manufacturing. By groups of countries, there are 456,000 workers at Japanese subsidiaries in the NIEs and 278,000 workers in ASEAN. The number of workers employed at the subsidiaries in the NIEs, ASEAN, and China amounted to 763,000, or 95.8 percent of total employment at Japanese subsidiaries in overall Asia. Among the NIEs, Korea and Taiwan hold a large number of workers employed at Japanese firms, both recording approximately 170,000, while among the ASEAN countries

---

5. The ratios of FDI to domestic capital formation reported here may underestimate the contribution of foreign firms in the host countries. As the FDI figures used here only account for financial resources received from foreign countries, they do not take into account capital formation by foreign firms with financial resources obtained in the host country. On the other hand, the figures may overestimate the true figure if the amount of FDI transferred was not used for capital formation but for other purposes such as payments for workers.

Table 4 Employment at foreign subsidiaries in selected Asian countries

Country	Year	All foreign subsidiaries	Japanese subsidiaries (1988)	
			Total	Manufacturing
Hong Kong	1988	108,032[a]	38,494	18,306
Taiwan	1986	266,837	171,851	166,424
Korea	1986	416,000	179,269	162,386
Singapore	1988	235,130	67,441	54,087
Malaysia	1988	251,823	70,324	57,456
Philippines	1982	502,835	36,183	24,414
Thailand	1985	182,635	109,831	96,115
Indonesia	n.a.	n.a.	61,611	52,257
China	n.a.	n.a.	28,775	21,283

n.a. = not available.
a. indicates manufacturing only.

Sources: World Investment Directory 1992, vol. 1, Asia and the Pacific, United Nations, 1992, and *Kaigai Shinshutsukigyo Soran* (Statistics on Foreign Subsidiaries), Toyo Keizai Shinpo-sha, 1989.

Thailand registers a large employment at Japanese firms, amounting to 110,000.

To assess the impact of FDI on host country employment, we examine the share of workers working for foreign firms in overall employment. Such information is available for manufacturing employment for some Asian countries. According to the estimates provided by the United Nations Center on Transnational Corporations (UNCTC), which are shown in table 5, the pattern of importance of foreign firms in the host countries regarding manufacturing employment is similar to that found for capital formation. In Singapore almost 60 percent of manufacturing workers are employed by foreign firms, and in Malaysia one out of two workers is employed at foreign firms. Following these two countries, the Philippines has a large share of workers employed at foreign firms in total manufacturing employment, with one out of four workers in manufacturing employed at foreign firms. By contrast, the proportion of workers employed at foreign firms to total employment is rather limited in Korea (9.5 percent) and Thailand (8.8 percent).

If the sectoral pattern of employment at other foreign subsidiaries is similar to that observed for Japanese subsidiaries, where manufacturing employment amounts to 86 percent of overall employment, then the importance of employment at foreign subsidiaries in total employment observed for manufacturing overstates the importance of foreign subsidiaries in overall employment. This is because the share of manufacturing employment in total employment for these countries is significantly smaller than 86 percent.

It would be interesting to compare the differences in the contribution of foreign firms to host countries in capital formation and in employment

Table 5   Foreign firms' manufacturing sector activities in host countries (percentage of overall activities)

Host	Year	Employment	Sales	Exports
Korea	1986	9.5	21.5	29.0[a]
Hong Kong	1987	13.5[b]	17.5	n.a.
Taiwan	1986	10.0	13.9	18.5
Singapore	1988	59.5	53.0	88.1
Malaysia	1988	48.7	44.8	59.6
Indonesia	1990	18.8	n.a.	22.3[a]
Thailand	1986	8.8	48.6	5.8
Philippines	1987	27.3	40.8	34.7[a]
China	1990	0.1[a]	n.a.	12.6[a]

a. Values are for overall sectors.
b. 1990 figure.

Sources: World Investment Directory 1992, vol. 1, Asia and the Pacific, United Nations, 1992, and estimates by the Sanwa Research Institute based on data from country sources.

because such comparisons would tell us the pattern of technologies (labor-capital intensity) employed at foreign subsidiaries vis-à-vis local firms. This study could possibly provide empirical evidence on one of the hotly debated issues, characteristics of technologies adopted by foreign firms. A lack of information precludes one from pursuing such analysis for most sample countries. For China, where data are available, foreign firms are shown to adopt more capital-intensive production methods than do local firms, as the share of foreign firms in domestic capital formation (5.3 percent) was significantly higher than the corresponding value in total domestic employment (0.1 percent). This seems to indicate that foreign firms in China do not adapt their technologies to local conditions. One should note that factor-intensity comparisons using aggregate figures, as conducted above, have to be complemented by sectoral comparisons to draw more solid results.[6]

It was pointed out earlier that FDI in Asia responded actively to export promotion policies such as the setting up of export processing zones. One would therefore expect that FDI contributed significantly to export expansion. This assertion is borne out by the statistics given in table 5. The shares of exports by foreign firms in total exports are significantly higher than the corresponding shares for total sales in most of the sample countries, indicating high export propensity of foreign firms.[7] This pattern is particularly notable in Singapore and in Malaysia, where foreign firms are credited with as large as 88 and 60 percent of their respective manufactured exports. Following Singapore and Malaysia, the share of exports

6. For a brief review of the findings from earlier results on the comparison of the methods of production by local and foreign firms, which are mixed, see Reddy and Zhao (1990).

7. A similar observation is made by Pangestu (1991), Tambunlertchai and Ramstetter (1991), and Plummer and Ramstetter (1991).

carried out by foreign firms in total exports is high for the Philippines, Korea, Indonesia, Taiwan, and China, each registering the share as greater than 10 percent.

One apparent exception to the high export propensity of foreign firms is Thailand. In the case of Thailand, the definitions of foreign firms—foreign affiliates to be more precise—used in sales statistics and export statistics are different, making direct comparison difficult. Specifically, in the sales statistics, foreign firms are defined as firms in which foreign ownership is 10 percent or more. In the export statistics, 25 percent foreign ownership is used to define foreign firms. Accordingly, the coverage of foreign firms for sales is wider than that for exports. Such differences in the definition of foreign firms leads to underestimation of the contribution of foreign affiliates in export sales.

We have examined the contribution of foreign firms to the host countries in a variety of economic activities. There we found that foreign firms contribute significantly to the economic development of the host countries, especially in the manufacturing sector and in export activities. In the examination, we only dealt with direct effects of foreign firms. If indirect effects such as backward and forward linkages are included, the overall effect would be significantly greater.

Technology Transfer through FDI

Importation and assimilation of foreign technologies have been an important contributor to economic development. In general, foreign technology is imported through three different channels: importation of capital goods, technology trade such as patents and licensing, and FDI. In the postwar period, Japan's importation of capital goods and patents played an important role in upgrading its technological level, while FDI has become an important vehicle for technology transfer in recent years.[8] FDI has contributed significantly to technology transfer in countries such as Taiwan and Thailand, which adopted FDI promotion policies. According to a questionnaire conducted by the NIKKEI Research Institute of Industry and Markets (1992), 67 percent of the total number of technology transfer cases in Taiwan undertaken by Japanese firms was carried out through FDI, while the corresponding share for Korea was significantly lower, at 32 percent. These differences in FDI as a channel of technology transfer between Taiwan and Korea are attributable to the differences in FDI and technology policies.

Various factors have led to the increase in importance of FDI as a channel of technology transfer. For the technology recipient, inflow of FDI provides not only technology but also other benefits such as financial

---

8. For the experiences of technology imports for Japan and for Korea, see Urata (1990) and Kim and Lee (1990), respectively.

resources, managerial know-how, and a well-organized network. There are also reasons for the technology supplier to prefer FDI to other channels.[9] Firstly, it is well-known that the technology trade suffers from imperfect markets, which are caused mainly by imperfect information. As a technology recipient is likely to underestimate the true value of the technology in question, market transactions fail to take place. Secondly, being an intangible asset, technology has a characteristic of public good, making it difficult to protect the right of technology inventors. These special characteristics of technology make firms with technology rely more on nonmarket channels such as FDI for transferring technology.

It is difficult to quantify the extent of technology transfer being performed. Therefore, one frequently uses questionnaires to answer this question.[10] A NIKKEI Research Institute of Industry and Markets survey (1992) regarding technology transfer by 133 Japanese firms in Asia produced interesting findings. In response to the question, "To what extent (percentage terms) has your firm completed its technology transfer objectives, based on your expectations?" the average completion rate for rather simple technology such as operation of machinery and equipment was greater than 70 percent, but the corresponding rate for more advanced technologies such as development of new products was as low as 25 percent (figure 1). It should be noted from the figure that Japanese firms expect to increase technology transfer substantially in three years. This strategy is consistent with a recent shift in Japan's global strategy from one emphasizing interprocess production to one constructing a self-sufficient production system in the Asian region (Urata, forthcoming).

A number of obstacles to efficient technology transfer have been pointed out by both technology suppliers and technology recipients. Technology suppliers attribute limited technology transfer to a lack of technical skills of workers, a lack of aspiration for *kaizen* (improvement) by local workers, job-hopping, and myopic management style, among other things, while technology recipients point out the unwillingness of investors to perform technology transfer, lack of communication with local workers, and expensive equipment and machinery embodying technology as obstacles to efficient technology transfer.[11]

---

9. Caves (1982) provides a concise discussion on this point.

10. The share of workers from the parent firm in total employment is often used to quantify the extent of technology transfer. However, the indicator's shortcoming is that it does not take into account the differences in the importance of the positions or roles that personnel from parent offices and local workers play. For example, the low ratio does not necessarily indicate that technology transfer has been performed if an entire operation depends on a few personnel from the parent offices.

11. Although technology transfer is undoubtedly one of the most important contributions FDI provides to the host countries, there have been only a few empirical studies on the subject because of apparent difficulty in quantifying the extent of technology transfer performed. See Reddy and Zhao (1990) for a survey on the literature on technology transfer.

Level of Technology Transfer

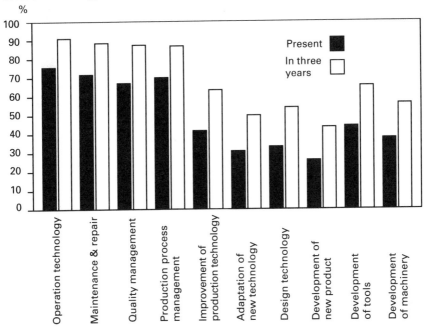

Figure 1. Survey on completion of technology transfer objectives by Japnese firms in Asia, 1991. Note: See text for explanations. Source: NIKKEI Industrial Research Institute, Tokyo, 1991.

Expansion of Networks through FDI

Through FDI, host countries not only obtain resources such as financial capital and technology but also gain access to foreign firms' networks. For example, foreign subsidiaries may use marketing channels established by parent firms to export their products and to purchase intermediate goods as well as capital goods for their production. The contribution of foreign firms to the host economies in this respect is important, since establishing these networks entails enormous financial and human resources. In this section, we examine the contribution of foreign firms to the host economies in expanding their sales and procurement networks. Because of data availability, we confine our analysis to the case of Japanese firms, and where possible a comparison will be made to the practices of the US firms.

Table 6 shows the changes in the pattern of sales and procurement of the Asian affiliates of Japanese manufacturing firms in the 1980s. Before analyzing the figures shown in the table, it should be noted that the magnitude of sales and procurement by the Asian affiliates of Japanese manufacturing firms appeared to have increased substantially during the

Table 6 Sales and procurement by Asian affiliates of Japanese firms (percentage of total sales and procurement)

Industry	1980				1989			
	Local market	Japan	Other Asia	Non-Asia	Local market	Japan	Other Asia	Non-Asia
Sales								
Manufacturing	63.9	9.8	12.8	13.5	63.9	15.8	9.7	10.6
Food	40.5	30.2	14.4	14.9	66.9	16.1	9.8	7.2
Textiles	61.1	4.0	21.0	13.9	70.5	14.9	8.1	6.5
Wood and pulp	33.1	30.8	10.8	25.3	34.4	35.9	20.2	9.5
Chemicals	85.0	8.9	3.8	2.3	78.1	10.3	8.8	2.8
Iron and steel	85.4	10.1	1.3	3.2	87.7	4.2	4.2	3.9
Nonferrous metals	74.5	2.6	17.2	5.7	73.3	12.1	12.8	1.8
General machinery	65.5	5.5	7.1	21.9	56.9	18.2	5.9	19.0
Electric machinery	51.6	16.2	10.2	22.0	37.4	26.9	16.7	19.0
Transport machinery	89.7	1.9	2.9	5.5	92.1	1.6	2.2	4.1
Precision machinery	56.3	9.1	25.3	9.3	55.0	22.2	7.8	15.0
Petro and coal products	n.a.	n.a.	n.a.	n.a.	100.0	0.0	0.0	0.0
Other	60.9	6.0	22.3	10.8	78.5	12.1	4.3	5.1
Procurement								
Manufacturing	42.2	41.5	8.7	7.6	49.8	38.9	6.1	2.4
Food	75.4	1.6	3.1	19.9	87.7	3.3	4.3	5.2
Textiles	38.9	29.3	14.0	17.8	43.1	22.4	6.4	28.1
Wood and pulp	65.2	1.8	24.2	8.8	92.8	2.3	4.4	0.5
Chemicals	53.3	30.8	1.8	14.1	56.3	34.7	1.9	7.1
Iron and steel	26.6	53.3	5.2	14.9	36.0	56.1	4.3	3.6
Nonferrous metals	20.6	42.1	2.7	34.6	59.3	18.1	4.3	18.3
General machinery	44.5	54.8	0.0	0.7	53.6	42.5	3.2	0.7
Electric machinery	49.6	46.0	3.8	0.6	42.4	44.6	12.5	0.5
Transport machinery	38.2	61.1	0.0	0.7	57.7	41.8	0.1	0.4
Precision machinery	12.1	74.8	12.3	0.8	42.1	45.2	11.0	1.7
Petro and coal products	n.a.	n.a.	n.a.	n.a.	89.5	10.5	0.0	0.0
Others	40.5	27.8	27.9	3.8	36.0	48.4	7.3	8.3

n.a. = not available.

Sources: Kaigai Toshi Tokei Soran (Statistics on Foreign Investment), Ministry of International Trade and Industry, Japan no. 1, 1981, and no. 4, 1991.

1980s. Although accurate figures are not available, the sample surveys conducted by the Ministry of International Trade and Industry (*Kaigai Toshi Tokei Soran* [Statistics on Foreign Investment], no. 4, 1991) indicate that manufacturing sales and procurement by these affiliates increased, respectively, from ¥6.1 trillion and ¥4.9 trillion in 1980 to ¥14.3 trillion and ¥11.6 trillion in 1989, indicating the expansion of sales and procurement networks of the host countries by the Japanese firms in Asia.

Turning to the changes in the destinations of the sales of the Asian affiliates in the 1980s, one finds that the share of exports in total sales remained the same, at 36.1 percent. However, there is a notable shift in the export destinations toward Japan, as Japan's share in total manufacturing sales increased from 9.8 percent in 1980 to 15.8 percent in 1989. Export orientation intensified mainly in the machinery sectors over 1980–89. This tendency is particularly noticeable for the electrical machinery sector, where the export–total sales ratio increased from 48.4 percent to 62.6 percent over the period. The increase in the export–total sales ratio in the electrical machinery sector was attributable to rapid export expansion to the Japanese market, as the share of exports to Japan in total electrical machinery sales increased from 16.2 percent in 1980 to 26.9 percent in 1989. Other sectors that experienced a large increase in exports to Japan as a share in total sales include textiles, nonferrous metals, general machinery, and precision machinery. Indeed, the exports from the affiliates of Japanese firms to Japan—so-called "reverse imports" from the viewpoint of Japan—are reported to have increased remarkably since the mid-1980s (Japan External Trade Organization 1990). The remarkable shift in export destinations toward Japan from the rest of the world is obviously due to the substantial yen appreciation. Furthermore, export promotion policies by host country governments contributed to overall export expansion.

It is often asserted that expansion of exports to Japan from Asia was carried out mainly in the form of intrafirm trade and that, accordingly, exports to the "closed" Japanese market are only possible through the use of Japanese distribution channels. Considering that the shares of exports by Japanese subsidiaries in total manufacturing exports from the NIEs and ASEAN to Japan are estimated, respectively, at 12.5 and 19.1 percent by Hirata and Yokota (1991), this assertion appears to be rejected, despite the fact that the share of intrafirm trade in the Asian affiliates' exports to Japan was as high as 60 percent (table 7). Although the importance of intrafirm trade in the Asian affiliates' exports to Japan declined substantially from 1986 to 1989, it is still much higher compared with cases in which products are sold in other markets.

An international comparison is useful to see if the Japanese firms' behavior is exceptionally closed in their sales to home markets. Information necessary for such comparison is very limited and available only for the US firms for all affiliates, (and not for those in Asia only). According

Table 7 Intrafirm trade as share of overall transactions by sector for Asian affiliates of Japanese firms
(percentages)

Industry	1986 Local market	1986 Japan	1986 Other	1986 Total	1989 Local market	1989 Japan	1989 Other	1989 Total
Sales								
Manufacturing	8.9	76.5	23.7	24.0	6.5	58.9	37.2	21.0
Food	0.0	37.8	0.0	27.5	0.6	70.8	17.5	14.8
Textiles	8.0	57.7	2.5	10.7	4.8	50.4	17.2	13.4
Wood and pulp	0.0	27.7	0.0	7.1	16.6	65.1	15.2	33.6
Chemicals	2.6	83.9	1.5	5.8	4.2	40.2	35.1	11.5
Iron and steel	3.2	100.0	0.0	8.2	3.1	13.8	13.9	4.4
Nonferrous metals	15.1	99.2	0.6	36.3	4.4	16.5	6.5	6.2
General machinery	29.9	94.7	46.6	54.3	0.6	98.5	45.4	29.6
Electric machinery	9.6	73.0	32.1	31.6	12.9	60.3	43.9	36.7
Transport machinery	9.1	46.0	62.8	22.0	6.2	35.7	8.5	6.8
Precision machinery	59.8	86.1	59.5	65.4	16.2	50.8	55.4	32.8
Petro and coal products	0.0	0.0	0.0	0.0	64.0	0.0	0.0	64.0
Other	0.0	88.5	13.9	8.9	2.6	85.2	34.5	15.6
Procurement								
Manufacturing	6.8	66.6	34.3	37.3	4.1	62.6	23.9	29.1
Food	0.0	100.0	0.0	3.1	1.6	87.6	44.5	8.3
Textiles	15.5	46.7	12.2	18.0	4.7	19.3	23.7	14.5
Wood and pulp	27.9	93.8	0.0	23.5	2.6	0.0	0.0	2.4
Chemicals	5.5	24.4	67.5	20.9	2.8	83.8	33.6	33.7
Iron and steel	16.5	40.2	3.5	32.1	4.0	64.1	0.0	37.4
Nonferrous metals	0.0	65.1	0.0	6.9	4.5	42.0	3.0	10.9
General machinery	15.8	80.0	96.8	52.7	0.6	79.1	32.3	35.3
Electric machinery	6.2	78.1	55.9	49.9	5.1	65.3	29.8	35.1
Transport machinery	4.0	56.1	67.9	42.0	2.3	48.9	0.7	21.8
Precision machinery	26.1	95.8	62.7	84.6	3.6	96.1	86.2	55.9
Petro and coal products	0.0	0.0	0.0	0.0	0.0	0.0	0.0	0.0
Other	7.9	81.5	9.7	33.2	13.9	69.7	16.7	41.4

Sources: Kaigai Toshi Tokei Soran (Statistics on Foreign Investment), Ministry of International Trade and Industry, no. 3, 1987, and no. 4, 1991.

to the US Department of Commerce (1990), intrafirm trade as a share in total manufacturing exports of the affiliates of US firms to the United States was 89.0 percent in 1988, while the corresponding share for Japanese firms in 1989 was 61.6 percent. These findings indicate that US firms are more closed than Japanese firms in their export transactions. This is somewhat surprising because Japanese firms are frequently criticized for their closed-minded business practices.[12] Several reasons may be noted for the high share of intrafirm trade for US firms. One is a special arrangement that the US government imposes tariffs only on the value-added portion of imported products when the components used for the production at foreign affiliates are exported from the parents. This arrangement promotes intrafirm trade. Another reason may be that US imports from their foreign affiliates are more technology-intensive than the Japanese counterparts, leading to high intrafirm trade for US trade, thereby avoiding market imperfections often associated with technology.

What appears to be most important for the host countries is the fact that exports are carried out, and not so much which channels of exports are used. Indeed, it is the consumers—in this case, consumers in home countries—that are affected unfavorably from the closed channels.

Before closing the discussion on the sales pattern of foreign affiliates, we examine if foreign affiliates of Japanese firms are more export-oriented than those of US firms, an issue often debated. Lack of information on the sales behavior of Asian affiliates of US firms precludes us from conducting a comparison of the behavior of Asian affiliates of US and Japanese firms. Instead, we compare the behavior of all affiliates. For manufacturing, the export propensity of all affiliates of Japanese firms in 1989 was 20.6 percent, while the corresponding value for the US firms in 1988 was significantly higher, at 37 percent. From these findings we conclude that the affiliates of US firms have higher propensity to export than those of the Japanese firms in general. This result is extraordinary. However, before providing a conclusive statement, more careful comparison is needed by taking into account factors such as areas of operation, sectoral distribution, and length of operation.

We now turn to the pattern of procurement of intermediate goods by the Asian affiliates of Japanese firms (table 6). For the manufacturing sector, the ratio of local to total procurement increased from 42.2 percent in 1980 to 49.8 percent in 1989, resulting in lower dependency on foreign supply. Considering that there is positive correlation between the length

---

12. Using the information on intrafirm imports from foreign subsidiaries to the parents for US, European, and Japanese trade, Lawrence (1991) finds that the share of intrafirm imports in overall imports (not just those related to multinationals) is significantly higher for Japanese imports than the corresponding share for other imports. These findings appear to indicate the relatively closed nature of the Japanese market compared with other markets, but not necessarily the closed nature of Japanese firms' behavior, a point discussed in the main text.

of operation and dependence on local supply because it takes time to develop local procurement networks, and considering also that a large number of Asian affiliates have a short history, one would conclude that the local-supply ratio for the Asian affiliates established before the 1980s increased substantially in the 1980s. Over 1980–89, most of the manufacturing subsectors experienced an increase in the local-supply ratio as a result of an increase in the capacity as well as improvement in the capability of local firms in the production of intermediate goods.[13] One exception is the electrical machinery sector, whose local-supply ratio declined over the same period. This may be due to the physical as well as technological inability of local producers of intermediate goods to catch up with rapidly growing demand resulting from active FDI as well as rapidly advancing technological progress in that industry.

Among the foreign supply sources for the Asian affiliates, Japan has been most important. In particular, dependence on Japan for intermediate goods was high for the four machinery sectors and iron and steel, both relying on Japan for more than 40 percent of total procurement. Coupled with the observation that the export–total sales ratio is high for electrical and precision machinery, high foreign-supply ratios for these sectors indicate that intraindustry trade, probably interprocess trade, is taking place in these sectors.[14] Moreover, a large increase in the share of other Asian firms in sales as well as procurement in the electrical industry indicates that intra-Asia trade in electrical components expanded in the 1980s.

Intrafirm trade for the Asian affiliates of Japanese firms is more important for procurement than for sales. The share of intrafirm trade in total procurement is particularly high in procurement from parent firms in Japan. This may be understandable, as a large portion of parts and components are often produced according to specific designs shared with parent firms. It may be important, however, to point out that the importance of intrafirm procurement declined in the 1980s, leading to more open trading practices.

Finally, it is interesting to note that intrafirm trade in the procurement from the home country is significantly higher for affiliates of US firms

---

13. It would be interesting to compare the procurement pattern of Japanese subsidiaries with that of other subsidiaries. But a lack of data prevents such analysis. In this regard, one should note that Kreinin (1988) found that dependence in procurement of capital equipments on home country, not intermediate goods as we discuss in the paper, is significantly high for Japanese firms in his survey of approximately 20 firms from Japan, the United States, and Europe in Australia. One of the problems of his study is small sample size. In order to shed more light on the procurement practices of foreign affiliates, more information is required.

14. Although presence of interprocess trade is shown in various company documents, statistical support is hard to obtain. Urata (forthcoming) found some statistical evidence to support that interprocess trade takes place for electric machinery.

compared with affiliates of Japanese firms. Concerning procurement for overall sectors, for which the statistics are available, as high as 89.5 percent of imports from the United States by the Asian affiliates is conducted in the form of intrafirm trade, while the corresponding figure for the Asian affiliates of Japanese firms is significantly lower, at 63.2 percent in 1989. These observations once again point to the "closed" behavior of US firms. Here, the same explanations apply that were given to explain the high intrafirm export ratio for the US subsidiaries earlier.

Conclusions

The substantial realignment of the currencies of the Asian countries precipitated FDI in the region in the mid-1980s. Japan and the NIEs actively undertook FDI, while the NIEs and ASEAN countries received FDI hungrily. Through FDI, Japan and the NIEs achieved industrial adjustment by relocating overseas the industries and production processes that had lost comparative advantage at home. At the same time, the NIEs attempted to promote high-tech industries by attracting FDI. By contrast, the ASEAN countries and China pursued industrialization by attracting FDI mainly from Japan and the NIEs. Since the flow of FDI was accelerated as a result of liberalization of trade regimes, the pattern of production in Asia, which is realized by relocating production facilities through FDI, appears to be more or less consistent with the pattern of comparative advantage of the countries in the region.

FDI contributed to economic development of host countries not only by promoting capital formation, production, and employment, but also by upgrading technological capability through technology transfer. In addition, FDI contributed to export expansion by involving the host country in the sales network of the parent firms. FDI also contributed to upgrading the industrial structure of the home countries, as relocation of industries losing comparative advantage was carried out through rationalization and diversification in the home countries.

Because FDI was undertaken actively in a short period, the shortage of social capital such as transportation services and the shortage of human resources such as engineers and middle management have become acute problems in the host countries. These problems have to be solved, not only to attract more FDI but also to promote economic development. Construction of infrastructure and improvement of human capital through education should be carried out mainly by the public sector, as the social rate of return from such investment generally exceeds the private rate of return. Under the tight budget situation of most host country governments, foreign economic assistance plays an important role in the construction of social capital and the upgrade of educational services. Recognizing that the magnitude and quality of social capital and human resources are important in determining the contribution of FDI on the host countries, coordination between the public sector providing such services and the private sector undertaking FDI may prove effective in promoting economic development.

Reference

Caves, Richard E. 1982. *Multinational Enterprises and Economic Analysis.* Cambridge, MA: Cambridge University Press.

Hirata, Akira, and Kazuhiko Yokota. 1991. *"Hatten Tojokokuheno Eikyo"* (The Impact on Developing Countries). In Ippei Yamazawa and Akira Hirata, eds., *Senshinshokoku no Sangyochosei to Hattentojokoku* (Industrial Adjustment in Developed Countries and Developing Countries). Tokyo: Institute of Developing Economies.

Japan Development Bank. 1991. *Chosa* (Research) no.151 (July). In Japanese.

Japan External Trade Organization. 1990. "White Paper on International Trade." Tokyo: JETRO. In Japanese.

Kim, Kwang Doo, and Sang Ho Lee. 1990. "The Role of Korean Government in Technology Import." In Chung H. Lee and Ippei Yamazawa, eds., *The Economic Development of Japan and Korea.* New York: Praeger.

Kreinin, Mordechai E. 1988. "How Closed is Japan's Market? Additional Evidence." *World Economy* (December): 529–42.

Lawrence, Robert Z. 1991. "How Open is Japan?" In Paul Krugman, ed., *Trade with Japan.* Chicago: University of Chicago Press.

Lee, Chung H., and Eric D. Ramstetter. 1991. "Direct Investment and Structural Change in Korean Manufacturing." In Eric Ramstetter, ed., *Direct Foreign Investment in Asia's Developing Economies and Structural Change in the Asia-Pacific Region.* Boulder, CO: Westview.

NIKKEI Research Institute of Industry and Markets. 1992. *Nikkeikigyo no Ajia niokeru Gijutsuiten* (Technology Transfer by Japanese Firms in Asia). Tokyo: NIKKEI Research Institute of Industry and Markets.

Pangestu, Mari. 1991. "Foreign Firms and Structural Change in the Indonesian Manufacturing Sector." In Eric Ramstetter, ed., *Direct Foreign Investment in Asia's Developing Economies and Structural Change in the Asia-Pacific Region.* Boulder, CO: Westview.

Plummer, Michael G., and Eric D. Ramstetter. 1991. "Multinational Affiliates and Changing Division of Labor in the Asia-Pacific Region." In Eric Ramstetter, ed., *Direct Foreign Investment in Asia's Developing Economies and Structural Change in the Asia-Pacific Region.* Boulder, CO: Westview.

Ramstetter, Eric D., ed. 1991. *Direct Foreign Investment in Asia's Developing Economies and Structural Change in the Asia-Pacific Region.* Boulder, CO: Westview.

Reddy, N. Mohan, and Liming Zhao. 1990. "International Technology Transfer: A Review." *Research Policy,* no. 19.

Schive, Chi, and Jenn-Hwa Tu. 1991. "Foreign Firms and Structural Change in Taiwan." In Eric Ramstetter, ed., *Direct Foreign Investment in Asia's Developing Economies and Structural Change in the Asia-Pacific Region.* Boulder, CO: Westview.

Tambunlertchai, Somsak, and Eric D. Ramstetter. 1991. "Foreign Firms in Promoted Industries and Structural Change in Thailand." In Eric Ramstetter, ed., *Direct Foreign Investment in Asia's Developing Economies and Structural Change in the Asia-Pacific Region.* Boulder, CO: Westview.

Urata, Shujiro. 1990. "The Impact of Imported Technologies on Japan's Economic Development." In Chung H. Lee and Ippei Yamazawa, eds., *The Economic Development of Japan and Korea.* New York: Praeger.

Urata, Shujiro. 1991a. "The Rapid Increase of Direct Investment Abroad and Structural Change in Japan." In Eric Ramstetter, ed., *Direct Foreign Investment in Asia's Developing Economies and Structural Change in the Asia-Pacific Region*. Boulder, CO: Westview.

Urata, Shujiro. 1991b. "Globalization of Japanese Electronics Industry and Its Impact on Foreign Trade in Electronics Products." Paper prepared for OECD Development Centre project, Regionalization and Globalization. Paris: OECD. Mimeo (February).

Urata, Shujiro. N.d. "Japanese Foreign Direct Investment and Its Effect on Foreign Trade in Asia." In Takatoshi Ito and Anne O. Krueger, eds., *Trade and Protectionism*. Chicago: University of Chicago Press. Forthcoming.

US Department of Commerce. 1990. "U.S. Foreign Direct Investment Abroad, Preliminary 1988 Estimates." Washington: US Department of Commerce.

9

The Yen and the International Monetary System

TAKATOSHI ITO

As the Maastricht proposal to create one unified currency area has experienced a surprising defeat in Denmark and only a narrow approval in France, the future of the international monetary system—especially the possibility of issuing the European unified currency, ecu, to replace existing national currencies—is unclear, to say the least. The German mark will maintain its status as a strong currency in the European Monetary System (EMS) and remain its anchor. Although the US dollar is still the key currency in every aspect, its dominance in international financial markets seems to have been decreasing for decades. It may simply reflect the decreased weight of the US economy in the world, due to its low growth as compared with Japan and some European countries. However, it is unclear at this stage whether the yen or the ecu, if successfully issued, will take over the role of the key currency in the world, or at least share co-leader roles in the international monetary system.

Recently, many papers have been written on the subject of the internationalization of the yen (not meaning, necessarily, a yen bloc). Tavlas and Ozeki (1992), Frankel (1991 and 1992), Frankel and Wei (forthcoming), Kawai (1992), and Taguchi (forthcoming) have written on the same theme. What has been established can be summarized as follows. Although the use of the yen as the invoice currency or the reserve currency of

Takatoshi Ito is Professor, Hitotsubashi University, and Visiting Professor, John F. Kennedy School of Government, Harvard University. The author is grateful to C. Fred Bergsten, Richard Cooper, Jeffrey Frankel, Marcus Noland, Yuzuru Ozeki, Hugh Patrick, John Williamson, and the participants of the international seminar at Harvard University, who provided helpful comments.

central banks has increased, the pace is not as fast as Japan's rise in national income or as a number-one capital exporter.

When one pictures a yen bloc, it is natural to place it in the East Asian region. The Asian currencies have adopted the basket system to peg their currencies. The weight of the yen in their basket has not been significant (with an exception of the Singapore dollar). The Asian currencies have traditionally been more tied to the US dollar than the Japanese yen (Frankel and Wei; Taguchi). Although trade and investment links between Japan and other Asian countries have grown stronger, there is no particular bias, beyond the part explained by the proximity and high-speed growth of those economies, for trade in this region (Frankel 1992; Petri 1991 and 1992)

This paper looks at the role of the yen as an international currency and how it has changed recently, extending some results in the existing literature. The existing literature in general shows only a modest gain in the role of the yen in the past decade. This paper goes a step further to adjust statistics for the impact of structural changes due to the yen appreciation and oil price decreases from 1985 to 1987 and also due to changing export and import structures. Some changes are apparent gains in the use of the yen in invoicing, namely, effects of oil price decreases and the yen appreciation on compositional shifts in trade and finance, rather than active increase in the use of the yen or rebalancing the portfolio.

This paper also tries to identify reasons for a failure of the yen to become an international currency in the region. Relatively closed domestic capital markets and the political uncertainty of the Japanese relationship with Asian countries are identified as hurdles the yen must overcome to become a key regional currency.

Invoice Denomination

First of all, a currency is considered more internationally recognized if it is used to determine the value of international contracts—namely, exports and imports. A small nation may have difficulty asking its trading partners to denominate trade in its own currency because it is probably difficult for importers and exporters to obtain it and use it, respectively, in the international market. This was essentially the case for Japan before 1971 because of the tight currency control during the Bretton-Woods period, when the US dollar was essentially the only international convertible currency (to gold).

However, as the country's economy grows, there is incentive to use the currency in international trading. For exporters to and importers from that country, using its currency mitigates exchange-rate risks. For the trading partners, receiving or paying in a currency other than the US

Table 1 Invoice currencies of Japan's exports and imports by yen and dollar shares, 1970–91[a] (percentages)

	1970	1975	1980	1985	1986	1987	1988	1989	1990	1991
Exports										
in yen	0.9	17.5	28.9	39.3	36.5	33.4	34.3	34.7	37.5	39.4
in dollars	90.4	78.0	66.3	52.2	53.5	55.2	53.2	52.4	48.8	46.7
Imports										
in yen	0.3	0.9	2.4	7.3	9.7	10.6	13.3	14.1	14.5	15.6
in dollars	80.0	89.9	93.1	n.a.	n.a.	81.7	78.5	77.3	75.5	75.4

a. Imports, 1985 and 1986 are figures for April-to-March fiscal year.

Sources: Kawai (1992) for exports and imports invoicing. Original sources are, for exports until 1982, Bank of Japan; after 1983, MITI; imports until 1980, MITI; 1985, Ministry of Finance; and after 1986, MITI. (MITI, *Yushutsu kakunin statistics* and *Yunyu hokoku statistics*, 1991). Import ratios from Ministry of Finance, *Foreign Trade Statistics*.

dollar would not be too inconvenient if the currency can be obtained (for importers) from other sources, such as international capital markets, or used (for exporters) for other purposes, such as for imports. Consider the case of Japanese-Korean trade. If Japan exports parts to Korea, and Korea manufactures goods and exports mostly back to Japan, just enough to balance bilateral trade accounts, it does not matter whether these gross imports and exports are denominated in the dollar or the yen (or even in the won). However, it may be difficult for Japan to convince Korea to use the yen if Japan does not import enough from Korea. (We will explore this avenue further in a later section.)

Table 1 shows time-series statistics for yen and dollar shares of Japan's invoicing from 1970 to 1991. In 1970, the last year of the Bretton-Woods era, almost none of Japan's exports or imports were denominated in the yen. In 1991, 40 percent of exports and 16 percent of imports were denominated in yen. The share appears to have increased dramatically between 1970 and the mid 1980s, although leveling off in the second half of the 1980s. From this, we may conjecture that there may be more yen-denominated trade in the future.

However, even in 1991 Japan still lags in the use of its own national currency when compared to other advanced countries. Table 2 shows how much of the exports and imports of major industrially advanced countries are invoiced in their own national currencies and how much in yen. For example, the United States invoiced 96 percent of its exports in dollars in 1988, while receiving invoices for 85 percent of their imports in dollars. Japan used the yen as the invoicing currency in only 34.3 percent of its exports and 14.1 percent of its imports. Germany, a country that recorded large trade surpluses, as Japan did, used the deutsche marks in 81.5 percent of exports and in 52.6 percent of imports. In fact, Japan's invoicing ratios are lower than the typical European Community countries.

Table 2   Use of national currency and the Japanese yen in six industrially advanced nations (percentages)

	1980		1988	
	National currency	Yen	National currency	Yen
Exports				
Japan	29.4	29.4	34.3	34.3
United States	97.0	n.a.	96.0	1.0
Germany[a]	82.3	n.a.	81.5	0.5
France	62.5	n.a.	58.5	0.5
United Kingdom	76.0	n.a.	57.0	n.a.
Italy[a]	36.0	n.a.	38.0	n.a.
Imports				
Japan	2.4	2.4	14.1	14.1
United States	85.0	1.0	85.0	3.0
Germany	43.0	n.a.	52.6	2.5
France	33.1	1.0	48.9	1.3
United Kingdom	38.0	n.a.	40.0	2.0
Italy[a]	18.0	n.a.	27.0	n.a.

n.a. = not available
a. 1987.

Source: Tavlas and Ozeki (1992, table 17).

From tables 1 and 2, one may conclude that the yen is not yet functioning as the unit of account for Japanese trade. In contrast to European countries, Japan appears to lag in the use of the yen for invoices of exports and imports. Four preliminary observations, often cited in the literature, are made to explain these relatively low ratios of yen denomination for Japan's trade.

First, both exports and imports of the United States are denominated in the United States. Second, for other countries, exports tend to be denominated in national currencies. Hence, one argument goes that it is natural to have a lower own-currency ratio for imports for any country that depends on exports to the United States, such as Japan, and it would have a low own-currency ratio for exports, too.

Third, the international commodity markets, like crude oil and grain, are traded in terms of dollars. Countries with higher ratios of raw-materials imports tend to have higher dollar-denominated imports. Fourth, the use of a national currency lags the size of the nation's economy in relation to the rest of the world. Pure inertia maintains a currency's status long after the corresponding economy loses its dominant status in world trade.[1]

---

1. A conventional view is that, once an invoice currency is established (as the dollar), it would need a large change in economic environment to replace it, even though the economic power of that country has relatively declined in world trade, as is the case with the United

We will closely investigate these findings below. Some can be verified directly.

To begin with, we will investigate the structure of exports and imports, by commodity and by country. First, Japan's exports are decomposed by destination, by commodity groups, and by invoice currency ratios for each category shown in table 3.

Indeed, only 16 percent of Japan's exports to the United States are invoiced in yen. This contrasts with higher yen-invoice ratios for exports to other regions: 42 percent to the European Community and 50 percent to Asian countries. This is consistent with the fact that US imports, regardless of origin, tend to be invoiced in dollars (table 2). However, this aspect does not explain an increasing trend toward yen-invoiced imports in the 1980s, documented in table 1, because the ratio of US-destined exports rose slightly during the 1980s.

Note that half of exports to the European Community are invoiced in European currencies, and also about half of Japan's exports to the Asian countries are invoiced in dollars, to which many Asian currencies are pegged de facto (Frankel and Wei, forthcoming). Although it is the case that Japan has a higher yen-invoice ratio than other Asian countries, its ratio is not much different from that for exports to EC countries. Thus, there is no strong evidence that Japanese exporters' behavior toward Asian countries is much different from that toward EC countries.

The aspect of a low own-currency invoice ratio for non-US-destined exports is Japan's deviation from major European countries: that is, exports tend to be invoiced in exporters' currencies, as shown in table 2. Does this mean that the Japanese exporters are less powerful in business negotiations over the choice of invoice currency? Not necessarily.

One possible explanation is that Japanese exporters adopt a "pricing-to-market" strategy more often than other countries do (Marston 1990 and 1991).[2] The issues of invoice currency and the pricing-to-market

States. The shift from British pound sterling to the dollar took place in the 1950s and 1960s, even though the US economy surpassed, in terms of gross output, foreign reserves (gold) and net assets abroad in the 1920s. Japan became the world's largest creditor, while the United States became the world's largest debtor only in the late 1980s. See Matsuyama, Kiyotaki, and Matsui (1992) for important theoretical work on the choice of a transaction currency in the framework of international trade. They formulate a model of the "evolutionary approach to equilibrium selection, which is used to explain how the international medium of exchange emerges in the world economy." The model predicts that once the choice is established, it takes a very large disturbance to upset the equilibrium.

2. Marston showed that Japanese manufacturers have engaged in "pricing-to-market" behavior more than have their US counterparts. See also Ito (1992, chapter 10) for an example and references on this subject. Knetter (1992), however, compared manufacturers in the United States, United Kingdom, Germany, and Japan, and concluded that pricing behavior is very similar internationally for the same (narrowly-defined) industry. He argues that most of the difference arises in the varying composition of industries across countries.

Table 3 Destination of Japan's exports by currency and by commodity, 1991

	World			US			EC			Asia[a]		
	Millions of dollars	Dollars (percentages)	Yen	Millions of dollars	Dollars (percentages)	Yen	Millions of dollars	Dollars (percentages)	Yen	Millions of dollars	Dollars (percentages)	Yen
All commodities	294,790	46.8	39.4	87,923	83.4	16.5	57,238	6.8	42.0	85,162	45.9	50.8
Foodstuffs	1,639	55.6	41.2	239	76.3	23.6	148	22.7	64.8	950	55.7	42.5
Textiles	6,102	63.0	32.5	600	80.1	19.5	764	9.3	60.4	2,961	71.0	28.5
Chemicals	15,544	63.0	26.2	2,549	74.8	25.0	2,843	14.1	38.1	7,317	78.6	20.1
Nonmetals[b]	2,918	53.5	40.5	628	78.8	21.1	355	9.0	56.1	1,396	61.3	36.7
Metal products	18,864	76.8	19.5	3,506	89.3	10.6	1,058	22.4	43.6	9,287	78.8	19.9
Steel	13,013	87.7	9.4	1,982	99.1	0.9	427	44.2	16.2	6,659	88.6	10.9
Machines[c]	230,091	42.2	42.8	75,371	83.3	16.6	47,834	5.9	42.2	57,363	33.2	62.6
Generators[d]	7,067	40.7	48.8	2,020	83.2	16.6	1,031	9.1	42.8	2,220	25.9	67.5
TV	2,184	35.0	56.6	218	91.4	8.3	307	5.6	51.1	695	19.9	74.8
VCRs	5,822	42.1	39.7	1,608	91.4	8.6	1,017	2.5	29.8	1,343	27.7	62.3
Autos	57,342	44.2	35.3	24,300	86.1	13.9	11,382	0.5	36.8	4,291	19.1	69.8
Ships	5,333	13.7	86.2	67	97.6	2.4	417	35.1	64.2	558	22.8	77.2
Heavy[e]	3,207	41.0	51.5	470	73.3	26.6	335	5.9	49.9	1,791	45.4	51.7
Miscellaneous[f]	18,467	52.7	30.4	4,823	86.5	13.3	4,032	6.1	36.6	5,425	58.7	39.4

a. Korea, Taiwan, Hong Kong, Thailand, Singapore, Malaysia, Philippines, Indonesia, India.
b. Nonmetal mineral manufactured goods, such as cement, ceramics.
c. Generators, machine tools, computers, microprocessors, bearings, TVs, tape recorders, videotape recorders , semiconductors, autos, ships, cameras, copiers, watchs.
d. Generators and motors.
e. Heavy electric machinery.
f. Tire tubes, musical instruments, toys.

Source: Ministry of International Trade and Industry (Japan), *Export Confirmation Statistics,* 1991.

behavior are related, as invoice prices in contracts cannot be changed easily when the exchange rate fluctuates. Suppose a Japanese automobile maker exporting to US distributors writes a contract in dollars. Then his export price (in yen) has to decrease as the yen appreciates, and thus the pricing-to-market strategy emerges. Factors to consider in selection of the invoice currency are similar to factors discussed in the pricing-to-market literature. First, the Japanese exporters may be pursuing a market-share maximizing behavior in the short run as a part of a long-run strategy when sunk costs are large. Second, the Japanese parent firms may tend to protect their subsidiaries and trading partners from exchange rate risks, possibly because of the parents' readier access at lower cost to hedging technology.

In fact, it is notable that the yen-invoice ratio dropped from 1985 to 1987, the period of rapid appreciation, as shown in the first row of table 1. One interpretation is that this reflects the decision of many Japanese firms to cover more currency risk in order to alleviate their trading partners' anxiety over rapid yen appreciation.

In sum, Japan has made progress with respect to using its national currency for its exports. However, the level is still low, and that is true not only for exports to the United States, but to the European Community and Asian countries. This is likely related to the pricing-to-market behavior of Japanese exporters.

Next, we investigate the structure of imports by commodity and by country of origin, and invoice currency ratios for each category, as shown in table 4.

A salient feature of the invoice currency for Japan's imports is that its crude oil imports are invoiced 100 percent in dollars and, more broadly, that mineral and other raw materials, except for textiles, are almost all invoiced in dollars. This feature is evident regardless of the origin of the imports. One might observe that the raw materials from the European Community do not have a comparably high dollar-invoice rate, but the value of imports from EC countries is much lower than that from the United States or Asian countries. (For example, only 32 percent of imports from EC countries of "other raw materials" listed in table 4 are invoiced in dollars, but the amount of imports from the European Community for that category is one-twentieth of the aggregate amount of imports from the United States and Asia, where the dollar invoice share is 99.7 percent or higher.)

Imports of manufactured goods have a different characteristic. Again, imports from the United States are invoiced mostly in dollars, although the ratio is generally about 89 percent, leaving the yen-invoice ratio at about 11 percent. About 30 percent of imports of manufactured goods from the European Community and Asian countries are invoiced in the yen, although yen-invoiced ratios for subcategories are very different for imports from the European Community and imports from Asia.

Table 4 Origin of Japan's imports by currency and by commodity, 1991

	World			US			EC			Asia[a]		
	Millions of dollars	Dollars (percentages)	Yen	Millions of dollars	Dollars (percentages)	Yen	Millions of dollars	Dollars (percentages)	Yen	Millions of dollars	Dollars (percentages)	Yen
All commodities	201,045	75.4	15.6	44,824	88.7	11.2	24,324	15.9	31.4	56,412	76.5	21.6
Foodstuffs	32,605	72.4	22.2	10,451	85.1	14.8	3,082	22.2	40.3	9,380	73.1	26.3
Raw materials[b]	72,442	97.2	1.9	7,770	98.5	1.5	811	50.0	22.1	18,692	97.4	2.4
Textiles[c]	2,357	77.4	12.5	512	99.9	0.1	79	53.9	19.6	327	79.9	19.7
Ore[d]	7,058	98.1	1.2	727	99.0	1.0	115	88.2	2.7	1,606	97.1	2.4
Misc.[e]	13,688	91.8	5.9	4,943	97.8	2.2	466	32.2	29.0	3,500	90.5	8.9
Minerals[f]	49,338	99.5	0.3	1,587	99.9	0.1	150	73.9	16.9	13,257	99.7	0.3
Crude oil[g]	26,079	100.0	0.0	263	100.0	0.0	16	100.0	0.0	4,236	100.0	0.0
Manufactured[h]	95,997	60.0	23.7	26,601	87.2	12.6	20,430	13.5	30.4	28,339	63.8	32.8
Chemical[i]	14,270	51.7	32.5	4,476	84.6	15.1	4,685	12.3	58.5	1,671	69.8	28.0
Machine[j]	30,984	52.5	22.5	13,254	87.4	12.4	8,408	7.3	17.9	7,228	49.5	43.9
Other[k]	50,742	66.9	21.9	8,870	88.1	11.6	7,336	21.5	12.6	19,438	68.5	29.0

a. Korea, Taiwan, Hong Kong, Thailand, Singapore, Malaysia, Philippines, Indonesia, India.
b. Raw material and fuel.
c. Wool, cotton, silk, etc.
d. Iron ore, copper ore, scrap metal, etc.
e. Raw hide, soybeans, lumber, and pulp, etc.
f. Crude oil, coal, natural gas, etc.
g. Crude oil.
h. Manufactured goods.
i. Chemical compounds, phamaceutical goods, medical products, cosmetics, etc.
j. Motors, electric machines, aircrafts, autos, etc.
k. Wood and textile products, various alloys, precision instruments, etc.

Source: Ministry of International Trade and Industry (Japan), *Import Reporting Statistics,* 1991.

One additional observation is obvious. There is no bias for yen-invoiced trade with Asian countries.[3] Although the share of yen-invoiced imports from Asia is higher than that from the US, it is lower than that from EC.

One might wonder at this point how much of the rise in Japan's yen-invoiced imports over the decade is due to the changing structure of Japan's imports. In particular, oil prices declined sharply in 1986 and stayed low for the rest of the 1980s while prices of other primary commodities (raw materials imported into Japan) were in general lower in the second half of the 1980s than in the first half. As the share of oil and raw materials in Japan's imports decline, the share of yen-invoiced imports also declines because the yen-invoiced share of oil and raw materials is lower than that for manufactured goods (as shown in table 4). In order to estimate the effect of structural change, as opposed to a genuine change in the yen-invoicing practice, I calculated the yen-invoiced import ratio for nonoil imports, taking advantage of the fact that all crude oil imports are invoiced in dollars, and I calculated the yen-invoiced ratio for non–raw material imports by assuming that all raw material imports, not including textiles, are invoiced in dollars, while about 95 percent of them are in fact invoiced in dollars. The ratios are shown in table 5.

From this table we learned the following interesting facts. The overall yen-invoiced ratio climbed from 2.4 percent to 15.6 percent in 12 years from 1980 to 1991. This was more than a 13 percentage point gain, or a sixfold increase. Some part of the increase is suspected to be explained by the fact that the ratio of oil imports in Japan's total imports decreased from 37.5 percent in 1980 to only 13.2 percent in 1991. Excluding oil imports, which are for understandable reasons invoiced in dollars, Japan's yen-invoiced imports increased from 3.8 percent to 18.0 percent—a gain of 14.2 percentage points, or three times as much. In fact, the calculated nonoil yen-invoiced ratio shows a steady gain of the yen-invoiced imports, about one percentage point a year since 1985. In sum, the adjustment for crude oil imports does not change the trend. One slight difference between the nonoil yen-invoice ratio and the overall yen ratio shows up in the movement from 1985 to 1986, when the overall yen ratio gained 2.4 percentage points, while after adjusting for a decrease in crude oil imports, the nonoil yen-invoice ratio gained only in 1.5 percentage points.

The non–raw material, yen-invoiced ratio is also shown in table 5. It shows that for goods other than crude oil, iron ore, and other raw materials, the yen-invoiced ratio has increased from about 7 percent in 1980

3. Frankel (1992), and Frankel and Wei and Petri (forthcoming) showed, using gravity equations, that most of the increases in trade among Japan and Asian countries are explained by the relatively faster growth and geographical proximity of the countries in the region. The evidence here sheds light on a different aspect of the same phenomenon: there is nothing special about Japan's trade with Asian countries compared with, say, trade with the European Community, in terms of the ratio of yen-invoiced imports or exports.

Table 5 Yen-invoiced trade and adjustment, 1980–91 (ratios)

Year	Total imports[a]	Yen ratio[b]	Oil ratio[c]	Raw material ratio[d]	Nonoil yen ratio[e]	Non material yen ratio[f]
1980[g]	140.528	2.4	37.5	65.0	3.84	6.86
1983	113.378	3.0	37.2	59.4	4.78	7.39
1985	114.111	7.3	26.7	55.4	9.96	16.37
1986	105.654	9.7	15.4	41.6	11.47	16.61
1987	130.970	10.6	13.8	39.1	12.30	17.41
1988	161.070	13.3	10.1	33.7	14.79	20.06
1989	184.465	14.1	10.2	33.3	15.70	21.14
1990	204.841	14.5	13.5	36.2	16.76	22.73
1991	201.045	15.6	13.2	34.8	17.97	23.93

a. Customs-based total imports.
b. Yen-invoiced ratio.
c. $100 \times (oil\ imports)/(total\ imports)$.
d. $100 \times (raw\ material,\ except\ textile\ material)/(total\ imports)$.
e. Yen-invoiced imports for goods other than crude oil, using the fact that all crude oil imports are invoiced in dollars. Author's calculation:
   $non\text{-}oil\ yen\ ratio = (non\text{-}oil\ yen\text{-}invoiced\ trade)/(non\text{-}oil\ trade)$
   $= (total\ imports) \times (yen\ ratio)/(total\ imports) \times (1 - oil\ ratio)$
   $= (yen\ ratio)/(1 - oil\ ratio)$
f. Yen-invoiced imports for goods other than raw material imports, except for textile materials, (that is, yen- invoiced imports for manufactured goods, foodstuff, plus textile materials), assuming that raw material imports (except for textile materials) are 100 percent invoiced in dollars; in fact they are about 95 percent denominated in dollars. Author's calculation:
   $non\text{-}material\ yen\ ratio = (non\text{-}raw\ material\ yen\text{-}invoiced\ trade)/(non\text{-}raw\ material\ trade)$
   $= (Total\ imports) \times (yen\ ratio)/(Total\ imports) \times (1 - raw\ material\ ratio)$
   $= (yen\ ratio) \times (1 - raw\ material\ ratio)$
g. 1981, 1982, 1984 are missing because the yen-invoiced trade is not available.

Sources: Ministry of Finance (Japan), *Customs Statistics*, various years; Ministry of International Trade and Industry (Japan), *Import Report Statistics*; Kawai (1992).

to about 24 percent in 1991. This again shows that the yen invoicing has been steadily increasing among manufactured goods. One difference between the overall yen-invoice ratio and the non–raw material yen-invoice ratio was evident in 1985 and 1986. The non–raw material yen-invoice ratio only increased 0.2 percentage points, while the overall ratio increased 2.4 percentage points.

In sum, the use of the yen as an invoice currency for Japan's imports is steadily increasing. In 1991, although it claimed only 15.6 percent in overall imports, the ratio is 18 percent for nonoil imports and 24 percent for non–raw material imports. Exports to and imports from European and Asian countries are increasingly invoiced in the yen.

The Yen as a Transaction Vehicle

When a currency becomes recognized internationally, not only are contracts denominated in the currency, the currency also is used for settle-

Table 6   Currency composition of the foreign exchange markets, April 1989

	London		New York		Tokyo	
Transactions per day (billions of dollars)						
April 1989	187		128.9		115.2	
April 1992	303		192.3		128.0	
Markets (percentages)						
interbank	n.a.		82.0		67.1	
customer	15.0		13.0		29.3	
others	n.a.		5.0		3.6	
Composition (percentages)						
April 1989	UK/$	27.0	DM/$	32.9	Yen/$	72.3
	DM/$	22.0	Yen/$	25.2	DM/$	9.7
	Yen/$	15.0	UK/$	14.6	UK/$	4.3
	SFr/$	10.0	SFr/$	11.8	SFr/$	4.3
	FFr/$	2.0	CAN/$	4.0		
	others	15.0	other/$	11.5	others	3.3
	cross[a]	9.0	cross	3.6	cross	6.1
	DM/yen	2.0	DM/yen	n.a.	DM/yen	1.0
April 1992	DM/$	23.0	DM/$	33.7	Yen/$	67.3
	UK/$	19.0	Yen/$	22.8	DM/$	14.1
	Yen/$	13.0	UK/$	9.3	UK/$	3.8
	SFr/$	6.0	SFr/$	7.9	SFr/$	1.7
	other	22.0	other	15.0	other	5.3
	cross	17.0	cross	11.3	cross	7.8
	DM/yen	3.0	DM/yen	2.8	DM/yen	3.9

n.a. = not available
a. "Cross" means the exchange between nondollar currencies.

Source: Bank of Tokyo, *Togin Shuho*, (Bank of Tokyo weekly) 5 October 1989.

ment—that is, actually paying for exports and imports. Moreover, financial transactions—hedges and speculations alike—are usually carried out in the currency of the greatest number of participants. Hence, the currency is traded in the interbank market as it becomes internationally used.

Currency transactions in interbank markets can be analyzed according to the composition of currencies in major foreign exchange markets or the transactions in the offshore markets. Tables 6 and 7 show currency composition of foreign exchange markets and offshore trading, respectively.

Table 6 shows the size of the major foreign exchange markets—London, New York, and Tokyo—in terms of their transaction volumes and currency composition in April 1989. In Tokyo, foreign exchanges are predominantly yen-dollar transactions. In the London market, the pound sterling and the deutsche mark have about a quarter of the market each. The yen is third, with only a 15 percent market share.

Table 7   Japan's offshore market assets, 1986–90
(billions of dollars, except where noted)[a]

	1986	1987	1988	1989	1990
Position vis-à-vis nonresidents					
Total assets	88.7	191.9	329.7	449.6	473.4
In yen	19.2	69.0	129.8	203.2	193.0
Share of total	21.6	36.0	39.4	45.2	40.8
In other currencies	69.5	122.9	199.8	246.5	280.3
Share of total	78.4	64.0	60.6	54.8	59.2
Positions vis-à-vis residents					
Total assets	5.0	46.9	84.5	158.0	131.6
In yen	n.a.	31.3	60.6	111.0	80.4
Share of total	n.a.	66.7	71.7	70.3	61.1
In other currencies	n.a.	15.6	23.8	46.8	51.3
Share of total	n.a.	33.3	28.3	29.7	38.9
Resident and nonresident					
total assets	93.7	238.8	414.2	607.6	605.0
In yen	n.a.	100.3	190.4	314.2	273.4
Share of total	n.a.	42.0	46.0	51.7	45.2
In other currencies	n.a.	138.5	223.7	293.3	331.6
Share of total	n.a.	58.0	54.0	48.3	54.8

n.a. = not available
a. End-of-year figures.

Source: Bank for International Settlements, *International Banking and Financial Market Developments*, May 1990. (Updated by Ministry of Finance)

In the New York market, deutsche mark–dollar transactions have a share of 32.9 percent and yen-dollar transactions 25.2 percent. The European currencies, combining deutsche marks with other EC currencies, have about half of this market, and the yen has about a quarter of the market. Although Japan is the number-one place of origin for imports and the number-two export destination for US trade (Canada being number one), Japan's shares in US total trade are only one-tenth of exports and a little less than a quarter for imports. Hence, the weight of the yen in the currency market reflects more than Japan's role in goods and services trade.

Table 7 explains the currency composition of assets in Japan's Offshore Market (JOM). The weight of the yen increased until 1989 but slightly declined in 1990. About 40 percent of nonresident assets were in yen, while about 60 percent of the residents assets were in yen. However, yen transactions in the JOM, or any other offshore market, may reflect assets placed there in order to avoid domestic regulations, and it does not necessarily imply actual transaction needs for the currency.

The Yen as an Asset

When a currency is considered safe and likely to keep its value, many international investors and central banks increase the share of that cur-

Table 8 Official foreign reserves in all countries' central banks, 1980–90 (percentages)

Currency	1980	1981	1982	1983	1984	1985	1986	1987	1988	1989	1990
Yen	4.4	4.2	4.7	5.0	5.8	8.0	7.9	7.5	7.7	7.9	9.1
USD	68.6	71.5	70.5	71.4	70.1	64.9	67.1	67.2	64.9	60.2	56.4
UKL	2.9	2.1	2.3	2.5	2.9	3.0	2.6	2.4	2.8	2.7	3.2
DM	14.9	12.3	12.4	11.8	12.7	15.2	14.6	14.4	15.7	19.3	19.7
FFr	1.7	1.3	1.0	0.8	0.8	0.9	0.8	0.8	1.0	1.3	2.1
SFr	3.2	2.7	2.7	2.4	2.0	2.3	2.0	2.0	1.9	1.7	1.5
NGu	1.3	1.1	1.1	0.8	0.7	1.0	1.1	1.2	1.1	1.1	1.2

Source: Tavlas and Ozeki (1992, table 25).

rency in their portfolios. Then the currency performs the function of an international store of value. The definition of a "safe" currency encompasses political aspects (no drastic shift in political regime), regulatory aspects (no surprise capital controls), and economic aspects (low inflation and strong economic growth).[4] Hence, it is instructive to look at whether a currency's recognition as an international currency depends upon the degree to which central banks and institutional investors of other countries hold it.

Table 8 shows the composition of currencies among central banks' foreign reserves. In 1990 about 60 percent of central banks' foreign reserves were held in dollars and about 20 percent in deutsche marks. The yen is a distant third with 9 percent. It appears that shares of nondollar currencies, especially the yen and the deutsche mark, have increased in the last 11 years. However, close scrutiny reveals that most of this change seems to have occurred along with the sharp appreciation in the yen and European currencies after the Plaza Agreement of September 1985. If the central bank just held a fixed portfolio of the currencies, without selling or buying them, from the end of 1984 through 1985 (and to a lesser extent, through 1986), then the mark-to-market composition should have changed drastically due to the dollar depreciation during the period.

A back-of-the-envelope calculation shows the magnitude of the problem. From the end of 1984 to the end of 1985, the yen and most European currencies appreciated against the dollar by 25 to 30 percent. The dollar share of central bank reserves in 1984 was 70 percent. Without active rebalancing of portfolio, how much should the mark-to-market dollar share have decreased in one year? When the value of nondollar currencies, with a 30 percent share, increased in value against the dollar, with its 70 percent share, the new share should be about 37 percent against 64

---

4. The dollar is considered to be the safest asset in a world-scale crisis due to US military power and reasonably large oil reserves. The "safe haven" effect usually explains appreciation of the dollar at the outbreak of regional wars, with increased political uncertainty in a country important to advanced nations, and during oil crises.

percent, or, put differently, a 20 percent increase in the nondollar share, with a 10 percent decrease in the dollar share in the new mark-to-market asset value. In fact, for dollar and deutsche mark shares at the end of 1985, this is very close to the case.

To verify this effect more accurately, a decomposition into capital gains and active rebalancing of foreign reserve portfolio changes from 1984 to 1985 for all central banks is calculated in table 9. After this decomposition is done, the yen still seems to be the currency of active gains among the central banks. This seems to reflect active intervention, mainly by the US federal reserve banks and the Bank of Japan, which were buying yen and selling dollars according a plan drawn up in the Plaza Agreement. However, capital gains of the yen, held by central banks worldwide, exceeded active rebalancing by 7 billion SDR to 2 billion SDR for the yen. Other European currencies, held by central banks worldwide, increased their share in the portfolio in 1985 purely because of the appreciation of their currencies.

When only the Asian central banks are considered, the yen share still increased in 1985 but decreased significantly after 1985, as shown in table 10. It peaked at 30 percent in 1987 and then declined to 17.5 percent in 1989. This is consistent with the yen fluctuation after 1985, too. It is notable that among central banks of Asian countries, the yen share exceeds that of the deutsche mark.

Table 11 shows the currency denomination in yen and dollar shares of the external debts of five Asian countries. The share of yen-denominated debts increased throughout the 1980s and overtook the share of the dollar-denominated debts in all countries but Korea by 1988.

The yen-denominated debt tended to increase in the countries that depended on official development assistance (ODA) from Japan, such as Indonesia and Philippines, since some parts of ODA are yen-denominated loans. When countries borrow in the international lending markets, it tends to be denominated in the dollar, with interest rates tied to the London Interbank Offer Rate (LIBOR).

Korea, for example, relied heavily on international bank lending in the beginning of the 1980s, and then mostly grew out of it. At the same time, it became wealthy enough so that it did not qualify for Japan's ODA. This growth strategy is reflected in the currency denomination of their debts.

Strategic Exchange Rate Policy

In this section, I will explain why the use of the yen as an invoice currency is rather limited, even in trade between Japan and the Asian countries and how to interpret findings summarized above from the viewpoint of

Table 9 Composition of changes from 1984 to 1985

	1984 Dec31 FX/$[a]	1985 Dec31 FX/$[a]	appreciation vis-à-vis $ (a − b)/b = c	asset share 1984[d]	asset value 1984 d / 100 × 405.8[k] billion SDR[e]	asset of 1984 adjusted for 1985[k] billions SDR[f]	asset share 1985[g]	actual asset value 1985, billions SDR[h]	capital gains f − e = i	active rebalance h − f = j
JA	252.00	200.00	0.26	5.8	23.54	30.44	8.0	32.42	6.90	1.98
UK	0.8626	0.6904	0.25	2.9	11.77	15.09	3.0	12.16	3.32	−2.93
DM	3.1580	2.4400	0.29	12.7	51.54	68.45	15.2	61.59	16.91	−6.86
FF	9.6550	7.4850	0.29	0.8	3.25	4.30	0.9	3.65	1.05	−0.65
SF	2.6060	2.0540	0.27	2.0	8.12	10.57	2.3	9.32	2.45	−1.25
GU	3.5590	2.7485	0.29	0.7	2.84	3.77	1.0	4.05	0.93	0.28
US	1.0	1.0	0.00	70.1	284.47	291.91	64.9	262.97	7.44	−28.94
$/SDR	1.04695	0.9802								
Total	405.8	405.2								

FX = foreign exchange
JA = yen
UK = pound sterling
DM = deutsche mark
FF = French franc
SF = Swiss franc
GU = Dutch guilder
SDR = Special drawing rights

a. New York closing rate of foreign exchange rate per dollar in December 1984.   UK is a reciprocal of usually quoted rate. Taken from Toyo Keizai Shimpo, *Money Market Index*, 1988.
b. New York closing rate of foreign exchange rate per dollar in December 1985.
c. Foreign exchange value appreciation against the dollar, as calculated.
d. Taken from Tavlas and Ozeki (1992, table 25); see table 8 of this paper.
e. Foreign reserve value at the end of 1984, taken from International Monetary Fund, *International Financial Statistics*.
f. Value of a portfolio at the end of 1984, marked to the exchange rates at the end of 1985.
g. Taken from Tavlas and Ozeki (1992, table 25), see table 8 of this paper.
h. Foreign reserve value at the end of 1985, taken from International Monetary Fund, *International Financial Statistics*.
i. Capital gains as defined in the table.
j. Active rebalancing as defined in the table.
k. Formula is Assets (1984) × [$/SDR(1984) × FX/$(1984)]/[$/SDR(1985) × FX/$(1985)], or (5) × [(1) × 1.04695]/[(2) × 0.98021]

Sources: Toyo Keizai Shimpo, *Money Market Index*, 1988; International Monetary Fund, *International Financial Statistics*, various issues; Tavlas and Ozeki (1992, table 25).

Table 10 Currency composition of foreign reserves in selected Asian countries' central banks,[a] 1980–90 (percentages)

Currency	1980	1981	1982	1983	1984	1985	1986	1987	1988	1989	1990
Yen	13.9	15.5	17.6	15.5	16.3	26.9	22.8	30.0	26.7	17.5	17.1
Dollar	48.6	54.4	53.2	55.7	58.2	44.8	48.4	41.2	46.7	56.4	62.7
Pound	3.0	2.5	2.7	2.9	3.5	4.1	3.6	3.9	4.2	6.4	4.9
Deutsche mark	20.6	18.9	17.6	16.7	14.6	16.4	16.7	16.7	17.4	15.2	14.2
French franc	0.6	0.6	0.7	0.8	0.6	0.9	1.1	1.0	0.5	0.5	0.2
Swiss franc	10.6	5.1	5.6	6.6	4.9	4.93	5.1	5.7	3.4	3.0	0.5
Guilder	2.8	3.1	2.6	1.8	1.9	2.1	2.2	1.5	1.0	0.9	0.5

a. Korea, Taiwan, Hong Kong, Thailand, Singapore, Malaysia, Philippines, Indonesia, India.

Source: Tavlas and Ozeki (1992, table 25).

Japan and an Asian country, which compete with each other in the US market.

Let us consider a case, such as that of Korea or Taiwan, in which a country typically imports semimanufactured materials from Japan and exports finished products to the United States. In the US market, the goods are imperfectly differentiated from Japanese manufactured goods. What is the optimal strategy for this country for selecting denominations of currency for trade and for assets and debts? (We assume here that the contract export and import prices denominated in the contract currency cannot be changed frequently, so that pricing to market is not perfect.)

Suppose that the country's imports from Japan and exports to the United States are denominated in dollars. Suppose further that the country's currency is pegged to the dollar. The yen appreciation vis-à-vis the dollar will automatically give a price advantage in the US market to this country's producers, who are in competition with Japanese exporters, provided that the intermediate-goods imports from Japan are also denominated in dollars. This is essentially what happened in the second half of the 1980s.[5]

Japanese producers began losing sales in the US market to other Asian producers. One way to lessen the exchange rate effects on Japanese producers is to denominate intermediate-goods exports from Japan to other Asian producers in yen. This way, the cost of the importing country's imports must increase as the yen appreciates against the dollar. The cost increase presumably is passed on, though maybe only partially, in the export price, which is denominated in dollars. Then the competition in the United States between goods made in Japan and goods made in Korea, for instance, with Japanese parts becomes less favorable to Korean producers. Hence, the steady increase in the yen-denominated exports to

---

5. This is the reason that the United States persuaded Asian countries to cut back on the dollars in their currency basket because the decrease in Japan's exports to the United States was largely made up by an increase in the Asian exports.

Table 11　External debts in five Asian countries by currency denomination, 1980–89

	1980	1981	1982	1983	1984	1985	1986	1987	1988	1989
Indonesia										
(billions of dollars)	15.0	15.9	18.5	21.6	22.3	26.8	32.5	41.4	41.2	40.8
Yen (percentage)	20.0	19.3	21.0	23.3	25.0	31.7	33.9	39.4	39.3	35.2
Dollars (percentage)	43.5	44.4	43.1	42.3	41.4	30.7	26.0	19.2	18.5	19.5
Thailand ($ billions)	3.9	5.0	6.0	6.9	7.2	9.8	11.5	14.0	13.3	12.4
Yen (percentage)	25.5	23.2	24.0	27.3	29.2	36.1	39.9	43.1	43.5	40.9
Dollars (percentage)	39.7	40.5	38.0	32.5	29.9	25.5	20.6	17.8	20.8	23.6
Korea ($billions)	15.9	18.4	20.2	22.2	23.8	28.3	29.3	24.5	21.3	17.3
Yen (percentage)	16.6	14.1	12.3	12.5	12.8	16.7	22.0	27.2	29.5	26.6
Dollars (percentage)	53.5	60.2	63.7	64.4	66.0	60.3	49.4	33.8	32.4	35.1
Malaysia ($billions)	4.0	5.7	8.2	11.9	13.2	14.7	16.6	18.0	16.1	14.5
Yen (percentage)	19.0	16.9	13.3	14.2	21.2	26.4	30.4	35.7	37.1	36.6
Dollars (percentage)	38.0	51.5	62.3	65.8	61.5	50.6	45.0	36.3	35.6	34.2
Philippines($billions)	6.4	7.5	8.8	10.5	11.2	13.8	19.2	23.5	23.5	23.0
Yen (percentage)	22.0	20.6	19.2	20.0	20.0	24.9	25.5	35.2	40.5	32.6
Dollars (percentage)	51.6	51.1	53.9	51.2	52.7	47.8	48.1	42.4	34.7	36.9
Total										
(billions of dollars)	45.2	52.4	61.7	73.0	77.8	93.5	109.7	121.5	115.5	108.1
Yen (percentage)	19.5	17.8	17.2	18.5	20.3	25.8	29.3	36.0	37.9	35.7
Dollars (percentage)	47.3	51.3	53.4	53.2	52.9	44.7	38.5	29.0	27.0	28.1

Source: Tavlas and Ozeki (1992, table 24); original source, World Bank.

Asian countries can be understood as a defensive move by Japanese firms in response to the large yen appreciation in 1986–87. This does not happen in a collusive way. If Japanese producers and parts makers start losing money from their exports of parts to Asia as the yen appreciates (and the dollar depreciates) and sales are denominated in dollars, then not all parts producers will tolerate it, and each of them may decide to inflate export prices.

Given that a growing portion of imports are denominated in yen, the Asian country now has less resistance to putting increased weight on the yen in the basket formula of its exchange rate. When the yen appreciates against the dollar, the Asian country's currency partly appreciates against the dollar and partly depreciates against the yen. The cost of imports from Japan increase slightly, and the cost of other imports, denominated in the dollar, decreases slightly, in exchange for a slight disadvantage in export competition to the US market. Hence, increased yen-denominated imports may encourage the country to place more weight on the yen in its currency basket.

Another way in which Japan, if we assume that banks and producers conspire, can prevent the other Asian country from realizing a cost advantage during a yen appreciation is to denominate lending to Asian countries in yen. This trend is evident in statistics. However, it may be just a reflection of Japanese banks, acting independently from manufacturers, trying to limit exposure to exchange rate risks by denominating lending in yen. Also, it may be that the ratio of the yen-denominated debt went up quite independently from any development in price competitiveness of manufactured goods and was put into effect as a part of ODA policy.

Political Economy of Currency Negotiation

In the first half of the 1980s, US trade deficits and the Japanese trade surpluses were growing rapidly. In response to increasing criticism on this issue, the Reagan administration launched an attack on Japanese financial regulations. The so-called yen-dollar group meetings took place in 1983–84 to discuss, among other things, liberalizing Japanese financial markets.[6] One objective of the working group was to open up Japanese domestic financial markets to US investment banks and securities firms. Another objective was to deregulate Japanese financial products to make them attractive for foreigners so the yen would appreciate through increased investment. At the time, the US administration actively sought yen appreciation as a remedy for the soaring trade imbalance between the two countries.

However, deregulation in the Japanese financial markets, encouraged by the United States, lowered the barriers for both inflows and outflows of capital. Since the US interest rates were in general higher than the Japanese interest rates at the time, and since the Japanese saving-investment balance continued to show a surplus of saving, outflows of Japanese capital to the rest of the world, particularly to the United States, exceeded inflows into Japan. The result was further yen depreciation, just the opposite of the pretext for the yen-dollar negotiations.

Whatever the intention was, deregulation due to the yen-dollar group helped the yen to become an "international currency." More Eurobonds became available in the yen, and domestic financial markets became more "liberalized" for foreign as well as domestic investors.

In September 1985 financial ministers and central bank governors of the Group of Five countries gathered in the Plaza hotel in New York to discuss exchange rate levels. In order to correct huge US trade deficits, it was agreed that the dollar should depreciate. The central banks started heavy intervention during the week of 22 September 1985, followed up by some changes in domestic monetary policy. The monetary authorities

---

6. See Frankel (1984) for a detailed examination of these meetings.

of the G-5 managed to lower the value of the dollar against the yen by about 40 percent between September 1985 and August 1986. As a result, the weight of the yen-denominated assets in portfolios of central banks and private investors appreciated accordingly.

After the Plaza Agreement, the yen, along with European currencies, promptly appreciated against the dollar.[7] The yen, which was traded at 240 to the dollar at the time of the Plaza Agreement, appreciated to 230 the following week and then to 200 in three months. It further appreciated to near 150 by the summer of 1986. The Louvre Accord in February 1987 has been seen as implementing a target zone, an attempt to keep the value of the currencies of the G-7 countries within a narrow band. The second half of the 1980s is marked by active exchange rate management.

Although the yen appreciated more than 50 percent against the dollar, the trade imbalance between the United States and Japan did not begin to really correct itself until 1987. This was partly due to pricing-to-market behavior of the Japanese and US manufacturers (Marston 1990 and 1991) and partly due to the standard J-curve effect, showing a lagged response.

From 1987 to 1990 the Japanese trade surpluses declined in parallel with the decline in the US trade deficits. By 1990 the Japanese surpluses were within 1 percent of GNP, a level which does not provoke political tensions.[8] Thus the currency issue, including the issue related to the international monetary regime, was not a major concern at the end of 1990. In 1991 and 1992 the issue became active again in European countries as they pursued a common currency as outlined in the Maastricht treaty. However, the yen was left alone in the controversy surrounding Maastricht and the subsequent turmoil in the European Monetary System.

Stumbling Block in Japan's Domestic Markets

The role of the yen, as measured by the degree to which it is used among other things, will increase if that role parallels the role of trade. There are two stumbling blocks to the fulfillment of this prediction. First, Japan's domestic financial markets have to be deregulated further. Second, a political gap between Japan and Asian countries must be bridged.

It is well-recognized that in order to attract foreign investors, a "thick" market for short-term, risk-free assets is necessary. Investors, including foreign central banks, can park their funds in such a market. A typical short-term, risk-free asset is a Treasury bills market. In Japan, T-bills should not be confused with financing bills, or FBs. The latter is issued

---

7. See Ito (1992, chapter 11) for details of the appreciation process.

8. However, the Japanese trade surpluses have increased since 1991. In 1992 they will reach a record high in level, at about 3 percent of GNP.

Table 12 International comparison of short-term capital market, September 1989 (in trillion yen)[a]

	Japan		US		UK		Germany	
Interbank	call	25.0	FF,RP	24.8	call	2.5	call	23.1
	bill	11.3			deposit	19.7		
Open market	TB	3.3	TB	56.7	TB	1.2	TB	0.8
	FB	2.0			bill	2.9	bill	5.3
	RP	4.9	CD	55.2	CD	9.8		
	CD	19.9	CP	70.6	CP	0.7		
	CP	11.1	BA	8.9				

a. Conversion to yen made at the exchange rate at the time of writing report cited at the source.

Source: Bank of Japan and Ministry of Finance, Short-term capital market research group (1990).

mostly to the Bank of Japan, with low yield, and a majority of the outstanding balance is held by the Bank of Japan. In Japan, six-month T-bills were first issued in 1986 and three-month T-bills in 1989.[9] As of March 1991 the T-bill market has a balance of only ¥8 trillion, while call and bills (*tegata*) markets combined had a market size of ¥40 trillion. Currently the Bank of Japan operates its monetary policy mainly through interbank and bills market.

Table 12 shows the size of the short-term capital markets in Japan, the United States, the United Kingdom, and Germany. A most notable difference in Japan, compared to the United States, is a relatively small size of the T-bill market.[10] The volume of T-bill issues has been increasing, but the size is still smaller than that of the United States. Since the T-bill market is an important place for foreign investors to park their yen-denominated funds, its shallowness hampers capital flows into Japan.

Table 13 summarizes the market size of the short-term capital market in Japan. It shows that interbank markets are much "thicker" (i.e, large and diverse enough to absorb idiosyncratic shocks) than open-market instruments.

Proposals to make the T-bill market attractive have been discussed by policymakers and academic economists in Japan, partly because that would establish a market where the Bank of Japan can conduct open-

---

9. See Ito (1992, 121–24) for a description of Japan's short-term financial market. Note the difference between T-bill (*tanki kokusai*) and FB (*seifu tanki shoken*) interest rates and method of issuance. It is also confusing that FBs were once translated T-bills, before what are now called T-bills were issued. Books written on the Japanese economy or Japanese financial market before the mid-1980s have the old names, giving the false impression that T-bills existed before 1985.

10. For details of short-term market instruments, see Ito (1992, chapter 5).

Table 13 Short-term capital market breakdown in Japan, March 1991 (billions of yen)[a]

Calls	27,065
Bills	14,043
Treasury bills	8,211
Financing bills	16,356[b]
Repurchase agreement	11,047
Certificates of deposit	19,803
Commercial paper	11,210

a. Outstanding balance at the end of March 1991, except calls and bills are average outstanding balance over the month of March 1991.
b. In March 1991, out of 15,356 billion yen FBs outstanding, 13,890 billion yen were held by the Bank of Japan, thus not circulating in the secondary market. The correct market size is like 1,000 billion yen.

Source: Bank of Japan, *Economic Statistics Annual, 1991*, March 1992.

market operations in the manner of the Federal Reserve Bank, and partly because the yen can thus be "internationalized." It is presumed that a market size of ¥30 trillion to ¥40 trillion is needed to conduct open-market operations in Japan.

I have proposed the following scheme to increase the size of risk-free markets in Japan (Ito 1990). First, it is easy to increase the size of T-bill issues to an outstanding balance of ¥10 trillion. Financing bills can be auctioned to the public instead of being issued to and held at the Bank of Japan. This will add another ¥10 trillion to ¥12 trillion. Then, outstanding near-maturity long-term bonds, predominantly 10-year bonds in Japan, can be used. In each year during the 1980s, at least ¥10 trillion worth of long-term bonds were issued. Then near-maturity bonds can be treated like T-bills. They are the same in terms of being risk-free. Two aspects differentiate T-bills and long-term bonds. First, long-term bonds come with interest-bearing coupons, while T-bills are issued with discounts. Second, long-term bond interest is subject to withholding and securities transactions taxes, while T-bills are exempt from both. In order to create near-maturity long-term bonds, coupons can be stripped (i.e., ownership to coupon-payments and ownership to principal payments are separated) so that the principal part becomes a de facto discount bond. This requires improvement in the method of registering bonds because the current infrastructure does not allow stripping. Then near-maturity long-term bonds must be granted exemption from the securities transactions tax, imposed on the face value so that it becomes prohibitively expensive as the maturity date nears. Lastly, investors, including foreign central banks, must be exempt from the withholding tax without much red tape. With these innovations, there will be a ¥10 trillion to ¥12 trillion market for near-maturity long-term bonds, which will be traded as T-bills.

More attractive capital markets, both short-term and long-term, will invite more foreign investment, and with more foreign investment, the yen will be used more widely in the world.

Let us return to the second point: political problems between Japan and Asian countries. Although trade between Japan and its Asian neighbors is increasing at a faster pace than between Japan and other regions, the political distance sometimes poses a problem.[11] Unless Asian countries come to regard Japan as a trustworthy country that poses no political threat, there is little prospect that Asian countries will form some kind of the yen bloc, in terms of the use of the yen or bilateral investment flows. Although there is an increase in Korean and Taiwanese investments to other ASEAN countries, they have invested little in Japan.

One scenario for enhancement of political and economic ties between Japan and its Asian neighbors envisages increased Japanese imports of Asian goods. That is, the trading structure would become more horizontal and less vertical. By exporting to Japan, Asian countries will automatically earn yen. Some could be used in their imports, but they also would have more incentive to manage funds in yen. By increasing exports to Japan, Asian countries will have more incentive to denominate their exports in yen. The share of the yen-denominated imports to Japan would then increase, too.

Summary

The findings described in the preceding sections reveal the use of the yen from various perspectives, summarized as follows. Although Japanese exports and imports increased sharply, the use of the yen as a unit of account, as a vehicle currency, or as an asset in portfolio has not risen to a status parallel to commodity flows. Exports from and imports to Japan are predominantly denominated in dollars instead of yen, although the yen-invoice ratio has been steadily increasing. This seems to be a result of Japan's trading structure (little intraindustry trade with its Asian neighbors), and Japan's relatively closed capital markets. The share of yen in foreign currency transactions in the world market is less than the share of deutsche mark.

More than half of Japan's exports to Asian countries are denominated in yen, but only a quarter of Japan's imports from Asian countries are denominated in yen.

---

11. It is still a prevalent feeling among some Asian countries that Japan has not apologized for its atrocities before and during the Second World War. One such example is Japan's handling of the issue concerning "comfort women" during the war. The Japanese government first denied any government involvement in forcing women from Asian countries into prostitution but later admitted to having recruited them for this purpose. The government still maintained, however, that the women offered their services voluntarily.

The yen is more important in the Asian region. This is reflected, for example, in the official reserve currency composition among the Asian countries. However, even there, a major increase in the 1980s occurred because of the appreciation of the yen instead of active rebalancing. The yen-denominated external debt among the Asian countries has risen steadily compared with debt denominated in other currencies, mostly in dollars.

The future of yen use in the international financial and capital markets, especially in the Asian region, will increase if Japan's domestic capital markets are further liberalized and the political distance between Japan and Asian neighbors can be narrowed. Developments in these areas are likely over the next 10 years.

References

Black, Stanley W. 1991. "Transactions Costs and Vehicle Currencies." *Journal of the International Money and Finance* 10: 512–26.

Frankel, Jeffrey A. 1984. *The Yen/Dollar Agreement: Liberalizing Japanese Capital Markets.* Washington: Institute for International Economics.

Frankel, Jeffrey A. 1991. "Is a Yen Bloc Forming in Pacific Asia." In R. O'Brien and S. Hewin, eds., *Finance and the International Economy.* New York: Oxford University Press.

Frankel, Jeffrey A. 1992. "Is Japan Creating a Yen Bloc In East Asia and the Pacific?" *NBER Working Paper* 4050. Cambridge, MA: National Bureau of Economic Research (April).

Frankel, Jeffrey A., and Shang-Jin Wei. N.d. "Yen Bloc or Dollar Bloc: Exchange Rate Policies of the East Asian Economies." In T. Ito and A. O. Krueger, eds., *Macroeconomic Linkage: Saving, Exchange Rates, and Capital Flows.* Sapporo, Japan: University of Chicago Press (forthcoming).

Ito, Takatoshi. 1990. *"Kijikasai katsuyo in yoru tannki kinnyu shijou kakushin no teigen"* (Proposal to innovate the short-term capital market using near-maturity long-term bonds). *Ekonomisuto* (3 July).

Ito, Takatoshi. 1992. *The Japanese Economy.* Cambridge, MA: MIT Press.

Kawai, Masahiro. 1992. *"En no Kokusai-ka"* (Internationalization of the Yen). In T. Ito, ed., *Kokusai Kin-yu no Genjo* (Current Status of International Finance). Tokyo: Yuhikaku (May).

Knetter, Michael M. 1992. "International Comparisons of Pricing-to-Market Behavior." *NBER Working Paper* 4098. Cambridge, MA: National Bureau of Economic Research (June).

Marston, Richard C. 1990. "Pricing to Market in Japanese Manufacturing." *Journal of International Economics* 29: 217–36.

Marston, Richard C. 1991. "Price Behavior in Japanese and U.S. Manufacturing." In Paul Krugman, ed., *Trade with Japan: Has the Door Opened Wider?* Chicago: University of Chicago Press and National Bureau of Economic Research.

Matsuyama, Kiminori, Nobuhiro Kiyotaki, and Akihiko Matsui. 1992. "Toward a Theory of International Currency." *Review of Economic Studies.*

Petri, Peter A. 1991. "Market Structure, Comparative Advantage, and Japanese Trade under the Strong Yen." In Paul Krugman, ed., *Trade with Japan: Has the Door Opened Wider?* Chicago: University of Chicago Press and National Bureau of Economic Research.

Petri, Peter A. N.d. "The East Asian Trading Bloc: An Analytical History." In J. Frankel and M. Kahler, eds., *Japan and the U.S. in Pacific Asia*. San Diego: University of Chicago Press (forthcoming).

Taguchi, Hiroo. N.d. "On the Yen Bloc." In T. Ito and A. O. Krueger, eds., *Macroeconomic Linkage: Saving, Exchange Rates, and Capital Flows*. Sapporo, Japan: University of Chicago Press (forthcoming).

Tavlas, George S. 1991. "On the International Use of Currencies: the Case of the Deutsche Mark." Essays in International Finance, Princeton University (March).

Tavlas, George S., and Yuzuru Ozeki. 1992. *The Japanese Yen as an International Currency*. Occasional Paper no. 90. Washington: International Monetary Fund (January).

10

Human Capital Flows

GLENN A. WITHERS

The present era is one of mass migration. According to the International Organization of Migration (1990), over 80 million people are living outside their countries of birth. Fifteen million of these are refugees. As Stephen Castles (1992, 1) has put it:

> Never before have so many people left their countries in search of work, a better life or simply a safe refuge. There are few countries in the world not affected by migration, as countries of origin, receiving countries, or often as both.

Yet people flows are all too rarely discussed in the context of trade and development. This seems odd. We know that human capital is central to productivity, growth, and development and that internal and international migration represents major human-capital reallocations. Using the standard global general equilibrium modeling methods to document gains from free trade, it has been estimated by Hamilton and Whalley (1984) that removal of all barriers to migration would double world GDP.

Of course, population movements have been an enduring feature of human geography. The classic 19th century migrations from Europe to North America and Australasia were major voluntary movements, and these host countries continue to attract migrants, though from more diverse sources. The United States now receives over 600,000 settlers each year.

Glenn A. Withers is Director of the Economic Planning Advisory Council in Canberra and Professor of Economics at La Trobe University. The views expressed are those of the author only and do not necessarily represent the views of EPAC or the Australian government.

Western Europe itself became a major host country for migration after the Second World War, attracting millions from the Mediterranean countries and now attracting many from the Maghreb, the Levant, and from Eastern Europe, as the borders there crumble. West Germany has been receiving 1 million immigrants per year since 1989.

There have been major pan-African migrations—to South Africa, Zimbabwe, Nigeria, Cote d'Ivoire, and Gabon—and there are substantial Latin American migrations within South America and north to the United States.

Asia has not been immune to these developments. Indeed, the 1970s and 1980s were a period when "Asia entered the world migration arena" (Castles 1992, 3). This was brought home most starkly during the recent Gulf War, when 500,000 of the 3 million Asians working in the Middle East returned home. Intra-Asian movements have themselves burgeoned. The regional press is replete with stories of Korean workers in Japan, Indonesian migrants in Singapore, Thai workers in Malaysia, and so on.

Some indication of the magnitude and diversity of the Asia-Pacific flows was given by Australia's National Population Council (1991, 104), which estimated that:

- 25 million tourists visit the region annually;

- 5 million guest workers from the region presently work outside their homelands;

- 500,000 students from the region are studying abroad;

- 600,000 people settle permanently and legally in another country each year;

- 200,000 people or more obtain illegal entry into other countries each year;

- 2 million refugees have fled their home countries since 1975.

The conclusion is that human capital flows are substantial and increasing, globally and in the Pacific region itself. The astute observer will also note that the data upon which such an observation is made are relatively imprecise. But the broad nature of the phenomenon is not in doubt.

The World Bank (1990) has attempted to pull together much of the global information and provide projections to the year 2000. Its summary view of the pattern of immigration and emigration is given in figures 1 and 2.

The Origins of Population Flows

Neoclassical economic analysis would see the underlying choice process for migration as one of comparing streams of pecuniary net returns for alternative locations, suitably discounted for time and risk. In this way migration is merely the locational dimension of human capital theory (Sjaastad 1962).

It is certainly true that much modern international migration has a strong economic element of this kind. The predominant flows are clearly South-North, reflecting major differences in present and future real-income prospects and in employment opportunities.

Recognition of this leads to some important predictions globally and for the Asia-Pacific region. Globally, the contrast is strong between countries of high living standards and robust economies but aging and declining population levels, and the poorer countries with large, rapidly growing populations. There is pressure then for migrants to seek to compensate for demographic aging and to meet short- or medium-term labor market needs (Organization for Economic Cooperation and Development 1991).

In terms of the Pacific region, the key observation is that there are quite disparate patterns of development and growth in labor structure among Asia-Pacific economies. There are countries with substantial present or emerging labor shortages—such as Taiwan, Japan, Singapore, South Korea, Thailand, and Malaysia. There are countries with considerable trends toward excess labor supply. These include such populous nations as China, India, and Bangladesh. The prediction is that globalization and porous borders will mean increasing pressure on the advanced industrial countries and labor-shortage countries of the region with respect to international people flows.

One set of projections supporting this conclusion is seen in tables 1 and 2, taken from the Pacific Economic Cooperation Council's *Human Resource Development Outlook 1991–92*. Some individual projections illustrate the problems in any simple economic methodology, and projections for a number of crucial economies, notably those of South Asia, are not presently constructed. But overall, the potential for economically based intraregional pressure for labor movement is evident. Of course, sectoral disaggregation would refine this very gross analysis, since it may be that particular shortages or surpluses that are hidden by the overall picture do provide substantial impetus for migration. Further work, analyzing the data by industry and occupation, is needed to allow for this.

At the same time, it must be stressed that a purely economic interpretation of migration is too narrow. There is also an important explanatory role played by cultural, social, political, environmental, and historical factors. Migration has its strong economic motivations, but it is also a social process based on communicative networks, information, and expectations.

The phenomenon of "chain migration," for instance, is well-documented, based on family reunion and affiliation with existing expatriate communities, however established. Colonial and military linkages carry

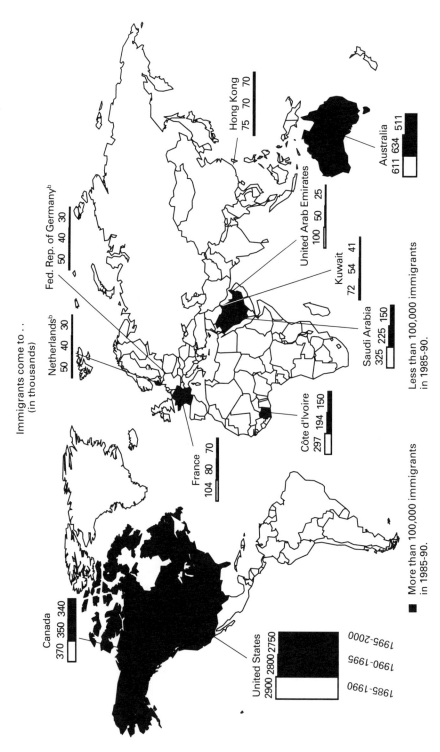

Immigrants come to . .
(in thousands)

Canada
370 350 340

United States
2900 2800 2750

1985-1990
1990-1995
1995-2000

France
104 80 70

Côte d'Ivoire
297 194 150

Netherlands[b]
50 40 30

Fed. Rep. of Germany[b]
50 40 30

Hong Kong
75 70 70

United Arab Emirates
100 50 25

Kuwait
72 54 41

Saudi Arabia
325 225 150

Australia
611 634 511

■ More than 100,000 immigrants
   in 1985–90.

   Less than 100,000 immigrants
   in 1985–90.

Figure 1. Destinations of immigrants. a. The countries and territories specified receive the largest totals of net immigrants. b. Tied for tenth place.
Source: World Bank, *Finance and Development,* June 1990.

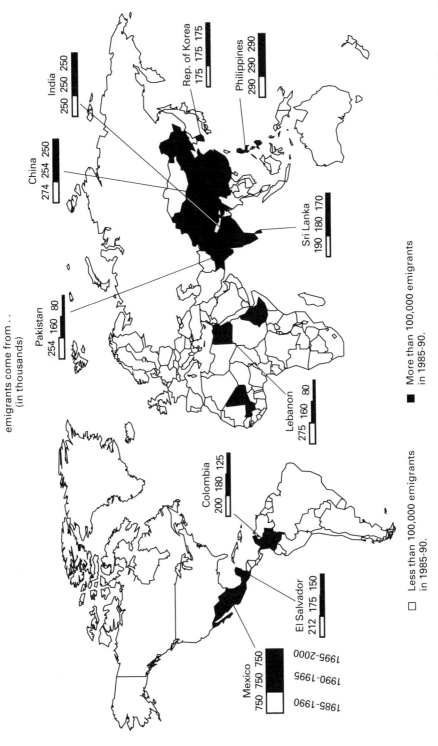

emigrants come from . . . (in thousands)

India
250 250 250

China
274 254 250

Pakistan
254 160 80

Rep. of Korea
175 175 175

Philippines
290 290 290

Sri Lanka
190 180 170

Lebanon
275 160 80

Colombia
200 180 125

El Salvador
212 175 150

Mexico
750 750 750

1985-1990
1990-1995
1995-2000

☐ Less than 100,000 emigrants in 1985-90.

■ More than 100,000 emigrants in 1985-90.

Figure 2. Sources of emigrants. a. The countries and territories specified receive the largest totals of net immigrants. *Source:* World Bank, *Finance and Development*, June 1990.

327

Table 1   Projected growth in labor demand and supply in 14 PECC economies, 1991–92
(percentages except where noted)

	Actual labor (millions) 1990	Labor demand growth		Supply growth	Excess supply growth	
		1991	1992		1991	1992
Australia	8.0	1.51	2.01	2.30	0.79	0.29
Canada	13.7	−2.22	2.48	0.90	3.12	−1.58
China	683.6	−0.40	0.70	1.60	2.00	0.90
Hong Kong	2.8	−2.30	0.40	0.90	3.20	0.50
Indonesia	75.9	1.90	3.00	2.40	0.50	−0.60
Japan	62.7	0.22	1.52	0.40	0.18	−1.12
Malaysia	6.8	5.60	5.30	2.90	−2.70	−2.40
New Zealand	1.6	2.40	2.20	0.80	−1.60	−1.40
Philippines	24.7	1.60	3.70	2.80	1.20	−0.90
Singapore	1.3	2.90	3.40	0.60	−2.30	−2.80
S. Korea	30.2	3.40	2.90	1.80	−1.60	−1.10
Taiwan	8.3	1.40	2.40	1.70	0.30	−0.70
Thailand	30.5	7.10	4.90	1.80	−5.30	−3.10
United States	123.9	−0.95	1.65	1.00	1.95	−0.65

PECC = Pacific Economic Cooperation Committee

Source: PECC. 1992. *Human Resource Department Outlook, 1991–92.*

migration consequences—as they did for Britain, France, and the United States. A broader political economy also operates, related, for example, to foreign investment and trade. For instance, Japan is now said to have over 1 million executives and technicians overseas working for Japanese firms. Finally, the consequences of political upheaval, civil war, famine, drought, and environmental disaster lead to refugee and humanitarian flows, which even the broadest interpretations of neoclassical theory have trouble accommodating.

To take this latter point further, some of the largest forced international migrations in history have occurred in recent times in Asia (Hugo 1991). Over the last 15 years, some 2 million refugees have left Indochina, and 4.2 million Afghans have relocated in Iran and Pakistan.

The potential for further movement in the region is also clear. A major backlog remains in clearing refugee camps in countries of first asylum. Further, refugee-like migrations within the region are possible as a result of problems of political suppression, environmental fragility, ethnic conflict, secessionism, and the political instability that can be variously found or predicted in the region.

There is then a major need to understand noneconomic as well as economic origins of the movement of people—and their intermixture—in explaining who settles where and when.

The process of movement is also determined largely by the policies of the receiving countries. Policy itself will be discussed separately below, but it is important to point out here the significant distinctions often

Table 2 Labor demand and supply balance in 14 PECC economies, 1991–92 (millions)

	Labor demand		Labor supply		Excess supply	
	1991	1992	1991	1992	1991	1992
Australia	8.12	8.28	8.18	8.37	0.06	0.09
Canada	13.40	13.73	13.82	13.95	0.43	0.22
China	680.87	685.63	694.54	705.65	13.67	20.02
Hong Kong	2.74	2.75	2.83	2.85	0.09	0.10
Indonesia	77.34	79.66	77.72	79.59	0.38	−0.08
Japan	62.84	63.79	62.95	63.20	0.11	−0.59
Malaysia	7.18	7.56	7.00	7.20	−0.18	−0.36
New Zealand	1.64	1.67	1.61	1.63	−0.03	−0.05
Philippines	25.10	26.02	25.39	26.10	0.30	0.08
Singapore	1.34	1.38	1.31	1.32	−0.03	−0.07
S. Korea	31.23	32.13	30.74	31.30	−0.48	−0.84
Taiwan	8.42	8.62	8.44	8.58	0.02	−0.03
Thailand	32.67	34.27	31.05	31.61	−1.62	2.66
United States	122.72	124.75	125.14	126,39	2.42	1.64
PECC 14	1075.58	1090.25	1090.72	1107.73	15.14	17.48

Source: PECC. 1992. *Human Resource Development Outlook, 1991–92.*

established in admission policies. The following categories represent some of the more common classifications:

- tourists

- business visitors

- overseas students

- temporary contract workers

- permanent settlers

- refugees or asylum-seekers

- professional transients

- illegal workers

- dependents (family reunion)

And these distinctions have meaning and importance, particularly for migration management by nations. However, these distinctions may disguise as much as they display. In particular, one of the great lessons of migration policy is that such categories are functionally artificial, whatever their administrative validity. Students seek to become permanent settlers. Asylum claimants may really be economic migrants. Settlers may return home. Professional transients may seek to be accompanied by family dependents, and so on.

The point is an important one, for the major single finding of a 1986 OECD Conference on the Future of Migration (OECD 1987) was that old views of a sharp dichotomy between the experience and interests of European "guest worker" countries and New World "settler" countries were fundamentally flawed. Instead, there was recognition of much convergence in the migration experience, whatever its administrative designation, and an awakening recognition that common longer-term underlying forces were at work in producing migration inflow pressures on all OECD economies. Equally clear was the recognition that simple definitions of immigrant receiving and sending countries were unsatisfactory. The diversity of forms of movement meant that most countries were involved in important flows both across and within their borders. Many countries in the world were seen to be simultaneously countries of immigration and emigration.

The conclusion on origins of population movement is that the impetus sustaining the mass migrations of the last 15 years shows no signs of dissipating. For both economic and noneconomic reasons major movements of people across borders are likely to continue. And the process of movement will affect many countries in increasingly common and complex ways.

Economic Consequences

Immigration economics has had something of a revival in recent years. As far as the New Palgrave Dictionary of Economics is concerned, the field is little more than the 1967 Harris-Todaro model. But it has now attracted the systematic attention of theorists such as Bhagwati, Ethier, Rivera-Batiz, and Stark and many others, and it has begun to develop an impressive array of supporting empirical studies. In particular, studies in North America and Australasia permit us to draw some important empirical conclusions based on the experience of the countries in those regions.

It is evident that a larger population results in a larger economy simply because more people generate greater demand—whether it be for consumption, housing, or investment—and contribute workers to produce what is being supplied. Population scale generates economic scale.

What is of more interest from the "New World" empirical studies is the question of the short-run balance of these effects and the implications for longer-run productivity growth and distribution of wealth.

As regards the short run, much research effort has gone into establishing the connection between migration or population and other macroeconomic indicators such as inflation, nominal wages, and the unemployment rate. The almost universal finding is that there has been no strong effect on these variables, even for the case of Australia, where some 20 percent of the population is overseas-born and migrants and their children have contributed almost 60 percent of the postwar growth of the labor force. The demand and supply effects of immigration have basically neutralized each other. The research is well-surveyed in Wooden (1990), US Department of Labor (1987), Employment and Immigration Canada (1989) and, for all countries, in Salt (1991).

The significance of this finding deserves explicit enunciation: migrants have not robbed jobs; they have created as many as they have taken. This is important because it means that one common source of domestic opposition to migration may be based on an economic fallacy. It is also important because it implies that migration is not a useful instrument for short-term macroeconomic policy manipulation. And it further implies that seeking to meet labor shortages through general migration entry may also be based on an economic fallacy, since such a policy neglects the new labor demands generated by migrant-related expenditures. The labor-shortage countries should recognize this paradox in determining their own policies on migration.

This economic ineffectiveness proposition is paralleled in the demographic literature by the also near-universal finding that the seemingly simple proposition of increasing the intake of young migrants to compensate for the aging of the host population does not in fact work. Effects of realistic levels of migration on dependency ratios are small and transitory due to the aging of the migrants themselves, so that a large and rising future migration inflow is needed to offset this effect (OECD 1991).

It is also now increasingly well-established that the migration experience in North America and Australasia has been such that migrants pay their way in providing tax funds for government services, including infrastructure funding and welfare services. Indeed, illegal migrants actually provide a handy surplus to other taxpayers due to their contributions via indirect tax and their limited share in benefits (Simon 1989; Whiteford 1991). They also often embody the source-country spending on education, a major gain in skills transfer for the recipient nation and hence a loss to the source country.

This is not to say that there will not be short-term phases of surplus or deficit because of expenditure lumpiness and life-cycle and integration effects. And significant economic and political debate can develop around these effects. This has certainly been the Australian experience on the related issue of the balance of payments effects of migration, where a clear life-cycle effect is evident: an early improvement in the foreign debt due to savings repatriation, then a deterioration due to lumpy investment needs, followed by longer-term benefit due to returns on investment through export or import replacement.

What then of longer-run effects of migration on economies? Average well-being is determined ultimately by labor productivity, not by the scale

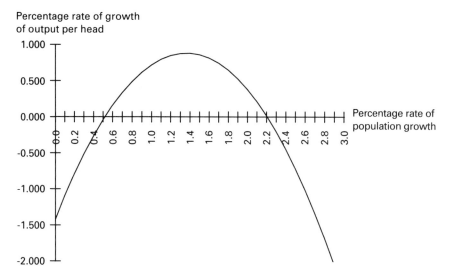

Percentage rate of growth
of output per head

Percentage rate of
population growth

Figure 3. Population growth and growth in output per head in Australia. *Source:* Nevile
(1990). Copyright with the Commonwealth of Australia. Reprinted with permission.

of the economy per se. Such long-run per capita effects of population
growth depend centrally upon the nature of that growth and whether it
generates economies or diseconomies of scale.

Direct simulation analysis of this question using computable general
equilibrium models has proved inconclusive, since so much depends
upon what is most difficult to measure—namely, scale economies. However, indirect analysis of population growth and growth in output per
capita—over time and not dependent on direct estimation of scale effects—has usually found a positive relationship. Figure 3 from Nevile
(1990) is indicative of these findings.

The Nevile figure shows the effects of variability in population growth
on growth in per capita output. There has also been more precise analysis
of the composition of migration, where simulation can be useful. The
Centre for International Economics (1988), for instance, finds that the most
important contributions to average real income growth come not from
the quantity of labor but from the quality of the labor force. Skill level is
the key relevant determinant of labor force productivity, and as figure 4
shows, varying the skill level of a migration intake of fixed size can have
quite different outcomes for GDP per capita.

Success in capturing these potential benefits depends upon effective
use of such skills (e.g., recognizing qualifications) and upon the ability
to capitalize on source-country education and training. However, in the
latter respect, it must be remembered that the employment-generation
dimension of migration means that demands for new skilled jobs are

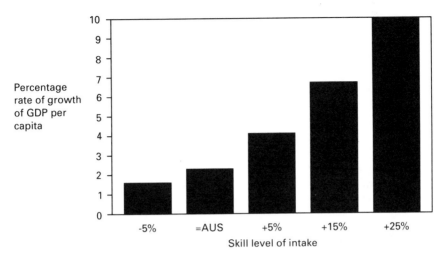

Figure 4. Gain in GDP per capita by skill level of intake, 1987-2030. *Source*: National Population Council, 1991. Commonwealth of Australia copyright. Reprinted with permission.

being created as well as skills being supplied. There need not be any automatic crowding out of domestic skill formation.

Increasing recognition of this has created what Borjas (1990) has called a "competitive market" for migration, whereby the United States, Canada, and Australia compete vigorously for skilled migrants to come to their countries.

The presumed benefits, however, can be challenged. Since people will be paid their marginal product, it is the migrant who gains most, with some potential gain for local capital owners and some potential loss for local workers. The loss to local workers can be offset if there are scale economies and/or externalities. The notion of skilled externalities is particularly important here, yet little explored. It involves the question of how much benefit spills over to a local worker by working with (migrant) co-workers of higher skill levels than would otherwise be the case. Is the benefit all captured by the higher skilled newcomer, or does it benefit others in the work place? Naturally a highly aggregative analysis should reflect such a benefit. But it will only do so in conjunction with other benefits. The separate contribution of skill externalities has yet to be properly explored empirically. Yet it is central to much policy toward human capital in this and other areas. Finally, a GDP per capita criterion disguises these distributional concerns, particularly for natives.

The same question arises in the context of structural change. Unskilled migration can help sustain declining industries and provide cheaper personal services, especially in the informal economy. The contrasting vision is that of tapping young, skilled, entrepreneurial migrants to assist in industrial restructuring to high value-added industries better integrated into world markets. Here, migration must be derived from industrial policy and national social values regarding the economic profile for the population and the "tone" or "form" of the society.

Naturally, the value-added approach also raises the question of source-country effects. There is a well-established theoretical framework for the review of such issues, and some good case-study work relating especially to Asian guest workers in the Gulf states (Appleyard 1989; Grubel and Scott 1977; Stahl 1982). But there is considerable confusion over the general outcome of the balance of costs and benefits and the circumstances under which these vary for particular economic situations. There remains much scope for extensive research on the consequences of international human capital movements for the source countries. It is undoubtedly a top priority for study. But an equal priority might be how much the North American and Australasian results carry over to other environments, even for receiving countries.

Another research priority that is beginning to be addressed is the question of linkages between migration and other international flows—trade, aid, and foreign investment, for example. Sassen (1989) has looked at this in a broad political economy framework, and a   National Bureau of Economic Research project (Abowd and Freeman 1991) has looked at such flows in terms of impact for the United States. The basic conclusions of the NBER project for the US labor market are that:

- immigrants have been absorbed with little adverse effect on the natives;

- foreign firms are at least as favorable to US workers in employment conditions as are domestically owned companies;

- the impact of import increases on US wages and employment has been, by contrast, very severe.

The reason for these results is quite straightforward: people flows and capital flows have been smaller and induce offsetting consequences in ways that trade in goods does not. For example, migrants create jobs as well as fill them, and foreign equity only leads to claims on domestic resources when profitable. Imports have no such significant direct counterbalancing benefits. Or, to interpret the argument another way, migrants and investors demand nontraded goods, imports do not.

It is important therefore to realize that there are important economic qualifications to the basic trade theory propositions on factor flows and world trade. Migration, investment, and trade are substitutes, and in the very long run, an efficient international division of labor would be obtainable by movement in any one or all of these. But in the shorter run, macroeconomic demand influences are important, and in the medium term, changes in the international distribution of income and wealth can play a role. Finally, factor movements relate to more than just economic effects.

Policy

If migration is basically neutral in its short-term economic effects and offers long-run potential for increased per capita income, why do comprehensive barriers to movement remain? Even the traditional immigration-receiving countries take only a very small share of the many who would like to live in those nations. Answering the question posed takes us firmly into the policy realm.

There is no country in the world that has completely open borders. A great degree of liberalization within trading blocs has occurred or is in prospect—for example, in the European Community and with the North American Free Trade Agreement. But other strong barriers remain, and the countries of Asia especially are among the most restrictive in terms of regulating foreign residence. Moreover, in some instances, trade liberalization itself may be a quite conscious attempted substitute for population movement. It has been suggested that many US citizens are supportive of NAFTA precisely because they prefer receiving Mexico's goods rather than its people. The modern permeability of borders shows how trade policy and migration can come together.

The explanation for policy choices no doubt lies as much in the limits to the economic criteria as in the economic effects. It was emphasized earlier that migration is also a social process. This is not so just for the migrants themselves, but also for the host societies in which they interact. There are major and distinctive social consequences, not only economic effects, that derive from human capital flows.

Some social consequences of migration are seen by many as enriching—greater diversity of ideas, attitudes, life-styles. But for many others this very diversity is seen as threatening, a challenge to "social cohesion." Social disharmony, as much or more than any perceived economic dislocation or loss, is likely to be the real reason why borders are not deliberately opened more than they are.

Yet the modern reality in this era of globalization is increasingly one of permeable borders and the mass movement of people. Japan, for instance, has long adopted an exclusionist border policy. Yet it has an estimated 150,000 to 300,000 illegal residents, as many or more than an immigration-receiving country such as Australia. Taiwan may have 200,000 illegals, and estimates run as high as 700,000 for undocumented migrants in peninsular Malaysia (Hugo 1991). These are situations of increasing policy concern in these countries.

How then can national concerns and sovereignty be best integrated with global realities? The answer is clearly neither wide-open doors nor strict exclusionism; it has to be a new and cooperative regime of international migration management.

Migration is inherently a controversial field. Countries traditionally have discerned competing interests and displayed considerable political sensitivity. On what basis can progress be made?

The analysis presented above highlights key components that should be recognized:

The forms of international human capital flows are complex and varied. They embrace everything from tourists to refugees. Attempts to focus only upon a subcategory of movement, such as permanent settlers, will miss considerable category overlap and flows overlap to the detriment of manageable policy (Withers 1991). Australian export education policymakers, for instance, chose to ignore the likely pressure for permanent residency by overseas students. Yet even prior to Tiananmen Square, two out of five PRC students were overstaying their visas. In the United States, 90 percent of South Korean graduate students remained as permanent residents (Sorowy and Inkeles 1985). Or again, activists for ecologically sustainable development in Australia often focus on immigration as a source of undesirable population pressure on a fragile environment. Yet annual settler migration inflow peaked in 1991 at 140,000, at a time when tourism to Australia was approaching 2 million people annually, with a much greater probable impact on key sensitive environments such as the Great Barrier Reef.

No country is isolated from international people flows. Even Myanmar has refugee and guest worker problems, including HIV-infected workers returning from Thailand. Modern communications, cheap transportation, financial liberalization, expanding tourism and overseas study, and all the other dimensions of globalization produce a world in which movement is easy and in which migration will affect all. Certain longerterm, underlying forces and pressures are at work, affecting all countries, even if the particular form and direction does vary.

There is a convergence that should be understood in the migration process. Administrative distinctions between movement types become very blurred as people change category and status. As a consequence, there is much that can be learned jointly about common elements of the migration process. Germany for decades denied that it was a country of immigration, but Turkish and other guest workers and Eastern Europeans claiming German ethnicity have made Germany today the country of immigration *par excellence*. The temporary labor migration to Western Europe of 30 million workers resulted in a permanent migration of 13 million people. Also, the migration experience and situation for any one country can change rapidly, reinforcing the value of learning from even the previously divergent experience of others. Of course, this is not to imply that all countries will be uniformly confronted with the same problems and challenges.

There is a need for more information and research to provide analytic insights and to codify experience in order to underpin policy development. The data deficiencies in documenting the very magnitude and character of human capital flows are many. And there are major lacunae in our knowledge, including sending-country economic consequences, social consequences, and linkages to other flows, to mention only some that have been highlighted above. To this might be added the need to analyze these impacts, particularly for newly emerging recipient countries such as Japan and Malaysia.

The rising high-level governmental and public concern with migration issues in Western Europe has pointed up the paucity of information upon which to base policy. Decades of denial by European countries that they were countries of immigration has revealed an abysmal ignorance of migration and an incapacity to deal effectively with present problems. European advisers have now sensibly turned increasingly to New World migration models and knowledge for some insight.

There are mutual benefits possible from greater policy exchange of knowledge and policy cooperation and coordination. At a minimum, there could be joint measures against illegal migration, protocols on return of funded overseas students, agreement on treatment of unsuccessful asylum claimants, agreement as to minimum rights for guest workers to prevent exploitation, strengthening opportunities for cultural and scientific exchange, provision of state-of-the-art advice on migrant selection systems, and so on. The focus would be upon monitoring and channeling flows in mutually acceptable ways.

There is a need for migration policy to go beyond entry controls and consider the settlement and integration of foreign residents. A major lesson of the European guest worker experience is that migrants deprived of basic political and social rights remain as a major disadvantaged class and that this disadvantage can be intergenerational and a source of social conflict. The effectiveness of alternative settlement and multicultural policies should be closely considered in order to understand the extent to which formal arrangements to foster social diversity and integration, such as in Canada and Australia, are successful.

There is a need to take migration policy beyond border control to get at root causes of international movements. This involves linking population growth and migration to trade and investment and cooperating with sending countries in formulating appropriate policies. This is the most ambitious and problematic task of all. The difficulties in influencing population growth and in improving the economic prospects of sending countries is well-recognized (US Commission for the Study of International Migration and Cooperative Economic Development 1990), and the role of trade and investment in this process is often paradoxical. For example, trade and aid can facilitate migration by reinforcing information flows and providing liquidity for family-reunion travel. The prospects are best for the long haul and in a situation where a culture of emigration and the associated linkages have not yet taken hold.

Individual countries can be urged to respond to these insights. Far more effective would be the bolder step of reinforcing or newly establishing appropriate international agencies to also facilitate this response.

The options appear to be as follows:

Broaden the role and function of an existing migration-related global international agency. The major candidates are the United Nations High Commissioner for Refugees (UNHCR), the International Labor Organization (ILO), the International Organization for Migration (IOM) and the Organization for Economic Cooperation and Development (OECD). Each has existing activities in the field. But

- UNHCR is appropriately specialized to a narrow constituency that needs effective single-purpose advocacy;

- ILO is appropriately concerned with many other labor issues as well but should play an important consultative role in relation to migrant work standards;

- OECD is too focused on its rich-country perspective.

This leaves IOM, which certainly has global ambitions and, with creative leadership, could play a new role of the kind needed, particularly if it can look beyond its European base and refugee movement origins to a broader vision.

Encourage the emergence of new regional groupings. This is less a concern for population movement than for trade movement, since the socially derived necessity for maintaining some significant barriers for some foreseeable future appears undeniable.

Given the substantial intraregional flows in the Pacific Basin, thought could be given to Asia-Pacific regional opportunities. More investigative groundwork on people flows and their impacts may be needed, and informed review of the possibilities by a group such as the Pacific Economic Cooperation Council (PECC) would be most useful. In fact, PECC's recent establishment of a Human Resource Development Working Group provides an appropriate vehicle. The results of such work, if promising, could then be taken up either

- through Asia Pacific Economic Cooperation (APEC), if it acknowledges the important economic content of the issue, or

- through a free-standing Asia-Pacific Migration Council or Committee.

If this task is too hard at this time, a final alternative that might act as a circuit breaker on this long-neglected issue is for a small group of sponsors to establish an eminent persons group, drawn from several major countries in the region, to consult, review the situation, and advise the Asia-Pacific community on the way forward.

International people movements are continuing to grow, and they represent a phenomenon that will not go away. Such flows of people are the tangible expression of our human interdependence. An improved international regime for managing this burgeoning process seems essential.

References

Abowd, J. M., and Freeman, R. B., eds. 1991. *Immigration, Trade and the Labor Market*. Chicago: Chicago University Press.

Appleyard, R., ed. 1989. *The Impact of International Migration on Developing Countries*. Paris: OECD.

Borjas, G. 1990. *Friends or Strangers: The Impact of Immigrants on the US Economy*. New York: Basic Books.

Castles, S. 1992. "The New Global Migrations." Paper presented at Evatt Foundation Conference, Sydney (April).

Ethier, W. J. 1985. "International Trade and Labor Migration." *American Economic Review* (September).

Employment and Immigration Canada. 1989. *Immigration to Canada: Economic Impacts*. Ottawa: Official Print.

Grubel, H.G., and Scott, A. 1977. *The Brain Drain: Determinants, Measurement, and Welfare Effects*. Waterloo, Ontario: Wilfred Laurier Press.

Hamilton, B., and Whalley, J. 1984. "Efficiency and Distributional Implications of Global Restrictions on Labor Mobility." *Journal of Development Economics* 14.

Hugo, G. 1991. "Recent International Migration Trends in Asia." In J.W. Smith, ed., *Immigration, Population and Sustainable Growth*. Adelaide: Flinders Press.

International Organization of Migration. 1990. "Background Document." Ninth IOM Seminar on Migration. Geneva: IOM.

National Population Council. 1991. "Population Issues and Australia's Future: Discussion Paper." Canberra: Australian Government Publishing Service.

National Population Council. 1992. "Population Issues and Australia's Future: Final Report." Canberra: Australian Government Publishing Service.

Nevile, J. 1990. *The Effect of Immigration on Australian Living Standards*. Canberra: Australian Government Publishing Service.

Organization for Economic Cooperation and Development. 1987. *The Future of Migration*. Paris: OECD.

Organization for Economic Cooperation and Development. 1991. *Migration: The Demographic Aspects*. Paris: OECD.

Pacific Economic Cooperation Council. 1992. *Human Resource Development Outlook, 1991–1992*. Singapore: Human Resource Development Task Force, PECC.

Rivera-Batiz, F. 1982. "International Migration, Non-traded Goods and Economic Welfare in the Source Country." *Journal of Development Economics* 11 (1).

Salt, J. 1991. "The New Flows of Migration." Background paper, Migration Working Party. Paris: OECD.

Sassen, S. 1989. *The Mobility of Labor and Capital*. Cambridge: Cambridge University Press.

Simon, J. L. 1989. *The Economic Consequences of Immigration*. Oxford (UK): Blackwell.

Sjaastad, L. 1962. "The Costs and Returns of Human Migration." *Journal of Political Economy* (October).

Sorowy, L., and Inkeles, A. 1985. "University-Level Student-Exchange: the US Role in Global Perspective." In E. G. Barber, ed., *Foreign Student Flows: Their Significance for US Higher Education.* New York: Institute for International Education.

Stahl, C. 1982. *International Labor Migration and International Development.* Geneva: International Labor Organization.

US Commission for the Study of International Migration and Cooperative Economic Development. 1990. *Unauthorized Migration: An Economic Development Response.* Washington: Government Printing Office.

US Department of Labor. 1987. *The Effects of Immigration on the US Economy and Labor Market.* Washington: Government Printing Office.

Whiteford, P. 1991. *Immigrants and the Social Security System.* Canberra: Australian Government Publishing Service.

Withers, G. 1991. "Australasian Immigration, Economics, and Interdependence." *Australian Journal of International Relations* 1.

Wooden, M. 1990. "Economic Aspects of Immigration." In J. Sloan et al., *Australian Immigration: A Survey of the Issues.* Canberra: Australian Government Publishing Service.

World Bank. 1990. *World Population Projections; 1989–90.* Washington: International Bank for Reconstruction and Development.

11

Economic Growth, Environmental Issues, and Trade

KYM ANDERSON

The United Nations Conference on Environment and Development, held in Brazil in June 1992, was riding the second major wave of public concern with environmental degradation. The first wave of widespread public interest, in the late 1960s and early 1970s, focused mainly on industrial pollution within and between neighboring advanced economies. The foreign trade and investment issues raised at that time were confined mainly to the concerns of industrial capitalists and workers in rich countries that the imposition of stricter pollution standards at home than abroad would lower their international competitiveness, from which they sought protection.[1] Following a lull in interest brought on by the economic disruptions of the 1973–82 oil shock, the current wave of public concern for the natural environment is much more intense, more widespread, and likely to be sustained and to affect a much broader range of countries than was the case in the 1970s—not least through its effects on foreign trade and investment.

Kym Anderson is Counsellor, Economic Research, for the GATT Secretariat and Professor of Economics at the University of Adelaide. Bernard Hoekman, Patrick Low, Mari Pangestu, and other conference participants provided helpful comments on an earlier draft, but the views expressed are the author's alone and are not intended to reflect the views of the GATT Secretariat or GATT contracting parties.

1. See, for example, Baumol (1971), General Agreement on Tariffs and Trade (1971), Siebert (1974), and Walter (1975 and 1976). Such protection from import competition is, of course, not warranted on economic efficiency grounds because the environmental policy is aiming to eliminate an unjustifiable (implicit) subsidy rather than add an unjustifiable tax (Snape 1992).

This phenomenon is worthy of the attention of those concerned with trade policies affecting Pacific Rim countries, not only because environmentalism has already become a nontrivial influence on policy within Pacific economies, but also because, like regionalism, environmentalism poses a threat to the liberal multilateral trading system on which Pacific dynamism depends.

This paper seeks to address four sets of questions concerning this development. First, in what ways and why are environmental issues having a more pervasive influence on public policy? Second, how is this greater impact of the natural environment on policy going to affect trade specialization in various groups of countries as the world economy grows over time? Third, what impact will new trade liberalization initiatives have on the environment? And fourth, what are the implications for Pacific countries in particular, and how might they respond to these changes? While the greening of world politics has the potential to boost Pacific and global welfare broadly defined (although the gains will not be spread evenly and some communities could be made worse off), the paper concludes that there is a considerable risk that the policies adopted in response to environmental concerns will be so far from first-best as to worsen welfare in many countries through erosion of the global trading system. And in the process, they may even add to rather than reduce environmental degradation.

Why Environmental Issues Are Becoming More Pervasive

The list of environmental concerns has grown rapidly in recent years, and it has taken on more of a global orientation. Air, water, soil, and visual pollution at the local or national level is increasingly being seen as emanating from the production or consumption of not only industrial goods but also primary and service sector products. Some of that pollution is believed to be also damaging the environment on a global scale, through climate change and ozone depletion, for example. Hence, people are worried by the use of chlorofluorocarbons (CFCs) and the emission of carbon dioxide, not just at home but also abroad, particularly as economic growth and industrialization spread to poorer countries with laxer environmental policies. Likewise, more and more people are concerned about deforestation, species extinction, and animal rights at the global level, regardless of national boundaries. And ongoing integration of the world economy brings with it consumer concerns about the safety of imported products. Since personal values play an important role in international debates on these issues, the scope for friction between countries is considerable.

Fluctuate though it might with the business cycle, this heightened concern for the environment and for product safety is likely to keep growing. One reason is that, even though uncertainties remain, the scientific basis for many of these concerns is perceived to be more solid now than was the case 20 years ago. Another is that the world's population and real per capita income have each increased by about 40 percent since 1970, and the annual volume of output and consumption has doubled. These increases are adding continually to the demand for the goods and services provided by the natural environment (including essentials for human health such as clean air, potable water, filtered sunlight, and natural medicines; raw materials; the capacity to absorb wastes; and aesthetic and recreational services such as those obtained from visiting or even just ensuring the existence of unspoiled wilderness areas with a diverse abundance of plant and animal species).

Unfortunately, the supply of these environmental goods and services is not unlimited, and markets for many of nature's services are incomplete or absent.[2] Markets are underdeveloped because of disputed, ambiguous, or nonexistent property rights or because of the high cost of enforcing those rights. It is true that the more advanced economies have established institutional structures to help handle the tasks of arriving at a social consensus on appropriate environmental policies for that society, of allocating property rights, and of enforcing policies. The same is true in some traditional societies before they begin to "modernize." But the creation of appropriate new institutions is often slow in modernizing, poor economies, where population and consumption growth will be concentrated for the foreseeable future, and they are largely absent at the international level, where cooperation among sovereign governments is required for efficient solutions. Hence, there is growing interest in rich countries—particularly on the part of proposers and drafters of international environmental agreements—in using one of the few instruments currently available to them—trade policies—to influence environmental outcomes in other countries. Already, we have seen the use of trade provisions on affected products (e.g., in the Montreal Protocol on CFCs), but there are also proposals to use trade sanctions on unrelated products in the hope of persuading poorer countries to adopt stricter environmental policies (e.g., threats to provide less access to textile and other markets of industrial countries unless logging is curtailed).

---

2. This does not apply equally to all environmental resources of course. The dooms-dayers such as Meadows et al. (1972) have been proved spectacularly wrong in predicting the exhaustion of minerals and energy raw materials, for example, because they have failed to take into account economic feedback mechanisms. Beckerman (1992) and Crowson (1992) note that the cumulative world consumption of many minerals during the past quarter century exceeded "known reserves" at the beginning of the period, and yet today's revised "known reserves" exceed those of 25 years ago!

Economic Growth, Environment, Trade, and Welfare

The standard theory of changing comparative advantages in a growing world economy, which has been developed without consideration of environmental concerns, can readily be modified to incorporate at least some of them. As espoused by Krueger (1977) and Leamer (1987), this theory suggests that when a poor country opens up to international trade, its exports initially will be specialized in primary products. This is because its stocks of man-made capital, relative to natural resources, are comparatively low. If those nonnatural capital stocks per worker expand more for this country than they do globally, the country's comparative advantage will gradually shift from primary products to manufactures and services (except for those primary products in which competitiveness is retained through the development of new technologies involving sufficient factor-intensity reversals). This shift will begin at an earlier stage of economic development, and the nonprimary exports will tend to use unskilled labor more intensively the more natural resource–poor or densely populated the country. If the country continues to expand its capital per worker relatively rapidly, its exports will tend to become steadily more capital-intensive over time. In the case of manufactures not subject to factor-intensity reversals, this process then leaves room in international markets for later-industrializing countries to follow suit in exporting their way out of poverty.[3]

With the help of the Leamer triangle depicted in figure 1, that theory can provide a rough idea of different countries' comparative advantages as of 1989. The triangle illustrates countries' relative endowments of three factors, denoted N for natural resources, L for labor time, and C for man-made capital (human, physical, knowledge, and so forth). Proxies used here to represent the ratio of natural resources to labor and the capital-to-labor ratio are land area per capita and GDP per capita. (Crude though these proxies are, more sophisticated indexes are unlikely to change greatly the relative positions of the country groups shown in figure 1.) These ratios are measured in logarithmic terms along the NL and LC sides of the triangle, respectively, the midpoint of each being the world average, which is taken as the numeraire. Thus, point W represents the global average endowment of all three factors. Countries in space WAN—which includes Africa and Latin America—have below average per-worker endowments of man-made capital and above average per-worker endowments of natural resources. Consequently, they have a

---

3. There is simultaneously an expansion in the importance of intraindustry trade among industrial economies as they grow, for the reasons mentioned in Grant, Papadakis, and Richardson (1993), but that development does not negate the trends mentioned above.

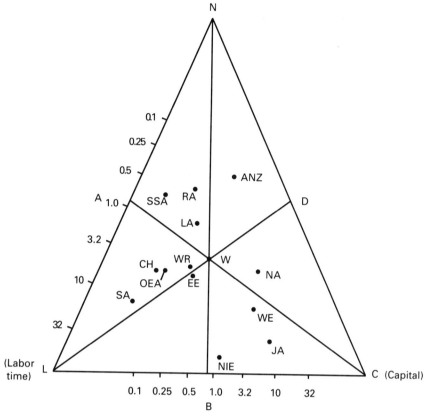

(Natural resources)

Figure 1. Relative endowments of natural resources, labor and capital, for various economies, 1989[a]. [a]The distance along NL from N measures the population density as a ratio of the world average (0.39 people per hectare of land). The distance along LC from L measures national product per capita as a ratio of the world average (US$3,980). Both scales are in logs. Along any ray from C to the NL line, the population density is constant, and similarly for rays from the other two corners of the triangle. W is the world's endowment point. Countries are represented as follows: ANZ Australia and New Zealand, CH China., EE the East European economies, JA Japan, LA Latin America, NA the United States and Canada, NIE East Asian's four newly industrialized economies, OEA other East Asian market economies, RA Russia and the 5 former Soviet central Asian republics, SA South Asia, SSA Sub-Saharan Africa, WE the West European economies, WR the 9 western republics of the former Soviet Union. The estimates used for per capita income for Eastern Europe and the former Soviet Union are $2,350 and $1,780 respectively, based on World Bank (1991) and other estimates reported in CEPR (1990, 33). The relative incomes and population densities within the former Soviet Union are derived from data in the report by the IMF et al. (1991). Purchasing power parity measures of income, if they were available for all countries, would show less differences across countries, but this would alter little the relative position of country groups in the above triangle. Source: Adapted from Leamer (1987) using data from the IMF et al. (1991) and the World Bank (1991). Permission to adapt Leamer model granted by the publisher. Copyright 1987, University of Chicago. All rights reserved.

comparative advantage in primary products and a comparative disadvantage in skill-intensive manufactures and services. The converse is true for Western Europe and Japan, which are located in the WBC space.

If there were no international environmental spillovers, this story need be complicated only slightly to allow for the fact that as a country's per capita income and industrial output grow, the value its citizens place on the environment increases. So do their demands for the implementation of costly domestic pollution abatement policies, at least after certain threshold levels of income and/or pollution are reached. Beyond that threshold, the severity of such abatement policies is likely to be positively correlated with per capita income, population density, and the degree of urbanization.[4] If all economies were growing equally rapidly, the progressive introduction of national environmental policies would tend to cause pollution-intensive production processes to relocate gradually from richer to poorer countries and from densely to sparsely populated countries.[5] These policies would also slow or reverse the growth in demand for products whose consumption is pollutive, especially in rich and/or densely populated countries. If more-advanced economies are net importers of products whose production is pollutive, or net exporters of products whose consumption is pollutive, these countries' optimal environmental policies would worsen their terms of trade to the benefit of poorer economies, and vice versa (Siebert et al. 1980; Anderson 1992a). Thus, countries that develop environmental policies will affect even those countries without (or with unchanged) environmental policies through trade and investment.

Given that the natural environment is part of the stock of natural resources, that it provides services that are valued increasingly as incomes rise, and that national environmental policies may need to be introduced to ensure the optimal use of the services of the environment, then a country's comparative advantage also will be affected by the distribution of environmental resources globally and the pattern of environmental policy interventions.[6] In terms of figure 1, this amendment is easy to accommodate if there are no international environmental spillovers, (given

---

4. Two recent papers reporting evidence that the demand for implementing and enforcing pollution abatement policies is income-elastic are Grossman and Krueger (1991) and Radetzki (1992). See also Deacon and Shapiro (1975) on the correlation between income levels and voter attitudes toward environmental priorities.

5. The term "pollution-intensive production processes" should be broadly interpreted to include activities such as mining in pristine areas or leisure services that may attract undesired local or international tourists.

6. This inclusion of environmental policies as a determinant of comparative advantage is in the spirit of Clarida and Findlay's (1992) analysis of trade, in which the government plays an active and potentially positive (rather than inactive or negative) role in development.

the proxies used to measure N, L, and C, namely, land area, population, and GDP): the closer countries are to point N and the farther they are from point C in the Leamer triangle, the weaker will be their density of economic activity (GDP per hectare), so the stronger will tend to be their comparative advantage in goods and services whose production is pollutive, all else being equal.[7]

The story becomes more complicated, however, when account is taken of policy reactions to international environmental problems such as the global commons, species depletion, or animal rights. The ban by the Convention on International Trade in Endangered Species (CITES) on ivory trade provides an extreme example: the strong comparative advantage that southern African nations had in elephant products virtually disappeared when the ban was introduced in 1989. Another example is the proposed limitation on imports into high-income countries of tropical hardwoods, the aim of which is to discourage deforestation. This, too, would reduce export growth and specialization in those products by developing countries still well-endowed with hardwood forests. A third example is the Montreal Protocol on phasing out the use of CFCs and halons. The protocol, through trade provisions, effectively limits the relocation from signatory to nonsignatory countries of industries producing or using CFCs, as well as encouraging nonsignatories to accede to the Protocol.[8] And there is the infamous tuna example, involving the United States' ban not only on the use of dolphin-unfriendly nets by its own tuna fishermen but also on the importation of tuna US authorities deem to have been caught in dolphin-unfriendly nets. The domestic US ban alone would have boosted Mexico's comparative advantage in tuna fishing, but the subsequent US ban on tuna imports instead reduced it.

In the latter two examples especially, the motive for trade policy action is a mixture of national competitiveness concerns and a concern in rich countries (typically not shared to the same extent by poorer countries) for the global commons. The clear conflict of interest between the two groups of countries, and the fact that trade measures are being used to

---

7. The extent of international relocation of productive activities due to the enforcement of environmental standards should not be exaggerated, however. Recent studies suggest the effect of such policies on comparative costs may be quite minor. See, for example, Leonard (1988) and Low (1992). As well, Tobey (1990) finds little evidence of actual changes in patterns of trade specialization in response to the imposition of environmental regulations since the 1960s. However, as noted by Leidy and Hoekman (1993), the absence of changes in trade patterns may simply be because import barriers were raised to offset any decline in competitiveness in affected industries.

8. For details of the Montreal Protocol see, for example, Benedick (1991) and Enders and Porges (1992). A list of the other major international environmental agreements with trade provisions is provided in GATT (1992, appendix 1).

achieve the first group's environmental objectives, increase the likelihood of trade disputes between the two parties. And these are but minor examples of a large and rapidly growing number of international environmental issues on which countries will have different views.[9]

This increasing use of trade measures to address environmental issues should concern the world at large and dynamic Pacific economies in particular for at least three reasons. First, trade policy measures typically will not be the best instruments for achieving environmental objectives. Their use in place of more efficient instruments thus reduces unnecessarily the level and growth of global economic welfare as conventionally measured and may even add to, rather than reduce, global environmental degradation.[10] Despite this, producer interest groups and some environmental groups are finding it mutually advantageous to use environmental arguments to support claims for import restrictions, particularly when stricter environmental standards are imposed on domestic producers.[11] The second concern, then, is that the environment will provide a convenient excuse to raise trade barriers. And third, should this lead to an escalation in trade disputes, it could be followed by retaliatory and counterretaliatory action, ultimately undermining the global trading system on which Pacific dynamism depends.

But there is also another important sense in which environmentalism is putting at risk the global trading system. It is closely related to the second concern mentioned above and has to do with the claim by some environmental groups[12] that liberalizing trade will harm the environment. We now turn to this point.

---

9. For a discussion of other environmentally related trade measures in use or under consideration, see GATT (1992, part III).

10. The ban on ivory trade again provides a case in point. By lowering the value of elephant products, the ban reduces the incentive for rural Africans to tolerate elephants trampling their crops and so ultimately could result in fewer rather than more elephants in some areas. In other areas, the value of the animal has fallen so much that it is no longer profitable to cull the herd. An unfortunate consequence is that bush land in national parks is being decimated by the increased number of elephants, which is of course endangering other species.

Even the threat of trade restrictions can be environmentally counterproductive. The talk of European import bans on tropical hardwood logs has encouraged Indonesia to ban log exports. But since felling has been allowed to continue, this policy has lowered the domestic price of logs and thereby raised effective assistance to Indonesia's furniture and other timber-using industries to extremely high levels (GATT 1991, 127). At that lower timber price, it is not surprising that less of each tree is now used.

11. See the discussion in Hillman and Ursprung (1992) and Hoekman and Leidy (1992), as well as the empirical evidence analyzed by Van Grasstek (1992) of voting behavior of US senators.

12. See, for example, Shrybman (1990), Ritchie (1990) and Arden-Clarke (1991).

Effects of Trade Liberalization on the Environment

Countries' actual trade patterns have been affected not only by the determinants of comparative advantage discussed above but also by the pattern of distortionary policies introduced by national governments. A distinctive feature of that global pattern of distortions is that poor countries have tended to discriminate against their primary and labor-intensive export manufacturing sectors in which they have a comparative advantage and to favor their import-competing industrial sector, while in advanced economies, those industries losing comparative advantage that are significant employers (agriculture, coal mining, textiles, cars) are the ones assisted most, especially via protection from import competition.

Economic policy reform, and particularly trade liberalization, leads to higher incomes in both sets of countries and an international relocation of production and consumption. Both of these effects worry some environmentalists. With respect to higher incomes, they simply assume that there will be greater demands on the environment due to increased spending. This ignores the fact that income growth also brings with it at least three pertinent changes in behavior patterns.

The first one, already alluded to above, is that as economies open up and incomes rise, more stringent environmental policies are put in place. This is partly because the demand for such policies has a high income elasticity after middle-income status has been attained. At the same time, more resources are available to spend on improving the environment. Also, the political cost of instituting such policies falls with the opening up of the economy to trade and investment. It falls because liberalization expands the opportunities to acquire more environmentally benign production processes and consumer products and thereby lowers the cost of (and hence the opposition to) implementing stricter standards.

Secondly, higher incomes in poor countries inevitably lead to lower population growth rates. This, along with the increased employment opportunities resulting from trade liberalization, is likely to reduce the rate of environmental degradation due to population pressures in developing countries. In rural areas, it means fewer people denuding hillsides to eke out a subsistence income, while in urban areas it means fewer squatters in shanty towns with poor sanitation and water (World Bank 1992).

And thirdly, the increase in the value of poor people's time in developing countries will raise the relative price of wood and charcoal as sources of household fuel. Since four-fifths of the timber harvested in developing countries is used as household fuel, this alone could have a major beneficial impact in reducing deforestation and carbon dioxide levels.

But, in addition to not appreciating these behavioral changes, environmentalists are often misguided in terms of the environmental impact of trade liberalization through its effects on the international location of production and consumption. Two of the world's most distorted commodity markets are those for coal and food: both tend to be priced well above international levels in advanced economies and well below them in developing countries (particularly the former centrally planned economies). Yet it is not difficult to demonstrate that liberalizing trade in these commodity markets is more likely to improve than to worsen the global environment. We begin with coal, the consumption of which damages the environment, and then consider food where it is an activity of production that is damaging the environment.[13]

The Case of Coal

Coal, which supplies nearly one-third of the world's energy, is a major contributor to local and international environmental problems, including global warming and acid rain.[14] Since liberalizing trade in a commodity typically leads to an expansion in its global consumption, one might expect coal to be an example of trade reform worsening the environment. In fact, this need not be the case. On the contrary, if domestic taxes on coal consumption are introduced or adjusted to ensure that the coal price to consumers does not fall when trade is liberalized, both economic welfare and the environment would improve.

Coal import restrictions imposed by numerous industrial economies, together with their subsidies to domestic coal mining, ensure that industrial countries (which account for one-third of global coal consumption) import less coal than they would if their markets were unrestricted.[15] This has depressed the international price of coal (and hence of other energy sources). If those domestic-producer subsidies and import restrictions were to be replaced by a tax on coal consumption that kept the domestic consumer price at its present level, coal production would decrease and imports would rise, but consumption and hence domestically generated pollution from coal use would remain unchanged. Moreover, greater demand by those industrial countries for coal imports would raise the international price of coal (and other energy sources), thereby reducing energy consumption and hence pollution in the rest of the world.

---

13. Another important case of particular importance to East Asia, but which has been studied less, concerns trade in logs and timber products (see GATT 1992, 38, box 6).

14. This and the next section draw on Anderson (1992b).

15. Data from Jolly, Beck, and Savage (1990) suggest that the combined effect of import protection and direct producer subsidies was to cause the domestic producer price of coal to be above border prices in 1986 by about 100 percent in the United Kingdom, 240 percent in West Germany and 290 percent in Japan. See also Steenblik and Wigley (1990).

While industrial country reform alone would lower global pollution, it represents only half the story. This is because coal is priced at only a small fraction of the international price in many developing and former centrally planned economies (the latter accounting for about half the world's coal consumption).[16] Were these countries to reform their coal markets, their domestic prices would rise substantially, leading to less coal being burnt and hence less pollution from these countries. While the increase in their exports would depress the international coal price, more or less offsetting the increase that would result from liberalization by industrial economies, this would not cause increased pollution in other countries if the latter's tax on coal consumption was adjusted to prevent the domestic consumer price from falling below the prereform level.

Hence, coal trade liberalization in poorer countries—especially the former centrally planned economies—could add substantially to the positive environmental effects of liberalization in advanced industrial economies. And since such reform would at the same time add to welfare as conventionally defined, for the usual gains-from-trade reasons,[17] it contrasts markedly with proposals to reduce global warming by imposing carbon taxes globally—proposals on which international agreement in any case would be extremely difficult to reach.[18]

The Case of Food

Liberalizing trade in farm products concerns environmentalists mainly through its effects on production rather than consumption. In Western Europe, part of the fear is that lowering farm price supports in industrial

---

16. According to data published by the International Energy Agency (1992), during 1988–90 the domestic price of steaming coal used for energy, as a proportion of the West European import price, was 15 percent in Czechoslovakia, 20 percent in Poland, 32 percent in Hungary, and 27 percent in India. Prices in the former Soviet Union may have been even lower, especially when valued at the shadow exchange rate. Prices for steaming coal in China vary by region, but even at the overvalued official exchange rate, the Plan prices (which apply to about two-thirds of all coal) were well below half the US export price in 1989 (Albouy 1991, 5). Burniaux et al. (1992, 55) suggests the user price of coal in 1985 averaged less than 55 percent of border prices in all of Eastern Europe, the former Soviet Union, China, and India.

17. In fact, the welfare gains would be even greater than the above single-commodity, partial-equilibrium analysis suggests. This is because of the opportunities for substitution in consumption among coals of different quality (in terms of their pollutiveness) and between coal and other, cleaner fuels.

18. Evaluations of the costs and distributional consequences across countries of such proposals can be found, for example, in Nordhaus (1991), Burniaux et al. (1992), Cline (1992), and Winters (1992). Burniaux et al. model the effects of reducing carbon emissions both with and without current energy-user price taxes/subsidies in place. The results—consistent with the above conclusion—show that the level of emissions by the year 2050 would be 20 percent lower if present distortions in energy-user prices were to be removed.

economies would harm the local rural environment (via more depopula-
tion of villages, less manicuring of alpine pastures, and so on). But there
is concern also for what the higher international food prices that would
result from reducing agricultural protectionism in rich countries would
do to the natural environment in the tropics. Two undesirable consequences are feared there. One is that, through encouraging developing-
country agriculture, tropical deforestation would accelerate to make
available more cropping and grazing land and that this would add to
global warming and reduce the biodiversity of plants and animals. The
other perceived undesirable consequence is that the available farm land
in the tropics would be used more intensively with heavier doses of
chemical fertilizers and pesticides. This would add to soil and water
contamination in those countries and to chemical residues in the food
produced there.

These concerns are understandable, but they are based on a less-than-
complete picture of the environmental effects of liberalizing agricultural
support policies. (Also, they ignore the usual welfare effects of trade
liberalization, which would be positive for both rich and poor countries—
see Tyers and Anderson 1992, chapter 6.) To obtain a more complete
picture requires first examining the effect of reform on the total volume
and location of the world's food production, then to ask how that relocation would alter land use in the affected locations, and thirdly to examine what environmental policy changes might accompany food trade
liberalization.

According to one recent set of modeling results, even if all industrial
countries were to liberalize their food markets fully and agents adjusted
immediately, there would be almost no change in global food output: the
net decline in farm output in reforming industrial countries would be
matched almost exactly by the net increase in developing country output
(top of table 1). Developing countries' output would not increase more
because even in the long run it is expected those countries would continue
to insulate their domestic markets somewhat—that is, they would not
allow all the international price increase to pass to their producers and
consumers. The regional changes in production are shown in the rest of
table 1. Most of the production cutback is projected to take place in the
EC-12: three-quarters of the grain and two-fifths of the meat reductions
would occur there. While most of the output expansion would occur in
developing countries, according to these results, a little over a quarter
would come from the least densely populated rich countries of North
America and Australasia—in America's case partly because the acreage
set-aside program also is assumed to be abandoned as part of its reform.
Apart from China, with its contribution of one-fifth to the expansion of
grain (although this represents only a 2 percent increase in its own output), the developing country that is projected to expand most is Argentina. It accounts for more than one-eighth of the global expansion of both

Table 1 Effects on global food production of total liberalization of industrial countries' food policies, 1990 (percentages)

	Grains	Meats
Proportional change in production in:		
All industrial countries	–5	–6
Developing countries	3	8
Total world	–0.3	3.0
Shares of production decline in industrial countries due to:		
EC-12	73	61
EFTA	13	7
Japan	14	32
Total	100	100
Shares of production increase in other countries due to:		
North America	30	20
Australia/New Zealand	2	6
Argentina	13	14
Brazil	11	9
Other Latin America	11	20
China	21	5
South Asia	5	3
Other Asia	5	12
Africa/Middle East	2	11
Total	100	100

Source: Calculated from printouts used in Anderson and Tyers (1992) as reported in Anderson (1992c, table 8.2).

grain and meat. Other Latin American countries would supply much of the rest of the additional output, with the more densely populated countries of Asia and Africa contributing little, especially relative to their populations.

How the environment would be affected by these relocations of production depends on how the global use of farm inputs would alter following liberalization. With respect to intermediate inputs, several points can be made. First, it is clear from figure 2 that chemical fertilizer applications are strongly correlated with producer price incentives. Countries with relatively low producer prices such as Argentina, Australia, and Thailand use less than one-twentieth the amounts of chemical fertilizer per cropped hectare that high-priced countries such as Switzerland use. Even just within Asia, the range has been very wide for fertilizer, and wider still for pesticide use (table 2)—despite the provision in the poorer

Table 2 Ratio of producer price to border price of rice and use of chemical fertilizers and pesticides per hectare in Asian economies, 1970s

Country	Producer- to border-price ratio for rice, 1976–80	Use per ha. of paddy land, 1976–79	Pesticide use per ha. of paddy land, 1970–78
		(kilograms per year)	
Burma	0.37	9	0.16
Thailand	0.70	11	0.97
Sri Lanka	0.76	65	0.11
India	0.76	32	0.33
Philippines	0.77	29	1.36
Bangladesh	0.93	11	0.02
Indonesia	0.98	57	0.38
West Malaysia	1.73	97	1.92
Taiwan	1.85[a]	252	3.48[b]
South Korea	2.66[a]	311	10.70
Japan	3.75[a]	340	14.30

ha = hectare

a. From Anderson, Hayami, and others (1986, 128, 130, 133).

b. Based on application to all crops on all cultivated land during 1979–81, from Department of Agriculture and Forestry, *Taiwan Agricultural Yearbook*, Taipei, 1988.

Source: Barker, Herdt, and Rose (1985, 77, 89, and 237).

countries of considerable subsidies to users of farm chemicals. Moreover, the extent of contamination of soil, water, and air from farm chemicals depends on their use not only per cropped hectare but also relative to the total land area of a country. It happens that the highly protected countries of Western Europe and Northeast Asia crop a quarter and a sixth of their land, respectively, whereas the rest of the world crops only a tenth of its land on average. Hence, the extent of pollution from farm chemicals is even more strongly related to current producer support policies than figure 2 and table 2 suggest.

It follows that an international relocation of crop production from countries with high-priced food to those with lower prices would reduce substantially the aggregate use of chemicals in world crop production and in particular their very high use in Western Europe and Northeast Asia. While it is true their use in other countries would expand, that expansion would be from a low base and to still-modest levels in terms of their pollutive and food-contaminating effects (and it could be more or less offset by reductions in the subsidies currently offered to users of farm chemicals in those countries). And the same is true for the effect of liberalization on the use of inputs in livestock industries. The relocation of meat and milk production would be associated with a decline in the extent to which the world's livestock is fed grain (often mixed with growth hormones) rather than pasture. The greater use of the latter, less-intensive method would reduce not only air, soil, and water contamination associated with the disposal of animal effluent but also the chemical additives in the livestock products we eat.

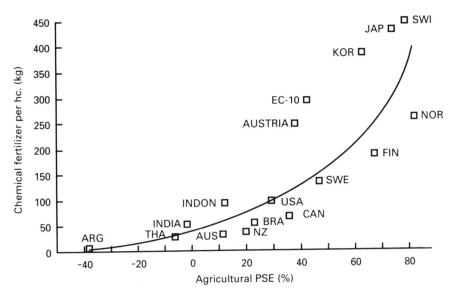

Figure 2. Relatio.iship between agricultural producer subsidy equivalent (PSE) for 1979-89 and use of chemical fertilizer per hectare of cropped land in 1985, various countries/country groups. Source: Data from Anderson (1992b, Table 2).

What about the use of labor and capital? If agricultural profitability was reduced in advanced industrial countries, labor and capital that would otherwise have been employed in agriculture would find employment mostly in the relatively unpolluting services sector or in industrial activities which for the most part already have basic environmental protection policies in place. By contrast, in the less-developed economies where food production would expand, the capital required for that expansion might otherwise be employed in smokestack manufacturing or mining activities, which could well be more pollutive than farming at the margin if adequate environmental policies are not in place. Also, some underemployed rural labor would be attracted into the expanding commercial farm sector. If these workers would otherwise be eking out a subsistence income by squatting on marginal hillsides, less deforestation and soil degradation on those hillsides would result. Also, the increased value of rural labor would raise the real price of wood for fuel (the main component being the value of time involved in collecting and chopping it). Cleaner fuels such as kerosene would then be used more, and forests would be depleted less. This effect on the environment could be very substantial because, as mentioned earlier, four-fifths of logs felled in developing countries are used as fuel.[19]

---

19. A similar set of comments could be made about the positive effects on the environment in rich and poor countries of liberalizing trade in textiles and clothing.

Finally, what about land use? Virtually all the econometric evidence suggests that, in practice, very little farm land would go fallow in liberalizing countries solely because of a fall in output prices. Instead, there would be an immediate decline in the value of land, which would in turn lead quickly to reduced use of land substitutes such as farm chemicals, irrigation water, and concentrated animal feeds. Over time, such use would fall even more because the decline in the price of land would reduce the bias in research toward the development of land-saving technologies (Ruttan 1971). Moreover, a lower price of land would reduce the incentive to clear remaining forests, wetlands, and other wildlife habitats in these countries. These positive environmental effects would add to the conventionally measured gains in economic welfare for the reforming countries.

But wouldn't there be more land cleared for farming in those countries where food production would expand? The answer is probably no in the case of North America and Australasia where, according to table 1, nearly a third of the extra grain and meat output would be produced. In these countries, there are strict deforestation regulations that prevent indiscriminate felling. In any case, in the United States the bulk of the increased grain output would come from bringing back into production farm land idled under the set-aside provisions of the price-support programs.

In the developing countries, the area used for food production may well expand, so the question becomes, by how much? Some of that extra land might be drawn away from plantation cash crops, which also use farm chemicals, so this shift may not represent a net addition to environmental damage. The concern of conservationists, however, is that more tropical forests would be felled, reducing their value as wilderness areas, sources of plant and animal biodiversity, and as absorbers of the world's ever-larger emissions of carbon dioxide. Yet empirical price response studies suggest there would be relatively little extra felling in response to aggregate output price increases. Consider, for example, the three countries that table 1 suggests would be responsible for producing two-thirds of the developing countries' extra grain and two-fifths of the extra meat following reforms abroad: namely, Argentina, Brazil, and China. A recent study of Argentina suggests a 10 percent permanent increase in the real price of farm products would cause the area farmed to increase by less than 5 percent even after two decades (compared with increases in farm labor and capital equipment use of 15 and 18 percent, respectively). Similar results were found for Brazil: a 10 percent product price increase there would in the long run increase land use in farming by 6 percent, labor use by 18 percent, and capital equipment use by 27 percent (Cavallo 1989; Lopes 1977; both quoted in Lutz 1992). As for China, a recent growth-accounting study found that during the 1965–85 period, none of China's rapid farm-output growth was attributable to land expansion (Fan 1991).[20] Since any liberalization of industrial countries' farm policies in the 1990s is unlikely to cause more than a 5 percent rise in food prices in developing countries, the annual expansion in the area used for farming that would result from such a reform would be at most a small fraction of 1 percent.[21]

An important qualification to the results reported in table 1 strengthens even further the likelihood of freer farm trade benefiting the global environment. It has to do with the effects in Eastern Europe and the former Soviet Union. The analysis reported in table 1 effectively ignored those countries by assuming they do not transmit international food price changes to their domestic markets. While that seemed a reasonable assumption when the results were generated, it is, of course, no longer so. A rise in international food prices now would boost farm incomes and employment there and, in so doing, reduce both the prospect of political instability and the incentive to divert resources away from agricultural relative to industrial activities. Given the present parlous state of pollution abatement by East European industry, this is a further way in which food policy reform could reduce European and global environmental problems.

Global Versus Regional Liberalization

The above discussion provides but two case studies of global trade liberalization. It cannot be inferred from them alone that global liberalization of all trade in goods and services, of the sort being negotiated as part of the Uruguay Round, would necessarily be beneficial for the environment, all else being equal. But what we do know from economic theory is that, in the absence of other distortions or market failures, radical reductions in all trade barriers will improve welfare as conventionally measured

---

20. The responsiveness of land use has been low in Southeast Asia also. In Thailand, for example, a 10 percent increase in the price of crop products is estimated to increase the demand for cropland by less than 1 percent (Phantumvanit and Panayotou 1990).

21. The study referred to in table 1 estimates that full liberalization by industrial countries would raise international prices of temperate foods by 25 percent. It is clear from the Uruguay Round negotiations that it will be difficult politically to deliver even as much as a one-third liberalization in the 1990s. Moreover, developing countries transmit only a fraction of any international price change to their domestic markets even in the long run, so 5 percent is probably an upper limit on the domestic price rise that could be expected from such reform this decade. According to the above econometric evidence, this would translate to less (in many cases much less) than a 3 percent increase in the demand for agricultural land over the decade—and during the past decade, the supply of farmland in developing countries grew at 5.5 percent as a result of logging.

(Hatta 1977). Indeed, *so long as optimal environmental policies are in place,*[22] welfare will improve even after taking into account any adverse effects of liberalization on the environment (Anderson 1992a).

Can the same be said about regional integration arrangements such as the North American Free Trade Agreement (NAFTA) or the EC 1992 single-market program and its evolving accords with the European Free Trade Association (EFTA) and the reforming economies of Eastern Europe? The global welfare effects (not counting the effects on the environment) are less clear-cut because trade diversion may offset trade creation, especially with the increasing propensity of countries to impose antidumping duties, voluntary export restraints, and other covert trade barriers both within regional blocs and against the rest of the world (Hoekman and Leidy 1993). And the environmental effects are even less certain because, in addition to the usual impact of production relocation and changes in relative prices faced by consumers, the regional agreements typically will have explicit or implicit provisions for harmonizing environmental laws to some extent.[23] On the one hand, one might expec ̀ standards to become stricter when new members have higher standards than existing members (EFTA versus EC-12). On the other hand, environmentalists fear that standards may be harmonized downward when a bloc admits members with lower standards (Mexico versus the United States and Canada; Eastern versus Western Europe). The latter risk is small for the cases mentioned, however, given the relative political strengths of the existing and joining countries. In those cases, then, the effect on the environment of creating or expanding a regional bloc is likely to be positive for the same sorts of reasons (and with the same provisos) as they are for global trade liberalization.

There are two differences between regional and global trade liberalizations that may be of some significance, however. The first is that if regional liberalizations become a substitute for global liberalizations, then to the extent that they apply only to a subset of the world economy, they will boost global income less and thus cause less greening of world politics (for the reasons mentioned above). And the other is that comparative advantages will change differently if the regionalism route is adopted instead of multilateralism. Specifically, suppose Mexico or Eastern Europe

---

22. This is a nontrivial proviso, especially the more an environmental problem spills over to other countries or involves the global commons.

23. Harmonization provisions such as minimum standards tend to be written into regional integration agreements, presumably to reduce the risk of member countries competing by undercutting each other's pollution tax rates, particularly in oligopolistic industries as a form of strategic industrial policy (Barrett 1991). A less likely motivation is to reduce the prospect that pollution taxes are raised by each country to ensure polluting industries are "not in my back yard" (the NIMBY prospect). For an analysis of the differing effects of these two scenarios, see Markusen, Morey, and Olewiler (1991).

were to adopt environmental policies much closer to those of the United States or European Community than to those of other middle-income countries.[24] Then the former's competitiveness in pollution-intensive industries would tend to be lowered to some extent, to the benefit of otherwise-similar economies outside those blocs—unless those blocs, as a consequence of enlargement, become sufficiently more powerful in imposing their standards on other countries.

Implications for Pacific Countries

This paper has sought to clarify a number of points concerning the nature and some of the trade effects of the greening of world politics. The first point is that the current wave of concern for the environment is much more intense, more widespread, and likely to be sustained and to affect a much broader range of countries than was the first wave of the early 1970s. This is partly because more is now known about the nature and the considerable extent to which we are degrading the natural environment. But the demand for many of nature's services is increasing also because of rapid population and income growth. The growth in the supply of environmental services, by contrast, is limited by their non-renewability and/or by incomplete markets for them, particularly in poorer economies and at the global level where cheap-rider problems are especially acute.

Second, because of genuine national differences in the demand for and supply of services from nature, countries will necessarily have different optimal environmental policies. In cases where there are no international environmental spillovers, attempts to harmonize domestic environmental policies across countries will be costly because they deny the existence of one of the determinants of comparative advantage. But it is necessary also to acknowledge that some environmental problems do spill over to neighboring countries and the global commons, both physically (acid rain, ozone depletion, global warming) and psychologically (species depletion, deforestation, animal rights). Since countries will differ also in their capacity and preparedness to reduce the overseas environmental impacts of their activities, the scope for friction between countries, brought about by this challenge to national sovereignty, is considerable. It is especially great when there are interactive environmental problems, as with global

---

24. Such adjustments can happen even without changes in environmental laws in the poorer new members of a bloc. For example, the lowering of trade barriers may result in some producer and consumer equipment from the richer countries being more competitive and less pollutive than local substitutes. An obvious case in point is second-hand cars, which have catalytic converters moving south from the United States or east from Germany.

warming and deforestation: poor countries see global warming as caused by rich countries' earlier deforestation and continuing high levels of carbon emissions while rich countries see tropical deforestation as reducing the world's capacity to absorb more carbon emissions as well as reducing its stocks of plant and animal species and of pristine wilderness areas. Since rich countries can better afford to worry about these problems, poor countries feel they should be paid to contribute to rich-country welfare through curtailing tropical deforestation activities.

Third, one of the few ways in which countries with a preference for strict environmental standards can influence the environmental policies of other countries is via trade measures. This should worry Pacific countries, partly because trade instruments are almost never going to be ideal for achieving global environmental objectives (their stick-and/or-carrot role in international environmental agreements being the main potential exception), and also because they are open to abuse by traditional protectionist groups seeking covert government assistance. They are thus likely to cause trade disputes and retaliation, which could ultimately undermine the global trading system on which Pacific dynamism depends. And that system is further undermined by the misinformation being circulated by some environmentalist groups in rich countries concerning the effects that multilateral trade liberalization would have on the global environment.

How might individuals and governments of Pacific countries respond to these developments? Opportunities, as well as challenges, present themselves. The main opportunities involve altering domestic production and consumption in response to changes in the terms of trade brought about by changes in other countries' environmental policies and preferences. As well as the traditional smokestack industries, this could affect service industries (e.g., promoting eco-tourism exports), primary sectors (e.g., marketing food exports as being relatively low in chemical additives), and high-tech activities (e.g., exporting antipollution equipment). But in addition, there is the opportunity simply to set an example within the Pacific region by not using trade measures for environmental purposes (e.g., adopting dolphin-friendly labeling provisions for tuna cans instead of banning imports of Mexican tuna into the United States, or limiting production rather than exports of logs from the Association of Southeast Asian Nations), and by giving higher priority to liberalizing trade in cases where it would have the additional benefit of reducing local and global pollution (e.g., freeing more of the market for coal in China, perhaps in return for greater access to developed-country markets for light manufactures).

The challenges that present themselves include minimizing not only the extent to which individual countries use the environment as an excuse to raise import barriers but also the tendency for the trend toward greater use of trade measures for environmental purposes to erode the global trading system. The GATT process itself offers one obvious channel. Another is during negotiations leading directly to international environmental agreements. And a third will be through the UN Commission to be set up to replace the UN Conference on Economic Development. By stressing there—just as several Asian delegations did at the Rio conference last June—that a Uruguay Round agreement probably would do more for the global environment in the 1990s than any conceivable series of international environmental agreements, perhaps those environmentalists opposed to trade liberalization will gradually be persuaded to switch their attention from trade measures and toward more appropriate environmental policy instruments.

References

Albouy, Y. 1991. "Coal Pricing in China: Issues and Reform Strategy." China and Mongolia Department, Discussion Paper No. 138. Washington: The World Bank (October).

Anderson, K. 1992a. "The Standard Welfare Economics of Policies Affecting Trade and the Environment." In K. Anderson and R. Blackhurst, eds., *The Greening of World Trade Issues*. Ann Arbor: University of Michigan Press, and London: Harvester Wheatsheaf.

Anderson, K. 1992b. "Effects on the Environment and Welfare of Liberalizing World Trade: The Cases of Coal and Food." In K. Anderson and R. Blackhurst, eds., *The Greening of World Trade Issues*. Ann Arbor: University of Michigan Press, and London: Harvester Wheatsheaf.

Anderson, K., Y. Hayami, and others. 1986. *The Political Economy of Agricultural Protection: East Asia in International Perspective*. Boston, London, and Sydney: Allen and Unwin.

Anderson, K. and R. Tyers. 1992. "More on Welfare Gains to Developing Countries from Liberalizing World Food Trade." Canberra: Australian National University. Mimeo (January).

Arden-Clarke, C. 1991. "The GATT, Environmental Protection and Sustainable Development." World Wide Fund for Nature Discussion Paper. Gland: WWF International (June).

Baumol, W. 1971. *Environmental Protection, International Spillovers and Trade*. Stockholm: Almqvist and Wiksell.

Barker, R., R. W. Herdt, and B. Rose. 1985. *The Rice Economy of Asia*. Washington: Resources for the Future.

Barrett, S. 1991. "Strategic Environmental Policy and International Trade." London: London Business School. Mimeo (December).

Beckerman, W. 1992. "Economic Growth and the Environment: Whose Growth? Whose Environment?" *World Development* 20 (4): 481–96.

Benedick, R. E. 1991. *Ozone Diplomacy*. Cambridge, MA: Harvard University Press.

Burniaux, J. M., J. P. Martin, G. Nicoletti, and J. Oliveira Martins. 1992. "The Costs of Reducing CO2 Emissions: Evidence from GREEN." Working Paper No.115. Paris: Economics Department, Organization for Economic Cooperation and Development.

Cavallo, D. 1989. "Agriculture and Economic Growth: The Experience of Argentina 1913–84." In A. Maunder and A. Valdes, eds., *Agriculture and Governments in an Interdependent World*. London: Dartmouth for the IAAE.

Clarida, R. H. and R. Findlay 1992. "Government, Trade and Comparative Advantage." *American Economic Review* 82 (2): 122–27 (May).

Cline, W. 1992. *The Economics of Global Warming*. Washington: Institute for International Economics.

Crowson, P. 1992. "Minerals: The Infinitely Finite." *The Mining Review* 16(4): 27–31 (August).

Deacon, R., and P. Shapiro. 1975. "Private Preference for Collective Goods Revealed Through Voting on Referenda." *American Economic Review* 65:943–55.

Enders, A., and A. Porges. 1992. "Successful Conventions and Conventional Success: Saving the Ozone Layer." In K. Anderson and R. Blackhurst, eds., *The Greening of World Trade Issues*. Ann Arbor: University of Michigan Press, and London: Harvester Wheatsheaf.

Fan, S. G. 1991. "Effects of Technological Change and Institutional Reform on Production Growth in Chinese Agriculture." *American Journal of Agricultural Economics* 73 (2): 266–75 (May).

General Agreement on Tariffs and Trade. 1971. *Industrial Pollution Control and International Trade*. GATT Studies in International Trade No. 1. Geneva: GATT Secretariat.

General Agreement on Tariffs and Trade. 1991. *Trade Policy Review: Indonesia*. Geneva: GATT Secretariat (August).

General Agreement on Tariffs and Trade. 1992. *International Trade 1990–91*, vol. 1. Geneva: GATT.

Grant, R. J., M. C. Papadakis, and J. D. Richardson. 1993. "Global Trade Flows: Old Structures, New Issues, Empirical Evidence." In M. Noland, ed., *Pacific Dynamism and the International Economic System*. Washington: Institute for International Economics.

Grossman, G. M., and A. B. Krueger. 1991. "Environmental Impacts of a North American Free Trade Agreement." Princeton University. Mimeo (October).

Hatta, T. 1977. "A Recommendation for a Better Tariff Structure." *Econometrica* 45: 1859–69 (November).

Hillman, A. L., and H. N. Ursprung. 1992. "The Influence of Environmental Concerns on the Political Determination of Trade Policy." In K. Anderson and R. Blackhurst, eds., *The Greening of World Trade Issues*. Ann Arbor: University of Michigan Press, and London: Harvester Wheatsheaf.

Hoekman, B., and M. Leidy. 1992. "Environmental Policy Formation in a Trading Economy: a Public Choice Perspective." In K. Anderson and R. Blackhurst, eds., *The Greening of World Trade Issues*. Ann Arbor: University of Michigan Press, and London: Harvester Wheatsheaf.

Hoekman, B. and M. Leidy. 1993. "Holes and Loopholes in Alternative Trade Agreements: History and Prospects." In K. Anderson and R. Blackhurst, eds., *Regional Integration and the Global Trading System*. London: Harvester Wheatsheaf.

International Energy Agency. 1992. *Energy Prices and Taxes* (fourth quarter 1991). Paris: IEA.

International Monetary Fund, International Bank for Reconstruction and Development, European Bank for Reconstruction and Development, and Organization for Economic Cooperation and Development. 1991. *A Study of the Soviet Economy*. Paris: OECD.

Jolly, L., T. Beck, and E. Savage. 1990. "Reform of International Coal Trade: Implication for Australia and World Trade." Discussion Paper 90.1. Canberra: Australian Bureau of Agricultural and Resource Economics.

Krueger, A. 1977. *Growth, Distortions and Patterns of Trade Among Many Countries*. Princeton, NJ: International Finance Section.

Leamer, E. E. 1987. "Paths of Development in the Three Factor, n-Good General Equilibrium Model." *Journal of Political Economy* 95 (5): 961–99 (October).

Leidy, M., and B. Hoekman. 1993. " 'Cleaning Up' While Cleaning Up? Pollution Abatement, Interest Groups and Contingent Trade Policies." *Public Choice* (forthcoming).

Leonard, N. J. 1988. *Pollution and the Struggle for World Product: Multinational Corporations, Environment and International Comparative Advantage*. Cambridge (UK): Cambridge University Press.

Lopes, M. 1977. "The Mobilization of Resources from Agriculture: A Policy Analysis for Brazil." Lafayette: Purdue University. Unpublished doctoral dissertation.

Low, P. 1992. "Trade Measures and Environmental Quality: The Implications for Mexico's Exports." In P. Low, ed., *International Trade and the Environment*, Discussion Paper 159. Washington: The World Bank.

Lutz, E. 1992. "Agricultural Trade Liberalization, Price Changes and Environmental Effects." *Environmental and Resource Economics* 2 (1): 79–89.

Markusen, J. R., E. R. Morey, and N. Olewiler. 1991. "Noncooperative Equilibria in Regional Environmental Policies When Plant Locations Are Endogenous." Boulder: University of Colorado. Mimeo (September).

Meadows, D. H. et al. 1972. *The Limits to Growth*. New York: Universe Books.

Nordhaus, W. D. 1991. "To Slow or Not to Slow: The Economics of the Greenhouse Effect." *Economic Journal* 101 (407): 920–37 (July).

Phantumvanit, D., and T. Panayotou. 1990. "National Resources for a Sustainable Future: Spreading the Benefits." Paper presented to a conference on Industrializing Thailand and its Impact on the Environment, held December. Bangkok: Thailand Development Research Institute.

Radetzki, M. 1992. "Economic Growth and Environment." In P. Low, ed., *International Trade and the Environment*, Discussion Paper 159. Washington: The World Bank.

Ritchie, M. 1990. "GATT, Agriculture and the Environment: The U.S. Double Zero Plan." *The Ecologist* 20 (6): 214–20 (November/December).

Ruttan, V. W. 1971. "Technology and the Environment." *American Journal of Agricultural Economics* 53 (5): 707–17 (December).

Shrybman, S. 1990. "International Trade and the Environment: An Environmental Assessment of the GATT." *The Ecologist* 20 (1):30–34 (January/February).

Siebert, H. 1974. "Environmental Protection and International Specialization." *Welwirtschaftliches Archiv* 110:494–508.

Siebert, H., J. Eichberger, R. Gronych, and R. Pethig. 1980. *Trade and Environment: A Theoretical Enquiry*. Amsterdam: Elsevier.

Snape, R. H. 1992. "The Environment, International Trade and Competitiveness." In K. Anderson and R. Blackhurst, eds., *The Greening of World Trade Issues*. Ann Arbor: University of Michigan Press, and London: Harvester Wheatsheaf.

Steenblik, R. P., and K. J. Wigley. 1990. "Coal Policies and Trade Barriers." *Energy Policy* 18 (4): 351–69 (May).

Tobey, J. A. 1990. "The Effects of Domestic Environmental Policies on Patterns of World Trade: An Empirical Test." *Kyklos* 43 (2): 191–209.

Tyers, R., and K. Anderson. 1992. *Disarray in World Food Markets*. Cambridge (UK): Cambridge University Press.

Van Grasstek, C. 1992. "The Political Economy of Trade and the Environment in the United States." In P. Low, ed., *International Trade and the Environment*. Discussion Paper 159. Washington: The World Bank.

Walter, I. 1975. *The International Economics of Pollution*. London: Macmillan.

Walter, I., ed. 1976. *Studies in International Environmental Economics*. New York: Wiley.

Winters, L. A. 1992. "Trade and Welfare Effects of Greenhouse Gas Abatement: A Survey of Empirical Estimates." In K. Anderson and R. Blackhurst, eds., *The Greening of World Trade Issues*. Ann Arbor: University of Michigan Press, and London: Harvester Wheatsheaf.

World Bank. 1991. *World Development Report 1991*. New York: Oxford University Press.

World Bank. 1992. *World Development Report 1992*. New York: Oxford University Press.

12

Implications of the Post–Cold War Politico-Security Environment for the Pacific Economy

Hadi Soesastro

In the multipolar world after the Cold War an effective regional framework could provide each country with a sort of safety net.
(Yoichi Funabashi 1991)

The shape of the post–Cold War order is far from clear. Many observers predict that the politico-security environment globally and in the Pacific will be characterized by uncertainty and fluidity. Noordin Sopiee (1992) has produced a 22-page list of parameters of the post–Cold War world. These include, among other things, the end of the ideological conflict between communism and anticommunism and the emergence of new ideological conflicts; the development of a more multipolar world with three emerging power centers; the arrival of a different United States; the rise of a doctrine of interventionism; consignment of the Third World to the periphery of global affairs; a turn to political regionalism; the spread of "people power," nationalism, and separatism; a fundamental change in the essence of power; the increasingly limited usefulness of military capability; and the rise of the primacy of economics and of economic conflict.

In examining the geostrategic implications of the end of the Cold War era, Zbigniew Brzezinski (1992, 5–13) suggested that "the future of world order will depend upon the resolution of basic problems within three important regions where order is at issue."[1] These regions are Europe, and how it will resolve the problem of widening and deepening of co-operation; the Pacific, and how this region will organize itself; and the Middle East, and how it will be pacified.

Hadi Soesastro is Executive Director at the Centre for Strategic and International Studies in Jakarta.

1. In an earlier article (1991, 1–20), Brzezinski identified four areas of concern, which include the Soviet Union and how it will be transformed.

How will the Pacific organize itself in light of the dramatic changes in the global and regional politico-security environment? And how will this reorganization affect the emerging Pacific economy? Brzezinski argued that, as is the case in the other regions, success in the Pacific would require US engagement and leadership. However, it is questionable whether, in view of the diminishing dominance of the United States, "hegemonic cooperation" could provide the basis for the post–Cold War regional order in the Pacific. Cooperation "after hegemony" requires the establishment of patterns of rule-guided policy coordination amongst the countries in the Pacific region. Robert O. Keohane (1984) has demonstrated that the demand for such a scheme can be based on the self-interests of the national actors concerned.

Thus, in addition to uncertainty and fluidity, security relations in the Pacific will also be characterized by experimentation. The experimentation concerns forms of global and regional multilateral organizations dealing with the management of regional and subregional security problems. The Pacific, particularly if compared with Europe, is the most underdeveloped in terms of regional institutions. In fact, the region has been generally resistant to institution building, especially on a multilateral basis. This resistance is particularly strong in Northeast Asia, which has little tradition of multilateral security arrangements before the coming of the West, during the era of imperial rivalries, or even during the Cold War (Evans 1992). Regional structures could help build relationships among the regional countries concerned that are stable and mutually beneficial. Such structures would be created to share risks and could be seen as "insurance policies."

The process of institution (or regime) building in the Pacific is likely to be a slow one. But the region has already begun experimenting. In the economic field, there are two regionwide processes of cooperation: Asia Pacific Economic Cooperation (APEC) and the Pacific Economic Cooperation Council (PECC). At the subregional level, more formal institutions have been established. In the realm of security, a number of proposals have been made. Some, such as the North Pacific Cooperative Security Dialogue and the idea of a regional, multilateral politico-security dialogue to be initiated by the Post Ministerial Conference of the Association of Southeast Asian Nations (ASEAN), have gathered momentum. In addition, new approaches to subregional conflicts and tensions have been applied to two problems: Cambodia and the Korean peninsula. Robert Scalapino (1992) has labeled this a "concentric-arcs" approach, involving consecutive combinations of countries based on the degree of involvement and of perceived national interest.

While positive developments are taking place in the direction of regional institutionalization and the creation of regional mechanisms for cooperation and confidence-building measures (CBMs), a question emerges as to whether the growing number of regional structures would indeed lead to greater regional stability. In this age of uncertainty and fluidity, nation-states, especially the less powerful ones, are tempted to buy insurance against all kinds of perceived uncertainties. Indeed, the sense of insecurity, heightened as a result of the fundamental changes in the global political arena, has prompted many countries to seek more of these "insurance policies," without duly considering the cost and the inconsistencies that might exist among insurance schemes.

This paper examines these costs and possible inconsistencies. The experimentation in the region is necessary, but it needs a logical structure, based on well-defined objectives. This paper will analyze four politico-security issues that have important bearing on shaping a regional order in the Pacific and implications for the Pacific economy: trends in the regional politico-security environment, the changing nature of global political relations, the "Asianization" of security in the Pacific, and trans-Pacific economic conflicts.

The Regional Politico-Security Environment

The strategic landscape in the Pacific region has been changing less rapidly than in Europe. To a number of observers, the transition to a post–Cold War world appears to be incomplete in the Pacific, as vestiges of the Cold War still prevail: the division of the Korean peninsula, the Northern Territories dispute between Japan and Russia, the continued entrenchment of Communist rule in China, North Korea, and Vietnam. Thus, it is believed that the Pacific, particularly East Asia, will be "the next area in which to expect major strategic change, with a growing impact on global affairs" (Heisbourg 1992).

While many parameters shape the new regional politico-security environment, there are essentially two main ones. First is the shifts in the regional balance of power, resulting from the collapse of the Soviet Union, the diminished power of the US, and the increasing strategic significance of the major countries in East Asia, including China and Japan. The second factor is the diversity of sources of regional conflicts, especially economic conflicts, across the Pacific as well as the many ongoing territorial disputes. Many of these conflicts are not new, but now they have surfaced as the East-West conflict has receded.

What is the current assessment of the stability of, and threat to, the Pacific region? Jusuf Wanandi (1992) argues that the Pacific region today is the most stable region in the world, but a number of geostrategic problems could emerge in the medium to long term. In addition to the shifting power configuration among the regional powers and the prevailing subregional conflicts, he suggested two other important factors: namely, internal sociopolitical development in the regional countries and the success of regional institution building. Robert Scalapino also concluded that the broad trends in the Pacific region are, on balance, favorable: while domestic or subregional violence could erupt, the likelihood of a conflict engulfing the entire area is very remote. Indeed, both argued that there is a golden opportunity for the regional countries to begin developing the necessary regional security structures to cope with future conflicts. They appear to suggest that current political realities are in line with this effort.

There are less sanguine views as well. In Northeast Asia, as Brzezinski (1992) sees it, there is a cluster of increasingly powerful states that coexist uneasily together and are not assimilated within any multilateral framework. There is great potential for conflict here: Japan's economic success could make it a political and even a military power, China is likely to emerge as a geopolitical contender in the Pacific region, and a unified Korea might emerge as a nuclear power. Since East Asia cannot achieve the degree of economic and political integration that had developed in Europe, Brzezinski believes, it is the security agenda that is critical in East Asia. James Schlesinger (1991) said that, although in both Western Europe and East Asia the focus is shifting from strategic to economic issues, US military forces in East Asia cannot be reduced as rapidly as in Europe.

Compared with Europe, a number of scenarios for the Pacific region point to "a striking range of possible negative outcomes, ranging from general multipolar instability, to preventive wars over nuclearization, and even to large-scale nuclear conflicts" (Moltz 1992). A "realist" perspective would view the competitive military environment, especially in Northeast Asia, as having a great potential for arms races and open conflict. Also, the presence of ongoing territorial disputes in both Northeast and Southeast Asia could spill over into the military arena. Is this indeed an inevitability? Will China use force to settle the seven-nations territorial disputes over the Spratly Islands in the South China Sea?

The scenario based on the "neorealist" school would predict that the shifting of alliances after the Cold War and the decline of US hegemony would lead to a breakup of the US-Japan Security Treaty. This in turn would create a wave of instability, as Japan is forced to "go it alone." The weakening of the superpowers would lead to a removal of the constraining effect on nuclear proliferation. To the neorealist, Japan poses the major threat to regional stability. The "idealist" school also shares the pessimism: unlike in Europe, it argues that in the Pacific region there are only few common principles upon which a formal political, economic, or military regime can be rooted. This scenario predicts that conflicts might even emerge to settle ideological disputes over how the region should be organized.

James Clay Moltz, however, offered a more optimistic scenario, based on the proposition that states may reject past behavior as dysfunctional as a result of learning (new knowledge). In addition, limited regional integration can still contain a number of factors for stability and war prevention. Although the Pacific region lacks explicit agreements and regional security organizations that are found in Europe, "the neoidealist" position predicts that "shared principles in the area of economic development and the lack of major powers with an interest in disrupting the status quo may create conditions of tacit cooperation in security affairs that could be as durable as [the] more explicit, regime-nested security relations in Europe" (Moltz 1992). He further suggested that the "new knowledge," which appears to have become a common ground for national policymaking and regional integration, includes a recognition of the primacy of economic goals over ideological aims, pessimism about the utility of warfare and heightened concern for its negative collateral costs, a commitment to expanded regional trade, and an acceptance of the concept of negotiated settlements as the best avenue for settling territorial and border disputes.

Two observations can be made here. First, while there is less agreement among observers as to Japan's future strategic posture, there appears to be a consensus that Japan is much more of a status-quo power than is China. Hence, any design for a regional, multilateral security structure must give careful attention to the manner in which China would be incorporated. Second, the momentum appears to be right as China is normalizing its relations with many countries in the region. Mutual economic interests definitely have been a major factor behind the improvement of these diplomatic relations. China's trade with South Korea may already have reached $5 billion, even before they established diplomatic relations in mid-1992. China-Taiwan economic relations are booming, and Taiwanese investments continue to pour into China, even though they have far from resolved their political disputes. China and Taiwan have both joined APEC. A phenomenon that is closely related to this development is the emergence of natural economic territories (NETs),[2] many of which involve portions of China, such as Guangdong–Hong Kong–Taiwan or Fujian-Taiwan.

These improved political relations based on mutual economic interests have no doubt greatly enhanced the stability of the Pacific region. Economic interdependence appears to have a stabilizing effect and thus could also enhance security. Economic interdependence, as Miles Kahler (1992) has shown, can have its strategic uses. Linkage strategies—namely, the manipulation of increasing economic interdependence for security objectives—can be successfully employed if political elites place a sufficiently high value on economic growth and opening to the world economy.

As these factors come into play in an ever-larger portion of the Pacific region, are we likely to see an expanded Pacific economy and the embryo

---

2. This term was first coined by Robert Scalapino (1991, 19–40).

of a security community of sorts that would encompass the entire region? It is generally believed that a Pacific economy is already emerging and that the borders of this regional economy might expand rapidly. The Pacific region, defined as encompassing the 15 APEC or 20 PECC economies, is a vast and diverse region already. The 28 Pacific countries and economies included in table 1 show the enormous economic diversity of the region. The addition of North Korea, Vietnam, Mongolia, Laos, Myanmar, and Cambodia, as well as Colombia and Ecuador, does not change the overall picture much. In 1990 the share of these eight countries in the region's total GDP was a mere 0.8 percent, and their share in the region's total value of exports was on the same order of magnitude. However, increased economic interactions between these countries, eventually leading to their integration into the Pacific economy, would greatly contribute to subregional stability and security, for instance, in Southeast Asia.

The point made here is that economic forces and the globalization of markets and production can bring greater stability to the potentially instable politico-security environment in the Pacific. This in turn requires the establishment of a collective decision-making system to manage the increased economic interdependencies. APEC should be seen as an experiment in this direction.

The Changing Nature of International Political Relations

The fall of the Berlin wall, the removal of the Iron Curtain in Central Europe, and to some extent the bamboo curtains in Asia not only mark the end of the Cold War but perhaps also symbolize the end of the era of the nation-state, which began with the Treaty of Westphalia of 1648. There is a parallel development in the economic realm: as tariffs are significantly reduced, international economic diplomacy is now focused on domestic economic structural issues that are viewed as impediments to trade.

Today, the nation-state is being pressured from many directions. It is being pressured from above to surrender some sovereignty to supranational political arrangements, including a revitalized United Nations. Such pressures are also a result of advances in communication, transportation, and globalization in general. Thus, as Scalapino (1992) described it, "a major paradox is unfolding": on the one hand, there is the propensity for countries to turn inward in order to improve the domestic sociopolitical and economic fabric of the society; on the other hand, there is the need to turn outward, increasing involvement in the regional and international arena. This pressure has released the competitive forces of nationalism and internationalism that are increasingly felt in many societies in the Pacific—especially in East Asia, where the economic transformation and

Table 1 The Pacific region in 1990—comparative data

Country	Population (millions)	Area (thousands of square kilometers)	GNP (per capita dollars)	GDP (billions of dollars)	Exports (billions of dollars)
Brunei	0.3	6	17,000	3.5	2.2
Indonesia	178.2	1,905	570	107.3	25.7
Malaysia	17.9	330	2,320	42.4	29.4
Philippines	61.5	300	730	43.9	8.2
Singapore	3.0	1	11,160	34.6	52.8
Thailand	55.8	513	1,420	80.2	22.8
China	1,133.7	9,561	370	364.9	69.5
Hong Kong	5.8	1	11,490	59.7	82.1
South Korea	42.8	99	5,400	236.4	60.5
Taiwan	20.6	36	8,690	169.9	66.4
Japan	123.5	378	25,430	2,942.9	287.7
Australia	17.1	7,687	17,000	296.3	38.9
New Zealand	3.4	269	12,680	42.8	9.4
Canada	26.5	9,976	20,470	570.2	131.3
US	250.0	9.373	21,790	5,392.2	393.1
APEC total	1,940.1	40,435		10,387.2	1,280.0
Chile	13.2	757	1,940	27.8	8.5
Mexico	86.2	1,958	2,490	237.8	30.0
Peru	21.7	1,285	1,160	36.6	3.3
Papua New Guinea[a]	3.9	463	860	3.3	1.2
Russia[b]	150.0	16,878	7,250	2,042.7	49.7
PECC total	2,251.1	61,776		12,735.4	1,372.7
Cambodia	8.5	181	120	1.0	0.0
Laos	4.1	237	200	0.9	0.1
Myanmar	41.6	677	200	8.2	0.4
Vietnam	66.3	330	230	15.0	1.3
Mongolia	2.1	1,565	950	2.0	0.1
North Korea	23.5	121	1,280	30.0	0.8
Colombia	32.3	1,139	1,260	41.1	6.6
Ecuador	10.3	284	980	10.9	2.7
Total Pacific	2,403.8	66,310		12,844.5	1,384.7

APEC = Asia Pacific Economic Cooperation
PECC = Pacific Economic Cooperation Council
a. Papua New Guinea is represented in PECC by the South Pacific Forum.
b. Figures refer to the former Soviet Union.

Source: International Bank for Reconstruction and Development, *World Development Report 1992*; The International Institute for Strategic Studies, *The Military Balance 1991/92*; International Monetary Fund, *Direction of Trade Statistics 1991*.

internationalization have been very rapid. That is why, Jusuf Wanandi (1992) has stressed the importance of domestic political institution building for regional stability.

The nation-state is also pressured from below. Economic development brings about greater diversity in the society, leading to increasing demands for greater freedom and decentralization of decision making so as to cope with specific local and sectional conditions. In addition, ever-smaller ethnic groups are asserting their sovereignty on the basis of self-determination. These pressures are real, although perhaps less urgent in East Asia than in Central Europe. Separatist movements in the region have died down by and large, but there is growing societal concern over the unequal distribution of economic gains.

The effect these pressures are having on international relations worries many nations, particularly in the developing world. Internal and external pressures for democratization, the policy of unqualified support for self-determination, and the elevation of human rights to a key global issue have heightened fears of increased intervention in the domestic affairs of sovereign states. Aid and economic assistance are increasingly linked to these issues. As a consequence, nations in East Asia and elsewhere have adopted defensive postures or have otherwise displayed feelings of political insecurity. The rise of an interventionist doctrine could become a source of North-South conflict, globally as well as in the Pacific. This can be damaging for the Pacific economy, where North-South cooperation has become one of its attractive features. As Noordin Sopiee (1992) put it: "The rise of such a doctrine would be generally threatening to the interests of the weaker nations since double standards will abound and it will be the strong who will determine its very selective application."

The crisis confronting the nation-state requires global or regional efforts to seek the optimum balance between the basic organizing principles underpinning political entities and the interaction of these entities. The policy of unqualified support for self-determination will lead to world disorder, for this principle is likely to be applied at ever lower levels. In this light, would it not be better, for instance, to recognize the rights of a minorities based on multilaterally agreed-upon criteria? Equally important is the issue of human rights and the need for similar multilateral or regional—rather than unilateral—agreements on its implementation. Indeed, this issue has become one of the most contentious in US relations with East Asia and will become a continuing source of trans-Pacific tensions. There is the feeling that, in the post–Cold War, the United States will become more interventionist on this front as it becomes less concerned with East-West security issues. Could the Pacific develop appropriate multilateral institutions where these new international issues can be taken up? This poses an equally important challenge for institution building in the Pacific. If the region fails to build such institutions, it is likely to see the fragmentation of the region into subregional groups. This certainly would be detrimental to the Pacific economy.

The Asianization of Security

The collapse of the Soviet Union and the United States' reordering of priorities have set in motion a process of Asianization, which could further accelerate. Asianization in the security field means the replacement of alliance relations and the pattern of patron-client relations that hitherto have prevailed. This new relationship, albeit providing greater flexibility and independence to those involved, is somewhat unstable, as it involves both cooperation and competition. In addition, the increasing Asianization of security relations tends to contribute to increased military expenditures on the part of most countries in the region (Scalapino 1992).

The Pacific region, especially Northeast Asia, is already heavily armed. China, the two Koreas, and Vietnam are among those that deploy the largest military forces in the world. Japan, South Korea, and China continue to increase their military spending, despite the end of the Cold War. The current high-profile Chinese naval presence in the South China Sea has reawakened the traditional anxieties of Southeast Asia toward China, defeating much of the confidence-building efforts made in recent years. China's recent moves to strengthen its claims on disputed areas in the South China Sea have exacerbated these anxieties. To offset China's growing naval presence, many Southeast Asian states may want to improve their naval capabilities. Although Malaysia's recent acquisition of two frigates from Britain and the signing of a tentative agreement with a Swedish shipyard for two submarines are not seen as a direct response to the Chinese naval buildup, the latter provides a convenient justification for such further spending (Cheung 1992). The Philippines, another party to the territorial dispute in the South China Sea, has also modernized its navy. Reports of China's planned purchases of aircraft carriers from Ukraine and the acquisition of 24 SU-27 aircraft have further focused the region's attention on China's intentions. China's aircraft buys would also provide a justification for the sale of F-16s to Taiwan by the US, which hitherto has been very cautious in transferring arms to both China and Taiwan.

As table 2 shows, until 1990 the nominal increases in defense expenditures in the ASEAN countries, except Singapore, had been modest, but the increases appeared to be rather dramatic in Northeast Asia, especially in rapidly growing Japan, South Korea, and Taiwan. Their combined share increased from 67 percent of total defense expenditures of the APEC countries (excluding the US) in 1980 to 74 percent in 1990. However, as a percentage of GDP, the military expenditures in Taiwan and South Korea have declined. The pattern that emerges from this sketchy picture is a general trend toward increased military expenditures in countries that are US allies or that are under the US defense umbrella. It might be that some implicit burden sharing has taken place. This burden sharing has become more explicit now, particularly with regard to Japan and South Korea, and may be expected to increase further to induce the US to retain its military presence in the region. Even nonaligned countries such as Indonesia and Malaysia are offering their facilities to the US Seventh Fleet, albeit on a commercial basis. This also signifies a kind of

Table 2 Defense expenditures in the Pacific, 1970–90

Country	1970 billions of dollars	1970 share of GDP	1980 billions of dollars	1980 share of GDP	1990 billions of dollars	1990 share of GDP
Brunei	n.a.	n.a.	0.20	4.0	0.23[c]	6.3
Indonesia	0.27	2.3	2.07	2.9	1.45	1.6
Malaysia	0.18	4.6	1.36	5.7	1.56	3.9
Philippines	0.11	1.9	0.61	1.7	0.98	2.3
Singapore	0.11	5.8	0.59	5.2	1.70	5.1
Thailand	0.24	3.9	1.10	3.3	2.06	2.6
China	4.88	n.a.	10.20	3.4	6.06	1.7
Hong Kong	n.a.	n.a.	n.a.	n.a.	n.a.	n.a.
South Korea	0.33	4.0	3.31	5.3	10.62	4.4
Taiwan	0.48	8.8	3.20	8.0	8.69	5.4
Japan	1.64	0.8	10.27	0.9	28.73	1.0
Australia	1.26	3.6	4.06	2.9	7.01	2.3
New Zealand	0.12	2.0	0.43	1.8	0.83	1.8
Canada	1.93	2.5	4.67	1.8	10.28	1.7
US	76.51	7.8	143.98	5.6	289.76	5.3
APEC total	88.06		186.05		369.96	
Chile	0.71	2.4	1.44	6.9	0.54	1.8
Mexico	0.21	0.7	0.82	0.4	0.68	0.4
Peru	0.16	3.0	0.40	2.1	0.64	3.5
Papua New Guinea[a]	n.a.	n.a.	n.a.	n.a.	0.05	1.4
Russia[b]	53.90	11.0	177.00	n.a.	225.38	11.0
PECC total	143.04		365.71		597.25	
Cambodia	0.06	5.9	n.a.	n.a.	n.a.	n.a.
Laos	n.a.	n.a.	0.02	7.0	0.02[d]	3.6
Myanmar	0.10	3.3	0.20	3.5	1.06	4.3
Vietnam	1.60[e]	28.0	n.a.	n.a.	2.32[d]	15.9
Mongolia	0.02	3.8	0.13	n.a.	0.27[c]	13.0
North Korea	0.75	24.5	1.34	9.9	5.23	10.9
Colombia	n.a.	2.8[f]	0.30	0.9	0.54	1.4
Ecuador	n.a.	n.a.	0.19	1.8	0.25	2.3
Total Pacific	145.57		367.89		606.94	

n.a. = not available
a. Papua New Guinea is represented in PECC by the South Pacific Forum.
b. Figures refer to the former Soviet Union.
c. 1988
d. 1989
e. North and South Vietnam
f. 1968

Source: The International Institute for Strategic Studies, The Military Balance (various issues).

burden sharing, which indicates that US military presence in the region is still desired.

The future size of the defense burden sharing cannot easily be predicted. East Asian countries recognize the need to contribute more to secure a continuing US military presence. The cost of the insurance for East Asia will definitely be higher. Thus, a peace dividend for East Asia

**Table 3 Defense expenditures and intraregional trade in the
Pacific, 1970–90** (billions of dollars, except where noted)

	1970	1980	1990
Defense expenditures in the Pacific	145.03	367.89	606.94
Intra-Pacific trade	60.94	377.99	939.34
Defense expenditures as share of intra-Pacific trade (percentages)	238.0	97.3	64.6
Defense expenditures in East Asia	9.63	34.47	70.71
Intra–East Asian trade	10.55	100.74	286.33
Defense expenditures as share of intra–East Asian trade (percentages)	91.3	34.2	24.7

Sources: International Monetary Fund, *Direction of Trade Statistics*, various issues; International Institute for Strategic Studies, *The Military Balance*, various issues.

is unlikely. In 1990 total East Asian defense expenditures amounted to about $70 billion, double what it was in 1980. However, as a proportion of intra–East Asian trade, the combined subregional defense expenditure was reduced to a quarter in 1990, from about one-third a decade earlier. Is it reasonable to expect a return to the 1980 level? For the entire Pacific region, defense expenditures have been reduced to about two-thirds of total intra-Pacific trade in 1990 from about 100 percent in 1980 (table 3). The region's total defense spending was about 4.7 percent of the region's combined GDP. Because US defense expenditures, as well as Russian military budgets, are declining, an increase in defense spending by East Asian countries would still mean a reduction of the level of the region's total defense spending. However, if burden sharing means the purchase of sophisticated military hardware, such as F-16s by Taiwan, to help the US economy, the region could end up entering a dangerous arms race. This will not enhance the region's stability, and it will also affect the region's welfare.

Defense burden sharing is but one important aspect of designing a Pacific security architecture, which must involve the United States. Other important aspects for US continued engagement in the security of the Pacific are its purpose and political acceptability at home. US officials have reiterated that, as a Pacific power, the United States will maintain a military presence in the region. Its engagement is said to provide geopolitical balance, to prevent development of a strategic vacuum, to be an honest broker, to reassure against uncertainty, and to maintain a working presence in case of regional contingencies (Baker 1991, 1–18; Solomon 1992). Even after the Cold War, the United States continues to claim a geopolitical and economic interest in the Pacific (Nye 1992, 83–96). But how easy will it be to convince the American public of this? Given the uncertain and fluid politico-security environment, this will not be easy.

Nonetheless, these decisions—whatever their outcome—should be couched in terms of the level of insurance the American people desire or the degree of risk they want to avoid.

US allies and other countries in the Pacific do not have a great deal of confidence that the US can be depended upon to maintain regional security indefinitely. This is why former US Secretary of State James Baker's proposed security structure for the Pacific was widely deemed inadequate. In his words, this structure can be illustrated as "a fan spread wide, with its base in North America and radiating west across the Pacific. The central support is the US-Japan alliance, the key connection for the security structure. . . . To the North, one spoke represents [the] alliance with the Republic of Korea. To the South, others extend to [the] treaty allies—the Association of Southeast Asian Nations (ASEAN) countries of the Philippines and Thailand. Further south a spoke extends to Australia. . . . Connecting these spokes is the fabric of shared economic interests now given form by the Asia Pacific Economic Cooperation (APEC) process" (Baker 1991, 5). This structure is not multilateral in nature; rather, it consists of a set of bilateral security relations. Baker justified this regional structure based on the diverse and decentralized character of the region's security concerns. However, if the United States cannot be relied upon in the future, this regional security structure will easily crumble. A structure with the United States as its hub also cannot accommodate the Asianization trend of security issues in East Asia. This is so because the the regional security structure should principally achieve the following: establish rules governing how Pacific countries should relate to one another, provide a basis for developing Japan's and China's politico-security roles in the region, and provide a forum for discussing nuclear proliferation and arms transfers in the region. These issues cannot be dealt with satisfactorily in a less than multilateral structure.

It is true that Japan and some other major East Asian countries remain strategically dependent upon the United States. Does this mean trans-Pacific relations must also be based on strategic dependence on the United States? A regional, multilateral security structure can provide an alternative to such dependency. Indeed, there are proposed structures for the Pacific that are aimed at easing such dependence, which should also be in the interest of the United States itself. Ideally, the structure should promote strategic interdependence across the Pacific. This would strengthen the integrity of the Pacific region, with highly beneficial effects on the Pacific economy.

US-Japan relations and US-China relations are both of critical importance to the stability of the Pacific region. The management of these bilateral relations is not easy, and the increased tensions in those relations have become a concern for the region as a whole. US-China relations are as complex as US-Japan relations. The tensions that have emerged in US relations with China are economic in nature (increased trade imbalance in China's favor), political (in the field of human rights), and strategic (the Taiwan problem). The management of these trans-Pacific problems cannot be left to bilateral channels alone.

Trans-Pacific Economic Conflicts

Perhaps the most serious cause of fragmentation of the Pacific region is economic tensions, particularly trade tensions, across the Pacific. These tensions have been exacerbated by the high and persistent US trade deficits, particularly with East Asia. The US trade deficit with East Asia has increased dramatically,[3] from $2 billion in 1970 to about $86 billion in 1990, amounting to about 90 percent of the total US trade deficit with the Pacific region (table 4). The high and persistent US deficit is due overwhelmingly to macroeconomic imbalances, but it has provided the excuse for the threats of retaliation through the use of the Super 301 provision of the 1988 Omnibus Trade and Competitiveness Act. East Asia also has become the main target of discriminatory measures and bilateral pressures to resolve trade problems. The increased prominence of bilateral and unilateral actions in US trade policy has become a major irritant across the Pacific.

Two developments could threaten the Pacific economy. The first is the development of a North American economic regionalism that does not include East Asia. Free trade agreements are essentially discriminatory; American assurances that the North American Free Trade Agreement (NAFTA) would not discriminate against East Asia are viewed with some skepticism. It is important, however, that other Asia-Pacific countries not overreact to NAFTA. The agreement of itself does not necessarily threaten East Asia, as Canada and Mexico already trade extensively with the United States, but a further enlargement of the agreement on a solely geographic basis could have serious implications. An important question has been put by Preeg (1992, 88): "Are regional free trade agreements 'building blocs' toward global free trade, or are they strategic economic groupings designed to become more competitive vis-à-vis other blocs? If the latter . . . how should East Asian countries and others not part of a major bloc respond?" This is exactly the problem. The unclear signals coming from North America, and especially from Washington, D.C., have provided the impetus for a second development that could threaten the Pacific: namely, the creation of a narrower, geographically or racially defined Asian regionalism, which the NAFTA concept has encouraged (Morrison 1992).

---

3. East Asia here includes Japan, China, Taiwan, South Korea, Hong Kong, and the ASEAN countries.

Table 4   US trade balances with the Pacific, 1970–90
(millions of dollars)

Country	1970	1980	1990
Brunei	n.a.	−223	47
Indonesia	71	−3,994	−1,784
Malaysia	−220	−1,351	−2,071
Philippines	−133	86	−1,451
Singapore	154	1,048	−2,077
Thailand	44	397	−2,597
China	n.a.	2,591	−11,489
Hong Kong	−597	−2,341	−3,110
South Korea	244	252	−4,888
Taiwan	−56	−2,561	−12,357
Japan	−1,588	−12,183	−44,485
Australia	336	1,311	3,704
New Zealand	−101	−198	−194
Canada	−2,695	−6,604	−10,821
APEC total	−4,519	−23,770	−98,053
Chile	137	795	101
Mexico	405	2,311	2,422
Peru	−148	−271	−74
Papua New Guinea[a]	5	−19	−32
Russia[b]	41	1,029	1,920
PECC total	−4,079	−19,925	−93,716
Cambodia	1	26	n.a.
Laos	8	−1	1
Myanmar	10	20	−3
Vietnam	351	1	7
Mongolia	−1	−2	−2
North Korea	n.a.	n.a.	n.a.
Colombia	109	409	−1,371
Ecuador	11	−89	−867
Total Pacific	−3,612	−19,561	−95,951
EC	1,500	18,873	2,541
Total world	779	−36,178	−123,914

n.a. = not available.
a. Papua New Guinea is represented in PECC by the South Pacific Forum.
b. Figures refer to the former Soviet Union.

Source: International Monetary Fund, *Direction of Trade Statistics* (various issues).

The proposal for an East Asian Economic Group (EAEG), initiated by Malaysia's Prime Minister Mahathir Mohamad in December 1990, was a response to the perceived trend toward economic regional blocs in Europe and North America. Mahathir argued that East Asian countries need to protect their interests by having their own economic arrangement. A further justification for the EAEG concept is the remarkable growth in intra–East Asian economic relations and the potential for their further enhancement through formal intergovernmental arrangements. However, this proposal was objected to on several grounds: the desire to maintain an open international trade regime, the desire not to undermine APEC, the desire not to antagonize the US, and primarily, because of the region's perceived strategic dependence on the United States.

Although the proposal has been watered down to a forum for consultations and renamed as the East Asian Economic Caucus (EAEC), it is essentially abortive. However, in nongovernmental circles, including in Japan, the idea remains alive, and there appears to be a growing number of proponents. An EAEG is seen by many as the most important insurance against a breakdown of the world trading system, exactly in the way Mahathir proposed it initially (*The Asian Wall Street Journal Weekly*, 15 June 1992). Many believe that the rise of geoeconomics in the Pacific has led to the emergence of an East Asian economic community characterized by a high degree of regional integration, manifested at its best by the emerging East Asian production structure with Japan at its core. Projections have shown that by the year 2000 or 2010, the combined GDP of East Asia will be as large as that of North America. Will this trend inevitably lead to a fragmentation of the Pacific region?

The US opposition to EAEG may have produced two effects. First, it may have accorded greater credibility to the proposal and contributed to a negative perception of the United States in the region because of the implied double standard—namely, the United States can be a member of both NAFTA and APEC, but East Asians cannot be members of an EAEG and APEC as well. Second, it may have helped the United States focus more on the Pacific. In opposing EAEG, the United States emphasized that the Pacific is one economic region and that APEC is the most appropriate forum for the region. For the United States, APEC has become an authoritative vehicle for defining a Pacific economic region that includes it. Thus far, East Asians believe, however, that high-level support and enthusiasm for APEC lagged behind the US rhetoric (Morrison 1992).

The above discussion suggests the need to address two problems relating to US policies toward the region. First, the application of its so-called three-track approach to trade, involving the General Agreement on Tariffs and Trade (GATT) in the first track, negotiations of free trade agreements in the second track, and unilateral initiatives in the third track. Where does APEC fit in this strategy? It has been suggested that Pacific economic relations and the US-Japan relationship in particular are three-track in concept, but they are ill-defined in practice and lacking in direction. The unclear application of the three-track approach generally makes other nations suspicious about US motives (Preeg 1992, 81–92). Second—and perhaps this explains why the US seems to lack a clear direction with regard to the Pacific—is its apparent lack of a clear sense of regional identity. This may be caused by its peculiar geographic position—that is, facing both the Atlantic and the Pacific. As Burenstam Linder (1986, 6) observed, "If Asian-Pacific growth causes the United States to focus rather more on the Pacific, this focus will serve to reaffirm the global economic alignment, even though US interests make the country not so much an integrated part of a dynamic Pacific Basin economy as a separate entity in a very special relationship with the Asia-Pacific community?"

Whatever the case, the United States is and should be seen as part of the Pacific economy, simply because of its strong economic interdependence with the region. Or should this derive essentially from some geopolitical notion and an appraisal of how economics are influencing this notion? There is as yet no theory of geoeconomics. The main element of such a theory would be to explain how economics shape geopolitics. Specifically, what is the role of economic interdependence in the formation of a security community, and what are the factors that promote economic "regionalization" or "regionalism"?

The simplest geographic definition of a region is often shaped by the perceived structure of relations among a group of neighboring countries. The term East Asia, for instance, once referred to Northeast Asia alone, but it now encompasses Southeast Asia as well. This is perhaps mainly due to increased economic interactions between the two subregions and the development of a greater sense of affinities (perhaps formed from their mutual experience as targets of US trade policies?). The definition of an *economic* region derives from both functional and geographic considerations, as clearly exemplified by the emerging NETs throughout many parts of East Asia. In fact, Pacific economic regionalization results from both factors. Regionalization differs from regionalism, the latter being the creation of preferential trading arrangements or the result of other types of institutional integration. "Optimal regionalization," as Detlef Lorenz (1992, 84–87) has suggested, should be aimed at improving the region's competitive potential, stabilizing challenges posed by heterogeneity through cooperation, and guaranteeing market access to other regions in the world. This is similar to the ideas embodied in the concept of Pacific "open regionalism" which PECC advocates.[4]

An economic region would inevitably have one or more core members, especially as its borders continue to expand to cover an increased portion of the geographic region. In this process, the functional aspect of regionalization may be compromised to accommodate other important, including geopolitical, considerations. A case in point was the acceptance of the former Soviet Union as a member of PECC. The strength or weakness of the core would determine the depth of the resulting integration. It has been taken for granted that at least the US and Japan—the two largest

---

4. The San Francisco Declaration was adopted at the PECC IX General Meeting in San Francisco in September 1992. It stresses that Pacific economic cooperation should contribute to a stronger, more open global economic system.

economies in the region—should be in the core and that in the absence of either one, the core would be weak. In addition, the great diversity of the Pacific region is often seen as an obstacle to the formation of a strong core. However, this may well constitute the region's greatest asset. Economic complementarities, for instance, could form the basis for the establishment of a strong core. Indeed, the so-called "flying geese" paradigm rests on this notion.

The Pacific region is the Pacific economic region. Economic forces will be the decisive factor in the creation of a Pacific regional structure. In the past, military security lay at the heart of international order. But the new order in the Pacific will be shaped mainly by the thickening web of economic interdependence. In any case, the emergence of a Pacific regional structure cannot be rooted in geopolitics alone (Cleveland 1984). The architects of the postwar international order were initially convinced that the way to structure world order for global governance was by creating a string of strong regional organizations, based on concepts of geopolitics. This turned out not to be workable, as the Central Treaty Organization[5] and the Southeast Asia Treaty Organization had shown. Seizaburo Sato also pointed to the region's geostrategic diversity, as reflected in the divergent security interests of countries in the region (Sato 1989). It remains to be seen whether the post–Cold War era will see a greater convergence of security interests among the Pacific countries. It also remains to be seen whether economic interdependence alone, in the absence of converging security interests, will provide a sufficiently strong foundation for the creation of a Pacific regional economy.

The theory is that economic interdependence, resulting from intensive economic transactions, brings about closer and stronger ties in trade, technology, and capital. These ties serve to multiply interconnections between countries, and they will force governments and the private sector to coordinate their actions. Economic interdependence is traditionally seen to exist only among industrialized countries, but in the Pacific this interdependence also encompasses the newly industrializing economies (NIEs) and developing economies. This phenomenon deserves explanation since, after all, the strengthening of interdependence derives from policy. For one thing, interdependence is rarely symmetrical. For another, interdependence is not without costs: it constrains the freedom of governments to act. Why, for instance, have the ASEAN countries opted for a strategy of economic interdependence? The answer can be found only in the economic imperative of security—namely, security in the sense of comprehensive security—as perceived by these nations, and this strategy will be employed so long as economic interdependence produces growth.

---

5. CENTO comprised Britain, Iran, Iraq, Turkey, Pakistan, and the United States. It was dissolved in 1979.

Table 5 Intra-Pacific trade, 1970–90

	1970	1980	1990
Intra-Pacific trade			
(billions of dollars)	60.94	377.99	939.34
Intra–North American trade			
Billions of dollars	22.08	102.22	229.86
Share of Intra-Pacific trade	36.2	27.0	24.5
Intra–East Asian trade			
Billions of dollars	10.55	100.74	286.33
Share of Intra-Pacific trade	17.3	26.7	30.5
Trade between North America and East Asia			
Billions of dollars	18.65	118.64	325.93
Share of Intra-Pacific trade	30.6	31.4	34.7

Source: International Monetary Fund, *Direction of Trade Statistics*, various issues.

Trade interdependence among the countries in the Pacific (with the exception of the centrally planned economies and those that have recently abandoned central planning) is most pronounced and needs little further elaboration here. Intra-Pacific trade increased from about 20 percent of total world trade in 1970 to close to 30 percent in 1990. As shown in table 5, throughout the 1970–90 period, intra–North American trade declined as a percentage of total intra-Pacific trade, while the share of intra–East Asian trade significantly increased from 17.3 percent to over 30 percent. As of 1990, intra-Pacific trade was accounted for, in order of importance, by trade between East Asia and North America (34.7 percent), by intra–East Asian trade (30.5 percent), and by intra–North American trade (24.5 percent). This shows that trade interdependence within East Asia is growing but also that trade interdependence between East Asia and North America (the United States in particular) is even stronger. In other words, the trend toward East Asian regionalization has been balanced by a parallel deepening of economic interdependence with other parts of the world. This resulted not only from the high and increasing interdependence between Japan and the United States, but also from the growing trade and investment interdependence between the United States and the rest of East Asia.

Economic interdependence in the Pacific is also characterized by capital flows, particularly the flows of foreign direct investment (FDI). These flows have produced a profound geoeconomic change in the region—namely, the emergence of a regional production structure with Japan as its core (Soesastro 1990). In 1990 the flows of Japanese FDI into the region was about two-thirds of total Japanese outgoing FDI and was almost four times the value of US outgoing FDI in the region. The stock of Japanese FDI in the Pacific region stood at a little over $200 billion in 1990, whereas the stock of US FDI was about $144 billion (table 6). It should be noted that US FDI stock values are based on historical costs and thus they tend

Table 6 Japanese and US FDI in the Pacific, 1990
(million of dollars)

	Japanese FDI		US FDI	
	Fiscal 1990	Cumulative[a]	1990	Investment position[b]
Brunei	—	109	−1	122
Indonesia	1,105	11,540	59	3,827
Malaysia	725	3,231	241	1,425
Philippines	258	1,580	48	1,655
Singapore	840	6,555	862	3,971
Thailand	1,154	4,422	237	1,515
China	349	2,823	−97	289
Hong Kong	1,785	9,850	439	6,537
South Korea	284	4,138	321	2,096
Taiwan	446	2,731	189	2,273
Japan	—	—	1,443	20,994
Australia	3,669	16,063	1,032	14,529
New Zealand	231	925	1,895	3,139
Canada	1,064	5,656	2,280	68,431
US	26,128	130,529	—	—
APEC total	38,038	200,043	8,948	130,659
Chile	30	311	293	1,341
Mexico	168	1,874	1,949	9,360
Peru	—	696	−346	600
Papua New Guinea[a]	9	226	68	232
Russia[b]	25	247	1	1
PECC total	38,270	203,397	10,913	142,193
Cambodia	—	n.a.	—	n.a.
Laos	—	n.a.	—	n.a.
Myanmar	—	n.a.	—	n.a.
Vietnam	—	n.a.	—	n.a.
Mongolia	—	n.a.	—	n.a.
North Korea	—	n.a.	—	n.a.
Colombia	59	131	115	2,043
Ecuador	—	n.a.	−19	389
Total Pacific	38,329	203,528	11,009	144,625
Total world	56,911	310,808	33,437	421,494

n.a. = not available.
FDI = Foreign direct investment
APEC = Asia Pacific Economic Cooperation
PECC = Pacific Economic Cooperation Council
a. Fiscal 1951–90.
b. Direct investment position on a historical-cost basis.

Source: Ministry of Finance, Japan; US Department of Commerce, *Survey of Current Business*, various issues.

to underestimate the true stock, and most US FDI in the region was undertaken much earlier than Japanese FDI. South Korea, Taiwan, Hong Kong, and Singapore have now become important investors in the region as well. They invest in both the developing countries and industrialized countries. The overall investment picture in the region is that of cross-investments in the entire region, but Japan remains by far the dominant source of investment, especially in manufacturing.

Another feature of the regional investment scene is that FDI flows into the United States from the region are higher than US FDI outflow into the region, the former surpassing the latter by $7 billion in 1990. Thus, the US position as a net capital importer can also be clearly seen in the regional context. Japan has become the main source of financing of the US current account deficits. The main destinations of the US FDI in the Pacific are the industrialized countries (Canada, Australia, New Zealand, Japan) plus Mexico. The United States has not followed the pattern of Japanese FDI toward globalizing and relocating industries in East Asia with the aim of strengthening international competitiveness. East Asia offers attractive production and export bases, but the United States has not taken advantage of them. Richard Solomon has articulated the importance of this development: for the United States, East Asia has become the focal challenge to its own economic competitiveness. If the United States meets this challenge, its leadership and its security role in the Pacific region will be enhanced. According to Solomon (1992), this is what the age of geoeconomics means for the United States.

Although macroeconomic policies are key to correcting the imbalances in US external accounts, enhancing US export competitiveness should also be seen as one of its main challenges. It could meet this challenge by integrating its production structure more closely with that of East Asia. This will mean a greater involvement of US capital and technology. Is the United States prepared to take this course? Many in the United States view economic interdependence with Japan and East Asia in general as posing a threat to the health of the US economy, leading "to the progressive decline of the US industrial base and the continued erosion of US technological leadership" (e.g., Cronin 1992). There is an equally strong perception of a clash of competing economic systems that places the United States at a competitive disadvantage. But this should provide more rather than less impetus for US integration of its production structure with East Asia.

This course requires that US-Japan relations be managed well. The management of this relationship appears to be more delicate in the post–Cold War era. Shared US-Japan security concerns are now less likely to mitigate their intensifying economic tensions and rivalry. The relationship will have to be based on mutual recognition of the value of economic interdependence. The Structural Impediments Initiative (SII), if conducted well, could definitely be a forerunner. Brzezinski (1992) suggested that an enlargement of NAFTA across the Pacific would create a larger framework for a cooperative US-Japan relationship. The notion of a Japan-US Free Trade Area has also been launched several times. In time, a Japan-US FTA will have to be expanded into a Pacific Free Trade Area (PAFTA). However, this arrangement would result in a totally different Pacific economy. What about the alternative: APEC, which ideally would be based on a notion of open regionalism? APEC is an experiment, and open regionalism is also still on the drawing board. However, this is an experiment worth undertaking. It certainly is wrong to view APEC simply as insurance in case the Uruguay Round ends in a failure. What if APEC itself fails? Will the region end up with a single PAFTA or with both a competing NAFTA and an East Asian Free Trade Area (EAFTA)? Or is APEC basically seen as a forerunner of PAFTA? These are the bottom-line questions.

Conclusion

It may be appropriate to entertain the idea of a PAFTA, but it is important to recognize that a PAFTA is a different kind of insurance from an APEC, which ideally would be based on open regionalism. APEC has greater flexibility. Through its flexible agenda setting, it is "modular multilateralism" in operation: multilateral because it will involve many players and modular because it can accommodate shifting actors according to the issue at hand. The leadership in APEC is also likely to be "issue-specific" rather than hegemonic. This flexibility is what the uncertain environment of the post–Cold War world demands and what is suitable for this vast, diverse region.

The splitting of the Pacific economy into NAFTA and EAFTA will be an accident. But it can still happen, however small the odds. It could happen if East Asian countries overreact to NAFTA. The implications will be far-reaching: it will fulfill the nightmare of a three-bloc world. This will not be in the interest of any one of the blocs. As Joseph Nye (1992) aptly stated, a three-bloc world runs counter to the thrust of global technological trends. While regional trade will certainly grow, many firms would not want to be limited to one-third of the global market and would resist such restrictive regionalism. Furthermore, restrictive regional blocs run against nationalistic concerns of some of the lesser states that need a global system to protect themselves against domination by large neighbors. A US-led NAFTA and a Japan-led EAFTA definitely would lead to contentious relations. In addition, the hegemon role in each bloc will be played by the country that is trusted least by other countries in their respective blocs: Japan in East Asia and the United States in the Western Hemisphere. This will create instabilities within each region (Krause 1991). The cost of an EAEG as insurance appears then to be too high.

How can this accident be prevented? Two things need to be done. First, a bargain will have to be made; there should be a quid pro quo—the surrender of a further enlargement of NAFTA in exchange for giving up of any kind of an East Asian restrictive economic grouping. Second, new efforts must be made to make APEC compellingly attractive. A pragmatic agenda for APEC, as proposed by Andrew Elek (1992), for instance, would focus on tackling four kinds of impediments to economic transactions in the region:

- market access barriers, including the heavy protection of some aspects of agriculture in Northeast Asia and North America, and the protection of textiles and clothing producers by Australia and North America;

- uncertainty about future market access, as countries increasingly resort to arbitrary and discriminatory measures to deal with losses of market share because of imports and to threats of unilateral trade retaliation, mostly aimed at East Asia;

- physical bottlenecks, as shortfalls in infrastructure are serious impediments to trade in the most rapidly growing parts of the region, including coastal China, Indonesia, and Thailand;

- differences in domestic rules and legislation, since divergent standards relating to safety, quality, and environmental matters and different approaches to commercial legislation can introduce distortions to regional trade and investment.

As its agenda stands now, APEC definitely needs to return to the drawing board. This proposed agenda would make a good start. APEC should not limit its economic agenda to issues of low politics alone. It should be ready to address issues of high politics as well. This would include efforts to develop a Pacific leadership in global economic development—for instance, through regional trade liberalization—or to help mediate US-Japan economic tensions. In addition, the region should also address regional politico-security issues. When the processes for current Pacific economic cooperation were conceived in the early 1980s, the countries involved strongly felt that this cooperation should be strictly confined to economic matters and that the agenda of any Pacific regional scheme should be free from politico-security issues, as their inclusion might jeopardize the exercise. As the Cold War is over, such inhibitions may no longer be operative. But the question remains whether the region should develop a single overarching regional structure to deal with economic, political, and security issues or whether two separate structures should be evolving. The latter seems to be more realistic, and both will be equally important because they could reinforce and strengthen each other. In this sense, the post–Cold War politico-security environment can have a positive influence on the Pacific economy.

References

Baker, James A., III. 1991. "America in Asia: Emerging Architecture for A Pacific Community." *Foreign Affairs* 70, no. 5 (Winter): 1–18.

Brzezinski, Zbigniew. 1991. "Selective Global Commitment." *Foreign Affairs* 70, no. 4 (Fall): 1–20.

Brzezinski, Zbigniew. 1992. "Order, Disorder, and US Leadership." *The Washington Quarterly* 15, no. 2 (Spring): 5–13.

Cheung, Tai Ming. 1992. "Fangs of the Dragon—Peking's Naval Build-up Sparks ASEAN Reaction." *Far Eastern Economic Review* 13 (August).

Cleveland, Harlan. 1984. "The Future of the Pacific Basin." *Pacific Viewpoint* 25, no. 1.

Cronin, Richard. 1992. "Japan-US Relations in a Post-Cold War Environment: Emerging Trends and Issues for US Policy." Summary of a CRS Seminar, *CRS Report for Congress* (24 March).

Elek, Andrew. 1992. "Pacific Economic Cooperation: Policy Choices for the 1990s." Paper presented at the PECC Trade Policy Forum, Batam (16–17 July).

Evans, Paul. 1992. "Non-Governmental and 'Track Two' Diplomacy: Problems and Prospects." Paper presented at the 6th Asia-Pacific Roundtable on Confidence Building and Conflict Reduction in the Pacific, organized by the Institute of Strategic and International Studies (ISIS) Malaysia, Kuala Lumpur (21–25 June).

Funabashi, Yoichi. 1991. "Japan and the New World Order." *Foreign Affairs* 70, no. 5 (Winter): 64.

Heisbourg, M. Francois. 1992. "The International System and the New Geostrategic Map." Paper presented at the Conference on Towards A New Global Order, organized by the Swedish Institute of International Affairs, Stockholm (17–20 May).

Kahler, Miles. 1992. "Strategic Uses of Economic Interdependence." Paper presented at the Conference on Pacific Security Relations after the Cold War, held in Hong Kong 15–18 June, organized by the Institute on Global Conflict and Cooperation (University of California, San Diego).

Keohane, Robert O. 1984. *After Hegemony—Cooperation and Discord in the World Political Economy.* Princeton, NJ: Princeton University Press.

Krause, Lawrence. 1991. "Can the Pacific Save US-Japanese Economic Relations?" Paper prepared for the Commission on US-Japan Relations for the Twenty First Century, Washington (July).

Linder, Staffan Burenstam. 1986. *The Pacific Century: Economic and Political Consequences of Asian-Pacific Dynamism.* Stanford, CA: Stanford University Press.

Lorenz, Detlef. 1992. "Economic Geography and the Political Economy of Regionalization: The Example of Western Europe." *American Economic Review* 82, no. 2 (May): 84–87.

Moltz, James Clay. 1992. "Conceptualizing Security Threats in the Pacific." Paper presented at the Conference on Pacific Security Relations after the Cold War, held in Hong Kong 15–18 June, organized by the Institute on Global Conflict and Cooperation (University of California, San Diego).

Morrison, Charles E. 1992. "The United States in Post-Cold War Asia." Paper presented at the 6th Asia-Pacific Roundtable on Confidence Building and Conflict Reduction in the Pacific, organized by the Institute of Strategic and International Studies (ISIS) Malaysia, Kuala Lumpur, (21–25 June).

Nye, Joseph S., Jr. 1992. "What New World Order?" *Foreign Affairs* 71, no. 2 (Spring): 83–96.

Preeg, Ernest H. 1992. "The US Leadership Role in World Trade: Past, Present, and Future." *The Washington Quarterly* 15, no. 2 (Spring) 88.

Sato, Seizaburo. 1989. "The Interrelations between Global and Regional Security Issues in the Pacific-Asian Region." In Robert A. Scalapino et al., eds., *Asian Security Issues: Regional and Global.* Berkeley: Institute of East Asian Studies, University of California.

Scalapino, Robert. 1991. "The United States and Asia: Future Prospects." *Foreign Affairs* 70, no. 5 (Winter): 19–40.

Scalapino, Robert. 1992. "Developments in the Asia Pacific Region in the 1990s—An Overall Assessment." Paper presented at the symposium on The Changing Asia-Pacific Scene in the 1990s: Security, Cooperation, and Development, organized by the China Center for International Studies, Beijing (1–12 August).

Schlesinger, James. 1991. "New Instabilities, New Priorities." *Foreign Policy* no. 85 (Winter): 24–39.

Soesastro, Hadi. 1990. "Southeast Asia's Expectation of Japan with Respect to Investment." *JASA—A New Era of Cooperation.* Kuala Lumpur: Institute of Strategic and International Studies Malaysia.

Solomon, Richard H. 1992. "America and Asian Security in an Era of Geoeconomics." Address before the Pacific Rim Forum, San Diego (15 May).

Sopiee, Noordin. 1992. "The New World Order: Implications for the Asia Pacific." Paper presented at the 6th Asia-Pacific Roundtable on Confidence Building and Conflict Reduction in the Pacific, organized by the Institute of Strategic and International Studies Malaysia, Kuala Lumpur (21–25 June).

Wanandi, Jusuf. 1992. "Developments in the Asia Pacific Region." Paper presented at the Symposium on The Changing Asia-Pacific Scene in the 1990s: Security, Cooperation, and Development, organized by the China Center for International Studies, Beijing (10–12 August).

Index

Africa 100, 161, 324
Aggarwal, Raj 57
Aggressive unilateralism 118, 120
Agriculture
    environmental effects of trade
      liberalization in 351–56
    in China 356–57
    in Europe 100, 146, 149, 354
    in GATT 71, 176–77
    in Mexico 176
    in NAFTA 176–77
    in Northeast Asia 354, 386
Air transport, trade negotiations in 87–88
Andean Group 54
Anderson, Kym 203
Andriessen, Frans 143
Antidumping
    in NAFTA 171, 175
    in the Australia–New Zealand free
      trade area 81
    in the European Community 80, 116
    in the United States 116
    in the Uruguay Round 120
Article XII (GATT) 89, 94
Article XVI (GATT) 177
Article XXIV (GATT) 7, 71, 100, 103, 155,
    160–62, 179
ASEAN Free Trade Area, proposed 112,
    186, 268
Asian newly industrializing economies
    (NIEs). *See also specific country*
    business–government relations in 53
    economic interdependence of 381

high–technology trade in 43
intraindustry trade 32
inward FDI 225, 274, 277–79, 280–81,
    295
outward FDI 225–26, 246, 274, 276,
    281–82, 295
shift in comparative advantage of 86
triangular trade of 123
Asianization of security issues 372–77
Asia–Pacific Economic Cooperation
    (APEC)
    and GATT-plus arrangements 128
    as "Asian OECD" 9
    as form of superregionalism 163
    as "modular multilateralism" 385
    as source of discipline over
      NAFTA 128
    founding of secretariat in
      Singapore 163
    market access issues in 386
    need for regional public goods
      improvement within 219, 386
    possible evolution into free trade
      area 8, 9
    post–Uruguay Round agenda
      for 218–20, 386
    proposed sectoral liberalization in 219
    role in migration policy 338
    role in policy harmonization 219, 386
    US support for 379
Asia-Pacific region
    absence of trade discrimination in 188
    basic indicators 371

Asia-Pacific region (continued)
  classification of regional groupings 227
  complementarities in trade in 203
  core membership of 380–81
  defense expenditures in 373–75
  demand and supply of labor in 12,
    325, 328–29
  FDI in 11, 273, 382
  future competition with Eastern
    Europe 154
  implications of European integration
    for 154–56, 214
  implications of NAFTA for 178–79,
    213–15, 220
  intensity-of-trade indexes for 195,
    200–04, 205
  intraindustry trade indexes for 208
  intraregional trade within 183–86, 382
  migration to and from 324, 328
  nature of trade growth in 187–88
  potential leading countries within 125
  prospects for economic
    integration 8–9, 101, 124, 126, 128,
    217
  shares of world trade 183
  trade liberalization in 187
  US trade deficits with 377–78
  weak integration of Canada and
    Mexico in 202
Asia-Pacific Migration Council,
  proposed 338
Association of Southeast Asian Nations
  (ASEAN)
  intraregional trade 51
  inward FDI 225–26, 275, 277, 281–83
  outward FDI 274, 275
  potential for regional leadership 125
  proposed free trade area in 112, 186,
    268
  prospects for RTA with United
    States 162, 216–17
Australia 76, 81, 208, 211–12, 217, 324,
  332, 336
Austria 145, 147
Automobiles
  FDI in 283
  in NAFTA 166–68, 174, 179

Baht Economic Zone 230
Baker, James A., III 376
Balance of power, regional 367
Balassa, Bela 34
Baldwin, Robert E. 116

Baltic republics 150
Bank of Japan 318–19
Basel Convention 172
Batam Economic Zone 234
Batam Industrial Park 236, 244, 248
Batam island 236, 240, 244, 247–48, 266,
  268
Bergsten, C. Fred 35, 83, 95, 121
Bergstrand, Jeffrey H. 34
Bhagwati, Jagdish 112, 116, 118, 330
Bicycle theory 7
Bilateral trade arrangements. See
  Regional trade arrangements
Bintan Integrated Development
  Project 244
Bintan island 241, 248–49
Borjas, G. 333
Bowen, Harry P. 25
Brainard, Robert 29
Bryant, R. C. 95
Brzezinski, Zbigniew 365, 368
"Bubble economy," in Japan 279
Burden sharing 373–75
Burniaux, J. M. 351
Business practices, restrictive 26, 72,
  81–83, 84, 121, 203, 276. See also
  Keiretsu

Cabotage 88
Cairns Group 7, 178
Canada 97, 100, 164–77, 202
Canada–US FTA 97, 113, 116, 164–77
Capital controls, in Europe 137
Capital formation 27, 28, 284
Capital goods, trade in 22, 29
Capital markets 317–20
Castles, Stephen 323
Catalytic liberalization 85
Central American Common Market 100
Central banks, foreign reserves
  of 310–12, 314
Chaebol 72
Chain migration 325
Chemical fertilizers 352–55
Chile 6, 100
Chile-Mexico bilateral trade
  arrangement 100
Chile-Venezuela bilateral trade
  arrangement 100
China
  agriculture in 356–57
  inward FDI 263, 276, 277, 282, 286
  open-door policy 250–51, 253

options for regional integration 216
outward FDI 275
potential for regional leadership 125
security issues 369
territorial disputes 368, 373
trade and relations with Hong
    Kong 191, 202, 249–56, 257–60
trade and relations with Korea 369
trade and relations with
    Taiwan 249–51, 257–61
trade and relations with United
    States 376–77
Cline, William R. 83, 351
Clinton, Bill 173
Closer Economic Relations
    arrangement 226
Coal, environmental effects of trade
    liberalization 350–51
Cold War, impact of end of 4, 12, 66,
    161, 365–87
Commodities, trade in 23
Commodity markets, use of dollar
    in 302, 305
Common Agricultural Policy (EC) 100,
    146, 149
Common trade policy (EC) 146
Comparative advantage
    and environmental issues 344–48
    created versus innate 56–58
    dynamic 41, 122
    East Asian shift in 86
    in high–technology trade 44
    revealed 44
    static versus dynamic 56
    versus competitiveness 41
Competition
    among multinational corporations 39
    -enhancing effects of RTAs 114
    for skilled migrants 333
    future, between Eastern Europe and
        Asia–Pacific region 154
    in intraindustry trade 38
Competition policy
    extraterritoriality and 79
    in European Community 80
    in future trade negotiations 78–81
    in GATT 78–81
    in NAFTA 171
    intrafirm trade and 38
    need for harmonization 79
Complementarity, economic
    as basis for regionalization 232–33,
        381
    in Asia–Pacific region 203

in GSC 251–52
in SIJORI 241, 244
Computers, trade in 39, 166
"Concentric-arcs" approach to regional
    cooperation 366
Contingent protection 77, 90, 116,
    118–20, 155. See also Antidumping;
    Subsidies and countervailing
    duties
Convention on International Trade in
    Endangered Species (CITES) 172,
    347
Convergence in world trade policies 7
Cooling-off period for trade disputes 93
Cooper, Richard N. 57, 188
Cooperative economic groupings in East
    Asia 227. See also Regional trade
    arrangements, Subregional
    economic zones
Corporate Average Fuel Economy
    (CAFE) standards 168
Countervailing duties. See Subsidies
Cultural issues, impact on global trading
    system 81–86
Cultural linkages, in SREZs 234, 252–53,
    264
Currencies. See also specific currencies;
    Strategic exchange rate policy
    as store of value 310–12
    central bank holdings of 310–12, 314
    use in invoicing 300–08, 312–16
    used in SREZs 264
Currency union, in Europe. See
    European Monetary System
Customs unions, theory of 191
Cyprus 150

Dango 82
Debt, external. See External debt
Defense expenditures, in Asia–Pacific
    region 373–75
de la Torre, Augusto 49
Delors, Jacques 142
Denmark 138
Derogations, as subsystem of global
    trading system 69
Developing countries. See also specific
    country
    as leaders of the global trading
        system 7
    environmental issues in 349
    intraregional trade among 53
    regional integration among 71, 160–61

Developing countries *(continued)*
  regional integration with developed
    countries 117, 156, 157
  resistance to strengthening GATT 92
  special and differential treatment
    for 118
Direct foreign investment. *See* Foreign
  direct investment
Discrimination, trade, 68, 116, 127, 155,
  188, 191–93, 202, 216, 377, 386
Discriminatory integration 50, 136,
  154–55, 186–89, 193–94, 213, 216–20
Dispute-settlement procedures
  in NAFTA 172, 173–75
  in the Uruguay Round 120
Distribution system, in Japan 72, 82, 121
Dollar, US 299–305, 311, 314
Dornbusch, Rudiger 85, 126
Drysdale, Peter 202
Dunkel, Arthur 164
Duty drawbacks 168

East African Common Market 100
East Asia
  advantages and disadvantages of
    trading bloc in 121–25
  intraregional trade 183–86
  Japan as hegemon in 125
  perspective on regionalism 113–17
  relative absence of RTAs in 49, 101,
    186
  shift in comparative advantage 86
  support of Uruguay Round 127
  triangular pattern of trade 123
East Asian economies
  bilateral trade shares 126
  extraregional orientation 122
  factor endowments 197
  industrial policy in 121
  interest in supporting
    multilateralism 127
  migration policy 335
  need to promote intraregional
    trade 128
  perception as unfair traders 118
  shares of world trade 119, 183
  similar patterns of industrialization 122
  trade and relations with Japan 123,
    125–26, 212, 320
  trade and relations with United
    States 54, 117–21, 124, 128, 179, 202,
    214–17, 372–78
  trade barriers in 121

East Asian Economic Caucus,
  proposed 112
East Asian Economic Group 6, 101, 112,
  124, 128, 378–79, 385
Eastern Europe
  accession to European Community 10,
    113, 142–43, 148
  future competition with Asia–Pacific
    countries 11, 154
Economic and Monetary Union, in
  Europe 5, 137–38, 146, 152
Economic complementarity. *See*
  Complementarity, economic
Economic growth effect, of RTAs 115
Economic integration. *See also* Regional
  trade arrangements
  definition 189
  general theory of 189–93
  intraindustry trade and 209
  "market" versus "institutional" 188–89
  trade resistances and 190–91
Economies of scale 34, 114
Education participation rates 27
Ehlermann, Claus–Dieter 153
Electronics, trade in 45, 166, 277, 279
Eminent persons group
  for migration policy 339
  for the Uruguay Round 98
Endogenous growth theory 41
Energy policy, bilateral agreements
  in 104
Enterprise for the Americas Initiative 6,
  54, 101, 113, 163, 213, 218
Entrepôt trade 19, 253, 261
Environmental issues
  as cover for protectionism 360
  comparative advantage and 344–48
  economic theory of 344–48
  effect of increasing incomes on 349
  effect of trade liberalization on 349–59
  FDI and 283
  growing worldwide concern
    over 342–33
  harmonization of policy in 358, 359
  in NAFTA 164, 172
  institutional structures to address 343
  international differences in attitudes
    toward 359
  market failures and 343
  trade disputes arising from 12, 347–48
  use of trade policies to address 12,
    343, 360
Europe. *See also* Eastern Europe;
  Western Europe

high-technology trade in 44
implications of integration for
    Asia–Pacific trade 154, 156, 214
integration as reconstruction
    strategy 161
migration to and within 336, 337
obstacles to growth 4
European Central Bank 138
European Community
    accession of new members 10, 113,
        135, 140–41, 144–46, 148–57
    agriculture in 100, 146, 149
    antidumping policy of 80, 116
    competition policy of 80
    deepening of integration 113, 135,
        136–40, 151
    Economic and Monetary Union 5,
        137–38, 146, 152
    effect of enlargement on Asia–Pacific
        region 154–56, 214
    effect of enlargement on GATT 155
    foreign and security policy 139–40,
        153–54
    intraregional trade 50
    judicial and domestic affairs 140
    own-currency invoicing 305
    preoccupation with internal affairs 5,
        118, 153–54
    trade and relations with Japan 82, 83
    trade and relations with United
        States 89
    unilateral trade measures by 91
    "variable geometry" of integration
        in 138
European Council 139
European Court of Justice 80, 139
European Economic Area 54, 113, 135,
    142–43, 145, 156
European Free Trade Association
    (EFTA) 10, 113, 135, 142–43, 144–48,
    154, 161
European Monetary Institute 137
European Monetary System 113, 137–38,
    152, 299, 317
European Political Area 142–43
Exchange rate policy, strategic 312–16
Exchange rates. See Currencies
Export-GDP ratios 18, 19
Export-Import Bank of Japan 281
Export processing zones 237, 241, 283,
    286
External debt 312, 315
Externalities, and resistances to trade 193
Extraregional import ratios 197–200

Extraterritoriality, in competition
    policy 79

Factor costs, relative 243, 253
Factor endowments 24–29, 197, 200
Factor intensity, estimation of 24
Farming. See Agriculture
Fifth-freedom rights 88
Financial deregulation, in Japan 316, 317
Financing bills, in Japan 317–18, 319
Finger, J. Michael 76
Finland 145, 147
Fisheries 147
"Flying geese" pattern of
    development 50, 122, 381
Foreign debt. See External debt
Foreign direct investment. See also
    Multinational corporations
    and domestic capital formation 284
    and employment 284–85
    and expansion of sales
        networks 289–95
    and exports 286, 291, 293
    and intrafirm trade 291–93
    and procurement of inputs 293–95
    and technology transfer 286–89
    as means of industrial adjustment 295
    benefits and drawbacks 273, 283,
        289–91, 295
    by small and medium-sized firms 281
    environmental issues relating to 283
    factors promoting 279–80
    impact on development 283–95
    in manufacturing 277, 283
    in NAFTA 173
    in nonmanufacturing sectors 276
    labor and capital intensities of 286
    policies to promote 280, 281, 283, 295
    shortages of social capital and 295
Foreign direct investment, inward
    in ASEAN countries 225–26, 275, 277,
        281, 283
    in Asia–Pacific region 11, 273, 382
    in China 263, 276–77, 282, 286
    in Korea 284–85, 287
    in NIEs 274–75, 277, 280
    in SIJORI 240, 242, 246–48, 264
    in Singapore 276
    in SREZs 234, 264
Foreign direct investment, outward
    by ASEAN countries 274–75, 277
    by China 275
    by Japan 38, 225, 274–80, 382, 384

Foreign direct investment, outward
(*continued*)
  by NIEs 225–26, 274–75, 281–82
  by Singapore 264
  by Taiwan 281
  by United States 274, 382–84
Foreign exchange markets 309–10
Foreign reserves 310–12, 314
Frankel, Jeffrey A. 126, 307
Free trade areas. *See* Regional trade
  arrangements
Freight and insurance costs. *See*
  Transport costs
Fujian 250, 260, 264
Fukasaku, Kiichiro 209
Funabashi, Yoichi 95

Garten, Jeffrey E. 48
General Agreement on Tariffs and Trade
  (GATT). *See also specific articles*;
  Global trading system; Uruguay
  Round
  absence of system performance
    evaluation within 68
  agriculture in 71, 176–77
  as indirect mechanism for free
    trade 105
  derogations from 67, 69, 71, 91
  developing countries and 92
  extension to nongoods trade 86–88
  impact of European enlargement
    on 155
  ineffectiveness against discriminatory
    protection 116
  key principles 69
  market access issues 86–88
  Mexican accession to 76
  need for institutional strengthening 91
  need for new approaches 85
  Secretariat 92
  status of nongovernment entities
    in 68, 78
  system analysis of 69–75
  textiles and apparel in 71, 120, 169
  Tokyo Round 82
  Trade Policy Review Mechanism 77,
    92, 93, 120
GATT-plus arrangement 121, 127, 128
Generalized System of Preferences 50,
  94, 100, 277
Geoeconomics 380, 384
Geographic proximity. *See also*
  Locational factors

as determinant of RTA formation 54
as rationale for SREZs 233–34, 236,
  252–53
Germany 57, 141, 149, 302, 324, 336
Global trading system. *See also*
  General Agreement on Tariffs
  and Trade
  as organizational framework 73–74
  competition policy and 78–81
  differing views on importance of 66
  domestic institutions and 72
  impact of cultural issues on 81–86
  impact of end of Cold War on 66
  impact of NAFTA on 11, 175
  maintaining openness in 88–96
  major-power leadership of 92–96
  nonconventional issues and
    arrangements 69, 71, 72
  organizing principles 10
  performance-oriented goals for 67,
    74–75, 104–06
  political economy of 77–78
  prospects for 117–21
  weaknesses of 68
Globalization of markets 370
Goh Chok Tong 229
Government procurement 177
Graham, Edward M. 86
Gray-area measures 116, 118, 120
Great Britain 100, 138, 151–52, 318
Greater South China (GSC) Economic
  Zone
  basic indicators 239
  comparison with SIJORI 263–64
  component areas of 226
  cultural linkages in 252–53
  economic complementarity
    within 251–52
  investment in 257–61
  political considerations in 249–51
  relative factor costs in 253
  role of Hong Kong in 191, 231,
    249–58, 261
  role of Taiwan in 252
Greenaway, David 31
Grimwade, Nigel 44
Grinols, E. 90
Grossman, Gene M. 43, 46
Group of Seven 4, 95
Growth triangles 229–30. *See also specific
  arrangements*; Subregional economic
  zones
Guangdong 250, 251, 260, 262–64
Gulf War 324

Habibie, B. J. 229, 240
Hamilton, B. 323
Harassment, contingent protection as 90
Hardwoods, tropical, trade in 347
Harmonization
  of competition policies 79
  of environmental policies 358, 359
  use of APEC to achieve 219, 386
Helpman, Elhanan 43, 46
High-technology trade
  as share of total manufacturing
    trade 24, 43
  determinants of 47
  in Europe 44
  in Japan 44
  in NIEs 43
  in United States 44
  intrafirm 35, 38
  intraindustry 35
  multinational corporations and 45
  policies to promote 46, 295
  revealed comparative advantage in 44
  trends in 18, 24, 43–45
Hindley, Brian 116
Hirata, Akira 291
Honda Motor Co., Ltd. 166–67, 180
Hong Kong
  as example of free trade 187
  dollar 264
  economic role in GSC 191, 231,
    249–58, 261
  sectoral composition of economy 262
  trade and relations with China 191,
    202, 249–56, 257–60
Hub–and–spoke type of RTAs 97
Hufbauer, Gary C. 6, 26, 86, 92, 97
Human capital flows. See Migration
Human capital formation 28
Human rights 372

Iceland 156
Import licensing 168
Import shares of GDP. See Trade shares
  of GDP
India 218
Indonesia 229–31, 240–41, 243–44,
  247–49, 266–68, 373
Industrial estates 240, 267
Industrial policy 29, 57, 121
Industries Assistance Commission
  (Australia) 29, 58, 77
Infrastructure
  in GSC 251

in SIJORI 244, 248
intraregional 128
joint development in SREZs 235, 236
use of APEC to address 386
Institution building 12, 91, 366, 371, 372
Institutional versus "market"
  integration 188–89, 220
Integration, economic. See Economic
  integration; Regional trade
  arrangements
Intellectual property protection 94, 118,
  120, 164, 178
Intensity-of-trade indexes 195, 200–05
International Labor Organization 338
International Organization for
  Migration 338
International Trade Organization,
  proposed 69
Internationalization of the yen 299–321
Interregional trade intensity indexes 115
Intrabloc trade. See Intraregional trade
Intrafirm trade
  and oligopolistic behavior 10
  by multinationals 35, 38, 292
  determinants of 39–40
  extraterritoriality and 38
  FDI and 291–93
  measurement of 196, 203, 208–12
  RTAs and 50
  trends in 35–37
  welfare implications 10
Intraindustry trade
  adjustment costs and 32
  and economic integration 209
  as measure of trade resistance 196
  benefits of 10, 32
  competition in 38
  determinants of 34–35, 210–11
  in Japan 32, 34, 211–12
  in manufactures 33, 208–09
  in NIEs 32
  in the United States 34
  measurement of 31–33, 196, 208
  political-economic stability of 33
  technological change and 34
  trends in 17, 18, 32
  variability 34
Intraregional trade
  and political linkages 52
  determinants of 54
  in ASEAN 51
  in Asia–Pacific region 183–86, 382
  in developing countries 53
  in East Asia 128, 183–86

Intraregional trade *(continued)*
  in European Community 50
  measurement of 48–49
  shares of total trade 51–52
Investment. *See also* Capital formation;
    Foreign direct investment
  in GSC 257–61
  in SREZs 264
  international agreements on 86–87, 173
Invoicing, currency denomination
    of 300–08
Ivory, trade in 347

J-curve 317
Jackson, John H. 91
Japan
  barriers to East Asian integration
    posed by 125
  "bubble economy" of 279
  business practices 26, 38, 72, 81–83, 84,
    121, 203, 276
  capital markets in 317–20
  cultural differences with United
    States 81
  factor endowments of 200
  FDI by 38, 225, 276–80, 382, 384
  financial deregulation in 316, 317
  formation of yen bloc 51
  high-technology trade in 44
  intraindustry trade 32, 34, 211–12
  migration policy 335
  obstacles to growth 4
  openness to trade 19, 121
  own-currency invoicing 302–08, 312–16
  participation in SREZs 232
  perception as unfair trader 118
  RTAs involving 8, 49, 100, 101,
    215–16, 385
  sectoral composition of trade 304, 306
  security issues 368, 369
  share of regional trade 125
  that can say "no" 85
  trade share of GDP 200
Japan, foreign relations
  with other Asian countries 320
  with the European Community 82, 83
  with the United States 8, 83–84, 384
Japan Sea Economic Zone 229, 236
Johor. *See* Johor–Singapore–Riau growth
    triangle
Johor-Singapore-Riau growth triangle
    (SIJORI)
  as vehicle for ASEAN cooperation 243

  basic indicators 239
  comparison with GSC 263–64
  component areas 229
  economic complementarities in 241,
    244
  effects on Johor 246
  effects on Riau 247–49
  FDI in 241–43, 246, 248
  founding of 229
  infrastructure needs of 244
  political commitment to 239, 241, 264
  rationale for 238–39
  relative factor costs in 243
  role of Singapore in 229, 238–49
Joint development–type SREZs 235–36
Jones, K. 92

Kahler, Miles 369
Keiretsu 38, 72, 81, 203, 276. *See also*
    Japan, business practices
Keohane, Robert O. 366
Knetter, Michael M. 303
Korea
  accession to OECD 9
  chaebol 72
  defense expenditures 373
  economic liberalization in 280, 281
  external debt 312
  FDI in 284–85, 287
  import-diversification system 122
  intellectual property dispute with
    United States 94
  potential for regional leadership 125
  potential inclusion in SREZs 230–32,
    268
  trade and relations with China 369
Kotlikoff, Laurence J. 24
Kravis, Irving B. 36
Kreinin, Mordechai E. 294
Krueger, Anne O. 344
Krugman, Paul R. 86, 123, 194

Labor, demand and supply of, in
    Asia–Pacific region 12, 325, 328–29
Labor issues, in NAFTA 172
Labor shortages, migration and 331
Land use 356–57
Latin America 213, 214, 324
Latin American Free Trade
    Association 100, 161
Lawrence, Robert Z. 38, 293
Leamer, Edward E. 24, 35, 344

Leamer triangles 344–47
Lee Kuan Yew 240
Leidy, M. 347
Leutwiler Report 77
Lincoln, Edward J. 32
Lipsey, Robert E. 35
Locational factors, as determinant of
    trade 26. *See also* Geographic
    proximity
Lorenz, Detlef 380
Louvre Accord 317

Maastricht Treaty 5, 136–40, 150–53, 157,
    177, 178, 299, 317
Macdonald Commission 99
Mahathir Mohamad 112, 186, 241, 378
Major trading powers, future leadership
    role 92, 94, 96
Malaysia 229–30, 234–35, 241–43, 246,
    266–67, 335, 373
Malta 150
Managed trade, NAFTA as 179
Manufactures. *See also specific industry*
    FDI in 277
    intraindustry trade in 33, 208–09
    trade in 22, 32–33, 43–45, 198–99,
        208–09
Market-Oriented Sector Selective Talks 83
Market access issues
    after the Uruguay Round 7, 75–77,
        86–88
    as rationale for SREZs 235
    in NAFTA 176–77
    in services and investment 86–88
    in the Uruguay Round 86–88
    use of APEC to address 386
"Market" integration 188–89, 212, 219–20
Marston, Richard C. 303
Maskus, Keith 25
Matsuyama, Kiminori 303
McGee, T. G. 236
Mercosur 54, 113
Messerlin, Patrick 90, 116
Metropolitan-spillover-type
    SREZs 235–36
Mexico. *See also* North American Free
    Trade Agreement
    accession to GATT 76
    agriculture in 176
    bilateral trade agreement with
        Chile 100
    economic reforms in 115, 168, 171,
        175, 177

nature of participation in NAFTA 164
US ban on tuna from 347
weak integration into Asia–Pacific
    region 202
Michalski, Anna 141
Migration and migrants
    and consumption of social services 331
    and economic adjustment 333
    "chain" 325
    classifications of 329, 336
    destination countries 149, 323, 324,
        326, 328, 335–37
    economic consequences of 330–35
    empirical analysis of 332
    history of 323
    in NAFTA 173
    international competition for 333
    labor shortages and 331
    noneconomic factors 325–28, 335
    OECD conference on 330
    prospects for global 328
    skill levels of 332–33
    source countries 149, 324, 327–28, 334
    theory of 330
    trade liberalization as substitute
        for 335
Migration policy
    APEC role in making 338
    eminent persons group for 339
    in East Asian 335
    need for cooperation on 337
    role of international agencies 338
    settlement and integration policies 337
Ministry of International Trade and
    Industry (Japan) 57
"Modular multilateralism" 385
Moltz, James Clay 368
Montreal Mid-Term Review 92
Montreal Protocol 172, 343, 347
Multi-Fiber Arrangement 71, 169
Multilateral Trade Organization,
    proposed 120
Multilateral trading system. *See* Global
    trading system
Multinational corporations (MNCs) 29,
    35–40, 241–43, 292. *See also* Foreign
    direct investment

Nation-state, decline of 370–72
National Population Council
    (Australia) 324
Natural economic territories 369. *See also*
    Subregional economic zones

Neutrality, political 144, 147, 155, 161
Nevile, J. 332
New Zealand 81, 187, 210, 217
Newly industrializing economies. *See*
    Asian newly industrializing
    economies
Noland, Marcus 25, 26, 38, 121
Nondiscrimination 74, 104
Nontariff barriers 19–22, 116, 165. *See
    also* Contingent protection;
    Quantitative import restrictions
Nontraditional trade arrangements, as
    subsystem of global trading
    system 69, 71
North American Free Trade Agreement
    (NAFTA)
    accession of third countries to 128,
        179, 180, 215–17
    agriculture in 176–77
    and open regionalism 164–75
    and US–East Asia relations 213, 220,
        377, 385
    antidumping in 171, 175
    APEC as discipline for 128
    as managed or free trade 179
    automobiles in 166–68, 174, 179
    differences from other regional
        arrangements 164, 166
    dispute settlement in 172, 173–75
    environmental issues in 164, 172
    FDI in 173
    impact on global trading system 11,
        175
    labor issues 172
    linkages to Uruguay Round 175–78
    market access issues in 176–77
    migration and 173, 335
    risk of delay in concluding 5
    rules of origin in 117, 165–70
    textiles and apparel in 169–70, 179
    trade diversion caused by 124, 160,
        166, 169, 170, 214
    unresolved issues 164
    US preoccupation with 213
North Pacific Cooperative Security
    Dialogue 366
Northeast Asia. *See also specific countries*
    agriculture in 354, 386
    defense expenditures in 373
    resistance to institution building in 366
    security issues 368–69, 373
    SREZs in 231–32
Northern Growth Triangle 229–30
Nye, Joseph 385

Organizaation for Economic Cooperation
    and Development (OECD)
    accession of Asian countries to 9
    Conference on the Future of
        Migration 330
    proposed free trade and investment
        area 127
    role in migration policymaking 338
Okimoto, David I. 57
Okita, Saburo 13
Oligopolistic behavior, and intrafirm
    trade 10
Open–door policy, in China 253
Open regionalism 11, 128, 163, 180, 220,
    380, 385
Openness
    indicators of 18–23, 196
    maintaining, in global trading
        system 88–96
"Opting out" of European
    integration 138
Overseas production ratios, Japan 280
Own–currency invoicing 301–05

Pacific Basin. *See* Asia–Pacific region
Pacific Economic Cooperation
    Council 163, 366, 325, 338, 380
Pacific Free Trade Area, proposed 8, 9,
    385
Papadakis, Maria 44
Pangestu, Mari 281
Park Yung Chul 34
Performance–oriented goals for
    GATT 67, 74–75, 104–06
Performance requirements 86
Petri, Peter A. 26, 29, 54, 307
Philippines 76, 284, 373
Plaza Agreement 316–17
Political commitment to economic
    integration 156, 239, 241, 264
Political economy
    of antiprotection 77–78
    of GATT 77–78
    of international currency
        negotiations 316–17
Population flows. *See* Migration and
    migrants
Population growth 332
Porter, Michael 57
Portugal 156
Preeg , Ernest H. 377
Prestowitz, Clyde V., Jr. 85
"Pricing-to-market" strategy 303–05, 317

Prisoner's delight 11, 187–88, 212
Product cycle theory 40, 42, 191
Protection
    and regionalism 115–16
    balance sheet for 77
    contingent 77, 90, 116–20, 146, 155
    discriminatory 116, 127
    environmental issues as cover for 360
    political forces opposing 77–78
    theory of 191

Quantitative import restrictions 120, 168,
    176

Regional balance of power 367
Regional conflicts 367
Regional trade arrangements (RTAs). *See
    also* Regionalism
    among developed countries 99
    among developing countries 49, 100,
        161
    and intrafirm trade 50
    as insurance against trade
        discrimination 97, 103–04, 118, 367
    between developed and developing
        countries 117, 156, 157
    competition–enhancing effects of 114
    criteria for success 162
    definition of 48
    determinants of formation of 48, 54–55
    economic growth in 115
    evaluation of 98–99
    hub–and–spoke–type 97
    importance of political commitment
        to 156
    in ASEAN 112, 186, 268
    interest of small countries in 97–98, 103
    large-country advantage in
        negotiating 97
    measurement of 48, 195
    relationship to global trading
        system 69, 71, 98, 120
    relative absence in East Asia 49,
        100–01, 112, 186
    technical and financial support for 156
Regionalism. *See also* Regional trade
    arrangements
    and global trading system 96–104, 117,
        127
    and security issues 369
    as competitive strategy 119
    East Asian perspectives on 113–17

environmental effects of 358–59
factors promoting 96–97, 380–85
history of 47, 99–102
policy responses to 102–06
prospects for 8, 101, 124, 126, 162,
    216–17
revival in 1980s 111
trends in 48–54, 96–97, 154, 155
welfare implications 10
Reserves, foreign currency 310–12, 314
Resistances to trade, 190–96
Resource endowments. *See* Factor
    endowments
"Results-oriented" approach to trade
    negotiations 77
Retaliatory trade conflicts 89, 93
Revealed comparative advantage, in
    high-technology trade 44
Riau islands. *See* Johor–Singapore–Riau
    growth triangle
Richardson, J. David 57
"Roll-up" problem 167
Rules of origin 117, 165–70, 179–80
Russia 217, 231–32

Safe haven, RTAs as 97, 118
San Francisco Declaration 380
Sassen, S. 334
Saxonhouse, Gary 53, 122
Scalapino, Robert 236, 366, 368, 370
Scale economies 34, 114
Schlesinger, James 368
Schott, Jeffrey J. 6, 48, 86, 97, 113, 117
Schumpeter, Joseph 42, 43
Section 301 118
Sectoral composition of world trade 22,
    23, 304, 306
Security and strategic issues
    Asianization of 12, 372–77
    in China 369
    in Europe 139–40
    in Northeast Asia 368–69, 373
    regionalism and 369
Self-determination 372
Services, trade in 23, 77, 86, 120, 173
Shenzhen 250, 263
SIJORI. *See* Johor-Singapore-Riau growth
    triangle
Singapore
    APEC secretariat in 163
    as example of free trade 187
    dollar 242, 264, 300
    inward FDI 276, 284–85

Singapore *(continued)*
  outward FDI 264
  role in SIJORI 229, 238–49
Single European Act 136
Small countries, interest in regional
  arrangements 97–98, 103
Smith, David A. 26
Social capital, shortages of 295
Softwood lumber dispute 174
Solomon, Richard H. 384
Sopiee, Noordin 365, 372
Soviet Union 150. *See also* Russia
Special and differential treatment 118
Special economic zones 231, 234, 237
Strategic exchange rate policy 312–16
Structural Impediments Initiative (SII) 8,
  72, 83–84, 125, 384
Subregional economic zones (SREZs).
  See also Greater South China
  Economic Zone;
  Johor–Singapore–Riau growth
  triangle
  description and categorization of 226,
    235–36
  cultural linkages in 234, 252–53, 264
  currencies used in 264
  distinguished from other
    arrangements 237–38
  in Northeast Asia 231–32
  Japanese participation in 232
  joint development–type 236
  market access and 235
  metropolitan spillover–type 235–36, 265
  rationales for 162, 232–35
  economic effects 265
  effects on nonparticipating regions 265
  geographic expansion of 267–68
  impact of FDI liberalization on 11, 234
  investment in 264
  political and social effects of 265–67
  prospects for 230–32, 267–68
  relations between component areas 266
  role of geographic proximity
    in 233–34, 236, 252–53
Subsidies and countervailing duties 26,
  170–71, 174, 176–77, 220, 350,
  354–55
Suharto 240
Summers, Lawrence H. 123, 194
Sung Yun-Wing 191, 253, 257
Super 301 9, 118, 377
Superregionalism 163, 179
Sweden 145, 147

Switzerland 135, 142
Systems analysis of GATT 69–75

Taiwan
  economic liberalization 250
  economic role in GSC 252, 261–62
  impact of GSC SREZ on 261–62
  outward FDI 281
  resistances to trade in 192
  trade and relations with China 249–51,
    257–61
Tariff-rate quotas 176
Tariffs 20, 71, 76, 146, 155, 165
Taussig, Frank W. 57
Techno-nationalism 39
Technological change, and intraindustry
  trade 34
Technology. *See also* High–technology
  trade
  appropriability of 42
  policy 46, 295
  transfer of 286–89
Technology gap theory 40–42
Technology trade theory 40
Territorial disputes 368, 373
Textiles and apparel
  environmental impact of trade
    liberalization in 355
  FDI in 277
  in GATT 71, 120, 169, 170
  in NAFTA 169–70, 179
Thailand 229–30, 268, 281, 285–87
Third–country accession to NAFTA 128,
  179, 180, 215–17
Tiananmen Square 336
Tobey, J. A. 347
Tokyo Round 82
Tourism 54, 230, 242, 245, 248–49,
  256–57, 264, 324, 336
Trade bias indexes 206, 207
Trade blocs 12, 97, 102, 113, 123–24,
  126–27. *See also* Regionalism;
  Regional trade arrangements
Trade creation 114–15, 192–93
Trade diversion 96, 114–15, 160, 166,
  169, 170, 192–93, 214
Trade intensity indexes 195, 200–05
Trade liberalization
  as substitute for migration 335
  catalytic 85
  environmental impact of 349–59
  in agriculture 351–56

in Asia-Pacific region 187
in coal, environmental effects of 350–51
through APEC 219–20
Trade policy. *See also specific policy areas*
convergence in 7
in the European Community 146, 155
in the United States 116
outlook for major initiatives in 5–8
to address environmental issues 12, 343, 360
transparency in 77
Trade Policy Review Mechanism (GATT) 77, 92, 93, 120
Trade-related investment practices 86
Trade shares of GDP, as trade resistance measure 194, 196–200
Transfer of technology 286–89
Transparency in trade policy 77
Transport costs 22, 54
Treaty on European Union (Maastricht Treaty) 5, 136–40, 150–53, 157, 177, 178, 299, 317
Triangular trade in East Asia 123
Tripolarity of the global economy 3, 51, 92–96, 121
Tumen River Delta Area 229, 232–32, 265
Tuna, US ban on Mexican 347
Turkey 150

Unilateralism, aggressive 118, 120
United Kingdom. *See* Great Britain
United Nations Development Programme 232
United Nations High Commissioner for Refugees 338
United States
aggressive unilateralism by 118
antidumping policies of 116
capital markets in 318
FDI by 274, 382, 384
high-technology trade in 44
intraindustry trade 34
migration to 323
military presence in Pacific 373–77
obstacles to growth 4
opposition to EAEG 379
own-currency invoicing 301
potential for additional RTAs 8, 101, 162, 216–17
preoccupation with NAFTA 213

support for APEC 379
three-track approach to trade 379
United States, trade and foreign relations
with Asia–Pacific countries 377, 378
with Canada 174
with China 376–77
with Europe 89
with Japan 8, 83–84, 101, 384
Uruguay Round
alleged inattention of major powers to 98
and NAFTA 164, 174–78
dispute settlement in 120
East Asian support of 127
eminent persons group for 98
focus on system strengthening 104
goals of 91
implications for Asia-Pacific trade 214–15
importance of successful conclusion 7
on antidumping 120
on intellectual property protection 86
on investment 87
on services 87
on subsidies 120
on textiles and apparel 169, 170
prospects for 4, 5, 65, 119–20, 178
US-Japan free trade agreement, proposed 8, 101

"Variable geometry" of integration in European Community 138
Venezuela 100
Voluntary export restraints (VERs) 71, 116, 119
Vietnam 217
Viner, Jacob 96

Wanandi, Jusuf 367, 371
Western Europe, immigration to and within 324, 336, 337
Western European Union 139
Whalley, John 323
White Paper of 1985 136
Wolf, M. 76
World Bank 324
World Trade Organization, proposed 91

Xiamen 250

"Yarn forward" rule 169
Yellow Sea Economic Zone 229, 236
Yen
  and international monetary system 12,
    299–321
  appreciation of, and Japanese FDI 279
  role in East Asian currency baskets 300
  use as a store of value 310–12

use as a transactions vehicle 308–10
use as an invoice currency 300–08,
  312–16
Yen bloc 51
Yen-dollar agreement 316

Zhuhai 250

Other Publications from the
Institute for International Economics

POLICY ANALYSES IN INTERNATIONAL ECONOMICS Series

1   **The Lending Policies of the International Monetary Fund**
John Williamson/*August 1982*
    ISBN paper 0-88132-000-5   72 pp.

2   **"Reciprocity": A New Approach to World Trade Policy?**
William R. Cline/*September 1982*
    ISBN paper 0-88132-001-3   41 pp.

3   **Trade Policy in the 1980s**
C. Fred Bergsten and William R. Cline/*November 1982*
(out of print)   ISBN paper 0-88132-002-1   84 pp.
Partially reproduced in the book *Trade Policy in the 1980s.*

4   **International Debt and the Stability of the World Economy**
William R. Cline/*September 1983*
    ISBN paper 0-88132-010-2   134 pp.

5   **The Exchange Rate System**
John Williamson/*September 1983, rev. June 1985*
(out of print)   ISBN paper 0-88132-034-X   61 pp.

6   **Economic Sanctions in Support of Foreign Policy Goals**
Gary Clyde Hufbauer and Jeffrey J. Schott/*October 1983*
    ISBN paper 0-88132-014-5   109 pp.

7   **A New SDR Allocation?**
John Williamson/*March 1984*
    ISBN paper 0-88132-028-5   61 pp.

8   **An International Standard for Monetary Stabilization**
Ronald I. McKinnon/*March 1984*
(out of print)   ISBN paper 0-88132-018-8   108 pp.

9   **The Yen/Dollar Agreement: Liberalizing Japanese Capital Markets**
Jeffrey A. Frankel/*December 1984*
    ISBN paper 0-88132-035-8   86 pp.

10 **Bank Lending to Developing Countries: The Policy Alternatives**
C. Fred Bergsten, William R. Cline, and John Williamson/*April 1985*
    ISBN paper 0-88132-032-3   221 pp.

11 **Trading for Growth: The Next Round of Trade Negotiations**
Gary Clyde Hufbauer and Jeffrey J. Schott/*September 1985*
    ISBN paper 0-88132-033-1   109 pp.

12 **Financial Intermediation Beyond the Debt Crisis**
Donald R. Lessard and John Williamson/*September 1985*
    ISBN paper 0-88132-021-8   130 pp.

13 **The United States–Japan Economic Problem**
C. Fred Bergsten and William R. Cline/*October 1985, rev. January 1987*
    ISBN paper 0-88132-060-9   180 pp.

14 **Deficits and the Dollar: The World Economy at Risk**
Stephen Marris/*December 1985, rev. November 1987*
    ISBN paper 0-88132-067-6   415 pp.

15 **Trade Policy for Troubled Industries**
Gary Clyde Hufbauer and Howard F. Rosen/*March 1986*
ISBN paper 0-88132-020-X   111 pp.

16 **The United States and Canada: The Quest for Free Trade**
Paul Wonnacott with an Appendix by John Williamson/*March 1987*
ISBN paper 0-88132-056-0   188 pp.

17 **Adjusting to Success: Balance of Payments Policy in the
East Asian NICs**
Bela Balassa and John Williamson/*June 1987, rev. April 1990*
ISBN paper 0-88132-101-X   160 pp.

18 **Mobilizing Bank Lending to Debtor Countries**
William R. Cline/*June 1987*
ISBN paper 0-88132-062-5   100 pp.

19 **Auction Quotas and United States Trade Policy**
C. Fred Bergsten, Kimberly Ann Elliott, Jeffrey J. Schott, and
Wendy E. Takacs/*September 1987*
ISBN paper 0-88132-050-1   254 pp.

20 **Agriculture and the GATT: Rewriting the Rules**
Dale E. Hathaway/*September 1987*
ISBN paper 0-88132-052-8   169 pp.

21 **Anti-Protection: Changing Forces in United States Trade Politics**
I. M. Destler and John S. Odell/*September 1987*
ISBN paper 0-88132-043-9   220 pp.

22 **Targets and Indicators: A Blueprint for the International Coordination
of Economic Policy**
John Williamson and Marcus H. Miller/*September 1987*
ISBN paper 0-88132-051-X   118 pp.

23 **Capital Flight: The Problem and Policy Responses**
Donald R. Lessard and John Williamson/*December 1987*
ISBN paper 0-88132-059-5   80 pp.

24 **United States–Canada Free Trade: An Evaluation of the Agreement**
Jeffrey J. Schott/*April 1988*
ISBN paper 0-88132-072-2   48 pp.

25 **Voluntary Approaches to Debt Relief**
John Williamson/*September 1988, rev. May 1989*
ISBN paper 0-88132-098-6   80 pp.

26 **American Trade Adjustment: The Global Impact**
William R. Cline/*March 1989*
ISBN paper 0-88132-095-1   98 pp.

27 **More Free Trade Areas?**
Jeffrey J. Schott/*May 1989*
ISBN paper 0-88132-085-4   88 pp.

28 **The Progress of Policy Reform in Latin America**
John Williamson/*January 1990*
ISBN paper 0-88132-100-1   106 pp.

29 **The Global Trade Negotiations: What Can Be Achieved?**
Jeffrey J. Schott/*September 1990*
ISBN paper 0-88132-137-0   72 pp.

30 Economic Policy Coordination: Requiem or Prologue?
Wendy Dobson/*April 1991*
            ISBN paper 0-88132-102-8   162 pp.

31 The Economic Opening of Eastern Europe
John Williamson/*May 1991*
            ISBN paper 0-88132-186-9   92 pp.

32 Eastern Europe and the Soviet Union in the World Economy
Susan M. Collins and Dani Rodrik/*May 1991*
            ISBN paper 0-88132-157-5   152 pp.

33 African Economic Reform: The External Dimension
Carol Lancaster/*June 1991*
            ISBN paper 0-88132-096-X   82 pp.

34 Has the Adjustment Process Worked?
Paul R. Krugman/*October 1991*
            ISBN paper 0-88132-116-8   80 pp.

35 From Soviet disUnion to Eastern Economic Community?
Oleh Havrylyshyn and John Williamson/*October 1991*
            ISBN paper 0-88132-192-3   84 pp.

36 Global Warming: The Economic Stakes
William R. Cline/*May 1992*
            ISBN paper 0-88132-172-9   128 pp.

37 Trade and Payments After Soviet Disintegration
John Williamson/*June 1992*
            ISBN paper 0-88132-173-7   96 pp.

BOOKS

IMF Conditionality
John Williamson, editor/*1983*
            ISBN cloth 0-88132-006-4   695 pp.

Trade Policy in the 1980s
William R. Cline, editor/*1983*
            ISBN cloth 0-88132-008-1   810 pp.
            ISBN paper 0-88132-031-5   810 pp.

Subsidies in International Trade
Gary Clyde Hufbauer and Joanna Shelton Erb/*1984*
            ISBN cloth 0-88132-004-8   299 pp.

International Debt: Systemic Risk and Policy Response
William R. Cline/*1984*
            ISBN cloth 0-88132-015-3   336 pp.

Trade Protection in the United States: 31 Case Studies
Gary Clyde Hufbauer, Diane E. Berliner, and Kimberly Ann Elliott/*1986*
            ISBN paper 0-88132-040-4   371 pp.

Toward Renewed Economic Growth in Latin America
Bela Balassa, Gerardo M. Bueno, Pedro-Pablo Kuczynski, and Mario
   Henrique Simonsen/*1986*
(out of print)   ISBN paper 0-88132-045-5   205 pp.

Capital Flight and Third World Debt
Donald R. Lessard and John Williamson, editors/*1987*
(out of print)   ISBN paper 0-88132-053-6   270 pp.

The Canada–United States Free Trade Agreement:
  The Global Impact
Jeffrey J. Schott and Murray G. Smith, editors/*1988*
                          ISBN paper 0-88132-073-0   211 pp.

World Agricultural Trade: Building a Consensus
William M. Miner and Dale E. Hathaway, editors/*1988*
                          ISBN paper 0-88132-071-3   226 pp.

Japan in the World Economy
Bela Balassa and Marcus Noland/*1988*
                          ISBN paper 0-88132-041-2   306 pp.

America in the World Economy: A Strategy for the 1990s
C. Fred Bergsten/*1988*
                          ISBN cloth 0-88132-089-7   235 pp.
                          ISBN paper 0-88132-082-X   235 pp.

Managing the Dollar: From the Plaza to the Louvre
Yoichi Funabashi/*1988, rev. 1989*
                          ISBN paper 0-88132-097-8   307 pp.

United States External Adjustment and the World Economy
William R. Cline/*May 1989*
                          ISBN paper 0-88132-048-X   392 pp.

Free Trade Areas and U.S. Trade Policy
Jeffrey J. Schott, editor/*May 1989*
                          ISBN paper 0-88132-094-3   400 pp.

Dollar Politics: Exchange Rate Policymaking in the United States
I. M. Destler and C. Randall Henning/*September 1989*
                          ISBN paper 0-88132-079-X   192 pp.

Latin American Adjustment: How Much Has Happened?
John Williamson, editor/*April 1990*
                          ISBN paper 0-88132-125-7   480 pp.

The Future of World Trade in Textiles and Apparel
William R. Cline/*1987, rev. June 1990*
                          ISBN paper 0-88132-110-9   344 pp.

Completing the Uruguay Round: A Results-Oriented Approach to the
  GATT Trade Negotiations
Jeffrey J. Schott, editor/*September 1990*
                          ISBN paper 0-88132-130-3   256 pp.

Economic Sanctions Reconsidered (in two volumes)
  Economic Sanctions Reconsidered: History and Current Policy
   (also sold separately, see below)
  Economic Sanctions Reconsidered: Supplemental Case Histories
Gary Clyde Hufbauer, Jeffrey J. Schott, and Kimberly Ann Elliott/*1985,*
  rev. December 1990
                          ISBN cloth 0-88132-115-X   928 pp.
                          ISBN paper 0-88132-105-2   928 pp.

Economic Sanctions Reconsidered: History and Current Policy
Gary Clyde Hufbauer, Jeffrey J. Schott, and Kimberly Ann Elliott/
  December 1990
                          ISBN cloth 0-88132-136-2   288 pp.
                          ISBN paper 0-88132-140-0   288 pp.

Pacific Basin Developing Countries: Prospects for the Future
Marcus Noland/*January 1991*

ISBN cloth 0-88132-141-9	250 pp.
ISBN paper 0-88132-081-1	250 pp.

Currency Convertibility in Eastern Europe
John Williamson, editor/*September 1991*

ISBN cloth 0-88132-144-3	396 pp.
ISBN paper 0-88132-128-1	396 pp.

Foreign Direct Investment in the United States
Edward M. Graham and Paul R. Krugman/*1989, rev. October 1991*

ISBN paper 0-88132-139-7	200 pp.

International Adjustment and Financing: The Lessons of 1985–1991
C. Fred Bergsten, editor/*January 1992*

ISBN cloth 0-88132-142-7	336 pp.
ISBN paper 0-88132-112-5	336 pp.

North American Free Trade: Issues and Recommendations
Gary Clyde Hufbauer and Jeffrey J. Schott/*April 1992*

ISBN cloth 0-88132-145-1	392 pp.
ISBN paper 0-88132-120-6	392 pp.

American Trade Politics
I. M. Destler/*1986, rev. June 1992*

ISBN cloth 0-88132-164-8	400 pp.
ISBN paper 0-88132-188-5	400 pp.

Narrowing the U.S. Current Account Deficit: A Sectoral Assessment
Allen J. Lenz/*June 1992*

ISBN cloth 0-88132-148-6	640 pp.
ISBN paper 0-88132-103-6	640 pp.

The Economics of Global Warming
William R. Cline/*June 1992*

ISBN cloth 0-88132-150-8	420 pp.
ISBN paper 0-88132-132-X	420 pp.

U.S. Taxation of International Income: Blueprint for Reform
Gary Clyde Hufbauer, assisted by Joanna M. van Rooij/*October 1992*

ISBN cloth 0-88132-178-8	304 pp.
ISBN paper 0-88132-134-6	304 pp.

Who's Bashing Whom? Trade Conflict in High-Technology Industries
Laura D'Andrea Tyson/*November 1992*

ISBN cloth 0-88132-151-6	352 pp.
ISBN paper 0-88132-106-0	352 pp.

Korea in the World Economy
Il SaKong/*January 1993*

ISBN cloth 0-88132-184-2	328 pp.
ISBN paper 0-88132-106-0	328 pp.

NAFTA: An Assessment
Gary Clyde Hufbauer and Jeffrey J. Schott/*February 1993*

ISBN paper 0-88132-198-2	192 pp.

Pacific Dynamism and the International Economic System
C. Fred Bergsten and Marcus Noland, editors/*May 1993*

ISBN paper 0-88132-196-6	424 pp.

SPECIAL REPORTS

1   Promoting World Recovery: A Statement on Global Economic Strategy
    by Twenty-six Economists from Fourteen Countries/*December 1982*
    (out of print)   ISBN paper 0-88132-013-7   45 pp.

2   Prospects for Adjustment in Argentina, Brazil, and Mexico:
    Responding to the Debt Crisis
    John Williamson, editor/*June 1983*
    (out of print)   ISBN paper 0-88132-016-1   71 pp.

3   Inflation and Indexation: Argentina, Brazil, and Israel
    John Williamson, editor/*March 1985*
                            ISBN paper 0-88132-037-4   191 pp.

4   Global Economic Imbalances
    C. Fred Bergsten, editor/*March 1986*
                            ISBN cloth 0-88132-038-2   126 pp.
                            ISBN paper 0-88132-042-0   126 pp.

5   African Debt and Financing
    Carol Lancaster and John Williamson, editors/*May 1986*
    (out of print)   ISBN paper 0-88132-044-7   229 pp.

6   Resolving the Global Economic Crisis: After Wall Street
    Thirty-three Economists from Thirteen Countries/*December 1987*
                            ISBN paper 0-88132-070-6   30 pp.

7   World Economic Problems
    Kimberly Ann Elliott and John Williamson, editors/*April 1988*
                            ISBN paper 0-88132-055-2   298 pp.

    Reforming World Agricultural Trade
    Twenty-nine Professionals from Seventeen Countries/*1988*
                            ISBN paper 0-88132-088-9   42 pp.

8   Economic Relations Between the United States and Korea:
    Conflict or Cooperation?
    Thomas O. Bayard and Soo-Gil Young, editors/*January 1989*
                            ISBN paper 0-88132-068-4   192 pp.

FORTHCOMING

A World Savings Shortage?
Paul R. Krugman

Sizing Up U.S. Export Disincentives
J. David Richardson

The Globalization of Industry and National Governments
C. Fred Bergsten and Edward M. Graham

Trade and the Environment: Setting the Rules
John Whalley and Peter Uimonen

The Effects of Foreign-Exchange Intervention
Kathryn Dominguez and Jeffrey A. Frankel

The Future of the World Trading System
John Whalley and Colleen Hamilton

Adjusting to Volatile Energy Prices
Philip K. Verleger, Jr.